Popular Politics and Protest Event Analysis in Latin America

POPULAR POLITICS
AND PROTEST EVENT
ANALYSIS IN
LATIN AMERICA

EDITED BY MOISÉS ARCE AND TAKESHI WADA

University of New Mexico Press | Albuquerque

First paperback edition, 2025

ISBN 978-0-8263-6883-6 (paper)
ISBN 978-0-8263-6568-2 (cloth)
ISBN 978-0-8263-6884-3 (ePub)

Library of Congress Control Number: 2023949839

Founded in 1889, the University of New Mexico sits on the traditional home-lands of the Pueblo of Sandia. The original peoples of New Mexico—Pueblo, Navajo, and Apache—since time immemorial have deep connections to the land and have made significant contributions to the broader community statewide. We honor the land itself and those who remain stewards of this land throughout the generations and also acknowledge our committed rela-tionship to Indigenous peoples. We gratefully recognize our history.

Cover illustration by Felicia Cedillos
Designed by Felicia Cedillos
Composed in Utopia Std

To the late Federico Schuster

Contents

Acknowledgments

This collaborative project has a long history and we are very happy to see the progress we have made. The project seeks to highlight the contributions of protest event analysis (PEA) and country-specific event datasets to furthering our understanding of protest politics in the Latin American region. It is a product of a unique interdisciplinary collaboration of senior researchers and emerging scholars with different academic backgrounds (economists, historians, sociologists, and political scientists) in both the Global North and South, most of whom reside outside the United States. These scholars have systematically compiled and quantified large amounts of information on protests over the years, using a variety of non-English domestic news sources. The result is a unique collection of studies of protest events in ten Latin American countries: Bolivia, Brazil, Chile, Colombia, Costa Rica, Ecuador, Mexico, Nicaragua, Peru, and Venezuela.

Moisés Arce and Takeshi Wada, the coeditors of this volume, overlapped academically at the University of Missouri in 2005–2008. We soon realized that we shared common research interests related to protest event analysis and the consequences of economic liberalization on protest politics in the context of widespread democracy. We received Research Board Awards from the University of Missouri System and later put together a grant proposal to compile and quantify protest event data. This seed funding was the first step that started this research journey.

In 2014, we reunited at the University of Tokyo, Takeshi's new home department. There, we thought more closely about a common research question to draw a larger group of scholars from the Latin American region. We hosted several academic gatherings in preparation for this project. We put together workshops at the Latin American Studies Association meetings in Lima, Peru (2017), Barcelona, Spain (2018), and Boston, USA (2019), and at a virtual congress (2021). We also held two small conferences at the University of Tokyo (2018) and Tulane University (2020).

We are very thankful to the late Federico Schuster, professor and former Dean of the Faculty of Social Sciences at Universidad de Buenos Aires (UBA) for the energy and enthusiasm he brought to this project. We surely miss him. We are also very thankful to Nicolás Somma and Rodrigo Medel for their feedback and suggestions at different stages of this project. María Inclán made a tremendous effort in bringing together the chapters' findings and making this volume better integrated. We value her contributions very much. Paul Almeida provided critical support to bring the edited volume closer to publication and we are indebted to him for this support. We thank very much Angela Alonso and Jessica Rich for reading and commenting on several draft chapters of this volume.

This book would not have been possible without the help and support of several institutions and organizations. At Tulane University, Moisés Arce would like to acknowledge the support of the School of Liberal Arts, Ludovico Feoli, executive director of the Center for Inter-American Policy and Research (CIPR), and Thomas Reese, executive director of the Stone Center for Latin American Studies at Tulane University.

Takeshi Wada is grateful to Hiroyuki Ukeda, ex-director of Latin American & Iberian Network for Academic Collaboration (LAINAC), the University of Tokyo, and the Japan Society for the Promotion of Science (JSPS KAKENHI 26590087, 15KT0040, 18H00921) for their long-term support.

We are also very thankful to the reviewers for their detailed reading of our manuscript, as well as their recommendations for revisions. We thank Camilo Andrés Ordoñez Zambrano and Shawny Green for translating several chapters from Spanish to English. We thank Senior Editor Michael Millman and the editorial team at University of New Mexico Press for their invaluable editorial support throughout the publication process. We thank Katherine Harper for her diligent copyediting of this volume. We thank Max Weber and Tali Gorodetsky, undergraduate students at Tulane University, and Kenta Tasaka, graduate student at the University of Tokyo, for their outstanding research support.

CHAPTER ONE

Introduction

MOISÉS ARCE AND TAKESHI WADA

The study of the social consequences of economic globalization generated intense disagreements within scholarly circles as research sought to explain the impact of market reforms on popular politics across Latin America. One perspective associated exposure to worldwide market competition with material insecurities and other demobilizing changes for popular sectors of society (Roberts 2002; Kurtz 2004; Oxhorn 2009). As countries aggressively competed with each other to attract footloose capital, market forces were thought to homogenize policies and other economic institutions. This convergence propelled a "race to the bottom" in labor standards, which in turn severely weakened and fragmented popular sectors. Another perspective evoked the image of a "backlash" against globalization (Ellis-Jones 2003; Silva 2009; Simmons 2016). Protesters initially resisted austerity measures aimed to stabilize consumer prices, but later sought to roll back unpopular economic policies, such as the privatization of utilities, labor flexibility and other social sector reforms (López Maya 2003; Almeida 2007, 2014; Arce 2008). Protesters even forced embattled presidents who supported market policies to leave office early (Hochstetler 2006).

These sweeping economic changes overlapped with the onset of the third wave of democracy (Huntington 1991), turning Latin America into the second most democratic region in the world. The majority of countries in the region are, in fact, experiencing the longest uninterrupted period of democracy in their respective histories (Levitsky 2018). Existing research views political regimes as less binary (democracy or dictatorship) than a continuum in which democracies may go through recession—or even auto-cratization—periods (Bermeo 2016; Lührmann and Lindberg 2019). For example, over the decade 2007–2017, countries such as Brazil, Bolivia, and Ecuador regressed (Mechkova et al. 2017), but democracy eroded and even reverted into authoritarianism in Nicaragua and Venezuela (Pérez-Liñán and Mainwaring 2015). With the spread of democracy, existing research became less preoccupied about its viability and moved to questions related to its quality and significance (Roberts 2016).

The pace of this dual transition—from closed interventionist econo-mies to open markets and from autocracies to democracies—was highly uneven. It produced what Almeida (2010a) characterized as a "hybrid political-economic environment," where democracy provides challeng-ers with expanding *political opportunities* or new advantages (e.g., toler-ance of nongovernmental organizations, broader political party repre-sentation, greater institutional access), but globalization brings about *economic threats* to livelihoods and human welfare (e.g., rising consumer prices, privatization, extraction of natural resources) (Auyero 2007; Almeida and Chase-Dunn 2018).[1] The departure from import-substitution industrialization policies advocating protectionism and a strong role for the state to open market economies was also seen as a critical juncture (Roberts 2002). It removed the state from modes of political representa-tion, such as urban labor movements and their affiliated mass party organizations, while unleashing more pluralistic, heterogeneous, and decentralized patterns of popular representation (Collier and Handlin 2009; Yashar 2005). As globalization and democracy increasingly domi-nate the Global South, it becomes imperative to assess how they have transformed popular politics in the region. Which sets of actors are strengthened and which are weakened by globalization? Are new sets of social actors or forms of mobilizing strategies emerging under new, but often weakly institutionalized democracies? Have the claims (or demands) that move citizens into struggle changed as a consequence of globalization and democracy? To what do social actors commonly attribute their demands? More importantly, what are the implications of these changes for democracy and/or globalization?

In this volume, we argue that protest event analysis (PEA), with its ability to compare protest activities across different time periods, diverse social actors (workers, peasants, students, etc.), and a variety of countries, regions, and cities, is the ideal approach to grasp the effects of large-scale social changes and, therefore, to advance better and well-grounded explanations about the consequences of globalization and democracy on protest. Protest event analysis follows a rich tradition in the social sciences (McAdam 2010; Tilly 1986; Tarrow 1989). It is a method that allows researchers to "systematically map, analyze, and interpret the occurrence and properties of large numbers of protests by means of content analysis" (Koopmans and Rucht 2002, 231). In addition to examining the numbers and features of protests in their own right, researchers can associate protests with other events, structures, or developments. They can evaluate how national contexts influence the levels of protest mobilization or action repertoires (Hutter 2014). When longitudinal data are available, PEA can disentangle protest waves and cycles (Tarrow 1998) and see how protests co-vary with changes in their environment, as when the economy changes. Likewise, when cross-sectional data are present, researchers can examine the geographical variation of protest within countries. Overall, PEA is an important tool for social science research and "provides a solid ground in an area that is still often marked by more or less informed speculation" (Koopmans and Rucht 2002, 251).[2]

This volume offers the first comparative study of popular protests in Latin America using country-specific event datasets. Compared to commonly used large-N cross-national datasets, which draw heavily on international news sources (see Herkenrath and Knoll 2011), these country-specific event datasets systematically extract data from non-English domestic news sources to provide detailed information on the major components of collective action, such as actor (who), target (whom), action (how), claim (why), place (where), and time (when). The higher quality of measures used enables the contributors of the volume to employ original and innovative event methods such as cluster analysis, spatial analysis, social network analysis, and multivariate event count models.

Compared to case studies, which provide detailed, rich treatments on specific antimarket campaigns such as the "water war" in Cochabamba, Bolivia (Simmons 2016) and other massive demonstrations against neoliberalism in Latin America (Silva 2009), the strengths of the country-specific event analysis are its ability to make broad comparisons across time and space. By triangulating empirical findings and insights, our volume makes important contributions that complement many existing case studies on the consequences of democracy and economic globalization on protest politics.

This book brings together scholars with different backgrounds (historians, sociologists, economists, political scientists) from both the Global North and South. These scholars have compiled and quantified large amounts of information on protests using a variety of non-English domestic news sources across a diverse set of countries. They originally did so in order to study different research questions specific to their interests—not necessarily those related to how economic globalization and democracy have transformed popular politics, as in this volume. One of the potential drawbacks of these datasets is that the specific categories used to classify the collective action components may not be directly comparable, but by carefully formulating a central research question, we can overcome this and other limitations and make important contributions to the study of popular politics in the region.

In countries with longitudinal datasets, researchers explore long-term trajectories in collective mobilization. Five of the ten datasets, in fact, cover extensive periods, and in some cases, these precede the region's dual transition to economic globalization and democracy (see, for instance, chapter 2, on Mexico, by Takeshi Wada, chapter 3, on Bolivia, by Roberto Laserna, and chapter 4, on Colombia, by Mauricio Archila Neira and Martha Cecilia García Velandia). Here, contributors unveil changes and continuities over time concerning actors, actions, targets, claims, and/or places of collective action.[3] In countries with cross-sectional datasets, researchers use protest event analysis as a magnifying glass to study short-term sequential events on important moments of globalization or democratization (see, for instance, chapter 7, on Costa Rica and Nicaragua, by Paul Almeida, Luis Rubén González Márquez, and María De Jesus Mora, and chapter 8, on Chile, by Nicolás Somma and Rodrigo Medel).

Latin America is an ideal place to explore the transformation of popular politics, as the region is often seen as a harbinger of social change. The decline of the "union-party hub" (Roberts 2002, 42) associated with the import industrialization era opened the door to more autonomous and pluralistic forms of organization during the market reform period, including associational networks (Collier and Handlin 2009), neighborhood or community assemblies, and local networks of unemployed workers. Yashar (1999, 86) spoke of "neoliberal citizenship regimes" where politics became increasingly "more liberal and more local." The years covered by the country-specific event datasets also allow us to compare and contrast not only what popular politics looked like during economic hard times—that is, Latin America's debt crisis of the 1980s, also known as "the lost decade"—but also how it changed during the region's commodity boom (2002–2014), which led to sustained economic growth and significant reductions in poverty and inequality, particularly in resource-rich countries (see, for instance, chapter 5, on Peru, by Moisés Arce and Renzo Aurazo, and chapter 9, on Ecuador, by Santiago Ortiz).

Likewise, the country-specific event datasets allow us to examine how popular politics changed as democracy expanded or regressed throughout the region (see, for instance, chapter 6, on Venezuela, by Margarita López Maya). In the 1970s, in fact, there were only two democracies (Costa Rica and Venezuela) and one semi-democracy (Colombia) in Latin America, but twenty years later the number of democracies had swelled to eighteen.[4] Colombia also faced a prolonged civil war with high levels of violence and human rights abuses. With increasing democratization, popular sectors of society had to "recalibrate" their organizational and mobilizing strategies (Almeida and Johnston 2006, 13). For instance, claim-making related to the repressive character of authoritarian regimes became less salient, and forms of resistance typical of closed political systems, such as "oppositional speech acts" (Johnston 2005) and clandestine organizational structures (Johnston and Figa 1988), were superseded by other modes of organizing and representation (Almeida and Johnston 2006, 13). Protest repertoires also changed and moved away from violence with growing democratization (Wada 2023). Overall, the face of Latin American democracy changed, showing the political ascendancy of indigenous people, a larger political representation of women, and the rise of several leftist presidents across the region.

The contributions of this volume are threefold. First, whereas studies focusing on demobilization and depoliticization typically pay greater attention to aggregate levels of contentious activity (e.g., actions), a measure that is readily available in several large-N cross-national datasets, our approach using country-specific event datasets provides the full spectrum of major components of collective action (actors, targets, claims, etc.). Second, in contrasting case studies of particular protest movements in countries that experience many protests (e.g., the *piqueteros* in Argentina), our approach takes into account important temporal and spatial dimensions as the strength of these movements varies across time and space. Third and finally, our approach based on country-specific event datasets mirrors the advantages of big data, a methodology that is transforming the social sciences. By considering all of the major components of collective action across time and space, we can systematically map and analyze patterns in contentious action and, in turn, better explain the timing, scope, and pace of major political developments. Overall, our approach allows us to make more meaningful generalizations about the consequences of globalization and democracy on popular politics.

We begin this chapter by discussing the most important economic and political changes in the region, especially those resulting in the arrival of economic globalization and democracy. We use this information as a background to situate the different country chapters. Next, we turn to the social movements literature to develop a working hypothesis on the consequences of globalization and democracy on protest. We identify two ideal types of mobilization—reactive and proactive—that coexist and often overlap with each other, yet vary depending on different economic and political contexts. Then we introduce the features of protest event analysis and explain how this methodology enables us to examine these broad patterns of mobilization. We conclude this chapter by providing overviews of the country-specific event datasets central to this volume and the chapter contributions.

Economic Globalization

Since the mid-1970s, Latin America has increasingly turned from the state to the market to achieve economic growth. This trend was accelerated by the debt crisis in the early 1980s, which spurred governments across the region to embrace the economic program known as the Washington consensus: a broad array of policy changes including fiscal discipline, trade liberalization, privatization of state enterprises, and a general preference for the market rather than the state in determining prices, interest rates, and capital flows (Williamson 1990).

The Washington consensus was rolled out in two broad phases.[5] The early stages of reform—mostly in the 1980s and early 1990s—sought to stabilize macroeconomic policies by reducing fiscal deficits and controlling rampant inflation. These actions took place largely in an insulated policy-making environment, providing state and technocratic elites with substantial autonomy from popular sectors. Stabilization policies were also easier to execute, and their results were often immediate. By contrast, the later stages of reform—mainly from the mid-1990s until the early 2000s—sought to strengthen and reorganize the state through the privatization of natural resources, government utilities, pension systems, and social services. These policies were characterized as structural adjustment because they were about reforming the state and reducing its role in production. The politics during this later stage of reform were more complex and less predictable than those of the initial stage. Among other things, later reforms were more difficult to implement, took much longer to achieve results, involved a broader array of actors, and required the cooperation of a wider range of societal groups (Naím 1995; Graham and Naím 1998).

Using the KOF index of globalization (Dreher 2006; Gygli et al. 2019), figure 1.1 shows the average level of economic globalization for the Latin American region.[6] In the 1970s and 1980s, the index of globalization rises only from 0.40 in 1970 to 0.44 in 1989. However, with the launch of the second phase of reforms in the 1990s, globalization begins a steady climb. It rises from 0.45 in 1991 to 0.59 in 2001, and then it increases to 0.66 in 2017. It was in 1995 that the pace of globalization in the region, on average, was the steepest. In addition, the level of globalization in countries such as Argentina, Chile, and Mexico was consistently higher than the Latin American average, whereas countries such as Bolivia, Brazil, and Ecuador showed the opposite trend. At this writing, Chile is the most globalized economy in the region and Venezuela is the least.

The costs of economic globalization were an economic threat to popular

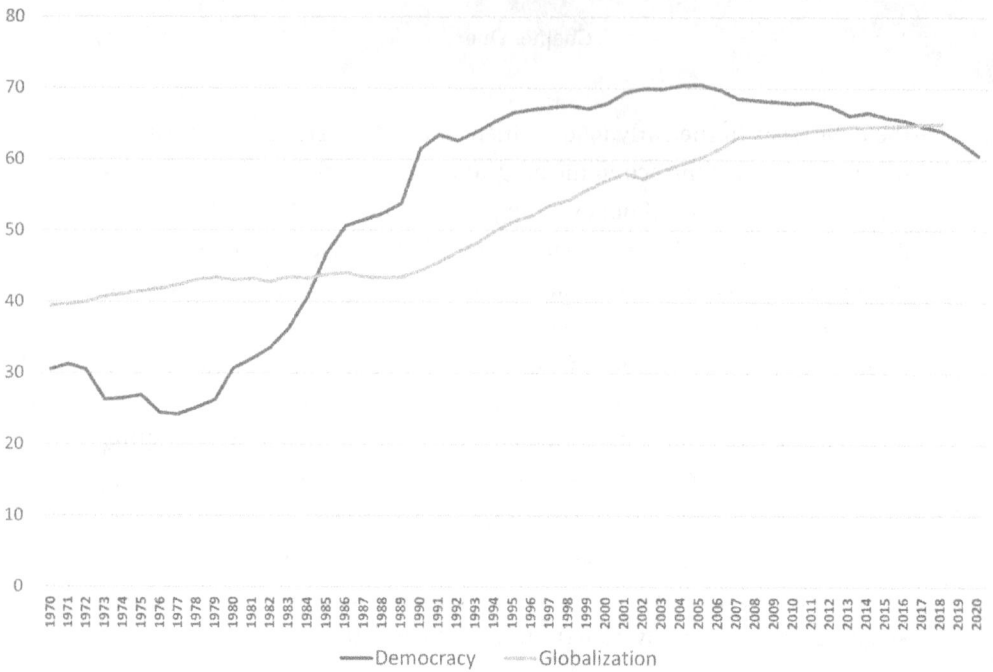

Figure 1.1 Globalization and Democratization in Latin America. Democracy scores are the electoral democracy indices from the Varieties of Democracy Project (V-Dem). Globalization scores are taken from the KOF index of globalization (Dreher 2006; Gygli et al. 2019).

sectors of society. Accordingly, both phases of reform triggered large-scale mobilizations across the Global South. The popular protests in response to stabilization policies were dubbed "IMF riots" because, in most cases, the uprisings followed agreements with the International Monetary Fund (Walton and Seddon 1994). They were also known as "austerity protests" because the recommended deep cuts in government spending magnified the severity of the ongoing economic crisis. When governments sought to remove subsidies and price controls to balance their budgets, popular sectors took to the streets to resist dramatic increases in the cost of living. In the 1989 popular revolt in Caracas, Venezuela known as the Sacudón or Caracazo, austerity reforms provoked violent urban rioting; this was followed by a heavy-handed use of military force that killed four hundred or more civilians (López Maya 2003). Walton and Seddon (1994) identified 146 antiausterity protests between 1976 and 1992 in Eastern Europe, Africa, Latin America, and Asia.

The mobilizations of the later stages of reform were related to a broad swath of policy changes supporting privatization, labor flexibility, and free trade agreements. Unlike the early stages of reform, where the costs of macroeconomic stabilization were widely shared by most of society, the burdens of structural adjustment policies were borne largely by specific groups or sectors. In the beginning, privatizations were widespread in the heavy industries and infrastructure sector, but later they extended to telecommunications firms, electricity providers, and extractive industries such as mining and petroleum companies. The sell-off of public sector utilities, in particular, sparked a series of important mobilization campaigns, such as water privatization in Bolivia (Laserna 2003; Perreault 2006), electricity privatization in Peru (Arce 2008), and electricity and telecommunications privatizations in Costa Rica (Almeida 2008a). Both the North American Free Trade Agreement (NAFTA) (Inclán 2008) and the Central American Free Trade Agreement (CAFTA) encountered popular resistance (Spalding 2014). In Costa Rica, challengers forced the national government to hold a referendum over the trade agreement (Almeida 2014, chapter 3).

While economic threats induced collective action during both phases of reform, the austerity protests were generally short-lived, and the overall market orthodoxy associated with the Washington consensus did not change (Almeida 2018). However, in the structural adjustment phase of reform, popular sectors regrouped and were able to roll back some of these policies. They also challenged officeholders seeking to expand market reform policies (Silva 2009). In so doing, as Roberts (2008, 328) noted, they "punctured the aura of inexorability that surrounded the trends toward economic liberalization and globalization." The later stages of reform thus spawned new ways of organizing and mobilizing civil society. One contributing factor to this wave of mobilization was democratization.

Democratization

Scholars initially emphasized the fragility of newly democratic regimes in the region, and their skepticism suggested the likely reversal to authoritarian rule (see Remmer 1991). Yet despite the severity of the economic crisis of the 1980s and the economic and social costs associated with austerity and structural reforms, the majority of these democracies survived. Peru (1992–2000) remains the only short-lived exception to this regional trend. Research at the time spoke of the "resilience" of Latin American democracies (Mainwaring 1999).

As shown in figure 1.1, democracy in the region took off in the late 1970s and reached a high point in the early 1990s. Based on the electoral democracy index[7] from the Varieties of Democracy Project (V-Dem), the average level of democracy rose from 0.25 in 1978 to 0.64 in 1991. In the 1990s and early 2000s, the level of democracy increased moderately—the highest mark being 0.71 in 2002—but starting in 2006 the average in the region began to decrease. While democracy has become more robust in countries such as Costa Rica, Chile, and Uruguay, the quality of democracy has eroded significantly in Venezuela and Nicaragua and, to a lesser degree, in Honduras and Ecuador. Here, we examine the major trends in the development of democracy and how it provided challengers with expanding political opportunities or new advantages in the context of economic globalization.

Both democracy and economic globalization need to be examined jointly to capture the aforementioned "hybrid political-economic environment" and its impact on popular politics. From this perspective, there are two broad puzzles related to the advantages associated with democracy that facilitate claim-making in the context of market reforms. One revolves around the variation of societal responses across the region, with high episodes of mobilization in some countries but not in others. The other is tied to the apparent delayed reaction to the economic threats induced by market reforms. In both instances, we argue that PEA is well-equipped to systematically assess the variation of protest across geographical areas and over time, allowing researchers to disentangle how national contexts or changes in the economy influence the levels of protest mobilization (Hutter 2014).

One way to examine the variation of societal responses to economic globalization is by taking into account the quality of institutional representation as embodied in political parties, institutions whose presence is conducive to social movement claim-making (Tilly 2004, 138). Here, research has shown that Latin American countries with strong and well-institutionalized parties experience lower levels of mobilization compared to countries with weak and poorly institutionalized parties (Arce 2010). Strong and bigger parties inhibit protests, but weak and smaller parties make possible more protests. Relatedly, Roberts (2012) draws attention to the ideological nature of party representation and the convergence of ideas in support of the Washington consensus in a context of economic crisis. He argues that when a conservative or business-friendly party initiated market reforms and there was an opposition party of the left in the legislature, it not only kept party competition stable but also allowed grievances related to economic globalization to be challenged through the institutionalized legislative process. By contrast, when a populist or center-left party initiated market reforms, it loosened the ties of those parties from their core constituencies (e.g., labor), destabilized party systems in the short term, and made them vulnerable to widespread social resistance in the long term, particularly when these popular constituencies regained their capacity to mobilize against the prevailing market orthodoxy. That said, some of the countries that are known to be at the low end of party system institutionalization (e.g., Bolivia, Ecuador, Venezuela, and Peru) (see Jones 2005) are the same ones that experienced dealignment in Roberts' view, leading to the collapse of traditional parties in some cases and/or explosive mobilizations in the streets in others. Conversely, countries that are known to have better quality of party representation (e.g., Chile, Uruguay, and Mexico) overlap with the group of countries that experienced stable, aligning party competition, thus advancing institutionalized channels to contest the ensuing market orthodoxy.

The main contribution of the works focusing on parties is to show the varied responses to economic globalization across the region. However, the analytic distinction between institutionalized party politics and popular politics has some limitations. Brockett (2005), for instance, states that this division is "more meaningful in institutionalized democracies than it is for the majority of the world's people." In several Latin American countries, in fact, political party activists have been at the forefront of major mobilizations, becoming "the most important and courageous protesters within their countries" (13). The fluidity of electoral rules affecting party competition in the region is also well-known (Remmer 2008), thus the separation between party politics and popular politics is not always clear-cut.

Turning to the delayed reaction to economic globalization, our second puzzle, the 2002 water war in Cochabamba, is often viewed as "the first victory against the neoliberal model" (Farthing and Kohl 2007). Alternatively, Roberts (2002, 1430) views the 1998 election of Hugo Chávez as the end of the hegemony of the Washington consensus. Several authors agreed that the response to market reforms and economic globalization was not immediate, and there are several interpretations about this delay. Some argued that both the economic crisis of the 1980s and its prescribed solution—the market policies of the 1990s—disarticulated popular sectors of society (Roberts 2002; Kurtz 2004; Oxhorn 2009). The delayed response could thus be a result of the overall decline in consumption, particularly in countries that experienced hyperinflation, as economic conditions were expected to deteriorate sharply before improving. Przeworski (1991) dubbed the period the "valley of transition." Other scholars argued that democracy was too shallow to advance opportunities for political actors to respond to these economic threats (O'Donnell 1994). The delayed response was also viewed as a period of recalibration because the shrinking of the state fundamentally changed its interaction with civil society (Stahler-Sholk et al. 2008).

Notwithstanding this delay, the reaction to economic globalization became more pronounced in or around the 2000s. The uninterrupted expansion of democracy in the region enabled popular sectors to recast existing organizations and forge coalition-building with other organizations to oppose market policies (Silva 2009). Grievances related to economic globalization became a powerful mobilizing force (Silva 2009; Simmons 2016) and produced a "master frame" (Roberts 2008, 341) for the repoliticization of popular sectors (Arce 2008).[8] Protests were no longer seen as a source of regime instability, but rather as part and parcel of the "normalization" of politics (Goldstone 2004; Moseley and Moreno 2010). Challengers were also actively engaged and interested in politics, opting to vote in some instances, but mobilizing in the streets in others (Boulding 2014; Moseley 2018; Boulding and Holzner 2021). Even when large-scale mobilizations sacked a few chief executives from office, democratic rule in the region did not crumble.

Economic Growth, the Commodity Boom, and Post-Neoliberal Regimes

Adverse economic conditions have always been a hallmark of political change in the Latin American region (Pérez-Liñán 2018). The growth record of the Washington consensus program—which was underwhelming—was no exception. GDP growth, in fact, hovered around 2 percent during the 1980s and 1990s (see table 1.1). Thus, economic performance was another element that aided challengers to contest the market model. It also paved the way for the left turn in the region (Levitsky and Roberts 2011) and the emergence of so-called post-neoliberal regimes.

Starting with the election of Hugo Chávez in Venezuela in late 1998, the region veered left, and by 2006, the election of left-wing politicians was a regionwide phenomenon. Brazil's Workers' Party (PT), for instance, was in power for fourteen years, from 2002 through 2016. The Peronist Party of Argentina ruled the country from 2003 until 2015. Chile's Socialist Party had two nonconsecutive terms in office, from 2006 to 2010 and again from 2014 to 2018.

Table 1.1. Economic and Social Indicators for Latin America

INDICATORS	PRE–DUAL TRANSITION, 1970–1979	STABILIZATION, 1980–1994	STRUCTURAL ADJUSTMENT, 1995–2001	COMMODITY BOOM, 2002–2014	POSTCOMMODITY, 2015–2019
GDP Growth	4.71%	2.10%	2.61%	3.67%	2.25%
GDP per Capita	$4,547	$4,751	$5,403	$6,540	$7,458
Resource Rents	4.62%	5.03%	3.47%	6.22%	3.59%
Inflation	31.94%	222.59%	13.42%	8.34%	21.70%
Poverty	—	—	49.31%	36.59%	26.90%
Gini	—	51.2	53.42	49.46	45.63

Note: GDP growth and resource rent figures do not include Venezuela during 2015–2019. Inflation figures do not include Argentina, Brazil, Nicaragua, and Venezuela during 1970–1979; Argentina, Nicaragua, and Venezuela during 1980–1994; Argentina and Venezuela during 1995–2001; and Argentina during 2002–2014. Poverty estimates do not include Argentina, Brazil, Colombia, Costa Rica, Ecuador, El Salvador, Honduras, Mexico, Paraguay, Peru, and Uruguay during 1995–2001; Argentina, Brazil, and Mexico during 2002–2014; and Brazil, Guatemala, and Venezuela during 2015–2019. Gini figures do not include Peru during 1980–1994 and Guatemala, Nicaragua, and Venezuela during 2015–2019.

Source: World Development Indicators.

With the exception of members of the Bolivarian Alliance of the Americas (ALBA), including Venezuela, Ecuador, Bolivia, and Nicaragua, the bulk of the left-wing governments in the region were moderate. Based on the KOF index of globalization (Dreher 2006; Gygli et al. 2019), Venezuela was the only country to show a significant drop in globalization, starting in 2002. The rest of the leftist governments supported international economic integration, while recognizing the risks of departing from the prevailing market orthodoxy. NAFTA and other bilateral free trade agreements between the United States and Latin American countries became a protective shield for the Washington consensus program. These governments were also bounded by growing international norms of respect for democracy, which made military coups costly (Cleary 2006). Altogether, this moderation not only served to diminish elite fears of radical redistribution, which were prevalent at the time of transition, but also helped leftist governments to secure their tenure in office.

Critics of the Washington consensus argued that the reforms had only served to improve macroeconomic figures: improvements at micro-level in the form of higher incomes or inequality were lacking. As luck would have it, the rise of the left unfolded during a commodity boom (2002–2014), due primarily to accelerating economic growth in India and China. Resource rents as a share of GDP rose from 3.47 percent in the late 1990s to 6.22 percent during the commodity boom period (see table 1.1). The boom tore open the Washington consensus and amplified the range of policy options that to date had privileged fiscal restraint. The export bonanza, in fact, gave leftist governments greater flexibility to expand social spending and pursue innovative social programs on behalf of the poor. Viewed as a backlash against the neoliberal Washington consensus, the bonanza aided the emergence of "post-neoliberal" or "neo-developmentalist" regimes.[9] The policies of these regimes brought about significant reductions in poverty and inequality throughout the region. For instance, as seen in table 1.1, the percentage of the population living in poverty decreased from 49 percent in the 1995–2001 period to 36 percent during the commodity boom period. The Gini coefficient also decreased.

Windfalls from commodities had other consequences for leftist governments themselves. The export bonanzas in Bolivia, Venezuela, and Ecuador helped to strengthen the power of incumbents (Mazzuca 2013, Weyland 2009). In these countries, state actors not only asserted their control over the revenues from natural resources in varying degrees, but also weakened democratic institutional checks and balances. In some instances, these post-neoliberal regimes compromised the fairness of elections by targeting political opponents through the courts. They skewed the political playing field to their advantage by deploying state resources as well as the media. In other cases, they wielded the power of incumbency to loosen restrictions on presidential term limits. Bolivia's Evo Morales (2006–2019), for instance, became one of the longest-serving presidents in the region (almost fourteen years). Ecuador's Rafael Correa (2007–2017) also amended presidential term limits and was voted into office in three consecutive periods. The weakening of institutional checks and balances eroded the quality of democracy in some of these countries and produced what scholars have characterized as the "illiberalism" of the left (Levitsky 2018). Returning to figure 1.1, the average level of democracy in the region dropped from 0.70 in 2006 to 0.63 in 2019.[10]

The end of the commodity boom reversed the political fortunes of the left. Several countries in the region swung back to right and center-right governments. The economic outlook of the region was no longer great. GDP growth hovered around 2 percent once again and resource rents dropped to 3.59 percent of GDP (see table 1.1). In some countries, the deteriorating economic conditions brought back some of the same deep cuts and economic reforms of 1990s, including the IMF's.

Reactive and Proactive Mobilization

To grasp the fundamental characteristics of protests that on the surface appear very complex and chaotic, this book identifies two broad patterns of mobilization: reactive and proactive. These two ideal types of mobilization are not mutually exclusive; rather, they coexist and sometimes overlap with each other. Reactive mobilization often follows the economy and speaks to the antiausterity protests, IMF riots, and water wars that became widespread as countries moved from the early to the later stages of economic liberalization.[11] In the context of globalization, reactive mobilization is a response to the economic threat, with the arrival of economic liberalization, of losing the material benefits available to class-based actors during periods of state-led development (Almeida 2007). In the presence of reactive mobilization, "bread and butter" issues (i.e., claims) were extensive, and protest actions such as strikes were a common strategy.

By contrast, proactive mobilization centers on politics and reveals a "rainbow of social actors" (Rich, Mayka, and Montero 2019) who have normalized protest politics (Goldstone 2004; Boulding 2014; Moseley 2018) and potentially moved the region's democracies closer to "movement societies" (Meyer and Tarrow 1998). Proactive mobilization is a response to expanding political opportunities or advantages afforded by the spread of democracy and speaks to a "second historical process of mass political incorporation" (Roberts 2008, 327). It involves the increasing presence of civic associations and urban dwellers and a broad set of claims dealing with political, environmental, and cultural rights. Protest actions such as demonstrations and marches are common strategies.

Reactive and proactive patterns of mobilization take into account economic threats linked to economic globalization amid expanding political opportunities under democracy. To elaborate, economic globalization and its two broad phases of reform, stabilization and structural adjustment, speak to one of the primary incentives stimulating collective action—threats (Tilly 1978; Goldstone and Tilly 2001). Threat-induced collective action is motivated by negative incentives or "bad news" that challengers may potentially avoid if they join in an action (Almeida 2010a). The economic upheaval of the 1980s, and its prescribed solution in the form of market reforms, carried substantial economic and social costs that motived popular sectors of society to fight for their livelihoods. Examples include higher consumer prices, food shortages, elimination of subsidies on consumer items, poor provision of basic government services, and the loss of existing rights.[12]

Almeida (2018) identifies different forms of threats, such as economic-related varieties linked to material conditions (e.g., austerity policies), ecological and environmental threats (e.g., pollution, mining practices), threats related to the erosion of rights (e.g., fraudulent elections), and repressive threats (e.g., human rights violations). These varied threats are not symmetrical, but rather are associated with different levels of collective action. In the context of the commodity boom, for example, an antimining campaign may activate local grassroots movements as well as transnational movements. Resistance over privatization policies and free trade agreements and protests demanding better public goods provision may trigger national social movements or even cycles of protests (Alonso and Mische 2017). Almeida and Pérez Martín (2020) further suggest that economic threats connected to market reforms and ecological threats related to changes in global industrial output are reactively mobilizing a large number of people at the time this book is being written.

Turning to democracy, research has argued that democratization advances systemwide political opportunities for challengers to respond to the economic threats associated with economic globalization (Meyer and Minkoff 2004; Almeida and Johnston 2006). Democracies encourage greater associational life by tolerating and legalizing civil society organizations. They also provide more opportunities for mobilization by opening channels of popular participation. In all, democracies capture several positive conditions in the political environment that are favorable for proactive mobilization (Almeida 2018). In this way, they motivate popular sectors to join in action as opportunities move them closer to the realization of their goals (Tilly 1978; Goldstone and Tilly 2001).

Contributors to this volume will demonstrate different actors (who), actions (how), claims (why) and even place (where) of contention across these two ideal types of mobilization. They will also show that when contexts are threat-heavy—as in the "lost decade" of the 1980s—we are more likely to observe reactive protests. But proactive protests are more likely to emerge when contexts are opportunity-heavy, given the "resilience" of Latin American democracies of recent years (Mainwaring 1999). However, the centrality of the state as a target (whom) of protest has not changed because in most cases the state remains both the problem and the solution to collective demands (Jenkins and Klandermans 1995). When state activities were centered on the production of goods and services, reactive mobilization was aligned mostly with the executive branch. However, as state activities recoiled from production, the state became mostly a regulator of such activities. In the twenty-first century, different state institutions and tiers of governments were common targets of proactive mobilization (Hochstetler 2012a; Chng 2012).

Because of the uneven pace of globalization and democracy across Latin America, these two ideal types of mobilization are not always clearly observable, and substantial variation remains across countries. The economic upheaval surrounding the periods of stabilization and structural reforms is distinct from the period of economic expansion associated with the commodity boom. Similarly, while the region has endured one of the longest uninterrupted periods of democracy, the election of populist candidates representing both left- and right-leaning political forces has undermined democracy in recent years. One way to show the convergence (or divergence) around these two broad patterns of mobilization in countries with vastly different political and economic contexts is by drawing on the methodological advantages of protest event analysis, as well as country-specific event datasets.

Protest Event Analysis

Protest event analysis (PEA), a highly original and increasingly popular method to examine protest mobilizations, is well suited for our objective of uncovering the patterns of popular reactions to economic threats and political opportunities across Latin America. PEA scholars adopt, to a large degree, common properties and components when they build country-specific event datasets, which in turn makes comparisons of their findings with other datasets meaningful. The social movements literature has contributed to our understanding of popular contention by establishing common properties to identify protest events as well as common components to understand collective action. The previous association of protest with disturbance, disorder, or even violence not only prevented the analysis of peaceful or symbolic manifestations, but also hindered the execution of comparative and historical analyses. Given that behaviors labeled as chaotic or violent are used to describe actions of which authorities, society, and institutions generally disapprove, their meanings also varied across time and cases. In other words, some behaviors may be seen as acceptable in some contexts but not in others. This makes it difficult to understand, interpret, and compare similar actions beyond specific contexts. However, the identification of common properties makes it possible to offer explanations applicable to a wide range of cases across space and time. Even though protest events are shaped by their own contexts, it is possible to recognize four main characteristics that apply to them all. The literature presents protest events as *collective* behaviors carried out by groups of individuals who seek to advance or protect their common interests. The latter are *contentious* insofar as they directly affect targets' interests or indirectly affect those of third parties. To grab a target's attention, these events are *public*, and they are *episodic* as they are performed outside institutions and without strict time or space regularities.

The identification of these properties also gave scholars an opportunity to identity other actions of protests and incorporate them into more structured comparisons. Knowing what a protest really is and having the theoretical tools to identify it served to define the scope of the analysis. These properties allowed scholars not only to demystify the intrinsic irrational component underlying violent and disorderly behaviors, but also to distinguish collective actions from other nonpurposive behaviors or even purely criminal endeavors. They analyzed different social phenomena, such as revolutions, rebellions, and massive grassroots mobilizations, with the same theoretical tools they used for low-intensity mobilizations and peaceful demonstrations. The intensity or historical relevance of certain events was no longer a condition to segregate them from broader comparisons.

Initially the identification of common properties led scholars to emphasize rational explanations. Under the logic of collective action, they explained protests in terms of expected gains (Olson 1965): The involvement of actors is mediated by a cooperative strategy when gains exceed costs, and successful contention is based on commitment through continued participation. This approach, however, failed to incorporate external factors that could influence individual as well as group behaviors. It also did not allow observation of the choice-making process that takes place inside groups.

Notwithstanding its limitations, the rational perspective provides two important insights to understand collective behaviors. Antagonism emerges as a necessary reality. As actors are motivated by rational

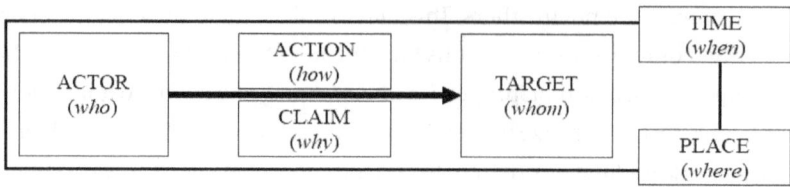

Figure 1.2. Collective Action Components

calculations, their collective actions are always directed to power holders (or targets). There is then an interaction between the actors demanding and the actors receiving the demand. The identification of antagonists helps to grasp other mechanisms of that interaction. These mechanisms condition the actions of antagonists, who are basically restricted to certain forms of interaction. Thus, an actor (who) carries out an action (how) to present a claim (why) to a target (whom) in a particular spatial region (where) at a temporal moment (when) (see figure 1.2).

The identification of these components opened a window to examine how collective action operates in place and time. The fact that the actor–target interaction is mediated by a limited number of actions—which are learned, shared, and performed through a deliberate process of choice that emerges from the struggle itself (Tilly 1993)—suggests the presence of stable temporal patterns. Both parties in dispute know more or less how to behave and what to expect (Tilly 2008). However, as the interest of actors and the opportunities to achieve these interests change, it is assumed that their collective ways of acting will also change (Tilly 1977). Despite operating within limits of well-established actions, actors have room to constantly experiment with new actions when searching for tactical advantages.

Strategic selections give leverage to actors during disputes. Innovative or even prohibited actions can be used to grab the target's attention (McAdam, Tarrow, and Tilly 2001; Tarrow 2012), and the selection of culturally accepted actions may enhance an actor's identification with protests (Cohen 1985; Kane 1997; Sewell 1999; Goodwin and Jasper 2003; Tilly 2005). The range of alternatives constitutes a "toolkit" of habits, skills, and styles actors can take on to build up tactical advantages (Swidler 1986; Williams 2004). Under this logic, actors are equipped with more than one way to bring up their claims to their respective targets, which will vary from place to place, from time to time, and depending on the set of antagonists (Tilly 2008).

Scholars interested in analyzing protest events have sufficient theoretical tools to distinguish protests from other collective behaviors (common properties) and know what to look for when observing changes and continuities in protest patterns (common components). However, these contributions would not have gone very far without the generation of new sources of information. The construction of datasets following protest event analysis (Beissinger 1998; Koopmans and Rucht 2002; Fillieule and Jiménez 2003; Soule 2013) expedited the collection of protest events (Orbuch 1997) under coordinated criteria involving the identification of sources, data collection, and codification processes (Kriesi et al. 1995). The datasets central to this volume follow these theoretical tools and reproduce many of these techniques to explain popular politics in Latin America.

To sum up, the social movements literature presents protest events as public, episodic, collective, and contentious phenomena that involve actors, targets, claims, actions, and places at a given time. Temporal changes between and within any of these five collective action components result from a continuous interaction process observable in protest event datasets over time. However, collective action is always permeable to the effect of external factors, and these variables have a significant effect on mobilizing strategies in Latin America and elsewhere. Considering the hybrid environment of economic threats and expanding political opportunities, the contributors to this volume draw on the main collective action components outlined above to examine popular politics in the region.

Overview of the Country-Specific Event Datasets

Country-specific event datasets allow researchers to quantify and visualize the level of popular mobilization in a given country. Here we follow Tarrow (1989, 8), one of the pioneering efforts in compiling protest event data, and define a "protest event" as disruptive public collective action aimed at institutions, elites, authorities, or other groups on behalf of the collective goals of actors or of those they claim to represent. Examples include marches, roadblocks, strikes, hunger strikes, sit-ins, takeovers, clashes, stoppages, invasions, destruction of property, and so on.

However, because protest events are dynamic—actors and targets in conflict change during struggles, goals and demands shift, and the number of protesters expands one day and contracts the next—a note on temporal and spatial boundaries is warranted. Popular protest can be recorded and counted using different temporal and spatial units (figure 1.3). The contributors to this volume examine protests at one or more of the three units: action, event, and campaign (table 1.2). A campaign consists of a series of actions and events carried out by the same actors in pursuit of the same demands and goals. Here, both one-time mobilization at one place and multiple protest activities in various places over time are counted equally as one campaign. Intuitively, a campaign is close to a phenomenon called social movement.

Datasets with longitudinal data provide a "bird's-eye" view of the

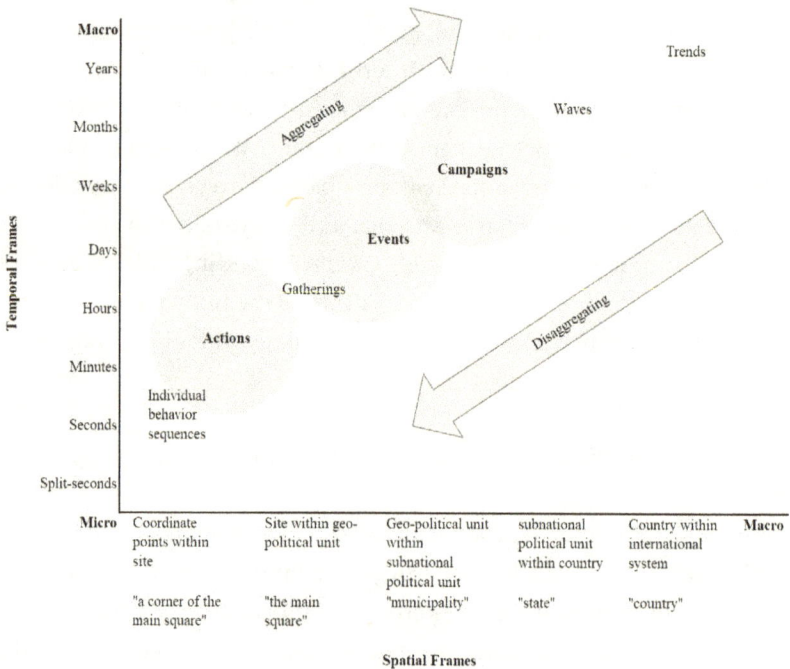

Figure 1.3. Three Units of Popular Protest: Action, Event, and Campaign. The graph is based on McPhail and Schweingruber (1998, 169, Figure 1).

Table 1.2. Summary of the Datasets

CHAPTER	COUNTRY	COVERAGE	UNIT	ANALYSIS	SOURCES
3	Bolivia	1970–2018	Event	Longitudinal	6 (n)
10	Brazil	2011–2016	Event	Cross-sectional	1 (n)
8	Chile	2009–2018	Event	Longitudinal	5 (n), 13(r), (o)
4	Colombia	1975–2019	Event	Longitudinal	9 (n), 11(r), (o)
7	Costa Rica	1983–1983	Campaign	Cross-sectional	4 (n), (o)
9	Ecuador	2007–2017	Campaign	Longitudinal	2 (n)
2	Mexico	1955–2018	Campaign	Longitudinal	3 (n)
7	Nicaragua	1990–1990	Campaign	Cross-sectional	3 (n)
5	Peru	1980–2015	Event	Longitudinal	3 (n)
6	Venezuela	1983–2012	Event	Longitudinal	1 (n), (o)

Notes: Chapter indicates the chapter in this volume. Sources includes the following information: (n) indicates the number of national newspapers; (r) indicates the number of regional newspapers, and (o) indicates that other reports were used to build these datasets.

transformation of popular politics and allow researchers to study long-term trajectories in collective mobilization, exploring changes and continuities over time concerning actors, actions, targets, claims and/or places of collective action. By contrast, datasets with cross-sectional data offer a "magnifying glass" view, enabling authors to analyze protest campaigns that occurred at critical moments of globalization or democratization. The bulk of these datasets draw on the print media, coding events using national and regional newspapers.

Overview of the Volume

The empirical chapters are divided into two major parts. Part I—the bird's-eye view—collects country-specific longitudinal analyses, and Part II—the magnifying glass view—presents country-specific cross-sectional studies of specific historical moments. In figure 1.4, using the KOF index of globalization (Dreher 2006; Gygli et al. 2019) and the electoral democracy index from V-Dem, we plot countries from Part I by their annual scores in Globalization (x-axis) and Democratization (y-axis). An upward move indicates democratization; a downward move signals autocratization. A move rightward means economic globalization and a move leftward denotes deglobalization (that is, increased state intervention in the economy). Gray-highlighted areas indicate the years that match the event data collected and analyzed by each chapter. The graphs will help us understand the varied paths toward economic globalization and democratization taken by each country, compare cross-national similarities and differences, and set up a baseline comparative framework that will be useful in reading the case-study chapters.

In chapter 2, "A Historical and Spatial Analysis of Popular Protests in Mexico, 1955–2018," Takeshi Wada traces shifting patterns of popular protest in Mexico as the twin processes of economic liberalization and political liberalization unfolded. Mexico's location on the graph in figure 1.4 shifts diagonally from bottom left (a combination of political authoritarianism and state-centered economy in the 1970s) to upper right (a region of democracy—albeit a limited one—and market-centered economy in the 2010s). The longitudinal study compares periods before, during, and after globalization and democratization using the Mexican Popular Contention Database (N = 2,321). The chapter applies cluster analysis to event analysis, which enables the author to identify actors, targets, and actions that followed similar paths of historical change. The results are presented in heatmaps that show declines in class-based actors such as workers and peasants, an increasing presence of urban groups and civic associations, and a shift from radical forms of action such as physical attacks and land invasions to moderate ones like demonstrations and marches, although a sign of a revival of violent means is also detected in parallel to the rise of organized crime.

Chapter 3, "Globalization, Democracy, and Conflict Events in Bolivia, 1970–2019," offers another longitudinal analysis that examines how the country's "hybrid political-economic environment" of democracy and globalization transformed its popular politics. Roberto Laserna draws on the Observatorio de Conflictos de CERES, a dataset recording protest events

Mexico

Bolivia

Colombia

Peru

Venezuela

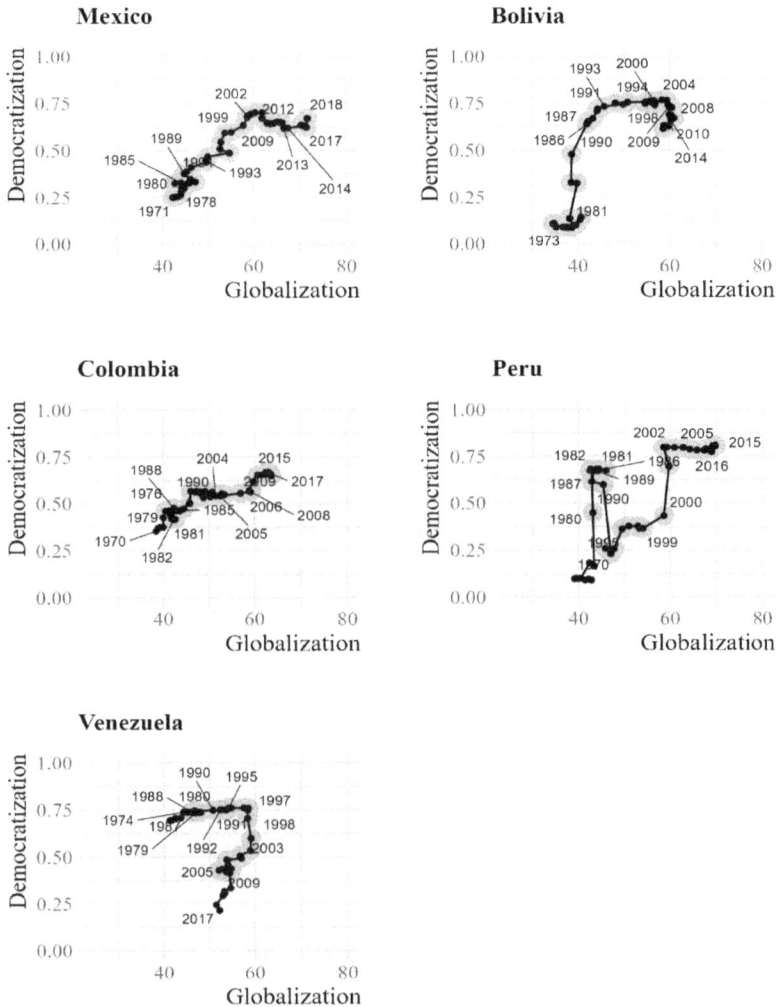

Figure 1.4. Trajectories of Democratization and Globalization (Part I chapters). Democracy scores are the electoral democracy indices from the Varieties of Democracy Project (V-Dem). Globalization scores are taken from the KOF index of globalization (Dreher 2006; Gygli et al. 2019).

from 1970 to 2019 (N = 19,440), and identifies three broad periods of political and economic change: state authoritarianism (1970–1985), democracy and open markets (1985–2003), and state populism (2003–2019). As shown in figure 1.4, the country's location starts from the area of authoritarianism and state-centered economy in the first period, moves upward (democratiza-tion) and rightward (globalization) during the second period, and goes downward (autocratization) in the third period. Laserna's analysis shows that class-based actors and material claims have declined, providing space to other actors and other types of claims: for instance, urban actors pursu-ing various political and social claims. Concomitantly, strikes have been replaced by marches and demonstrations as the main form of contention.

Colombia is a typical case of dual transition, as its evolution in terms of globalization and democracy (shown in figure 1.4) is close to the Latin American average. In chapter 4, "State Debt with a Social Agenda, Con-structed amid Social Protests in Colombia, 1975–2019," Mauricio Archila Neira and Martha Cecilia García Velandia use the Base de Datos de Luchas Sociales (BDLS), a database of social protests in Colombia from 1975 to 2019 (N = 26,119) compiled from sources as varied as daily newspapers, radio and television news stations, and the alternative press. Their longitudinal anal-ysis reveals that the recent neoliberal turn weakened workers, peasants, and other actors with class identity and decreased their material bases of existence (e.g., formal employment, access to land), while empowering oth-ers, such as urban dwellers, environmentalists, ethnic groups, and women. Persistent violence still plagues daily life in Colombia, despite the 2016 peace agreement between the state and guerrilla groups. As a consequence, the authors detect a major trend of growing "politicization" with proactive social protests and demands for more active participatory democracy, more respect for human rights, and more respect for differences of all kinds—regional, racial, ethnic, gender, sexual orientation, generational, religious, and linguistic.

Peru experienced a severe economic crisis during the 1980s that was conducive to the implementation of market policies in the 1990s and a sub-sequent significant expansion of globalization following the commodity boom in the 2000s. As shown in figure 1.4, the country moved rightward (globalization), but went downward (autocratization) when Alberto Fuji-mori was president in the 1990s. In chapter 5, "Protesting in Good and Bad Times: Peru, 1980–2015," Moisés Arce and Renzo Aurazo draw on the Base de Protestas Sociales del Perú (N = 20,468) to explore the protest landscape across different economic and political contexts. Using heatmaps, the authors show a shift from reactive to proactive mobilizations: a change from the dominance of labor actors and labor-related claims and strategies such as strikes during the economic transition of the 1980s to the rise of social actors and political claims and strategies such as marches and stoppages during the commodity boom of the 2000s. They also geocode data to show a shift of contentious activity from the capital city of Lima to peripheral regions across these periods.

Reactive protests are a recurrent phenomenon in daily life in Venezuela, as discussed in chapter 6, "Popular Protests, Deglobalization, and Authoritarianism in Venezuela, 1983–2012." Drawing on two complementary datasets—El Bravo Pueblo (N = 2,815) and Programa Venezolano de Educación Acción en Derechos Humanos (N = 36,137)—covering the period 1983–2012, Margarita López Maya explores the actions and claims of protesters across two broad periods of reform: before and after 1999, the year when Hugo Chávez came to power. In figure 1.4, the first period corresponds to the horizontal move toward the right (globalization) under democracy and the second to the downward and leftward moves of autocratization and de-democratization. The comparison reveals important similarities and differences in these two periods. For instance, the bulk of protest claims are and continue to be related to income (labor) conditions, poor provision of public goods, and human-rights demands. The repressive response of the state has not changed much before or after Chávez. However, starting with the Caracazo and continuing during the Chávez era, protest became more confrontational but also bidirectional, with mobilizations (against the government) and countermobilizations (in favor of the government). Overall, the analysis reveals the precariousness of institutional channels linking society and the state despite the long history of democracy in the country since the late 1950s.

Rather than tracing long-term historical changes, the four chapters in "Part II: A 'Magnifying Glass' View on Specific Protest Campaigns" zoom in on specific moments of globalization and democracy to reveal important dynamics of contention. Figure 1.5 shows the long-term trajectories of the countries; gray-highlighted areas are the specific moments examined in the chapters.

In chapter 7, "Local-Level Popular Protests in Central America at the

Costa Rica

Nicaragua

Chile

Ecuador

Brazil

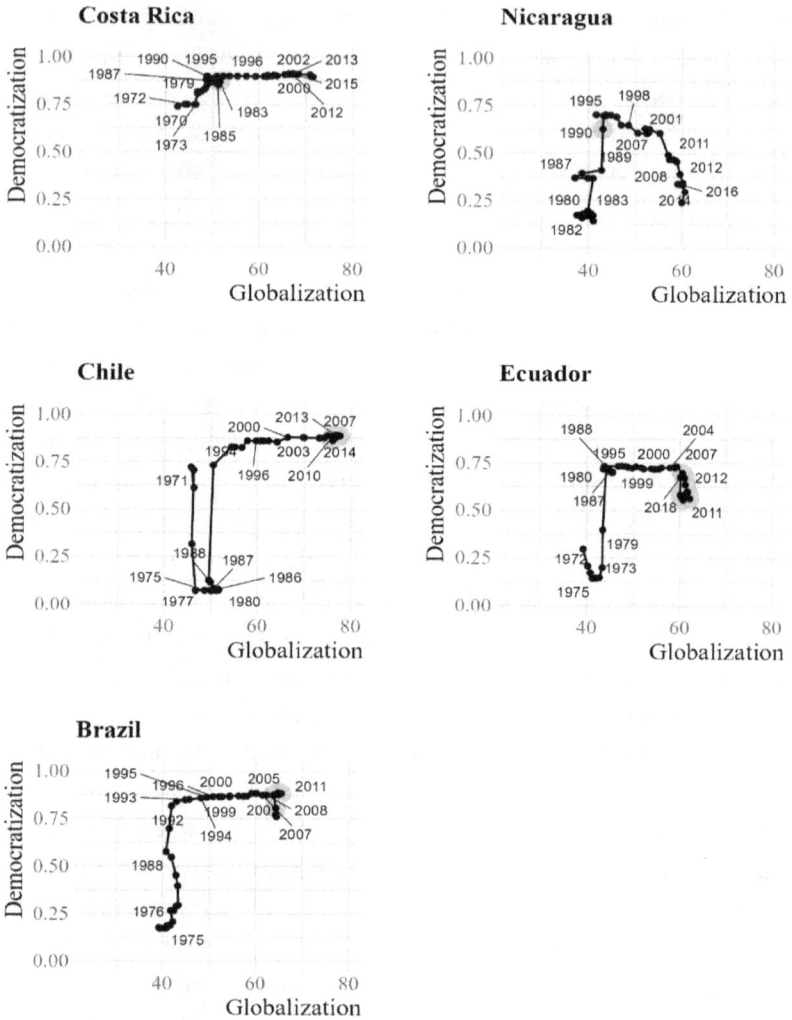

Figure 1.5. Trajectories of Democratization and Globalization (Part II chapters).
The data sources are listed under Figure 1.4.

Early Onset of Neoliberalism," Paul Almeida, Luis Rubén González
Márquez, and María De Jesus Mora focus on the very moment neoliberalism was launched under democracy. Intense reactive mobilization took
place in response to heightened economic threats, as in the 1983 anti-IMF

protest campaign against electricity price increases in Costa Rica and the 1990 anti-Chamorro protest campaign against austerity reforms in Nicaragua. Figure 1.5 confirms that these years correspond to early neoliberal reform: after these moments (the points bolded in the graphs), the locations of both countries start to move toward the right, indicating the process of neoliberal globalization. The focus on the early stage of neoliberal reform is valuable because the two countries offer an emblematic model of collective action observed in subsequent decades throughout the Global South. The authors detect considerable local variation in the occurrence of protests and ask why. They build a country-specific database of protest events for each of the two campaigns (N = 122 for Costa Rica and N = 642 for Nicaragua) from local newspapers and archival sources. Applying GIS mapping and negative binomial regression analysis, the authors discover that reactive popular protests were more likely to emerge in localities where communities were able to appropriate legacies from the state-led development era, including state infrastructures (e.g., major highways) and organizational assets (e.g., oppositional political parties) for mobilization tasks and tactics (e.g., roadblocks).

In contrast to chapter 7, Nicolás Somma and Rodrigo Medel examine the later stages of neoliberal reform in chapter 8, "A Group-Based Approach to Analyze the Protest Landscape in Chile at the Height of Neoliberalism and Democracy." This period (2009–2019) is important because the extent of both globalization and democracy in Chile was among the highest in Latin America and therefore the effects of economic and political transformations on popular politics can be more clearly revealed. In the 2010s, Chile reached the upper-right corner on the map in figure 1.5. As the highlight indicates, this chapter focuses on this interesting moment. Using the Observatory of Conflicts database (N = 23,398), the authors compare claims, tactics, targets, and places of protest by actor. The actor-centric comparative analysis or "group-based approach" reveals that workers and students—two major actors formed during the state-led development era—have adapted to democracy and market reforms and continue to be the most active players in the proactive Chilean protest landscape. Moreover, their application of social network analysis to protest event data uncovers the otherwise invisible patterns of actor alliances: Chilean workers were not only active but also the most connected to social actors of different types, while political parties were mostly isolated.

In chapter 9, "Protests and Citizens' Revolution in Ecuador under Post-Neoliberalism," Santiago Ortiz draws on the Registro del Centro Andino de Acción Popular (CAAP) to examine a protest cycle that occurred at a critical moment of democracy and globalization in Ecuador: the Citizens' Revolution of Rafael Correa (2007–2017). In this period, the country embraced a post-neoliberal regime with various policies to promote social justice, but with attacks on existing democratic norms and autonomous grassroots organizations. The period corresponds to the moment of de-democratization, as the country location on the figure 1.5 graph moves downward, a trend we also find in the Bolivian and Venezuelan graphs. Ortiz's analysis reveals how Correa's redistributionist approach made the government the main target of proactive contention. While the government funneled resources in response to increased contentious activity, it also fragmented various social organizations into pro- and anti-Correa camps.

Similar to the Ecuador chapter in this book, Luciana Tatagiba and Andréia Galvão's study of political contention in Brazil centers around the post-neoliberal period. Lula and Rousseff's Workers' Party (PT) governments implemented "neo-developmentalist" policies to achieve better distribution of income, but these generated strong oppositions. In chapter 10, "Dynamics of Political Contention in Brazil: From Deepening to Debacle of Neo-Developmentalism," the authors examine the nature of these oppositions by building a database of 1,285 protest events between 2011 and 2016 using *Folha de São Paulo* (FSP), one of the largest nationwide newspapers in Brazil. This period is critical because, as the downward move in figure 1.5 shows, contentious politics during the post-neoliberal and neo-developmentalist initiatives led to deterioration of democracy. Their event analysis uncovers vividly the rise of the anti-PT movement, composed of the middle and upper-middle classes. This new rightist movement, fueled by "antipetismo," used issues of corruption charges selectively, delivered Rousseff's impeachment after successful protest campaigns in 2015 and 2016, and paved the way for the election of Jair Bolsonaro in 2018. The empowered protest movement of the right, responding to the prevailing post-neoliberal regime, led to the resurgence of the neoliberal agenda, effectively restricting social and labor rights.

In the concluding chapter, María Inclán rounds out the book by summarizing the transformation of protest politics in the aftermath of economic globalization and democracy in the Latin American region. And, reversing the causal arrow, she also analyzes the implications of these changes for democracy and/or globalization.

Conclusion

This chapter has summarized the major economic and political developments in Latin America over the last forty years. We have argued that the arrival of democracy and economic globalization produced a "hybrid political-economic environment" of expanding *political opportunities* and *economic threats*, which in turn transformed popular politics in the region. To understand more thoroughly the fundamental characteristics of protests, we introduce two ideal-types of mobilization—reactive and proactive—and a working hypothesis that suggests when we are more likely to see these patterns emerge. When conditions are threat-heavy, reactive protests are common, but when conditions become opportunity-heavy, proactive protests are frequent.

By departing from previous approaches examining popular politics in Latin America, this book's contributors provide a unifying methodology based on protest event analysis using country-specific events datasets. Using fine-grained information related to the amount and main features of protest, contributors of this volume will show substantive differences across the two broad patterns of mobilization. In brief, actors (who), actions (how), claims (why), and place (where) of contention changed, but the target (whom) of protest did not. The convergence or divergence around these patterns of mobilization can be explained by taking into account the varied trajectories of both economic globalization and democracy.

Two other contributions can be drawn from our approach based on protest event analysis. First, research on the social consequences of economic globalization has focused for too long on the levels of mobilization (actions) and what these levels mean for democracy and/or contention against neo-liberalism. Empirical findings related to demobilization appear to be specific to certain periods (temporal dimension), whereas those of mobilization are concentrated on a handful of Latin American countries (spatial dimension) (see Hochstetler 2012b). By bringing forward the major components of mobilization (i.e., actors, claims, targets) and controlling for temporal and spatial dimensions, the contributors to this volume provide a more complete picture of mobilization in the aftermath of the region's dual transition to democracy and globalization.

Second, case study research and variations of this approach have dominated the study of popular protests in Latin America (for exceptions, see Boulding 2014; Moseley 2018). While it provides rich, detailed treatments of specific antimarket campaigns, the core limitation of the case study approach remains its focus on positive cases or successful mobilizations (see Hochstetler 2012b). By contrast, this volume traces the footsteps of big data, the game-changing approach that is transforming the social sciences. Specifically, building on contributions from protest event analysis (McAdam 2010; Tarrow 1989; Beissinger 2002; Koopmans and Rucht 2002; Hutter 2014), we have made the case that country-specific event datasets allow one to adequately examine large-scale social changes, while making it possible to identify generalizable patterns across the region. Having reviewed the main characteristics of these datasets and their places in our comparative framework, the chapters that follow take these comparisons to task.

Notes

1. Economic globalization can be understood as the increasing integration of national economies worldwide by means of foreign direct investment, trade liberalization, privatizing state-owned enterprises, and other market-oriented economic reforms. Different terms are used to denote this shift in economic strategies, including neoclassical economics, neoliberalism, economic orthodoxy, and the Washington consensus.
2. Ortiz et al. (2005) and Earl et al. (2004) discuss common biases associated with media coverage of protest events.
3. To explain long-term trajectories in collective mobilization, contributors

create and present distinctive periods based on specific country conditions.

4. Cuba remains the only open autocratic regime in the region.
5. This section follows Arce (2005).
6. The Latin American average corresponds to the following sixteen mainland countries: Argentina, Bolivia, Brazil, Chile, Colombia, Costa Rica, Ecuador, El Salvador, Guatemala, Honduras, Mexico, Nicaragua, Paraguay, Peru, Uruguay, and Venezuela.
7. The V-Dem electoral democracy index represents an answer to the question "To what extent is the ideal of electoral democracy in its fullest sense achieved?"
8. Simmons (2016) draws attention to the social and cultural aspects of grievances, which, when combined with material concerns, can play a critical role in shaping collective resistance.
9. The utility of these concepts is subject to ongoing debate.
10. To be clear, not all leftist governments attacked existing democratic norms. Under Lula's presidency in Brazil, for instance, the Worker's Party promoted greater civil society participation, elections were very competitive, and major violations of the rule of law were absent.
11. We use the term "water wars" broadly to denote widespread resistance to the privatization of public utilities such as water and electricity.
12. This section follows Almeida (2010a, 2018).

PART I

A "BIRD'S-EYE" VIEW ON THE TRANSFORMATION OF POPULAR POLITICS

CHAPTER TWO

A Historical and Spatial Analysis of Popular Protests in Mexico, 1955–2018

TAKESHI WADA

Introduction[1]

In Mexico, twin transformative processes of economic and political liberalization (or, roughly speaking, globalization and democratization) have not brought about the expected benefits of economic growth, inequality reduction, or political stability. While the reasons for this underachievement are complex, multifaceted, and beyond the scope of this chapter, the pages that follow attempt to shed light on the issue by uncovering changes in civil society or, more precisely, shifts in the patterns of popular protest in the liberalization processes. How have the processes of economic and political liberalization transformed Mexico's civil society? How has persistent inequality and poverty influenced the nature of popular protests? Has societal transformation contributed to political stability or hindered it?

In this chapter, we explore six specific questions related to shifting patterns of popular protest in Mexico. The first is whether democratization and globalization have increased or decreased the *level* of popular protest. Popular struggle may seem a destabilizing factor in politics. However, the dominant perspective in social movement and civil society studies suggests that protests and social movements are essential ingredients of democracy

(Cohen and Arato 1992; Ekiert and Kubik 1999). This is because the meaning and practice of citizenship are constructed, modified, and reproduced through popular struggle (Hanagan and Tilly 1999; Tamayo Flores-Alatorre 1999). In institutional political arenas, such as voting or lobbying by interest groups, popular groups are at a significant disadvantage compared to the resource-rich elite. It is not an exaggeration to say that appealing to protest is the only weapon available to popular groups (Piven and Cloward 1977). Whether this sphere of popular struggle and participation remains a viable option is important, especially when we consider the issue of the further deepening of democracy, an issue not just limited to the question of elections (Cleary 2007; Mattiace 2012).

The second question is about the *places* of protest. Do the stark contrasts in livelihood, poverty, inequality, and opportunities among Mexico's three regions—the richer industrialized north close to the United States, the metropolitan central valley including the capital, and the poorer rural south—affect Mexican citizens' decision to take to the streets?

What are the principal *claims* of contention? This is the third question. By examining the claims made in popular protests, we can understand where in politics, economy, or society Mexican citizens perceive problems to lie. In the process of democratization and globalization, are citizens primarily preoccupied with material economic issues such as poverty and economic inequality? Or are they more concerned with political rights such as the strengthening of democracy? Are new demands specific to twenty-first-century Mexico emerging?

The fourth question concerns the *actors* in popular protest. Who is the leading actor in the process of democratization and globalization? Are class-based organizations, such as workers and peasants, still mainstream? If indigenous peoples, women, and other marginalized groups enter the stage of political struggle, it might be a sign that they will contribute to the strengthening of democracy and political stability in the long run.

Fifth, to whom do the actors bring their claims? Who are their *targets* of contention? Have shifts in economy and politics led them to shift their targets, and if so, why?

The sixth question concerns the *actions*, methods, or forms of popular struggle. Not all popular struggles contribute to the deepening of democracy and political stability. Extreme radical actions and the use of violence likely cause instability: radical and violent actions can harm human lives and property, hinder rational dialogue, lead to security operations by police and military forces, and provoke further violence and countermobilization on the part of hostile social groups. Of concern is that the governing capacity of state institutions in Mexico is seriously compromised due to the development of organized crime and drug trafficking and the routinization of violence. In these circumstances, is the repertoire of popular protest also becoming more radical and violent?

Globalization and Democratization

PRE-LIBERALIZATION PERIOD

To examine the effects of economic and political liberalization in Mexico, we must understand the economic and political situation *before* these twin processes began. This pre-liberalization period spans the 1940s to the 1970s. It was characterized by a highly stable one-party political regime. Elections were held regularly, but in practice the official party, the Partido Revolucionario Institucional (PRI), won most elections. Real political competition happened not in the elections but around the informal process known as the *dedazo* ("big finger") through which outgoing presidents would handpick their successors (Langston 2006). Power resided more in the executive branch than in the legislative and judicial branches and at the higher levels of the state. In contrast to the "hard authoritarianism" of military dictatorships in South America, civilian control over the military was institutionalized in Mexico. In the face of political opposition, the regime's response was co-optation: that is, bringing the opponent into the political system by offering them a job or a policy concession (Eckstein 1977). This "soft authoritarianism" brought about more than a half-century of political stability.

The second political feature of the pre-liberalization period was corporatism (Wiarda 2004), which pertains to the way in which state and society relations are institutionalized. Three major social groups—the agricultural (peasants), labor, and "popular" (primarily middle-class) sectors—were

vertically incorporated into the official party as the Confederación Nacional Campesina (CNC), the Confederación de Trabajadores de México
(CTM), and the Confederación Nacional de Organizaciones Populares
(CNOP), respectively. Mexican corporatism was not just a formal arrange-
ment. It was fervently sustained and symbolically legitimized through an
ideology associated with the Mexican Revolution (social justice and land
distribution) as well as Mexican nationalism (catalyzed by the 1938 nationalization of the oil industry). Corporatism was a strategy of mobilizing and
organizing both the workers and the peasants and, over the years, served
as a mechanism of social control by keeping them apart from each other to
prevent the possible formation of a horizontal urban–rural coalition (Smith
and Green 2019).

The third feature was state-centered economic development. The Mexican state assumed a leading role in economic and social modernization
with its ambitious public works projects in the areas of irrigation, roads,
dams, communications, and port facilities and with its import-substitution
industrialization (ISI) policies. The state maintained a delicate balance
within the PRI between those forces promoting economic growth and
those pursuing social justice (land distribution, social security, redistribution). State intervention in the economy reached its height during the Luis
Echeverría government (1970–1976), when well over half the budget went to
special government agencies and state-sponsored companies (Smith and
Green 2019).

The fourth and final feature of the pre-liberalization period was its informal clientelist politics. The Mexican political system was built on dual pillars: the formal power centralized in the national government based on the
abovementioned features and the informal power based on a diffuse clientelist personal network (Fox 1994; Selee 2015, 163). Local political leaders
served as intermediaries for citizens in return for their loyalty to the official
party and assumed considerable decision-making ability in local governments.

In short, during the pre-liberalization period, power was concentrated
in high-level state executives, who exercised considerable influence over
the state, society, and market forces.[2] It was this power that was to be liber-
alized.

ECONOMIC LIBERALIZATION

Economic liberalization is the process of transforming from a state-centered to a market-centered economy. Economic growth in Mexico based on the state-centered ISI development model reached its limits in the 1970s. The Echeverría government was running large deficits and financing them in an inflationary manner, and by 1973 inflation was running at 20 percent, making it difficult to maintain a fixed exchange rate. Facing the pressure of the flight of capital, the peso was devalued by 60 percent in September 1976, then by another 40 percent the following month (Smith and Green 2019).

With Mexico's discovery of vast oil reserves, however, the José López Portillo administration (1976–1982) continued the familiar path of state-centered economic development. Mexico became excessively dependent on oil revenues. When the world slump in oil prices after 1981 reduced foreign exchange earnings, it had to default on eighty billion dollars in foreign debt in 1982. The debt crisis forced Mexico to change its traditional development model (Lustig 1992).

The decision in 1985 by the Miguel de la Madrid government (1982–1988) to seek entry into the General Agreement on Tariffs and Trade (GATT, the predecessor of the World Trade Organization or WTO) signaled Mexico's dramatic shift toward economic liberalization. De la Madrid and his successor, Carlos Salinas (1988–1994), reduced the state's role in the economy by cutting public spending, privatizing state-owned companies, and opening the economy through its entry into GATT in September 1986 and the North American Free Trade Agreement (NAFTA) in 1994. As a result of Mexican corporatism, the state, business, labor, and peasants signed a Pact of Economic Solidarity in 1987 to deepen the economic restructuring process (Teichman 1996). Within a decade, Mexico saw near-complete abandonment of the postwar policies of ISI and institutionalization of the market-centered economy.

Figure 2.1a (top graph) charts Mexico's processes of economic liberalization. It summarizes the number of privatizations of state-owned enterprises by year based on data from the World Bank and the Mexican government. The numbers are good indicators of when economic liberalization was implemented in practice. As mentioned above, in the case of Mexico, we can think of 1985 as a moment of transition from a state-centered economy to a market-centered one. Although data before 1983 are not available, we can identify peaks of privatization between 1988 and 1993 under the Salinas administration. NAFTA, a form of institutionalization of economic liberalization, came into force in January 1994. Privatization continued during the Ernesto Zedillo administration (1994–2000), but the number of privatizations was quite limited under the Partido de Acción Nacional (PAN) administrations of Vicente Fox and Felipe Calderón (2000–2012). The years under Salinas can be thought of as a period of market transition (Williams 2012), the Zedillo administration as one of market institutionalization, and the PAN administration as one of market maturity.

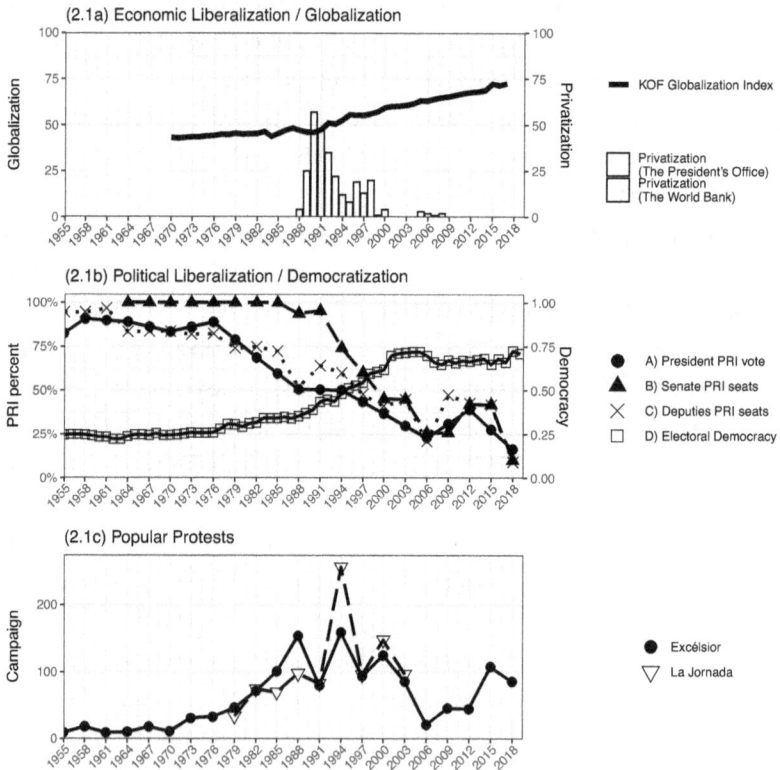

Figure 2.1. Economic Liberalization, Political Liberalization, and Popular Protests. a) The World Bank Group, DataBank website (http://databank.worldbank.org, accessed on March 13, 2021); KOF Globalization Index (Gygli et al. 2019; Dreher 2006); Presidencia de la República, *Informe de Gobierno 1983–2003* (cited by Chong and López-de-Sinales 2004: 11). b) Varieties of Democracy Project (V-Dem); Vicente Fox 2001, *Primer Informe de Gobierno: Anexo*, México: Presidencia; Enrique Peña Nieto 2017, *El Quinto Informe de Gobierno: Anexo Estadístico*, México: Presidencia (http://www.presidencia.gob.mx/quintoinforme, accessed on February 12, 2018). c) MPCD Version 2020.06 (Wada 2019).

The KOF Globalization Index (1970–2017), introduced in chapter 1, confirms this trajectory. The score had been constant until around 1990. The effect of neoliberal economic reforms, including privatization, can be seen in the line's upward trend from 1990 on (figure 2.1a), peaking at 72.48 in 2017, the final year for which data were available at the time of writing. In 2017, Mexico's degree of trade and financial liberalization was one of the highest in the world: it was ranked 51st of 203 countries and fourth in Latin America, behind Chile (40th), Uruguay (47th), and Panama (48th). Note that most of the countries above Mexico belong to the European Union.

POLITICAL LIBERALIZATION

The successful state-centered economic development was accompanied by the emergence of the middle class in Mexico. With the rise of the highly educated urban population, the stable one-party regime faced new political challenges. Some of the earliest came from provincial towns and cities as PAN won 26 of the 236 municipal elections between 1962 and 1978 (Gillingham 2012). The proven strategies of co-optation and selective repression had been mostly effective in countering a railroad workers' strike in 1959, Salvador Nava's electoral challenge for the San Luis Potosí governorship in 1961, and the resident doctors' movement in 1964. However, the most serious challenge to the regime came in 1968 in the form of the student movement. President Gustavo Díaz Ordaz sent army troops to Tlatelolco in Mexico City to repress it. The resulting student massacre eroded the PRI's legitimacy. Guerrillas then staged a series of bank robberies and kidnappings from 1971 on and independent peasant movements emerged, triggering liberalization processes (Trevizo 2011).

Facing the erosion of its legitimacy and the rise of extrainstitutional activities by opposition forces, the regime opted for a gradual process of political liberalization. In the 1977 electoral reform, the López Portillo administration eased the rules for registration of political parties, and the Communist Party thus gained official recognition. Opposition parties were guaranteed a total of at least one hundred seats in the four-hundred-member Chamber of Deputies. The basic idea behind this and subsequent reforms was to open the institutionalized political arena to opposition politicians and movements just enough for the PRI to be able to continue its hegemony and soft authoritarianism while preventing the further growth of extrainstitutional activism. In contrast to its South American counterparts, where abrupt democratic transition through elite pacts occurred, "protracted transition" (Eisenstadt 2000)—prolonged negotiations and deals over electoral rules and institutions between the regime and the opposition parties—characterized Mexico (Loaeza 2000; Ortega Ortíz 2000).

The next major challenge to the regime came in the 1988 presidential election, when the PRI split. Salinas, the PRI candidate, faced serious opposition in Cuauhtémoc Cárdenas, who led a breakaway faction. The PRI's controversial win further damaged its legitimacy, and Cárdenas founded the left-wing Partido de la Revolución Democrática (PRD) (Bruhn 1997). Facing electoral challenges from the left and from the conservative right in the PAN, at both the national and local levels, the PRI conceded local victories to the PAN through informally negotiated *concertacesiones* ("gentleman's agreements," originating in a Mexican slang combination of the words for "concertation" and "concession") but refused to engage PRD (Eisenstadt 2007). The 1994 electoral reform granted independence to the Federal Electoral Institute, and the 1996 reform under the Zedillo administration brought about the establishment of a more or less free and fair electoral system (Magaloni 2005).[3] The PRI lost control of the national Chamber of Deputies in 1997, the Mexico City governorship in the same year, and the presidency in 2000. Zedillo abandoned the time-honored dedazo by announcing that he would not himself designate his successor. The gradual political liberalization that began around the mid-1970s ended up, a quarter-century later, leading to elections that were more democratic.

Figure 2.1b shows the trend of political liberalization. The indicators reveal how the PRI's one-party rule gradually weakened and political opportunities were opened. Looking at the percentage of votes obtained in the presidential election and the percentages of seats won in the Senate and the House of Representatives ("Deputies"), until 1976 the PRI held a near-monopoly, at a level exceeding 80 percent, with political opportunities closed. The party's overwhelming advantage gradually eroded from the end of the 1970s with the economic crisis and the implementation of neoliberal economic reforms. The PRI's presidential vote and lower-house seat percentages dropped to the 50 percent–60 percent range, and its Senate seat percentage fell sharply beginning in 1994.[4] By the year 2000, the percentages had dropped below a majority, falling even further in 2006. With Enrique Peña Nieto's victory in the 2012 presidential election, the PRI vote increased by about 20 percent, but its popularity dropped to a historically low level in the 2018 elections.

The line (D) represents the electoral democracy score from the Varieties of Democracy (V-Dem) Project introduced in chapter 1. The trajectory of this measure of formal democracy is the opposite of the PRI's share of votes/seats. Mexico maintained a stable low score of around .250 from the 1950s to the mid-1970s. Mexico's one-party rule seems to be closer to semi-authoritarianism than to authoritarian regimes such as military dictatorships. (For instance, the score for Pinochet's Chile in 1978 was .072.) The score began to increase in the late 1970s with a series of gradual electoral reforms and local victories by the opposition parties, first by the PAN in the north during the 1970s and 1980s, followed by the PRD in the 1990s (Beer 2012; Gillingham 2012). Democratization processes continued into the time of Fox's presidency and hit their height in 2005 with a score of .720. During the presidencies of Calderón (PAN) and Peña Nieto (PRI), the democratizing processes stagnated; the score reached as low as .648 in 2008 and .649 in 2015. With Andrés Manuel López Obrador's presidential victory in 2018, electoral democracy reached its highest point (.725, 54th of the world's 179 countries).[5]

There are other indicators of democracy in the V-Dem dataset.[6] It is worth mentioning that Mexico has performed consistently poorly in the measure of egalitarian democracy, which takes into account degrees of material and immaterial equality. Mexico's score in 2018 was .420, 73rd in the world, well below its standing (54th) in the electoral democracy measure; this may have been one of the triggers of popular protest into the 2020s.

To understand the effects on civil society of the economic and political liberalization processes that began in the 1970s, it is necessary to systematically gather data on the political activities of Mexican civil society and delineate their evolution starting from the time when authoritarian rule by the dominant Institutional Revolutionary Party (PRI) was unwavering. This research builds a database of events of popular protest from the 1950s to the present using newspapers as its data source, as explained in the next section.

Methods

To understand historical changes in patterns of popular protest, it is indispensable to have a long-term record that enables historical and socio-spatial comparisons of the diverse activities of various social forces. This study uses the Mexican Popular Contention Database (MPCD), Version 2020.06. We set up this database of protest events in Mexico between 1955 and 2018 from data we gathered on incidents (events) of political activities of various social groups drawn from two sets of politically contrasting newspapers. *Excélsior*, founded in 1916, is close to the Mexican elites, and *Unomásuno* and *La Jornada* are more sympathetic to left-wing oppositions. *Unomásuno* was launched in 1977 by former *Excélsior* journalists. *La Jornada* was founded in 1984 by journalists who split off from *Unomásuno* after a dispute over management policies. Therefore, *Unomásuno* was used as a data source until the birth of *La Jornada*, and *La Jornada* was used afterward.[7]

Despite known limitations such as media bias in coverage, in practice newspapers provide us with the only systematic source of evidence that allows scholars to make chronological comparisons of political activities according to different social sectors (Hutter 2014; Jenkins and Maher 2016; Koopmans and Rucht 2002). Recent studies on Mexico have also adopted event analysis techniques (Cadena-Roa 2016; Inclán 2012; Strawn 2008; Trejo 2012; Trevizo 2011).

We sampled newspaper articles published during the periods two weeks before and two weeks after each triennial federal election between 1955 and 2018. The reason for collecting information from the 1950s is to be able to compare the periods of political and economic liberalization from the late 1970s onward with periods when Mexico's authoritarian regime was strong and state-centered economic development policies were firmly in place. Ideally, all newspaper articles from the 1950s to the present would have been used, but a lack of resources forced us to employ a sampling strategy. Mexico's national elections are usually held on the first Sunday in July, with newspapers the following day recording election events. Therefore, we gathered newspaper articles for a total of twenty-nine days per election, starting from the Monday two weeks before the election to the Monday two weeks after it.

The reason for focusing on the periods surrounding national elections is that the process of political liberalization in Mexico was particularly centered on electoral reforms, and so looking at election periods in chronological order makes it possible to understand the effects of political change directly. Except for the two federal elections under Carlos Salinas in 1991 (August 18) and 1994 (August 21) and the midterm election under Enrique Peña Nieto in 2015 (June 7), national elections were held regularly on the first Sunday of July, which also helped to control for other potential effects. In short, the data provide a snapshot of popular struggle during the twenty-two national elections between 1955 and 2018, as reflected in newspapers close to the elite and to the leftist oppositions.

The biggest advantage of event analysis is that it can quantify and provide a visualization of the level of popular mobilization. To do this, it is necessary to clarify what kinds of activities we count. Following Tarrow (1989, 8), the MPCD defines a "protest event" as disruptive public collective action aimed at institutions, elites, authorities, or other groups on behalf of the collective goals of the actors or of those they claim to represent. Examples of popular events based on the above include demonstrations, marches, hunger strikes, sit-ins, work suspensions, rallies, property destruction, physical attacks, land occupations, kidnappings, occupations of offices and buildings, obstructions of public transport systems, road blockades, and strikes.

Even if the object of analysis is defined conceptually as described above, there is still the problem of how to quantify the associated phenomena. Actual struggles are essentially dynamic: actors and targets in conflict can change during contentious processes; goals and demands shift flexibly; and the number of participants in protests expands one day and contracts the next. As shown in figure 1.5 in the introductory chapter, we must deal with the problem of quantifying phenomena whose temporal and spatial boundaries are not clear. The MPCD records (and counts) popular protests at three levels: action, event, and campaign. In this chapter, we will use the campaign level as the unit (N = 2,321). A campaign consists of a series of actions and events carried out by the same actors in pursuit of the same main demands and goals. It is important to note that both a one-time mobilization in a single location and multiple connected protest activities in various places over time may count equally as a single campaign. Intuitively, a campaign is close to a phenomenon called a social movement.

Popular Politics in Mexico

Do processes of democratization and globalization encourage political activities by civil society forces or discourage them? In this section, we introduce conflicting viewpoints from previous research and then compare them with our latest results.

The first perspective emphasizes the democratization process and assumes it will result in a politically active civil society and increase popular mobilization. According to this view, the transition from an authoritarian regime to a more democratic one expands "political opportunities" for social forces—intensified political competition among elites, increased access to political decision-making processes, shifting elite alignments, emergence of elite allies, and reduced risks of state control and repression—which encourages them to engage in a variety of political actions, including protests (Tarrow 2011). Some studies of Mexican civil society share this perspective and argue that as the PRI's one-party rule erodes and state control gradually weakens, civil society organizations find greater political space where they can mobilize their followers more autonomously (Bilello 1996; Favela 2010; Mattiace 2012; Monsiváis 1987; Pérez Arce 1990).

An alternative perspective is that the processes of political and/or economic liberalization will subdue popular groups and mobilizations. First, the inverted U-curve theory (Gurr 1970; O'Connell 2008) claims that it is difficult to engage in protest activity under an authoritarian regime because the risk of oppression is high and political opportunities are closed. The theory predicts a low level of protest activity under democracy as well, because citizens would only need to make claims through institutionalized political processes such as elections (Smelser 1962). In short, social movements and protests appear to be most prominent in semidemocratic/semi-authoritarian regimes between the authoritarian and democratic poles (Eisinger 1973; Ekiert and Kubik 1999). The idea of the inverted U-curve can be found in research on Mexican social movements (Inclán 2009; Inclán 2018, 31–32; Trejo 2014). Favela (2010) cites as a major reason for the increase in protests in Mexico since the late 1990s the semidemocratic nature of the Mexican political system: that is, that political liberalization has progressed but is still inadequate.

Others emphasize the effects of globalization and foresee a decline of civil society. Major social organizations that make up civil society—trade unions, cooperatives, farmer organizations, schools, universities, urban resident organizations—have benefited from close ties with the state. The main purpose of neoliberal economic reform elsewhere is to tear down just such a traditional state–society alliance. As a result, Castells (2010) argues that these social organizations are weakened, are less able to engage in mobilization, and tend to fall short on protecting the interests and values of their members. Research on Mexican society finds that this phenomenon of "atomization of the social network" has occurred (Zermeño 1990). Trade unions, farmers organizations, and urban resident organizations have served as important mobilizing structures of the ruling PRI. Under PRI corporatism, these organizations have enjoyed benefits due to state institutions such as the Ministry of Labor and Social Welfare, the Ministry of Agrarian Reform, various housing corporations, and agricultural banks. Zermeño (1998) claims that Mexico has entered an era in which citizens feel a sense of helplessness and disorder as a result of the introduction of a market-centered economy and trade unions, political parties, universities, and cooperatives no longer able to represent members' interests and values.

Now let us compare the timing of these liberalization processes with the ups and downs of popular mobilization. Figure 2.1c shows changes over time in the number of popular protest campaigns, as registered in the MPCD. The first finding, to our surprise, is that the graphs for the elite-oriented *Excélsior* and the left-wing newspapers are quite similar. It is true that the number of protest campaigns reported in *La Jornada* in 1994 was particularly high due to its extensive coverage of the Zapatista National Liberation Army's (EZLN) uprising in Chiapas[8] and the contentious presidential election. Still, the two sets of newspapers show very similar trends and peak years. The trend shown in figure 2.1c is quite similar to the one of indigenous protests reported by Trejo (2014, 339).

In the 1960s and 1970s, before the full-fledged liberalization of the economy and politics, there were very few popular protests. This was to be expected from the theories reviewed. From 1979 through the 1980s, the number of campaigns gradually increased. This is in line with the gradual expansion of political opportunities shown in figure 2.1b. This suggests that the liberalization of politics has stimulated political activities. This liberalization also involved an increase in freedom of the press, which likely contributed to the increase in news reports on protests. From 1988 through the 1990s, the number of popular protests reported reached the highest level. This coincides with accelerated processes of political and economic liberalization. In the midst of a major transformation of the political and economic system, the level of popular protests reached its peak.

After the 2000 regime change in politics and market institutionalization in the economy, the number of popular protests dropped sharply during the periods of the PAN governments (2000–2012). Mexico's electoral democracy score reached the highest level in its history (although still below .750), political opportunities were presumably more open than ever, and citizen mobilization appeared to have subsided. This result is not what would be expected according to political opportunity structure theory. It appears rather consistent with both the inverted U-curve—predicting that democracy would reduce protests (Inclán 2018) as political parties absorbed some of their responsibilities (Mattiace 2012) or were motivated to discourage radical mobilization (Trejo 2014, 332)—and the theory of declining civil society, anticipating a weakening of civil society organizations and their capacity to mobilize the masses with economic liberalization (Zermeño 1998).

In more recent years, however, with the PRI's return to the power (2012–2018), the level of mobilization increased. What does this finding of popular protests rising and falling mean for the deepening and stabilizing of democracy? To understand what is going on in civil society, we will examine the protest components—places, claims, actors, targets, and actions.

Places (Where)

Where did these protests occur? Scholars began to emphasize the importance of examining local politics and subnational variations (Cornelius,
Eisenstadt, and Hindley 1999; Correa-Cabrera 2013; Hiskey 2012). Map 2.1
shows the average number of protest campaigns by state according to
Excélsior.[9] The maximum number of campaigns to be represented by the
darkest color on the maps was set to 10, even when the average campaign
counts for Mexico City (the Federal District until January 28, 2016) exceeded
10 (24.0 in 1985–2000 and 19.8 in 2003–2018). This was done because if the
largest average campaign count from Mexico City had been used as the
maximum, the colors of most of the other states would have been too light
to be able to clearly discern the historical patterns. Counts for Mexico City
were very high because the capital city has been the country's main political center and because *Excélsior* is based there and provides greater coverage of the city than of the other states.

1955-1967

1970-1982

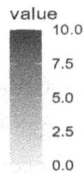

1985-2000

2003-2018

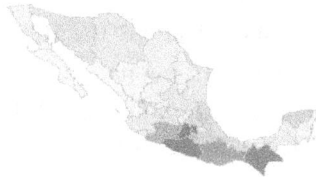

Map 2.1. Places: Average Number of Protest Campaigns by State (Excélsior). R's
mxmaps package was used to create the maps. MPCD Version 2020.06 (Wada 2019).

In the 1955–1967 period, during which the authoritarian hegemony was stable, the average number of campaigns was low across the country, including in Mexico City. For the 1970–1982 period that followed, in which the stability of both the political and economic systems began to unravel, most of the map remains light gray in color, meaning that protest campaigns were still not frequent, except in Mexico City.

During the period of political and economic liberalization (1985–2000), the color gets darker for most states, from the northern Sonora to southern Chiapas. The eruption of popular mobilization in this period, shown in figure 2.1c, was no longer just turmoil around the capital but had become a nationwide phenomenon.

In the post-liberalization period (2003–2018), the level of mobilization in richer northern Mexico returned to its pre-liberalization levels. Popular mobilization continued in poorer southern Mexico in the states of Michoacán, Guerrero, Oaxaca, and Chiapas, along with Mexico City and the surrounding State of Mexico. Possibly reflecting the effect of emergent regionalism (Klesner 2012), we find a polarization of protest locations opposing the rich and advanced north, where mobilization levels have gone back down, and the poor and less developed south, where intense mobilization has continued. In the next section, we will examine whether this trend is reflected in the nature of claims.

Claims (Why)

What are the demands, goals, and visions that drive Mexican citizens into struggle? Has the nature of their claims changed over the course of political and economic liberalization? The MPCD records concrete expressions of claims reported in the newspaper articles. We classified these claims into four types: material (economic), political, social, and cultural. Material claims include economic demands such as better wages, working conditions, and subsidies, as well as various forms of redistributive demands, including access to land and loans, education, and social security. Political claims refer to demands for a more democratic political system and for political rights, including physical and legal protection, freedom of association and expression, and access to information. Social claims are demands for democratizing social organizations such as trade unions, schools, peasant organizations, and social movements. It should be noted that social claims here are not about social rights for redistribution, which are coded as material claims in this study. Cultural claims concern respect for cultures, minorities, identities, and lifestyles. Examples include issues related to gender, sexuality, the body, indigenous and other minority groups, the environment, peace, antinuclear concerns, youth, and victims of various sorts.

The new social movement theory emphasizes the importance of these cultural claims and has been widely used as a theoretical framework to explain social conflict in Latin America (Almeida and Cordero Ulate 2015; Escobar and Alvarez 1992). Inglehart (2008) also predicts that, as countries develop and attain more wealth, intergenerational shifts will occur from "materialist" values emphasizing economic security (material claims in this study)—widespread among the older cohorts—to "postmaterialist" values emphasizing autonomy and self-expression (cultural claims here) among younger birth cohorts. It is important to determine whether or to what extent the main pattern of struggle is shifting from "old social movements" making material–economic demands to "new social movements" fighting over cultural codes such as lifestyle and identity (Melucci 1996; Touraine 1988) in places like Mexico where, unlike Europe, the informal sector has been expanding and economic and social disparities have remained enormous.

Figure 2.2 displays historical changes in claims. It should be noted that actors often make multiple types of claims in a campaign. Under the authoritarian regime up to 1970, it was difficult to mobilize people, regardless of type of claim. In the Echeverría era of political opening (1970–1976), the frequency of material, political, and social claims began to increase. From the late 1970s on, material claims increased dramatically, followed by political and social claims.

Given the timing of the increases, it appears that economic grievances triggered fights over political and social democratization. Tamayo Flores-Alatorre (1999, 268) made a similar point based on his political discourse analysis. Before the start of democratization and globalization around 1982,

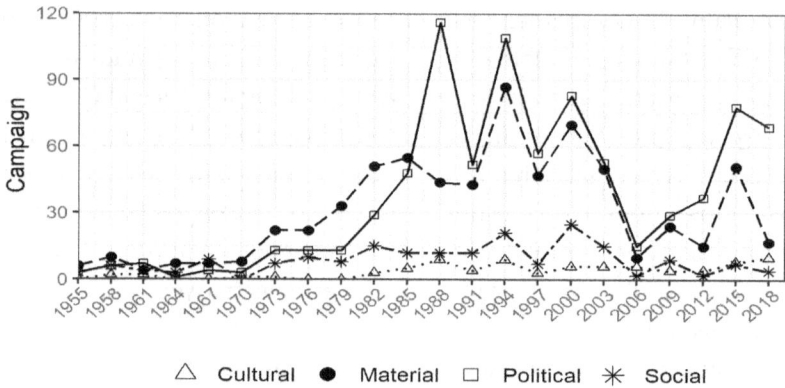

Figure 2.2. Types of Claims in Popular Protests (Excélsior, Campaign Counts). MPCD Version 2020.06 (Wada 2019).

Tamayo found that material–economic claims were central and often accompanied by other kinds of claims. This is because social actors realized that it was their leaders, trade union bosses, for instance, who prevented them from attaining material–economic benefits. Social claims and political claims were often made in pursuit of material–economic goals (Wada 2004).

In the liberalization period, the centrality of political claims is clear. Until 1979, demands for democratization of the state (political claims) and those for society (social claims) were made at about the same frequency. However, beginning in 1982, the frequency of social claims remained nearly constant, while political claims became more important. In the process of political liberalization, elections as an institutionalized form of political competition became the core issue for many civil society actors. The fact that social claims did not increase as much as political claims may reflect that corporatist controls within Mexican social organizations were still working effectively.

Tamayo's qualitative analysis (1999) echoes our quantitative findings. He discovered that the debt crisis in 1982 and subsequent neoliberal economic reform changed the priority in the types of claims made by Mexicans. Despite the growing importance of economic issues for ordinary people who were struggling in their everyday lives in the crisis, the elites pursued economic reforms abolishing social policies. In this context, people became aware of the importance of politics in implementing redistributive policies. Our evidence clearly backs this point. The lines representing material and political claims move in parallel for 1991–2009, indicating that many of the protest campaigns in that period had to make both types of claims simultaneously.

In the 2010s, political and material claims were decoupled, with political issues most prominent. Unlike the period before regime change in 2000, when most political claims were about voting rights and free and fair elections, those of the 2010s were about security issues and, more specifically, the government's inability to protect citizens from organized crime. We find a corresponding change in the target of contention (discussed below).

Finally, we do not find evidence indicating a shift from "old social movements" to "new social movements" yet.[10] Cultural claims were almost nonexistent until the 1970s and were scattered in the 1980s and 1990s. According to the data from *La Jornada*, not incorporated in this paper (the data after 2000 are not yet available for analysis), there were nineteen campaigns making cultural claims in 2000. This amounts to 13 percent of the total, outpacing the number of social claims. This evidence may suggest that cultural claims will become important for Mexicans in the twenty-first century.

Actors (Who)

Have the processes of democratization and globalization changed the key actors in popular protests? Some scholars anticipate that globalization and neoliberal economies will undermine class-based mobilization of workers and farmers (Castells 2010). Neoliberal economic reforms promote integration of national economies into a global economy by weakening the state's intervention in the market. The state loses its ability to implement its own financial, economic, and social policies to meet the demands of its citizens effectively. With the weakening of the state, civil society institutions that were developed and supported by it (e.g., unions, peasant organizations, political parties, and schools and universities) also weaken, and the identities that form the foundation of these institutions (e.g., "workers," "peasants," "party members," "students") no longer motivate people into mobilization.

Such a weakening of worker and peasant organizations has been pointed out in Mexico (Bensusán and Middlebrook 2012; Kleinberg 2000). Corporatism has underpinned the PRI's long-running one-party rule. Workers and peasants were incorporated into the ruling PRI through their own corporatist organizations, working to ensure loyalty to the government and at the same time secure material–economic interests and political privileges. However, as neoliberal economic reforms are implemented, the material–economic benefits provided through institutional organizations are diminishing (Teichman 1996). As a result, these institutional organizations are increasingly unable to protect their members from the adverse effects of reforms, resulting in dysfunction (Bizberg 2010, 33–35).[11]

If class-based actors in civil society are losing their capacity for mobilization, which social actors will play a central role in popular protest instead? Existing studies foresee the emergence of new actors but differ as to their nature. The new social movement theory predicts the rise of the educated middle class, who will assume the prominent role. In communities whose living environment is threatened by policies that prioritize economic growth, the mobilization of the middle class will take forms such as environmental, antinuclear, and peace movements. In societies where minority lifestyles are suppressed, middle-class movements that assert the identity and rights of, e.g., the LGBT and indigenous communities are likely to emerge (Habermas 1981; Mouffe 1988; Offe 1985).

Other researchers argue that, to counter the negative effects of the global economy and capitalism, actors based on identities such as race, ethnicity, locality, or religion will become active (Barber 1992; Castells 2010). This is because people who feel powerless in the face of global capitalism will be increasingly attracted to a local community where they can have a sense of control or, alternatively, to a worldview offered by a religion or an indigenous community that works from a logic different from global capitalism. Examples include the independence movements in Scotland and Catalonia, fundamentalist movements of Christianity and Islam, white supremacism in the United States, and indigenous movements in Latin America.

In the Mexican context, scholars have done research on various groups that can be classified as new social movements, such as women's movements (Tamayo Flores-Alatorre 1999), environmental movements (Foyer and Dumoulin Kervran 2015; Velázquez García 2010), and Alianza Cívica's electoral reform movement (Olvera 2010). Since the late 1980s, the number of nongovernmental organizations (NGOs) and nonprofit organizations (NPOs) in Mexico has grown rapidly. These are different from traditional class-based organizations as they are not organized around the workplace or universities (Pérez-Yarahuán and García-Junco 1998). Inclán (2019, 96) summarizes this emergent trend as the plurality of active civil society. Have these new and plural "civic associations" assumed a protagonist role in Mexican popular protest, replacing class-based organizations?

The findings from our data are presented in figure 2.3. The upper heatmap (2.3a) displays historical changes in protest campaign counts by category of actor.[12] The darker the color of the actor–year cell, the more frequently that actor engaged in protests *unrelated to electoral issues* ("nonelectoral protests") in that year. Most cells in the early years are light-colored because the total counts of protest campaigns were much lower than in the later years. To better understand the cross-sectional patterns of active and inactive actors at each historical moment, a heatmap of the relative frequencies (annual percentages) is also provided (2.3b). We find that those most active in 1955 were workers (the darkest cell in the upper-left corner indicates that 71.4 percent of all nonelectoral protest campaigns in 1955 were carried out by workers), followed by peasants, students, urban groups, and civic associations. We will present a separate analysis of actors in protests related to elections ("electoral protests") in which a vast majority were political parties. To improve the readability of the graph, we excluded the categories of actors that engaged in protests infrequently. The dendrogram to the right of heatmap (2.3a) displays the result of cluster analysis classifying actors by degree of similarity in historical patterns.

Until the early 1970s, the period before full-fledged democratization and globalization, workers, peasants, and students were the primary actors (2.3b). These actors arise from spaces of daily routine life such as workplaces, rural communities, and universities. The historical trajectories of workers and

2.3a. Frequency of Protest Campaigns by Actor Category

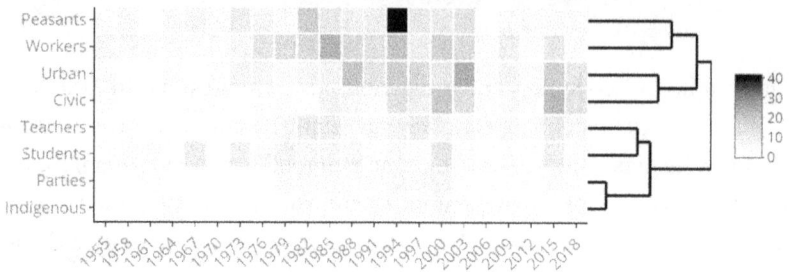

2.3b. Annual Percentages of Protest Campaigns by Actor Category

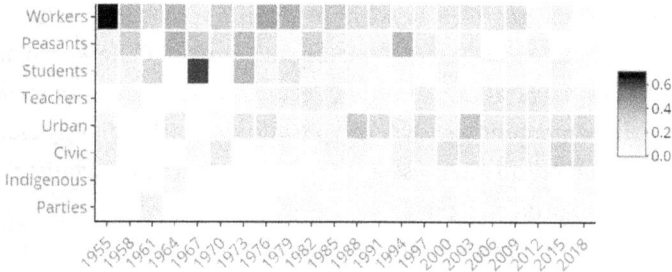

Figure 2.3. Actors in Non-Electoral Protests (Excélsior). a) Frequency of Protest Campaigns by Actor Category. b) Annual Percentages of Protest Campaigns by Actor Category. MPCD Version 2020.06 (Wada 2019).

peasants—the urban and rural corporatist pillars of the authoritarian regime—are so similar that in the dendrogram these categories were grouped together. The pattern of students is closer to the one of teachers.

When the state-centered ISI development model was exhausted, leading to chronic economic difficulties in the 1970s, it was the workers who first increased the protest frequency, reaching their peak in 1985 (2.3a). The enforcement of economic liberalization policies in the late 1980s and early 1990s—including the aforementioned Pact of Economic Solidarity—had a negative effect on the mobilization of workers and labor organizations, but the level of worker mobilization remained high in comparison with other social actors until the late 1990s.

While it may not be straightforward to grasp the upward trend of the peasant category due to its heavy fluctuations, the number of protest campaigns by peasants increased until the 1990s. There are two peaks of peasant mobilization, in 1982 and 1994. In 1982, autonomous peasant organizations were active, including the Coordinadora Nacional Plan de

Ayala (CNPA) (Trevizo 2011), and in 1994 the Zapatista uprising was covered extensively in the newspaper. It is important to note that the campaign frequencies of both workers and peasants declined after the regime transition in 2000.

Urban popular groups are the third most important category. This category is not necessarily limited to the poor, but the majority is composed of poor urban residents and workers in the informal sector. The actors in this category have maintained high mobilization levels since the mid-1980s, especially after the 1985 Mexico City earthquake, making them one of the principal actors in Mexico. The cluster analysis shown by the dendrogram puts this actor category together with civic associations rather than with workers and peasants because these groups continued to be active after the democratic transition in 2000.

We find so far that the three major actors during the liberalization period—workers, peasants, and urban popular groups—have a strong class element, and their identities are nurtured in everyday life contexts, such as workplaces and rural and urban communities. What about the new actors mentioned in the theories reviewed above? Of the categories shown in figure 2.3, indigenous people and civic associations fall into the category of new actors.[13]

While indigenous people are obviously not new to Mexico, there was little record of indigenous mobilization until the 1980s, according to our data. Only as of 1994 did the frequency of protest campaigns by indigenous groups begin to increase. According to *La Jornada* (not shown in this analysis), this category recorded twelve campaigns in 2000, accounting for 13 percent of the total. Given the timing of the growth of indigenous people's protests, the influence of the Zapatista uprising, which began in 1994, may have been decisive. What is new here is that indigenous people around Mexico began to engage in struggle based on their identity as indigenous people rather than as peasants (Eisenstadt 2011; Trevizo 2011)[14], and as a result, they were recognized and reported as indigenous people in *La Jornada* (less so in *Excélsior*).

Civic associations increased their presence from the mid-1990s on. Actors in this category are organized around specific issues, often a single issue, such as human rights (Acosta 2012), elections, the debt, antinuclear, race or gender discrimination, or victims of natural disasters. The rise of this type of civil society actor, which often has no basis for membership in everyday encounters, indicates that processes of political liberalization stimulated the activities of autonomous social actors that did not rely on the corporatist regime. Some scholars argue that NGOs and NPOs did not engage in politics and protest (Lindau 1998).[15] The current study reveals that, with the progress of democratization, a tactic of protest did become a strategic option for these organizations. These new actors remained active in the twenty-first century, and the dendrogram places civic associations and urban popular groups in the same cluster as the most active actors in recent decades.

In short, traditional class-based worker and peasant organizations were increasingly active in processes of economic and political liberalization until the 1990s. Beginning at the turn of the century, however, both of these actors showed less capability for engaging in protest activities. While problems of low economic growth, precarious employment, and income inequality continue to exist, the decreasing mobilizational capacity of class-based organizations—except for urban popular groups, which remained very active into the 2010s—may further weaken their ability to address these issues into the future. On the other hand, civic associations, which were marginal until the 1980s, gradually increased their presence starting in the 1990s and joined the ranks of major actors in the 2010s. A notable trend in civil society in the age of democratization and globalization, which had not been seen under the corporatist regime, is the rise of these issue-specific groups, reflecting the normalization of protest politics and the plurality of active civil society in Mexico as suggested by Inclán (2019). These new actors not only addressed political and economic issues but also raised public concerns about less visible social problems and cultural issues. In this sense, these new actors have the potential to further democratize Mexican politics and society in the twenty-first century.

Before we move on to the discussion of targets of contention, let us examine the actors in electoral protests, shown in figure 2.4. We compare the protest counts of the following three political lineages: (1) the PRI, (2) the PAN and conservative parties, and (3) the PRD, the National Regeneration Movement (MORENA), and left-wing parties. The results show that electoral protests occurred only sporadically until the 1970s, when

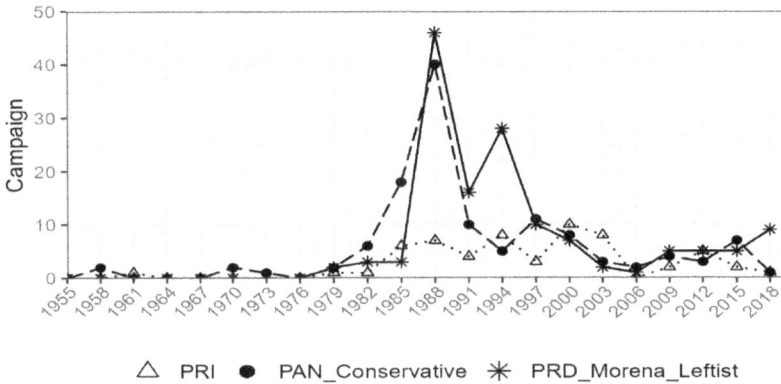

Figure 2.4. Actors (Political Parties) in Electoral Protests (Excélsior, campaign counts). MPCD Version 2020.06 (Wada 2019).

elections were not competitive. As elections became increasingly mean-ingful beginning in 1977, with more realistic chances of winning through a series of electoral reforms, more actors began to engage in electoral protest. In the 1980s, the conservative PAN led the struggles. From the 1988 presi-dential election, which the leftist coalition strongly condemned as fraudu-lent, the PRD and left-wing political parties took the lead in electoral pro-tests. These post-electoral protests are one of the features of Mexico's pro-tracted transition: driven by the poor reputations of formal electoral and judicial institutions, political parties tried to settle the disputes—mostly of local electoral contests—by way of concertacesiones (referred to as the *segunda vuelta* or "second time around" by the PRD) (Eisenstadt 2007, 39).

The graph also shows the process by which the PRI began to mobilize its members as electoral competition intensified with the PAN and the PRD. The 1996 electoral reform established a more transparent and fair electoral system and reduced the number of protest campaigns as the legitimacy of informal settlements via concertacesiones declined. Since 1997, the three political divisions have engaged in electoral protests at similar levels.

In short, the findings suggest that, given the transition from the one-party system in which the PRI dominated to a competitive electoral system involving three major political currents, disputes over election results were increasingly settled within the institutional framework—one of the world's more respected electoral institutions, according to Eisenstadt (2007, 39)—rather than on the street.

Targets (Whom)

To whom do the actors bring their claims? Have the shifts in economy and politics led them to change their targets, and if they did, why? Figure 2.5 shows the findings. The first heatmap (2.5a) displays the frequencies of nonelectoral campaigns in which protests were directed at target categories at least once. Electoral campaigns are excluded from this analysis because the targets in these campaigns in all periods were mostly rival political parties or electoral authorities. Reflecting the low level of mobilization during the pre-liberalization period, most of the cells are light-colored until 1976. During the liberalization period, it was the executive branches of the state and the business sector at which claim-making activities were directed. The executive branches continued to be the principal targets into the 2000s.

The second heatmap (2.5b) represents annual percentages and reveals important changes in the nature of the target that were not evident in the upper heatmap. First, an overall shift in target has taken place from socioeconomic power holders (shown in the lower left) to state institutions (in the upper right). During the pre-liberalization period (1955–1982), business corporations, landowners, rival peasant groups, social leaders (mostly labor union leaders) and rival worker organizations, and schools and universities were targeted quite frequently, but their relative weights have since declined. The business elite continued to be the major target until 1994, when economic liberalization processes were institutionalized in the form of NAFTA. After that, in the periods of market institutionalization and maturity, business sectors ceased to be the major target.

Second, the executive branch of the state became the focus of contention in the liberalization periods. While the federal and state governments were always the main targets, their relative importance increased from the 1990s

2.5a. Frequency of Protest Campaigns by Target Category

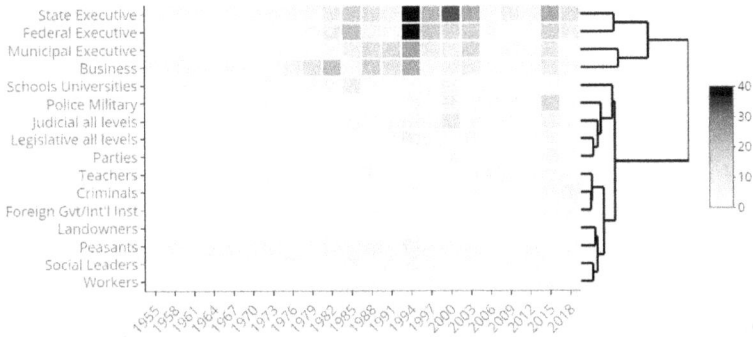

2.5b. Annual Percentages of Protest Campaigns by Target Category

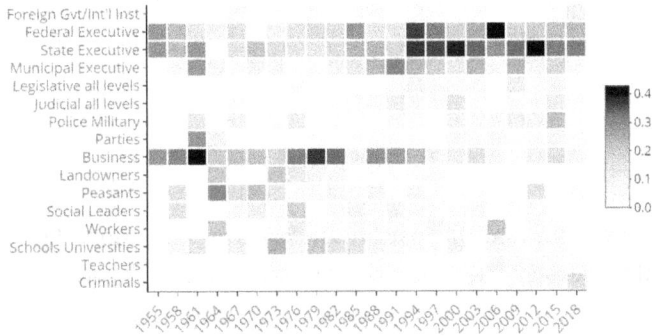

Figure 2.5. Targets in Non-Electoral Protests (Excélsior). a) Frequency of Protest Campaigns by Target Category. b) Annual Percentages of Protest Campaigns by Target Category. MPCD Version 2020.06 (Wada 2019).

onward, the period of neoliberal economy and political democratization. In particular, state governments became the most frequent targets, reflecting their increased power as a result of the fiscal decentralization initiatives (Cornelius 2000). Social actors also increasingly began to target municipal governments from the mid-1980s, when these became the locus of democratic struggle between the PRI trying to deflect contestation away from national arenas and opposition political parties trying to establish a political foothold (Selee 2012).

Third, the relevance of the legislative and judicial branches of government increased gradually during political liberalization (Beer 2003; Eisenstadt and Yelle 2012), but these institutions were still far from central in comparison with the executive branch. Fourth, given the serious security problems related to drug cartels since the 2000s, especially at the local levels (Trejo and Ley 2021), in recent years popular protests have begun to direct their claims at criminal groups.

In sum, the main targets of contention shifted from the socioeconomic elites to the state elites, in particular the federal and state executives. This change is likely an outcome of political liberalization. Economic liberalization and the market-centered economy did not place economic and social elites at the center of contention. The decline in the organizational and mobilizational capacity of labor unions and peasant organizations as well as the withdrawal of state institutions as a mediator of the labor conflict likely contributed to this change.

Actions (How)

This section examines shifting patterns in forms of contention. Have the ways in which Mexican citizens make claims become more radical or more moderate in the processes of political and economic liberalization? Figure 2.6 demonstrates the forms of action between 1955 and 2018 in two different ways. A wide array of descriptions of tactics reported in the newspapers were classified into nineteen major forms of action. For each of the major forms, the risk score is calculated and indicated in the graphs. Risk is defined as the prospect of one or more of the following eight outcomes taking place: property damage, injuries, killings, arrests, incarcerations, use of weapons, police and/or military mobilizations, and any other violence such as beatings. In calculating the risk, the information from *Excélsior*, *Unomásuno*, and *La Jornada* for the entire period was combined. Each time a form of action is employed, we count and add up the number of the occurrences of each of these eight outcomes. Thus, the maximum score is 8 and the minimum 0. We then compute the average risk for each action category. In the lower heatmap (2.6b), nineteen forms of action are arranged in descending order of risk, with physical attack being the highest risk (2.54) and boycott the lowest (0.00).

The upper heatmap (2.6a) displays the actual frequency of campaigns in which each form of action was used. Up until the 1970s most of the cells are light-colored because the absolute number of popular protest campaigns

2.6a. Frequency of Protest Campaigns by Form of Action

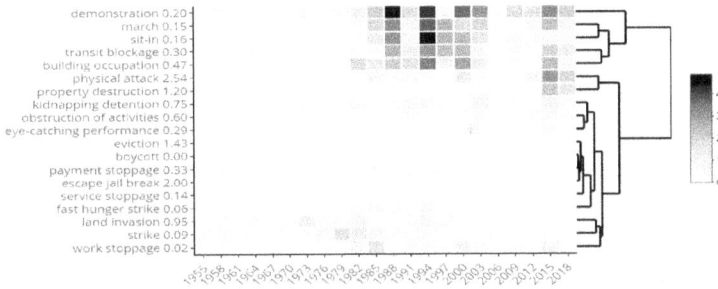

2.6b. Annual Percentages of Protest Campaigns by Form of Action

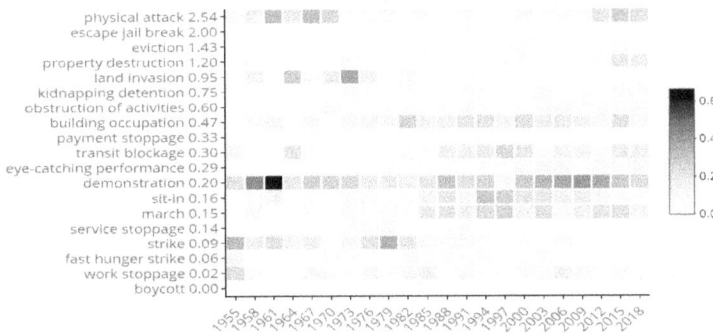

Figure 2.6. Forms of Action in Popular Protests (Excélsior). a) Frequency of Protest Campaigns by Form of Action. b) Annual Percentages of Protest Campaigns by Form of Action. MPCD Version 2020.06 (Wada 2019).

was low. To understand Mexican citizens' tactical selections at each historical moment, it is useful to look at the second heatmap (2.6b), which shows the percentages of each form of action used in each year (note that "year" here means a 29-day sampling period). In 1955, there were three campaigns featuring strikes. The 1955 strike cell in 2.6a is a light gray because the absolute number (3) is very low, but the corresponding cell in 2.6b is a darker gray because three campaigns constitute a third of the total of nine campaigns for this period. What we learn from this is that it was difficult for Mexicans to engage in protest in 1955, but when they did, their main tactic was the strike. In this way, the lower heatmap helps us to understand repertoires of contention at each historical moment.

The dendrogram for the upper heatmap (2.6a) classifies forms of action into two major clusters by similarity of historical patterns. One is the smaller cluster at the top composed of demonstrations, marches, sit-ins, transit blockages, and building occupations. The other, the larger cluster, includes the remaining forms, from physical attacks to work stoppages. The second cluster has three subgroups: physical attacks and property destruction; stoppages, strikes, and land invasions; and other tactics, which were rarely employed.

Four findings stand out from an inspection of the lower heatmap (2.6b) pertaining to this second cluster. First, the first two subgroups made up an important part of repertoires of contention from the 1950s to around 1985. This coincides with the pre-liberalization period. Second, once liberalization processes got underway, the weight of these forms of action was reduced considerably. In this sense, these forms are part of a declining repertoire in Mexico. Third, the use of many of these tactics was largely limited to specific actors in their routine life contexts. Strikes and work stoppages were employed overwhelmingly by workers; the land invasion strategy was available mostly to rural peasants and residents of urban communities. Actor-specific and rigid repertoire is one of the characteristics of the pre-liberalization period.

Fourth, there is a polarization of popular tactics in terms of risk. Physical attacks (2.54), property destruction (1.20), and land invasions (.95) were high-risk options for Mexicans, while strikes (.09) and work stoppages (.02) were low-risk choices. This probably reflects the political opportunity structure under the PRI's one-party authoritarian regime in the pre-liberalization period. On one hand, strikes and work stoppages were institutionalized forms of contention in the corporatist political system (hence the low risk). Leaders of major labor unions obtained resources by forging personal relationships with state administrators and using these to maintain the loyalty of members within the organization (Teichman 1996). It would have been out of the question to resort to radical high-risk tactics against the state administration. On the other hand, those actors outside of the corporatist system, such as the guerrilla activists of the 1970s, often had to employ violent and radical high-risk repertoires to confront the authoritarian regime. Favela's study of social movements also shows that during the period of authoritarianism, popular grievances and discontent tended to erupt in the form of radical struggle, with about 15 percent of the movements resorting to some form of violent means (Favela 2010, 113).

Let us now examine the first cluster in the upper part of the heatmap in 2.6a. This consists of three subgroups: demonstrations; marches and sit-ins; and transit blockages and building occupations. There are three findings. First, both the absolute (2.6a) and relative (2.6b) frequencies of these forms of action increase in a dramatic fashion as of around 1985. These are the major repertoires in the liberalization period, effectively taking the place of the earlier repertoire of the second cluster.

Second, these tactics in the first cluster are relatively low-risk. The highest-risk score is .47 (building occupations). As is clear in the heatmap in 2.6b, there has been a shift from a combination of high-risk violent tactics and lowest-risk institutionalized tactics to low-risk moderate tactics in between. This is good news. If moderate forms of action become the norm, popular protest as a form of communication between state and society will contribute to political stability in the long run.

Third, demonstrations occupy a special place in popular protest in Mexico. The dendrogram of the heatmap in 2.6a suggests that demonstration is quite dissimilar to the other four tactics in the first cluster, as it is only connected to them at the very end. The uniqueness of demonstration is clearly shown in the heatmap in 2.6b. Demonstration was Mexicans' main tactic for the entire period from the 1950s to the 2010s. Large-scale gatherings in Zócalo, Mexico City's historic main square, are representative of this popular tactic. Tarrow (2011) explains that demonstrations are likely to spread throughout society because they are "modular," meaning that a variety of social actors can employ them, against a variety of targets, and for a variety of demands and objectives.

In short, our analysis has detected a shift from actor-specific repertoires, both violent and institutionalized, to low-risk moderate repertoires, along with modular demonstration (i.e., proactive protests). The shift reflects the process of legitimation of protest activities and the normalization of protest participation (Inclán 2019). Before closing this section, we must point out an alarming trend. In figure 2.6, we observe a revival of the highest-risk tactics of physical attacks and property destruction from around 2012. This likely reflects the weakening of the state's governing capacity. The state apparatus has been increasingly unable to control organized crime, especially given the systemic infiltration of drug-related corruption in all institutional aspects of public agencies (Bailey 2012). Public security has deteriorated and state capacity has been impaired, especially since the Calderón administration's "drug war" in 2006. If this trend continues, it will have a serious impact on the prospect of democratic deepening in the 2020s.

Conclusions

The findings of this study are summarized as follows. First, the level of mobilization, especially that of popular protests making political demands, has increased in response to political liberalization. From our standpoint, that popular protest is an essential element of making democracy work; our finding that Mexican citizens are increasingly capable of making political claims in public space can suggest a trend toward the deepening of democracy.

Second, despite the opening of political opportunities after regime change in 2000, the number of protest campaigns has declined. This study points out three theoretical possibilities to account for this. One is that, as predicted by the inverted-U curve theory, social energy is directed more toward institutional politics than to protest politics under consolidated democratic institutions (Inclán 2009; Mattiace 2012; Trejo 2014). Another is that some social organizations were too weakened by the process of economic liberalization to carry out large-scale mobilizations ("social atomization") (Zermeño 1998). The third possibility is that time-proven authoritarian mechanisms of social control, such as the patron–client and corporatist relationship, remain resilient even in the period of electoral democracy (Fox 1994; Grayson 2004; Inclán 2012; Sabet 2008; Selee 2015). In some localities, residents continue to approach the local authority more as petitioners than as citizens with rights (Grindle 2009). As I will argue next, continued social pressure is essential to further strengthen democracy beyond elections.

Third, our empirical evidence does not fully support the view that the class struggle (the "old movements") will be replaced by "new social movements." Material–economic demands continue to be central (although we also find a decoupling of material and political claims in recent years), and active mobilization continues in the poorest southern states. These findings indicate that economic liberalization has not led to steady economic growth and reduction of inequality and that persistent poverty and inequality continue to define popular protest in Mexico in the early twenty-first century. Shefner and Stewart (2011) see that neoliberalism has brought about procedural, not substantive, democracy, which actually protects the elite's class privilege. Inclán (2018) argues that, in Mexico's protracted democratic transition, political elites are able to negotiate electoral reforms that democratize elections without being accountable to social actors and their demands. Mexicans "may have won political voice at the expense of economic voice" (Shefner and Stewart 2011, 373).[16] Our analysis of the targets also showed that citizens are finding it increasingly difficult to protest against socioeconomic elites. As Mattiace (2012, 415) states, the fact that many of the substantive demands that gave rise to the social movements that emerged after 1985 in Mexico remain unresolved provides a continued raison d'être for social movement activism today.

Fourth, if the old social movements survive in the age of democratization and globalization, what about the emergence of the new social movements? Cultural claims around lifestyle and identity—"postmaterial values" (Inglehart 2008)—have not become the mainstream in Mexico yet, but the number of protests making these claims has been increasing gradually. As indigenous people and civic associations become more important as actors, there is a chance that social issues of discrimination and cultural demands, which were not often addressed publicly in the past, will become major issues in the future. Here lies a possibility for further strengthening of democracy, encompassing its egalitarian dimension.

Finally, this study has limitations. While we examined places, claims, actors, targets, and actions separately, it is also important to analyze these elements simultaneously. (See Somma and Medel's chapter in this volume for such an analysis.) Different actors will have different demands and, depending on these demands, they will likely pick different targets and tactics. We should also consider using statistical analysis to measure the impact of democratization and globalization.

One of the significant changes in the patterns of popular protest in Mexico was the gradual shift in repertoires from high-risk violent and radical tactics, such as physical attacks and land invasions, to moderate tactics, such as marches, sit-ins, transit blockages, and demonstrations. This moderation reflects a process of normalization of protest politics (Inclán 2019) and may be conducive to further extension of democracy. Our evidence also demonstrates, however, a recent resurgence in violent forms of action, with criminal groups as a new target. This study has suggested the surge in drug cartels and the weakening of the state's governing capacity as the principal reasons behind this increase in violence. This emergent trend poses a threat to political stability in Mexico.

Notes

1. I would like to thank all the scholars and the students who helped me gather necessary materials to construct the protest event database used in this chapter, including, among others, Shoki Goto, Taeko Hoshino, Aki Sakaguchi, Ilán Bizberg, Carlos Alba, Karine Tinat, Charles Tilly, Sidney Tarrow, Anely Guerrero Molina, Antony Flores Mérida, Arisbeth Hernández Tapia, Emmanuel Hernández Velasco, Gustavo Baltazar López, Wako Yamaguchi, Kazuya Oki, and Luis Alberto Hernández Rodríguez. Generous research support was provided by the Japan Society for the Promotion of Science (JSPS) Grant-in-Aid for Scientific Research (KAKENHI 18H00921) and National Science Foundation (SES-99-00867).
2. Beer (2012) argues that this unbalanced power relationship between presidents and governors has often been exaggerated. Rubin (1996) also argues that the presence of the powerful Mexican state had been uneven and incomplete in terms of geography and domains of social life and that its hegemony had been contested regionally and culturally during the preliberalization period as well.
3. Brinegar, Morgenstern, and Nielson (2006) analyze how PRI's division between the president and the hard-liners ("dinosaurs") led to the 1996 electoral reform that precipitated the party's downfall.
4. The volume edited by Domínguez and Poiré (1999) describes how Mexican voters' preferences gradually shifted from the PRI to the opposition parties during the 1990s in a context of risk aversion and uncertainty generated by the limited and asymmetrical information about the ruling and the opposition parties.
5. It is worthwhile to mention, however, that the most recent V-Dem dataset

(version 12), released in March 2022, modified (lowered) the electoral democracy index as follows: .711 (2005), .646 (2008), .633 (2015), .674 (2018), and .628 (2021) (data accessed on July 1, 2022).

6. Refer to the V-Dem database for the definitions and operationalizations of different measures of democracy.

7. Interested readers are referred to the *Mexican Popular Contention Database (MPCD): Manual de uso e ingreso de datos* (Wada 2019). This manual contains information on how to build the database and how to use it, as well as points to keep in mind when obtaining information about popular struggles from newspaper articles. It explains methodological details that have been omitted from this chapter due to space limitations, such as the characteristics of reported protests and issues of bias, and provides notes on how to count popular struggles (units of analysis).

8. Inclán (2009, 2012) builds an event database on Zapatista-related protests in Chiapas, based mostly on the *La Jornada* reports.

9. Some campaigns spanned multiple states. When the latter are clearly mentioned in the news articles, the campaigns are recorded to each of the states. When the exact locations of a campaign are unclear (e.g., "the general strike happened in many states"), this campaign is not counted for this analysis.

10. In his study of indigenous protests, Trejo (2014, 339) also finds that ethnic claims for autonomy and self-determination never displaced demands for free and fair elections as the dominant indigenous claim.

11. The Confederación Nacional Campesina (CNC), a representative of corporatist peasant organizations, was unable to exert any influence over the process of economic reform promoted by the Salinas administration or the negotiation process for NAFTA; as a result, the CNC lost its legitimacy among peasants (Bizberg 2010).

12. The MPCD records actor/target information in the following four formats: (1) proper names of individuals (e.g., "Andrés Manuel López Obrador"), (2) positions and attributes of individuals (e.g., "president," "union secretary general"), (3) categories of a set of individuals (e.g., "peasants," "students"), and (4) proper names of organizations/institutions (e.g., "PRI," "Alianza Cívica"). Concrete descriptions recorded in the above formats are aggregated into broad analytical categories that form the basis of the analysis in this section.

13. Other actor categories based on identities include religious organizations, but this category is not included in the figure because its frequencies are low throughout the entire period.

14. By comparing indigenous mobilization in Chiapas in 1994 with the one in Oaxaca in 2006, Eisenstadt (2011) uncovers that indigenous peasants adopt individual, class-based, or ethnicity-based frames rather

pragmatically depending on land tenure institutions and on histories of
protest and repression.

15. Many NGOs and NPOs were born during the Salinas (1988–1994) and
Zedillo (1994–2000) administrations, which adopted a social policy of poverty alleviation entrusted to local grassroots organizations, thereby
inducing NGOs to concentrate on local community development projects.
These "independent" NGOs and NPOs, which relied on government funding, set themselves apart from political activity (Haber 1994).

16. On this point, Bizberg (2010, 40–42) claims that the weak mobilization
capacity of civil society can be a reason why democracy in Mexico is still
inadequate. Unlike the strong labor movements in Brazil and Poland, he
argues, Mexican social movements were not able to become the actors
leading the democratization processes and thus failed to continue to exert
pressure to dismantle the old regime and the elite privilege.

CHAPTER THREE

Globalization, Democracy, and Conflict Events in Bolivia, 1970–2019

ROBERTO LASERNA

Introduction

This chapter analyzes the relationship between politics and economics, considering, as a point of reference, the social action that is expressed in an open way in conflict events. The fundamental concern from the point of view of politics is democracy—its functioning and institutional strength, its capacity to represent society and enable it to achieve higher levels of economic well-being. In economic terms, our main analytical focus is the impact of globalization, as experienced by the national economy, as a means to openness or liberalization. While others have studied this topic, our approach offers a rare perspective, one that takes the long term into consideration, allowing us to understand globalization as a window to better understand the economy, democracy as another window that shows politics, and, finally, conflict events as a manifestation of social processes. This chapter explains how globalization and democracy affect observable changes in collective action in terms of actors, claims, and targets.

This chapter draws on a dataset containing information collected from media records of conflict events that were noteworthy enough to make the news between January 1970 and December 2019. The data can be disaggregated by different categories and studied within the context of their relationship to democracy and globalization. Of course, from such a broad viewpoint, the richness of detail and many nuances fundamental to the understanding of protests are lost. On the other hand, we get a more complete perspective and deeper understanding of these overarching processes.

The case of Bolivia provides relevant information to the overall perspective of Latin America that, especially due to generalization efforts, is at times overlooked. The relationship between globalization and democracy has been appropriately treated as a dual transition. It is characterized as "hybrid" because it is theorized that, while democracy expands opportunities to citizens, globalization represents a threat to various social actors (Almeida 2010a; Arce 2008). They can generate proactive and reactive protests, respectively (as described in the introduction of this volume). Therefore, although in some cases it is observed that protest actions increase at the same time as both processes, globalization provokes them and democracy makes them possible. In Bolivia, this exact pattern does not necessarily seem to occur—because democracy establishes institutional channels of representation and protest, or because globalization presents economic advantages, or both at the same time.

Having half a century of data, as in our case, offers the opportunity to differentiate the processes by time periods and detect nuances. In other words, in the fifty years that range from 1970 to 2019, there were a variety of situations in the intersection between politics and the economy. The data show that protest is not always "derived" from these processes, but contributes categorically to producing them. This is largely because situations are dominated by "political" actors at times, especially with broader projects, and at other times by "corporate" actors who are motivated by particular interests or demands and seem to be the ones who tend to respond or react to such processes.

Globalization and Democracy

In this book, the data measuring levels of democracy and globalization are used as independent variables, providing us with an important tool to understand these processes and at the same time to differentiate their pace. As seen in figure 1.4 of the introductory chapter, the first period in Bolivia extended to the mid-1980s, where both globalization and, fundamentally, democracy levels remained quite low. The country's globalization indicators are similar to the Latin American average, but remain small in parallel, and there is a virtual absence of democracy. It was a period ruled by military governments that, beyond projecting apparently ideologically distant discourses, reproduced economic statism, and political exclusion.

A second period was characterized by the intensification of both processes—expressly the opening to globalization and democratic institutionalization, with a notable increase in the levels of democracy that surpassed even the Latin American average, and in which processes of globalization were also accelerated. The pace was even faster than in the rest of the countries: Bolivian indicators were very close to the average, with a tendency to exceed it toward the end of the period. This period goes from the mid-1980s to the beginning of the first decade of the 2000s, where there are observable changes in both trends. It was a period of civilian governments with reduced majorities that were forced to make political pacts, increasing the relevance of Congress and related institutions and being taken into account as platforms for political action in a more systematic way.

Finally, a third period can be observed in which democracy declined, especially after 2006, and globalization also slowed down, as indicated by the increasing distance between the Bolivian indicators and the regional average. It was a period characterized by the rule of civilian governments that began under the circumstances of intense political crisis, to which the electorate responded by supporting a populist leader and breaking away from the parties and their methods of conciliation and pacts. In this period, there was also an extraordinary export boom that expanded consumption and the domestic market but discouraged investment and weakened institutions.

Defining exact dates to differentiate between one period and another is difficult, because, during the time of transition, aspects of the following period were emerging while those of the previous period still existed. These transitional junctures prevent more precise discussion of the periods and their corresponding data.

In Bolivia, the first period began in reality before 1970, but due to data availability, we mark that year as its inception and extend it until mid-1985. The second period goes from that point to the end of 2003. The third encompasses the following stretch of time until the forced resignation of Evo Morales at the end of 2019. But, as we touched on before, it is necessary to take the moments of transition into account, which correspond to the government of Hernán Siles Zuazo (1982–1985) at the end of the first period and the rapid succession of governments at the end of the second period, from the political debacle of Hugo Bánzer Suárez to the forced resignation of Gonzalo Sánchez de Lozada (2000 to 2003).

Siles Zuazo emerged from the elections of 1980, which were swiftly obscured due to the military coup led by Luis García Meza and then reinstated during the popular civil struggle in October 1982. Siles Zuazo presided over a coalition of nationalist parties that aspired to carry out a popular revolution, but whose policies of expanding fiscal expenditure ended up causing hyperinflation, disrupting markets, and impoverishing wage earners, who eventually repudiated such policies. This transition underwent an intense period of direct actions of a conflictive nature, cultivating demands for greater institutional stability. In the end, the coalition that supported Siles Zuazo began to break down and eventually accepted early elections, allowing for the emergence of a period of greater democratic institutional development and economic stability and openness.

The second moment of transition dates back to the end of the government of Bánzer, the former dictator turned democratic president. Bánzer, who was suffering from cancer, had to concede governmental authority to his vice-president Jorge Quiroga, who in turn completed his term and handed over the presidency to Sánchez de Lozada, who was forced to resign in October 2003. This period began with strong mobilizations in 2000 (the Water War) that could not be controlled even with a state of siege and continued with increasing virulence in September 2000 (peasant farmer blockades), January 2001 (coca growers in defense of legal markets), February 2003 (against taxes) and October 2003 (the Gas War). Even the common language demonstrates the intensity of this period in the use of the term "wars" when referring to the most outstanding conflict events framing this transition, closing the previous cycle and opening a new one.

Although the moments of transition are distinctive and constitute interesting objects for study in their own right, this chapter will discuss them in their double condition of marking a diffuse closure to the previous period and also the beginning of the new one. Let us look more closely at these three periods.

State Authoritarianism, 1970–1985

In September 1969, the Bolivian armed forces overthrew President Luis Adolfo Siles Salinas, justifying the coup with a Revolutionary Statute similar to the one that a year earlier had placed Juan Velasco Alvarado as head of the government of Peru. Shortly thereafter, General Alfredo Ovando signed the nationalization of Gulf Oil and took over the facilities of a mining company, emphasizing a nationalist and anti-imperialist discourse that did not prevent him from paying generous compensations in both cases.[1] Congress was shut down, the mayor's offices remained taken over, and General Ovando tried to conduct elections that would give him legitimacy. His comrades prevented him from doing so with a rapid succession of coups that finally succeeded in replacing him in October 1970 with another general, Juan José Torres. Torres managed to impose himself with the support of the workers' unions, with whom he established a "Popular Assembly" that some characterized as "soviet," because it demanded the delivery of weapons to popular militias (Mercado 1974). In those days, an impromptu guerrilla group drawn from the National Liberation Army and established by Ernesto "Che" Guevara in 1967 operated in a subtropical zone of La Paz province. The purpose of the guerrillas was to radicalize the process, but instead they succeeded in radicalizing the reaction to it (Ostria 2006). The military swept through the guerrilla columns, who were poorly trained, crudely armed, and disconnected from society, and wiped them out. However, this consolidated the guerrillas' unity and eventually they succeeded in raising Colonel Hugo Bánzer Suárez to power in another military coup.

Bánzer governed for seven straight years, first accompanied by civilians and political parties, followed by an exclusively military government from

1974 onward (Laserna 1980). Social and international pressure led him to call for elections in 1978, which were subsequently voided due to fraud in favor of the official candidate, who led a new coup. From that point on, there was a period of great instability, with brief military and civilian governments and frustrated electoral processes (1979 and 1980). The growing violence highlighted the political defeats of the military, whose image of order and security was insufficient to attract public support.[2] In October 1982, the weakened military surrendered to the Congress elected two years earlier and retreated to their barracks (Mayorga 1987).

Apart from the junctures that marked the beginning and end of that period, it was relatively stable: conflict events were violently repressed, and economic growth was based on mineral and oil exports, the prices of which increased significantly during those years. Public investment grew parallel to government spending, and optimism also stimulated borrowing.

In this period, civil liberties were not respected by the political powers or enforced by the military. Although the justice system maintained relative independence, it was ineffective in protecting citizens. Political parties lacked the space to attract and channel political representation outside of universities and unions. At times during this period, military action was used to repress protests. In addition to Bánzer's coup in 1971, which resembled a civil war due to the presence of armed civilians in direct actions, there were tense moments in January 1974 and November 1979. The first one was the so-called Masacre del Valle, when military troops dismantled blockages organized by peasants, killing more than fifty people (Laserna 1994). In November 1979, there was a vast peasant mobilization in the highlands that, even in the absence of assassinations or homicides, evidenced the strength of rural trade unionism, which had already achieved agrarian reform in the 1950s but now showed itself to be independent of governmental power (Dunkerley 1984).

As always, economic realism prevailed, putting an end to waste and forcing fiscal adjustments.[3] But adjustments require discipline and political will, which the military, by the end of the period, had already lost. Their decisions were incomplete and their attitude hesitant, which prevented them from reordering public spending and limiting borrowing, thus aggravating the crisis instead of resolving it.

When the military returned to the barracks, they left the government and the problems in the hands of civilians, which made the democratic transition extremely difficult, lasting from 1982 to 1985 during the presidency of Hernán Siles Zuazo. These last three years were therefore already transitional, even though they were strongly marked by the impact of a nationalist economic policy that, in a way, characterized the entire period.

This period can be summarized as politically authoritarian due to the predominance of militarism and economically nationalist due to the fact that the prevailing economic policy attempted to consolidate a relatively closed development model with a strong emphasis on national (and in fact, state) control of the economy. Global engagement was limited as economic policy sought to strengthen "inward growth" through protectionism.

Democracy and Open Markets, 1985–2003

In October 1982, Bolivia's government returned to civilian hands as a result of the recognition of the legitimacy of the July 1980 elections. A broad coalition of leftist-oriented parties had obtained the largest majority in these elections, including a fraction of the Movimiento Nacionalista Revolucionario (MNR)—which embraced the nationalization of mining, the elimination of large land holdings, and other reforms from the 1950s— the Communist Party, and the social democratic MIR (Movimiento de la Izquierda Revolucionaria). This coalition had won the three previous elections but did not achieve a sufficient majority to gain direct access to the government or an absolute majority in Congress.[4] Beset by social and congressional pressure, the Siles government was unable to control an economic crisis that led to hyperinflation and economic contraction, forcing him to resign after one year in office and call for elections in 1985, thus opening the stage for a new period.

In the 1985 elections, the largest majority went to the former dictator Bánzer, but it was Víctor Paz Estenssoro who managed to form a majority in Congress, governing until 1989 and following a radical program of fiscal adjustment and structural reform in line with what was later known as the

Washington consensus.[5] At the end of his term of office, the majority of the
electorate supported the architect of the economic stabilization reforms,
Minister Gonzalo Sánchez de Lozada, but in Congress the decision was different and Jaime Paz Zamora became president.[6] He maintained the principal policies, giving impetus to the privatization of many industrial and
service companies that had been created during the national revolution. In
1993, Sánchez de Lozada was once again victorious in the elections and this
time also won in Congress. He served as president until 1997. These four
years saw the greatest intensity and depth in the reforms aimed at democratic institutionalization and economic liberalization, with the capitalization of large state-owned companies, the reform of the pension system, the
creation of territorial mayor offices throughout the country, and the decentralization of public spending (Grebe 1998).

Democracy in this period was very intense and robust. The government
made concerted reforms to the Constitution, which allowed for the creation
of an Ombudsman, the Constitutional Court, and the Judiciary Council, in
addition to the consolidation of an Electoral Court that took charge of the
administration of the national identification system. Congress was
reformed, with the creation of single-member constituencies for half of the
deputies.[7] A modernizing and inclusive educational reform was implemented. Significant progress was also made in decentralization, through
the creation of assemblies at the departmental level, municipalization of
the country, by extending the jurisdictions of mayors to rural areas, and the
transfer of resources and local management responsibilities to mayoral
leadership (Laserna 2009).

In the economic sphere, relative continuity in the processes of economic
liberalization significantly reduced the presence of the state in productive
and commercial activities. Many unprofitable companies were transferred
to the private sector through competitive bidding and others were subject
to "capitalization." This process involved the transfer of state assets to a
Collective Capitalization Fund that would grant a universal old-age income
(called Solidarity Bond or Bonosol), initially managed by the Pension
Funds. It also involved the company's management being handed to a partner that capitalized it by contributing an equivalent amount to be used for
investments to expand the company's productive capacity. This secured

fresh investments in the oil and gas, electricity, telecommunications, rail-road, and aviation sectors (Pacheco 2008).

The reform of the pension system articulated the way forward for democracy and economic growth. The old pension system was broken. In many cases, workers' contributions had disappeared due to corruption and bad investments, and mechanisms had been developed to manipulate pensions, making them unsustainable. The system of individual capitalization combined with a universal old-age pension allowed the inclusion of independent workers, who were and remain the majority in the country.[8] In a short time, this system increased national savings and thus stimulated more transparent investments throughout the financial system.

The financial system and the Central Bank were also reformed with a more professional institutional framework, putting an end to the manipulation of savings and special credits for the benefit of oligarchic groups. Finally, the tax reform simplified the payment of taxes and created more efficient fiscal control mechanisms, with a more independent Comptroller's Office and better regulations.

In 1997, Bánzer Suárez won the general elections again and also the elections in Congress. However, his health was shaky and he was forced to resign a year before the end of his term. He handed over the government to his vice president, Jorge Quiroga. During this period, the political struggles and quarrels that seriously eroded the dynamics of the pacts and the continuity of the reforms became evident. In the 2002 elections, Sánchez de Lozada won again, but two populist movements had already shown their strength: one led by runner-up Evo Morales and the other by Manfred Reyes Villa, who finished third. The electoral results were very close. Sánchez de Lozada again managed to put together a broad congressional coalition, but it was weakly articulated. Thus, he could not resist the pressure of collective action and had to resign.

The last three years of this period, from 2000 to 2003, can be seen as the transition to the third period—state populism. In order to define the second period, we propose highlighting the two processes that most strongly characterized the political and economic spheres: the development of democratic institutions and the opening of the economy to globalization.

In other words, it is the period in which democracy and globalization were most vigorously deployed.

State Populism, 2003–2019

We characterize this third period as state populism because of the strong state emphasis that characterized economic policy under Evo Morales (even to the detriment of his support base of peasants, small merchants, and artisans), and the populism that characterized his political relationship with civil society. It should be noted, however, that these two rationales could not have been sustained without the abundance of resources provided by the mineral and hydrocarbon export boom, which was only a contextual factor because neither the export reserves, the infrastructure, or the prices on the international market were the result of the policies applied during this period.

Therefore, in October 2003, the third period began, characterized by the weakening of democratic institutions stemming from the populist style of Evo Morales's party, the decline of the global insertion of the Bolivian economy—despite the fact that there has rarely been such intense commercial exchange with the rest of the world—the weakening of economic actors, and the inefficiency of the state.

When Gonzalo Sánchez de Lozada resigned, his vice-president, Carlos Mesa, took over the government. He sought a direct relationship with citizens and tried to govern without links to political parties or Congress, and without using the unions and neighborhood networks, which were mainly controlled by rival politicians such as Evo Morales and Reyes Villa.[9] He was unable to complete his term, handing over the government to Chief Justice of the Supreme Court Eduardo Rodríguez, in a constitutional succession endorsed by Congress. Rodríguez was compelled to call for elections, which were won by an absolute majority by Evo Morales, the leader of the coca growers. During these years, a new hydrocarbons law was passed that increased state participation in the collection of revenues, albeit by sacrificing the investments necessary to maintain high levels of proved reserves for export.[10]

Morales's political strength was boosted by the weakening of the parties that had governed up until then and, limited by Congress, were unable to resist the statist and antiglobalization drive of the Movement toward Socialism (MAS). He had already been promoting a constitutional reform that, despite not formulating other proposals, was nevertheless attractive to an electorate eager to "change everything." A new constitution was approved in 2009, even though the law regulating its formulation was not complied with. Morales was able to run for a second term in 2010 and then for a third in 2015. Backed by an image of economic success due to the export boom, he tried to change the Constitution again via referendum in 2016, with the sole purpose of prolonging his stay in power. He lost the referendum but continued to attempt the extension with capricious interpretations of the Constitution and human rights conventions. Because the Constitution limited his reelection, he argued that it contradicted the principles of the Convention on Human Rights of San José, which proclaims that it is the right of every citizen to elect and be elected. In addition to having the Constitutional Court under his control, Morales succeeded in having them pass a resolution declaring the norms of the Constitution prohibiting reelection inapplicable. It was then absurd when the court declared inapplicable another part of the Constitution whose application was supposed to be monitored and defended in its entirety.

Based on such curious maneuvering, Morales ran for office again and, in October 2019, achieved a new electoral victory, but his support was greatly reduced in comparison to previous years. Fearful of losing in the second round, his supporters tried to force the results, but could not hide the manipulation of figures and data.[11] Morales and his entourage resigned and sought refuge abroad, fleeing accusations of fraud amid massive protests that spread throughout the country for three weeks. The collective opposition that he had hitherto skillfully navigated removed him from power. A new transition had thus begun in Bolivia, and is still underway. Its direction remains uncertain.[12]

Methods

The use of conflict events as a source of data for social and political analysis began at the Centro de Estudios de la Realidad Económica y Social (CERES) around 1983 as part of a program of studies on regional social movements in Bolivia, Ecuador, and Peru. At that time, we conducted a thorough inspection of the information recorded in three newspapers of national circulation from 1970 to 1985 and presented the results in several articles (Laserna and Mayorga 1985; Laserna 1991). The theoretical reference in the design of the data collection was provided by Alain Touraine's theory of social movements. In this, he proposed to consider the principles of identity, opposition, and totality to characterize the actors. In the process of transferring and creating variables, protagonists were translated into data according to how they defined themselves and presented themselves publicly, based on the definition of their target and the response the target gave (or did not give), or the delegation of that response to others; these, to a large extent, defined the type of relationship established in the event. The target might not recognize the protagonist (protest group) as opponents and need to be assigned to another one, or not recognize herself as a target and send another interlocutor (the police, for example). Therefore, we made an effort to recognize and record these variations and difficulties of the conflict event. Similarly, we collected data on the claims, the types of actions, the places where they took place, and their duration, considering that it is the combination of all these data that helps us to understand the context in which the events took place.

The idea was not to quantify social movements and even less to replace the concept with that of conflict events, but to present greater details to enrich the analysis. A social movement can express itself in campaigns and these campaigns in sequences of events. These considerations are well described in the introduction of this volume, which also helps to differentiate the varied empirical approaches used in this book when analyzing other national cases.

In our case, the recording unit of analysis is the event, a social fact classified as a "conflict" because it can be recognized that there is public mobilization of social actors (usually with a certain degree of violence) in pursuit of demands or immediate objectives or when they are very close to taking "de facto" actions (declaration of a state of emergency, strike, etc.). Therefore, it implies a group or collective action with public projection, even if it is carried out on private property (a strike in a factory, for example).

Once the recording was carried out, we compared the files, complementing the information provided by one media with the information provided by the others. We sought information that could be worked quantitatively by actors, claims, places, and the like. The consolidated record was transcribed into a coded dataset ready for quantitative analysis. Our intention was that the files and the quantitative analysis would also make it possible to identify other topics that merited more in-depth qualitative analysis.

It was fairly obvious from the beginning that this approach had its limitations. All events were treated as "equal" even when there were extreme differences in their demographic magnitude, degree of violence, or political influence. However, we could produce a "bird's-eye" view, like a satellite imagery, that was otherwise impossible. We also knew that not all events reached the press and that the press could filter them, excluding those that could be of little relevance to the journalist's opinion either because the actors were inconsequential or because the events occurred in remote places. This was especially true when the number of events increased significantly. The second time that we carried out an intense process of recording, around 1995, we sampled events not recorded in the mainstream media but mentioned in police reports, local media, and other sources. We found that the omission was insignificant when there was low conflict intensity but increased greatly in times of high conflict intensity, and that, in fact, twice as many conflicts occurred at those times. This suggests that the temporal curves are actually quite a bit steeper than what we found from our dataset.

Since the 2000s, CERES has kept the dataset updated, using the same methodology of filing and coding. The newspaper *Presencia* from La Paz ceased publication in mid-2001 and was replaced by *La Razón*. During the 2020 pandemic we were able to extract the data from the PDF files of the media, as they ceased to be published in print for several months.[13]

Popular Protests in Bolivia

We have recorded 19,440 conflict events from between January 1, 1970 and December 31, 2019 using the selected newspapers. Figure 3.1 shows the total

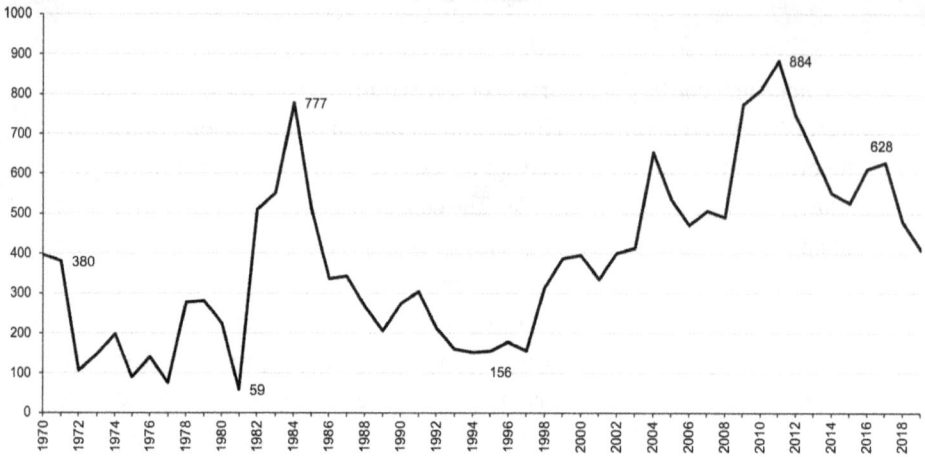

Figure 3.1. Conflict Events in Bolivia (1970–2019). CERES (2022).

number of conflicts per year during this period. One of the first things that can be observed is that the number of events varies significantly over time. Furthermore, it seems evident that the increase or decrease in the number of events can characterize the different crises that the country experienced.

To this effect, differences can be observed between the three major periods of democracy and globalization. The first (1970 to 1985) has, on average, some of the lowest figures in terms of the occurrence of conflict events. Corresponding to the period of military governments, Bolivia's general lack of civil liberties and respect for human rights meant either that the population was afraid to make their claims public or else their claims were made invisible due to censorship of the media by the government in power. By contrast, toward the end of the period, democracy was anticipated with a significant increase in conflict events in the transition years (1982 to 1985), when the number of events per year reached its highest figures. The return to democracy, therefore, seemed to free up both the possibilities to act and the expectations to achieve goals, but the pressure these events generated at the same time prevented the economic crisis from being controlled. Thus, in this first period we see that authoritarianism prevented actors from expressing themselves, even if their living conditions deteriorated. However, when they did, they managed to open up the political system and gain opportunities under democracy.

After this transitional period, and especially between 1986 and 1997, there was undeniable stability, with a tendency toward a decrease in the number of conflicts. During this second period, structural adjustment measures were implemented, prompting subsequent stabilization of the currency, consolidation of democratic institutions, and greater certainty for the population due to improved living conditions. Democracy seems to have been able to incorporate the social and political expression needs of actors, leading to the opening of the economy to globalization. While this reordered the economic landscape and reduced the role of the state, it also prevented the corporatism associated with the state economy from retaining privileges, allowing for new economic advantages in a more equitable manner.

As of 1998, the number of conflict events began to increase again, denoting a growing disenchantment of some sectors of the population that perceived their aspirations were not being satisfied. The international economic crisis—the effects of which were not adequately managed in the country—the weak credibility of democratic institutions, and greater demands for a deepening of social participation in the administration of the state, especially at the regional level, encouraged by the prospect of a strong increase in natural gas exports and oil revenue collections, all played important roles. The increase in the frequency of conflict events again seems to announce a transition that effectively took place by October 2003, when popular pressure forced President Sánchez de Lozada to resign, opening a new period that, for now, we can extend until November 2019, when Evo Morales resigned, cornered by massive protest mobilizations. In this third period, conflict events shifted toward corporate actors that, in a certain way, supported the nondemocratic control of institutions (hence the deterioration of democracy) and tried to take advantage of the resources coming from the unbalanced integration to the global economy (primary exports and consumer imports).

Comparatively, the first (state authoritarianism) and second periods (democracy and open markets) had lower levels of conflicts. But conflicts crested in the years of transition between the first and second periods, and then again between the second and third (state populism). In the first period, the level of conflicts was controlled by repression and, to a certain degree, conformity. The lower level of conflicts in the second period is partly due to the capacity of democratic institutions to process demands and controversies without repression. It is also due in part to the cost of the economic crisis, which affected people's daily lives and generated a broad demand for stability.[14] By contrast, the third period saw a greater frequency of conflicts, as these became the fundamental mechanism for accessing public resources. High commodity prices and corresponding resource rents were common across the first period (mostly in the 1970s) and the third (starting in the early 2000s). The statist orientation of both periods most likely increased expectations of redistribution and placed the government at the center of those struggles.

Actors (Who)

The so-called middle sectors (*sectores medios*) were, from 1970 to the present, the social group with the greatest presence in the scenario of conflict events in Bolivia (see figure 3.2). They had a significant participation in conflicts between 1970 and 1980, a period that corresponds to the time of dictatorships in the country. In the years of transition (1982–1985) and in the first years of the second period, chronologically from 1982 to 1994, their participation in conflict events decreased slightly, but was on average higher than in the third period, showing, in any case, a declining trend that gave way to other groups.[15]

In figure 3.2, it is evident that workers (*obreros*) and their parent organizations were, during most of the period under study, the second most important social group in the generation of conflicts. This participation reached its highest levels in 1981, which corresponds to the military dictatorship of Luis García Meza and the government of General Celso Torrelio. Nevertheless, these data must be qualified because this year corresponds to the one with the lowest number of conflicts registered in our dataset (see figure 3.1), which is explained by the enormous degree of violence and repression exercised by the state against social groups that dared to protest against or criticize the regime. It should also be remembered that the repression was especially hard on students, who, up to that moment, were

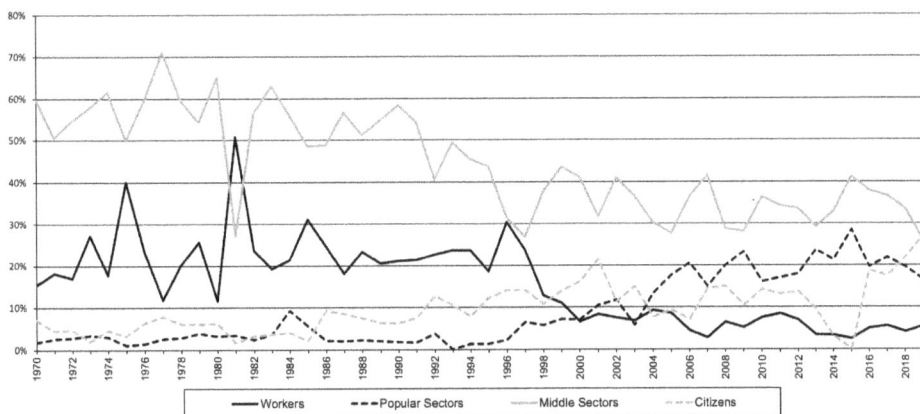

Figure 3.2. Social Actors in Conflict Events. CERES (2022).

the leading social actors in most of the conflict events in the country (see figure 3.3). Toward the end of the 1990s, workers had lower and lower participation rates in the conflict scenarios. This coincided with the capitalization of state enterprises and, therefore, with the decrease of the number of workers dependent on the state and the consequent weakening of their representative organizations.[16]

Figure 3.2 does not capture well the gradual emergence of other social actors throughout the period of study, each of which is still playing a small but growing role in the country's conflicts. One of these groups, which is quite broad and heterogeneous, is what we call the "popular sectors" (*sectores populares*), whose presence grew in importance in the last years of the third period. In the same way, the data generated by figure 3.2 show that the group called "citizens" (*ciudadanía en general*) has had a very oscillating presence: that is, it does not show a clear trend, so its behavior would not be related to major processes but to more circumstantial and perhaps temporary issues. This trend may also be due to the social heterogeneity for which we grouped them under this generic label. A more detailed analysis shows that one of the groups included in this broad category is made up of Bolivia's civic organizations. Although the demands of these entities are rather regional in nature, at certain times they have had a very relevant political presence, even replacing the parties and formal spaces for political deliberation.[17]

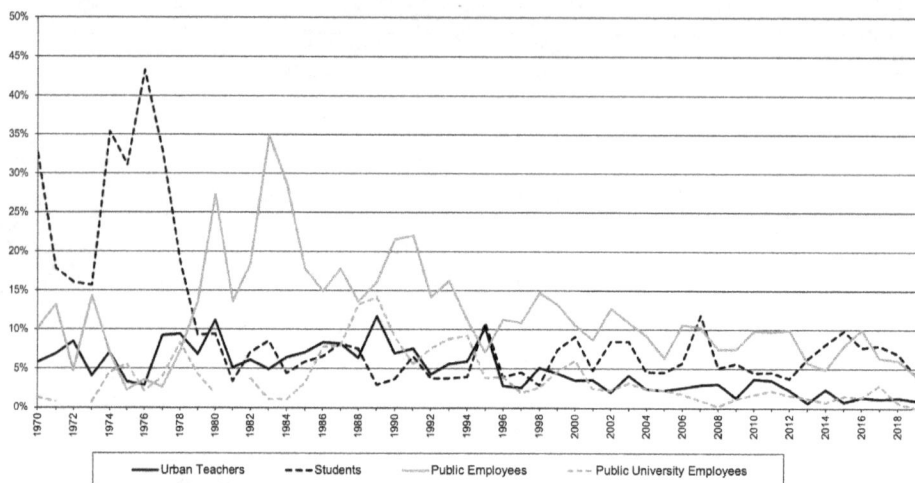

Figure 3.3. Middle Sectors. CERES (2022).

The "middle sectors" are, as we have seen, the most active protagonists of conflict events. This group includes students, public servants, urban teachers, rural teachers, university workers, professionals, small merchants, state bank employees, private-sector workers, and transportation workers, among others. Accordingly, it is appropriate to observe them in greater detail. Figure 3.3 shows only the actors with higher frequencies of participation. Based on the data, it was students who led the largest number of conflict events during the first period (1970 and 1978). Student groups also took on substantial relevance in the panorama of conflict events in the most recent period of state populism. Then, from the beginning of the transition to the second period and until recent years, it was generally public servants (*empleados públicos*) who were the main challengers (figure 3.3). Moreover, urban teachers (*magisterios urbanos*) were prominent, although their participation declined after the middle of the second period, when modernizing educational reform was promoted. Small merchants and transportation workers, usually referred to as informal workers, also increased their participation in conflicts, particularly during the third period (not shown in figure 3.3). In general, what the graph shows is that students no longer dominate the presence of middle sectors; rather, it is more diversified with the relative participation of the different actors. In the transition from the first to the second period, public servants achieved greater visibility; however, their participation has also been declining since the middle of the second period. Toward the third period, there was no clear performance from any of these actors in particular, but rather a highly varied and diverse presence of all groups.

When we disaggregate the "urban popular sectors" (figure 3.4), the information shows that their emergence was due almost exclusively to a greater role played by urban neighborhood groups (*vecinos urbanos*) or their organizations, the *juntas vecinales* (neighborhood councils). This event is not necessarily explained by a greater politicization of the neighborhood councils in relation to state policies. Instead, it is because these groups of citizens increasingly exercised public protest (rallies) or pressure (blockades) as a way to pressure the government to address needs with respect to neighborhood and community development—that is, to satisfy their expectations of urban improvement.

Claims (Why)

According to available data, the main claim over conflicts in the country was related to economic issues (*luchas económicas*); however, since 1994 such issues have become less and less frequent, to the point that in the last period of state populism, they were the second most frequent claim.

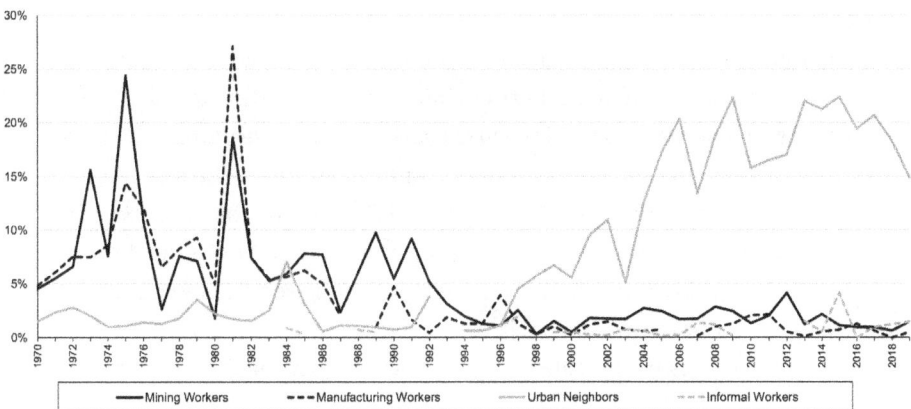

Figure 3.4. Urban Popular Sectors. Discontinuous lines indicate missing data. CERES (2022).

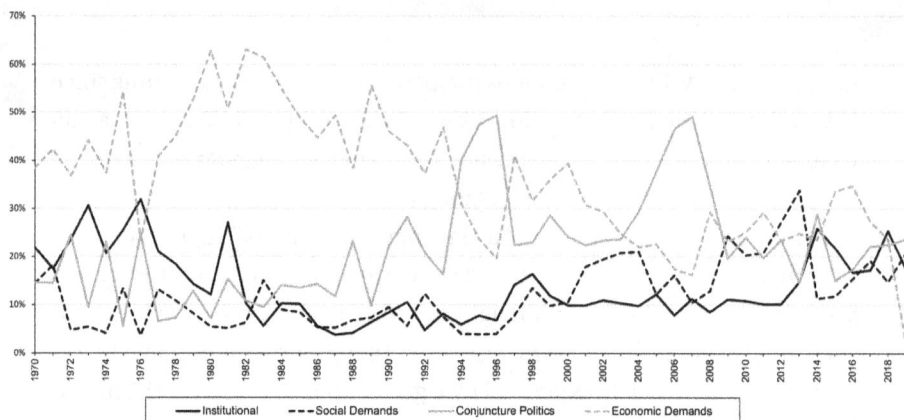

Figure 3.5. Claims of Conflict Events. CERES (2022).

To understand this phenomenon, we must take into account that two of the most common economic demands in the early periods, especially between 1970 and 1996, involved earnings, wage arrears, or salary increases (see figure 3.5). Since 1996, however, the proportion of conflicts demanding greater support from the state to specific regions or localities to address development issues or due to problems with royalties or oil revenues allocated to the regions has increased, as well as, to a lesser extent, claims for greater job stability or the creation of new sources of employment.

In the first period, between 1970 and 1985, another of the main demands of the groups in conflict was related to "institutional politics"—above all, greater democratic freedoms and respect for human rights—which was very much in line with the social and political circumstances the country was experiencing during a period characterized by dictatorial governments with iron fists up until the 1982 transition. However, after the return to democracy, the second most important trigger of conflicts developed into "political situations" (*político coyuntural*), a category by which we refer to issues related to management (appointments, regulations, etc.) rather than to the political structure itself. Their percentage of the total number of events shows an upward trend.

Most conflicts in the category of "political situations" were aimed at

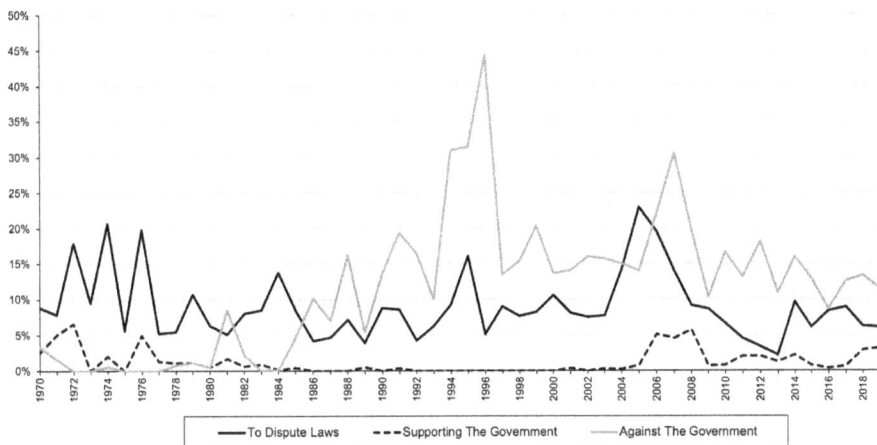

Figure 3.6. Political Situations. CERES (2022).

rejecting policies, actions, or measures taken by the government and, to a lesser extent, by local governments, or at demanding the change or amendment of legal provisions (see figure 3.6). The data show that these types of claims were especially intense at two moments. The first occurred between 1994 and 1996 and coincided with important changes carried out by the first government of Sánchez de Lozada, namely capitalization, popular participation, pension reform, and educational reform—measures that were strongly rejected at the time by the most organized sectors. The second began in 2004 and continues today: it corresponds to the worsening crisis of state and democratic institutions that Bolivia has been experiencing since the beginning of the 2000s, which has not been solved by either the Constituent Assembly or the "stability" of the Morales government, which managed to extend its term of office for fourteen years.

In recent years, there has also been a consistent increase in conflicts related to what we have called "social struggles" (*luchas sociales*), which are almost always linked to demands by the public for greater participation in appointments, dismissals, or changes of public servants (see figure 3.5). However, from 1997 on, the percentage of social struggles arising from problems related to the expropriation or appropriation of property, land, boundaries, and territory became more important (see figure 3.7).

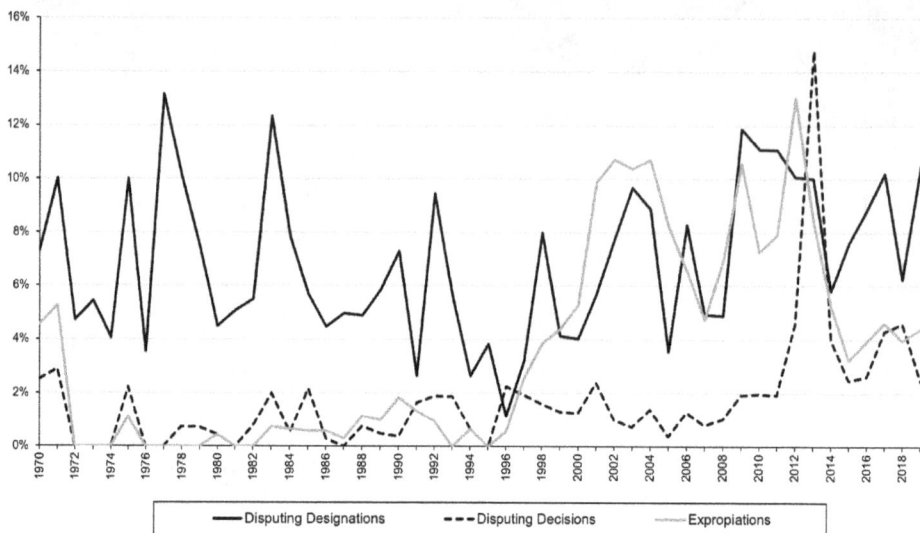

Figure 3.7. Social Struggles. CERES (2022).

Actions (How)

Figure 3.8 shows the change in the repertoire of collective action that has taken place during the fifty years we describe. In order to capture trends more clearly, we have eliminated from the graph some forms of conflict action that are less frequent, such as sit-down strikes (*huelgas de brazos caídos*); takeovers (*tomas*), or occupations of private spaces, offices, or factories; and civic strikes (*paros cívicos*). This does not detract from their importance. Takeovers usually represent intransigent and at times violent actions; perhaps that is why they are not used very often, as they can provoke equally violent responses. Civic strikes are also infrequent, but in general, they mobilize many people. Thus, they can be very influential and, in certain situations, decisive.

As shown in figure 3.8, the gradual decrease in the percentage of labor strikes in Bolivia stands out, especially after the period of democracy and open markets. Because the possibility of exercising this type of strike is only allotted to people who have a stable source of employment and are registered within the corresponding regulations, the decreasing proportion of this type of conflict can be explained in part by the decrease in the number of earners in the country. This decrease is the result of factors such

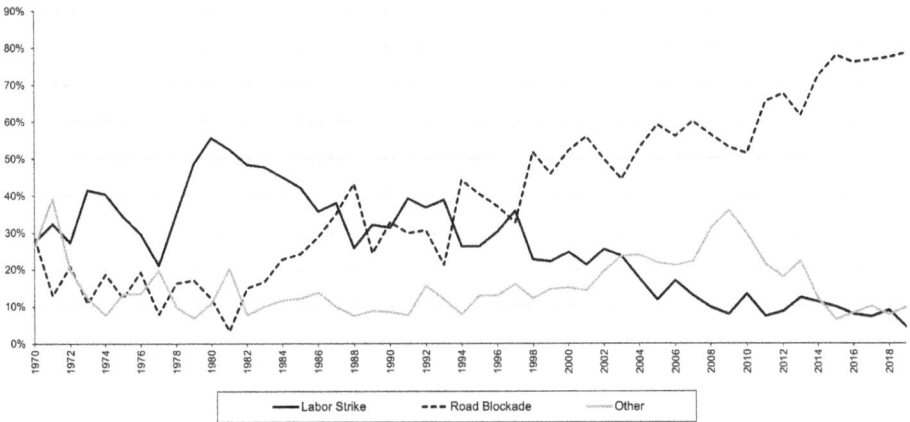

Figure 3.8. Actions of Conflict Events. CERES (2022).

as the privatization of some state enterprises, the bankruptcy or disappearance of others (particularly in the mining sector), the shrinking of the state, the liberalization of labor laws, and the greater political presence of informal groups. It should also be remembered that, even in the first period, labor groups were dominated by those who were more dependent on the state than the private sector.

The figure also shows that from the second period onward, blockades, marches, and demonstrations have tended to increase significantly in proportion to other forms of conflict and for approximately twenty-five years have become the main means of protest used by groups in conflict. These trends may be due to the fact that with the recovery of democracy came greater civilian liberties, and with them the possibility of protesting, dissenting, or presenting claims to the state. Democracy also led to not only the emergence of new social actors in the country, but also the increase in visibility of a number of other preexisting actors, in particular the excluded and marginalized sectors. On the other hand, the number of people in the "informal sector" of the economy increased dramatically. Most of the aforementioned social actors did not have stable sources of employment or strong social organizations through which to channel their claims, nor have they currently. Therefore, it is quite logical for them to turn to the streets as a way to express their demands.

With respect to other actions not shown in the graph, hunger strikes became more important after 1989 than in previous years, despite a recent decline. Moreover, takeovers and occupations were more frequent at the end of the second period, and in recent years they have been among the most frequent forms of conflict. At the same time, as shown, the proportion of road blockades, both in rural and urban areas, has increased with respect to the total.

All aforementioned forms of conflict that have increased in percentage terms over time correspond to what we have called "active adhesion conflicts" because they involve the subjects doing something out of the ordinary, such as leaving their homes or workplaces to occupy a road and prevent the movement of vehicles or pedestrians. By contrast, "passive adhesion conflicts" (*pasivas*), in which subjects generate conflict by ceasing to do something habitual, such as suspending work and productive activity through a strike, are a decreasing percentage of the total. Therefore, over these fifty years, the data show a clear reversal of the type of adhesion of conflicts (see figure 3.9). This is an alarming trend, given that the events of "active adhesion" (*activas*) presuppose a greater risk of violence and damage or harm to third parties or to the actors involved in the conflict event. Blocking a street or a road involves exercising violence on passersby as a pressure mechanism against others, such as the government or the mayor's office. This violence is often accepted by those who suffer it precisely because they are told that the adversary is the "other," but on occasions, the lack of response from the "other" has led to clashes between civilians, which can trigger more violence.

Targets (Whom)

The target is a peculiar actor within the development of a conflict because, in general, he, she, or it is defined as such by the social group or groups that trigger and then lead a social conflict—either because they demand certain behavior from the target or because they consider the target's actions and decisions to be harmful or beneficial to them. Figure 3.10 presents an overview of the social actors or institutions that were most often identified as the target during Bolivian conflicts.

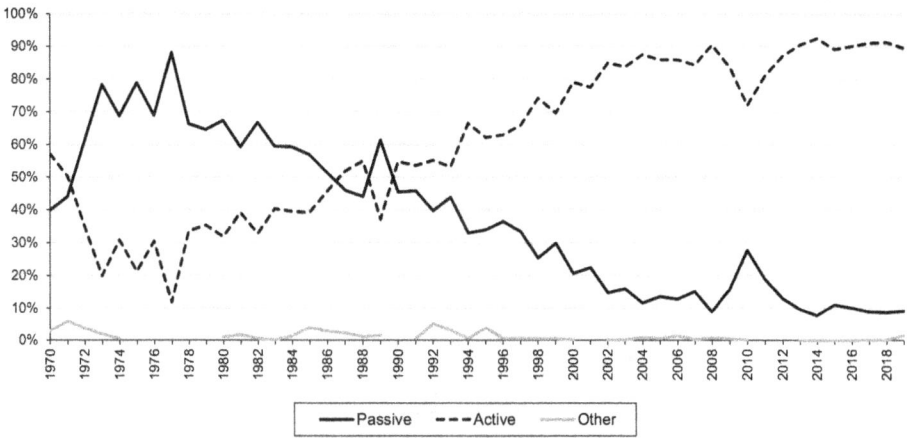

Figure 3.9. Types of Adhesion in Conflict Events. Discontinuous lines indicate missing data. CERES (2022).

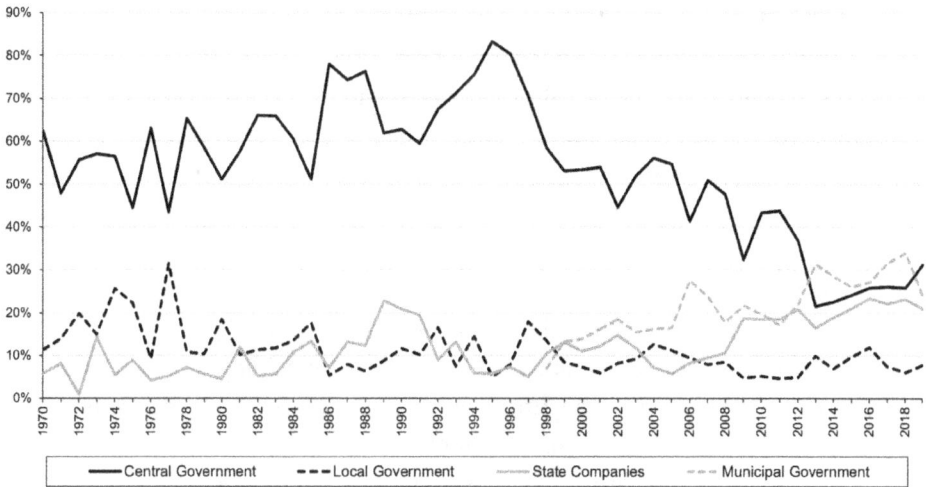

Figure 3.10. Targets of Conflict Events. Discontinuous lines indicate missing data. CERES (2022).

In general terms, the state at the central level (*estado central*) has been the most frequent target of claims. However, if we add to this other state targets, such as its apparatus at the local level—state companies and the police and armed forces[18]—we find that more than 80 percent of all conflicts during the last fifty years defined the state on some level as a target or interlocutor.

It should be noted that, after the adoption of the Law of Popular Participation, the municipal governments of the country have received claims more and more frequently. This trend has been especially noticeable for a little more than four years at this writing. The identification of state-owned companies as adversaries of conflict is also increasing rapidly, reflecting their growing importance in the economy since the nationalization policies that began in 2006.

Conclusions

After thoroughly reviewing the data in the light of the periodization proposed by the intersection of political and economic processes, it is now time to draw some conclusions. In Bolivia, over the long term, there tends to be a predominance of a statist orientation of social demands, fueled by both authoritarian and populist regimes. The first and third periods of the analysis, which were strongly marked by statist and protectionist policies (i.e., antiglobalization) altogether cover more than thirty years of the half-century under consideration.

We have not gone in depth into an analysis that could explain this coincidence between two apparently opposite leaders such as Bánzer and Morales, but we conjecture that they are brought together by the personalization of political leadership, or *caudillismo*. The *caudillo* seeks to bolster his popular image by projecting himself as a providential leader, which requires the strengthening of the state's position as a central actor in economic processes and as a protector against external threats. This, in turn, explains the tendency toward enclosure, except for foreign trade. This is fundamental for an extractive economy that sells natural resources—mainly minerals and hydrocarbons—and meets domestic consumption needs with imports. The "isolation" promoted by statism is, therefore, relative, referring mainly to foreign private investment and a fuller integration of markets. This also helps to explain the predominance of the state as a target in conflict events, even though it is more of an interlocutor than an adversary. Of course, there are marked differences in the frequency and intensity of collective actions between the authoritarianism of the first period, which did not deny the caudillo's personal relationship with corporate groups and also rejected and repressed public action as a sign of disorder, and the populism of the third period, which instead nurtured and encouraged such expressions because they helped to circumvent the limitations often imposed by existing norms and institutions.

The second period, in turn, showed a situation in which processes of democratic institutionalization and economic globalization were taking place at the same time, which in terms of conflict events looks more like a "plateau" of calmness. This could be explained by the capacity of democratic institutions to process the public's demands for representation, participation, and economic improvement, channeling them through parties, Congress, and municipal councils as well as defending them through laws and courts. This reduced the need for organized direct action by the people. They may also have found that their expectations and aspirations were more likely to be met in the open, expanded markets. This perception may have been reinforced by the redefinition of the role of the state. What would have been the point of mobilizing against an interlocutor that was trying to stop being the main actor for development?

Democracy and globalization have been marked by important changes in the presence of social actors, and these have brought about changes in motivations and forms of action. In general terms, and supporting a turn from reactive to proactive protests, as described in the introduction of this volume, we observe the declining presence of wage earners and the emergence of various social actors, including the informal sector, as well as the consequent change in the repertoires or forms of collective action, from increasingly infrequent labor strikes to increasingly frequent marches, demonstrations, and other street actions. There are also similar actor shifts from public servants (figure 3.3) to neighborhood groups (figure 3.4), and also shifts in claims, which became less and less related to employment conditions and more and more to living conditions, especially in the cities.

To conclude, while globalization and democracy have an effect on collective action, the latter also determines the degrees and paces of both. The impact is not unidirectional—it could be said that the relationship between the processes of global and political openness occurs through collective actions, in such a way that they show to a large extent the capacity of society to produce its political and economic environment, "opening" or "closing" it according to the force exerted by social actors and the degree to which that force shapes its institutional systems. Of course, these arguments need to be considered as part of a more complex scheme because, as we anticipated, the three processes on which we concentrate our attention are a sort of window to the fields of economy, politics, and society, in which there are other processes (economic performance, production, employment, consumption, elections, legislation, etc.) that were left out of this analysis.

Notes

1. It is seldom noted that a few days after Gulf Oil was nationalized, the government had to start negotiations so that the company would keep channels open with multilateral and cooperative entities. The nationalized company received US$79 million in compensation. correodelsur.com/ecos/20191027_a-50-anos-de-la-nacionalizacion-de-la-gulf-oil-co.html.

2. Because they take place in barracks and are led by very small groups, military coups succeed in imposing government authority only when they have social support. It may not be organized or quantifiable, but none is based exclusively on violence and repression. Even when that seems the case, it is only in appearance, and is based on the acceptance, tolerance, or silent support of an important part of the people. Sad as this may be, it should be remembered for a better understanding of social and political processes.

3. In November 1979, the government of Mrs. Lidia Gueiler Tejada attempted a fiscal adjustment with currency devaluation, which cost her popularity but allowed her to put the budget in order. The military men who replaced her by force talked a lot about frugality but could not prevent the economy from continuing to fall, as their policies were inconsistent and very limited, and resistance forced them to increase spending without control.

4. According to the Bolivian Constitution at that time, if a candidate did not reach an absolute majority, Congress became an Electoral College and elected among the three most-voted candidates. This rule was modified in 1993, eliminating the third party in the congressional election.

5. Paz Estenssoro had governed the country twice before, between 1952 and 1956 and from 1960 to 1964. He was reelected for a third term that year but was overthrown a few months later by a military coup led by his vice president, Air Force general René Barrientos. For a description of his economic policy of stabilization and openness, see Morales and Sachs (1988).

6. Paz Zamora had been Siles Zuazo's vice president (1982–1985) and led the social democratic MIR, a party belonging to Socialist International.

7. This reform has not been studied in depth but there are many indications

that it had good intentions but poor results. The constituencies were very large and heterogeneous, and the deputies, who were not known by the voters, dissociated themselves from the parties and weakened them.

8. This possibility did not become a reality due to people's distrust. The memory of the robberies of retirement funds was very much alive, and the resistance of the union elites to the new system was still understandably strong, due to the fact that their sectors' "complementary funds," which they had formerly managed, were eliminated. These funds not only broke the unity of the system but were also instruments for capturing state subsidies mandated in the name of solidarity with the elderly.

9. Evo Morales led the peasant coca growers' movement, which little by little assumed a sort of representation of anti-imperialist sentiment in opposition to the US antidrug policy toward the country. He also wielded coca as a symbol of cultural resistance, which allowed him to build bridges with indigenous movements. Manfred Reyes Villa had been a popular mayor in Cochabamba. He had a military background and tried to emulate the early Bolivarianism of Hugo Chávez. They both had parties organized around their personal image and projected themselves as caudillos with sensitivity to the changing moods of the popular masses.

10. The law was enacted by Rodríguez but presented as the spearhead of the "nationalization" promoted by Morales, which in fact only expropriated the part that belonged to Bolivian citizens, forcing the companies to sign new contracts.

11. In the 2009 Constitution, a second round of voting was introduced in the event that there was no winner by absolute majority or a victory by more than 40 percent of the valid votes and a distance of ten points over the runner-up.

12. Morales's resignation was followed by those of his collaborators, forcing the second vice-president of the Senate to assume command of the nation. Jeanine Añez, the second woman to hold that office in Bolivia, had to navigate a country troubled and affected by the COVID-19 pandemic leading up to the October 2020 elections, which were won by Morales's former minister of economy, Luis Arce Catacora, with a platform that basically promised a return to social stability and economic bonanza. In March 2021, former President Añez was arrested, accused of having orchestrated a coup to overthrow Morales. She has been subjected to several trials in conditions that were considered inadequate by human rights organizations.

13. Barrett et al. (2020) present an interesting methodology, also based on events recorded in the media but using an automated clocking system. By identifying news items from various global media sources using grammatical algorithms, the authors developed a Registered Social Unrest

Index based on the number of articles about conflicts (registered events) relative to the number of articles about the country's current affairs.

14. Inflation was 12,338 percent in 1985, but the adjustment program managed to lower it to 230 percent in 1986 and 13 percent in 1987, despite the fact that the price of tin, one of Bolivia's main export products since the 1930s, fell in 1985.

15. Other categories with lower participation frequencies not shown in the graph include political activists, a group with relatively continuous activity, and colonizers, mostly coca producers, who significantly increased their presence and ended up having enormous political influence in recent years.

16. It is worth highlighting the difference between the behavior of labor unions dependent on state entities or companies, which are much more prone to conflict, and those dependent on private entities or companies, which are less active in all periods, except in times of high political conflict intensity.

17. The term "general public" is used when the conflicts are led by representatives of the majority of the actors and living sectors of the population without any of them being clearly responsible for leading or directing them. In the first period, civic organizations played a relevant role, even in contributing to the democratic transition, as studied by Calderón and Laserna (1983). In the transition that started with the resignation of Evo Morales in November 2019, civic organizations once again played a leading role in channeling the protest of urban sectors.

18. Both entities were excluded from the graph because of their low frequency. The same was true of transportation companies and merchants, who occasionally appear as "adversaries" in neighborhood group mobilizations.

CHAPTER FOUR

State Debt with a Social Agenda, Constructed amid Social Protests in Colombia, 1975–2019[1]

MAURICIO ARCHILA NEIRA AND
MARTHA CECILIA GARCÍA VELANDIA

Social movements become visible to us through the wake of their action. That wake is their way of struggle; but like any wake, it is misleading: its form, its texture, its internal plotline, and its visibility change as time goes by, depending on the place of observance and the type of gaze.

—RAÚL ZIBECHI

Introduction

This chapter studies the evolution of protests in Colombia between 1975 and 2019 based on the processes of democratization and globalization, in which the country is close to the Latin American average. As in other parts of the continent, globalization has weakened actors with class identity such as workers and peasants, while empowering others such as urban dwellers, environmentalists, ethnic groups, and women. But both struggle to broaden democracy not only in representative but also in truly participatory terms, heralding the emergence of a new citizenry. This should be strengthened by the peace agreement signed in 2016 between the state and the largest and oldest guerrilla group in the continent; unfortunately, this important step has not ended violence against social leaders. In this regard, the failure of the state not only to implement the peace agreement but also to stop the violence marks the recent mobilization in the country. The instrument used for the Protest Event Analysis is a database of social protests (the Base de Datos de Luchas Sociales, or BDLS) that has 26,119 records beginning in 1975. This is how we capture the wake that makes social movements visible, as Raúl Zibechi states in the epigraph.

Globalization and Democratization: Colombia between 1975 and 2019

During this time, the country lived through great structural transitions that framed the trajectory of the social struggles of the period: its population doubled, moving from twenty-three million to a little over forty-eight million inhabitants, although the birth rate fell. Illiteracy fell more among women, but still affects 5 percent of the female population. The proportion of women heads of household grew, reaching 40.7 percent. Life expectancy grew to an average of seventy-six years, which increased the number of long-lived people: for every one hundred people under fifteen years of age, there are 40.5 individuals over age sixty-five (Departamento Administrativo Nacional de Estadística [DANE] 2018).

In terms of globalization and democratization—the "dual transition" that articulates this book, as Moisés Arce and Takeshi Wada point out in the introduction—between 1970 and 2019 Colombia had an evolution similar to the Latin American average, especially in economic terms.[2] As figure 1.4 in the introductory chapter shows, the line of globalization in the country was very similar to that of the rest of the continent, except for a lag between the 1990s and the middle of the second decade of this century.

By contrast, Colombia's trend toward democratization differs from the rest of the continent. Until the mid-1980s it was higher than the Latin American average; that was a time when most of the region was subject to military dictatorships. Although Colombia was not the best example of a democracy due to the weight of traditional bipartisanship and authoritarian traits in the management of public order, it stood out in the continental scenario because it maintained the elections formally. However, from the second half of the 1980s to 2015 the country fell below the Latin American average, marked in most countries by the return to democracy and consequently by stronger institutions, something not possible in Colombia due to the persistent armed conflict. Precisely, the signing of the peace agreement with the insurgency in 2016 allowed the country to once again figure above the average of democratization in the continent in the last five years of the period.

During these years the country transformed from primarily rural to urban. Today 77.1 percent of the population lives in urban centers and 36.7 percent are concentrated in the ten principal cities. The rural–urban flow has been fed by forced displacement, with currents of migrants moving to metropolitan areas, although with a preference for intermediate cities, on the periphery of which informal housing has grown, producing adverse impacts on the natural environments, the conurbation, and the quality of life of the receiving populations (Ruiz 2011, 142).

Beginning in the 1980s, internal forced displacement in Colombia assumed enormous dimensions, and in 2018 numbered 7,816,500 people forced to leave their territories (ACNUR-UNHCR 2018, 35), a statistic that grants Colombia the dishonorable first place in the world in internal forced displacement. A little over 50 percent of the displaced are women, and 35 percent are children. It is estimated that close to 15 percent of the total Afro-Colombian population and 10 percent of the indigenous population have been displaced, some of whom lived in collective territories recognized by the state. Eighty-seven percent of residents expelled from their regions lived in the countryside. More than 8.3 million hectares have been vacated or abandoned by force and 99 percent of municipalities have been sources of displacement. In the words of Myriam Hernández (2015, 16), "In light of the preceding statistics, it is not excessive to characterize Colombia as *a displaced nation.*" One of the consequences of this has been the *de-peasantization* of the national territory. At the same time that cities grew at a rapid pace, the landscape and vocation of the countryside changed following the exodus of its inhabitants: small farms growing various agricultural products were converted into large and uniform tracts of land cultivated with oil palm, or cleared for mining, or set aside for the cultivation of coca (Hernández 2015, 18).

Beginning in the 1980s the industrial model of development (which had reigned since the 1930s) was weakened, and processes of deindustrialization were accelerated, as well as, among other things, the trend toward more flexibility in workplace arrangements; the weakening of the agrarian economy and the internal marketplace; the reduction of trade barriers; the return to the extractive economy in mining; and reprioritization of extractivist projects in mining, oil, agro-industry, and fisheries. This coincided with the Latin American tendency to implement the economic adjustments proposed by transnational banks.

Oil became the leader in export, overtaking coffee. Open-sky mining was consolidated as a national objective, and grew on average 17 percent per year, while the agro-industrial and industrial sectors exhibited a relative stagnation (Santa María et al. 2013, 4). Nevertheless, during the '80s—the "lost decade" for development in Latin America—despite an uninterrupted succession of civilian governments, Colombia experienced a great macroeconomic stability, with one of the highest rates of growth in the region.[3] It did so while also experiencing a multiplication of violence, together with its settings and its agents.

In the 1990s, the role of the state transformed: it ceased to intervene directly in economic activity in order to act in consonance with the Washington consensus, that conjunction of reforms that deepened Latin America's entry into globalization. In this way, the productive system of the country reaffirmed its integration with global markets and the policies of liberalization of commerce, deregulation of financial and labor markets, privatization of public enterprises, and fomenting of direct foreign investment were all made explicit. Concurrently, an institutional and legal framework was created, aimed at strengthening property rights (Gaitán et al. 2011, 13). Meanwhile, the cultivation of coca leaf and the trafficking in cocaine constituted the largest share of illegal exports and made Colombia the drug's primary global producer. This entry of the country into narcotrafficking limited its chances for well-being and maintenance of the institutions of the economy (Rocha 2001, 430).

Beginning with the Political Constitution of 1991, the state debated with itself about broadening democracy, consolidating a social safety net, and attending to the requirements of the free market focused on regulatory activities to facilitate private productive activity. The new Constitution conferred a central role to civic participation, privileged social spending, deepened the process of decentralization, and established more than seventy-five civil, political, economic, social, cultural, environmental, and collective rights, liberties, and civic guarantees. However, at the same time, it prescribed the financial takeover of health care, pensions, and areas of public goods (Suárez 2015; Archila Neira et al. 2020). The legislative program included reforms to public education, labor, and tax and environmental law. The setting in motion of these policies of structural adjustment reduced the state's resources and hence its redistributive capacity, which led to the sharpening of socioeconomic asymmetries within the country.

In the first decade of the twenty-first century the Colombian economy opted for an extractive-exporting development model and saw itself enormously favored by the high demand for, relative scarcity of, and speculation in commodities, which pushed the volatility of their prices in international markets. This increased the cost effectiveness of investments associated with natural resources and contributed to environmental degradation and increases in vertical foreign investment and land conflicts.[4] Concomitantly, over a third of the continental area of the country was involved in mining activity, either through solicitation or concession of mining licenses or designation for the development of such activities in strategic mining areas. This statistic is alarming, because Colombia is the country with the most biodiversity per square kilometer on the planet, and because the institutions that regulate such activities are insufficient to protect and adequately maintain renewable natural resources (Negrete 2013, 24).

The process of economic turn to extractivism was reaffirmed with the signing of over a dozen free trade agreements. In addition to the traditional liberalization of duties, these included a long list of topics and mechanisms for deregulation and strict obligations for signatory nations in areas of agriculture, public purchases, services, access to goods, investments, intellectual property, labor and environmental standards, and e-commerce.[5] To depend on a productive paradigm that is primarily extractive makes the economy ever more vulnerable and dependent on international prices of primary goods, which is problematic because of the extreme volatility of commodity markets.

These forty-five years yielded a transition from the first period of *Violencia* (1946–1964) to the second (1985–2016) with continuities in modalities and geographies, but differences in actors, motivations, and, above all, the scale of the violent acts, particularly because of the resources of the narcotics trade, which financed all of the victimizers (González et al. 2002).

Closing out the period, the state signed a peace agreement with the Revolutionary Armed Forces of Colombia (FARC)—the largest and oldest guerrilla group on the continent—after more than fifty years of armed conflict. After this, 13,193 FARC members laid down their arms (ARN 2020, 2). However, breaches and delays in the implementation of the agreement made analysts and academics warn "If ex-combatants do not achieve holistic reintegration and have security guarantees, the risk that some will join some illegal armed group is high" (Corredor and Ramírez 2018, 19). This was no sooner said than done: toward the end of August 2019, three of the leaders of the former FARC—among them negotiators of the agreement and senators designated by this group—announced by video that they were taking up arms again and would coordinate efforts with the Army of National Liberation (ELN) and other splinter groups of the FARC, in order to save the peace that had allegedly been betrayed.

Methods: The Database of Social Struggles in Colombia

Following this wake has been a long-standing effort taken on by the Social Movements Team of the Centro de Investigación y Educación Popular (CINEP). To that end, it created its database of social struggles (BDLS), containing information about social mobilization in Colombia from 1975 to the present.[6] We carry out our Protest Event Analysis through this database not only in order to analyze the protests diachronically, but also to observe their relation to democratization and globalization processes in the Colombian historical context.

The registry of data in this database takes as a point of departure the concept of *visibility*, as suggested by Zibechi in the epigraph of this chapter. Because of this, we understand the footprint that social actors have left in the consulted sources. It reflects the will of the actors to make their protest public, as well as the way in which those outside the protest, including consulted mass media, perceived that act.

The BDLS is framed in the field of social movements. The central category to capture information is *protest* or *social struggle*, and this is where the criterion of visibility is actualized. We define it as the total of collective social actions of more than ten people that intentionally articulate demands or that push for solutions to injustices, exclusions, or inequalities before the state at its various levels, private entities, or individuals.

Not every social movement is made visible through protest, nor is all protest an expression of a social movement. Social struggle (or protest) has the quality of public challenge and is defined by three criteria: that it challenges power (not just the state's, but also that existing in civil society), is collective and social in the Weberian sense—that is, its meaning is evident to others and it seeks to affect the conduct of others—and is brought about in person in public spaces.

From this conceptual entry point, we have elaborated the following categories that engage with variables about which the BDLS provides information:

> *Temporal-spatial register of each struggle*: establishes the dates of initiation and finalization of the protest, its duration, the places where the conflict expressed by the social struggle emerge, and the places where the public events take place (which sometimes do not coincide).
>
> *Scope of the protest*: seeks to capture the geopolitical coverage of each collective social action. We distinguish seven levels: international, national, departmental, regional, subregional, municipal, and submunicipal. This categorization is framed in political-administrative divisions of the country yet recognizes that the scope includes environment as well as circumstances and situation (Restrepo 2019).
>
> *Actors*: defined based on three complementary criteria: the existence of a specific social conflict, the identity generated around it, and the

intentionality of the action undertaken. These criteria are summarized in the *what*, the *who*, and the *why* of the collective social action. The *what* refers to the existence, beyond the will of actors and antagonists, of a social conflict forged by injustices, inequalities, or exclusions. The *who* incorporates the subjective dimension in the way that actors publicly identify themselves. This identity or mode of social cohesion does not necessarily translate into a formal organizational expression. The *why* or the intentionality of the action determines the modality of the specific actor, choosing between various areas of conflict and diverse identities.

We include eleven actors: wage earners; peasants; urban inhabitants; students; ethnic groups—indigenous, black, Afro-Colombians, *palenqueros*,[7] and *raizales*[8]—victims of the internal armed conflict; women; the LGBTI population (Lesbian, Gay, Bisexual, Transgender, and Intersexual); independent workers; entrepreneur associations (within which those in commerce and transportation stand out, often without constituting social movements, but on occasion recurring to protest actions); and the incarcerated.

Modalities of action, type of struggle, or repertoires: includes work stoppages or strikes; mobilizations (marches, public meetings, rallies); squatting in rural land, ethnic territories, and urban areas and housing; occupation of entities (transitory, nonpermanent); roadblocks; disturbances (confrontations that involve clashes with public forces); hunger strikes; and actions of resistance or civil disobedience. The BDLS does not register armed actions of guerrilla or paramilitary forces, for these correspond to another category of quantification measuring political violence, in addition to these armed actors not being considered social movements.

Motives or claims: seeks to capture the perspective that actors have over the causes of the social conflict. This is the most complex variable, because each social actor has their own agenda. Given that normally there is more than one motive in collective social actions, and with the goal of avoiding the duplication of entries, we choose the motive formulated explicitly as the principal demand, or that was represented as such by the consulted source. We have tried to construct categories that cut across various actors in order to avoid the bias of assigning exclusive motives by social sector.

We have incorporated twelve categories of motive, ranging from material to political or cultural demands. They are: working conditions (wages, employment, labor stability, et al.); land and housing; public services and physical infrastructure; social services (primarily education, health-related, and services for vulnerable populations); breaches of laws and agreements; human rights; demands related to authorities; public policies at all levels of the state; environmental demands; solidarity with other actors in the conflict; commemorations; and struggles against other protests.

Conveners: refers to the organizations that convene to protest—although the press rarely highlights them. The majority of the categories coincide with the relevant actors, but also include NGOs, churches, political parties and movements, and even local or regional authorities.

Adversaries or targets: defined as the entities or groups to whom the demands of social struggles are directed. These include executive agencies; state or mixed enterprises at local, regional or national levels; private enterprises, cooperatives, or civil society; armed forces and police; and irregular armed groups. To a lesser extent, we see demands directed at legal and judicial power. We have also included a "without specific adversary" category for demands directed at society more broadly.

These categories—referencing the who, the how, the why, the when, and the where—are based in well-defined and mutually exclusive theoretical constructs. They inform the index of the BDLS, affording those coding events, as well as external users, the highest level of precision with regard to the meaning of each term. Each category contains subcategories, a hierarchy that was established so as not to lose richness of detail. This structure of data also allows for highly specific analysis by spaces, periods, actors, motives, adversaries, or combinations of these.

The primary sources we consulted to capture information on social mobilization that could be included in the BDLS are:

Nine daily newspapers and one weekly from Colombia's five main cities, all of which claim national coverage, and eleven regional or local newspapers.

Radio and television news stations.

The websites of newspapers, magazines, and radio or television news channels.

Journalistic and opinion magazines.

Bulletins, websites, and accounts in virtual networks maintained by social organizations and NGOs.

Alternative press.

Academic books and articles.

Testimonials collected directly, either orally or in writing.

The use of diverse sources seeks to increase the quantity of events that can be registered, free the data from the bias of any individual source, and to make it possible to triangulate sources to obtain diverse perspectives on the same event and thereby facilitate the validation of the data.

We have presented the structure of the BDLS in order to explore through the data it provides the transformation of popular protest in Colombia spurred by economic globalization and the vicissitudes of democracy in the period between 1975 and 2019. In the Protest Event Analysis in the next section, we placed particular attention on which actors have been weakened and which strengthened, and on the innovative strategies and forms of mobilization that have emerged during this period, as is proposed in the introduction to this book.

Popular Politics in Colombia, 1975–2019

The BDLS registered 26,119 protests that took place between 1975 and 2019. Compared with other Latin American countries, this could be seen as a low figure, but in the Colombian context, taking to the streets to protest is a brave act that can be very costly, given the potential for violence.

One can trace four periods of peak-to-peak pendulum, nearly corresponding to decades, over the graph in figure 4.1: 1975–1987, 1988–1999,

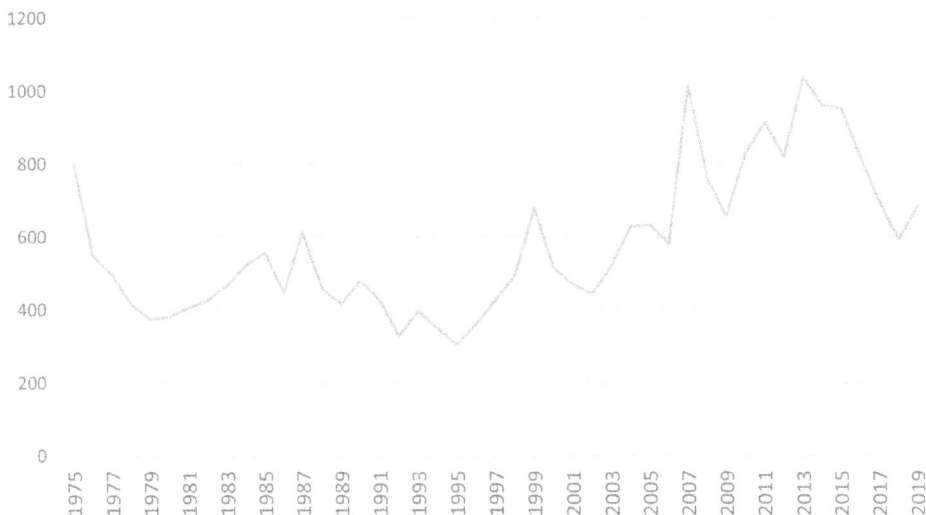

Figure 4.1. Trajectory of Social Struggles in Colombia, 1975–2019. BDLS (2022).

2000–2007, and 2008–2019. But different from the cycles as conceived by the relevant literature (Tarrow 1997), we find peaks in 1975, 1988, 1999, 2007, 2011, and 2013, as well as troughs in 1980, 1992, and 1995. For their part, 2002, 2006, 2009, and 2018 were relatively low years in the context of recent decades. The peaks and troughs respond not only to specific aspects of the national and global situation, but also to changing public protagonisms and social identities in these protests.

In general, the trajectory of these forty-five years of social struggles is associated with the democratic behavior of the country. Theories about social movements, particularly those that study the political process, illustrate that relation, indicating that protest tends to be more peaceful, autonomous, and proactive and less local in character to the degree that societies democratize according to the Western liberal model. Likewise, it is said that struggles respond to structures of political opportunity, which are often associated with the deepening of democracy (Tilly 2004; Tarrow 1997; see also Arce and Wada in the introduction to this volume).

Also, in the Colombian case it can be cited that, broadly speaking, social protests and the movements expressed in them tend to increase in moments of greater democratic dynamism, particularly during the opening of dialogues with the insurgency, as illustrated in the peaks of 1985–1987, 1999, and 2013. On the other hand, closures of civic participation and, above all, repressive policies, inhibit protest. But every rule has its exceptions: for example, the low number of social struggles registered between 1991 and 1992, just when the new political Constitution was being developed and implemented, a juncture in which one might expect a broad mobilization of the citizenry to push for the inclusion of demands and claims. The other notorious example was the peak of 2007, when Álvaro Uribe-Vélez (2002–2010) governed, a president of an authoritarian mold who could not exactly be characterized as incentivizing social mobilization, except when it was expedient for him. Each of these instances has a particular explanation, as we shall see below.

The first period of peak-to-peak pendulum (1975–1987) inherited the protest boom of the last years of the bipartisan pact known as the National Front. It corresponds to what Arce and Wada (see the introduction to this volume) call the "lost decade" previous to the adjustment policies. During this time a peak of social struggles took place, emerging separately but converging due to the political influence of the left. These included squatting on lands by peasants and indigenous people, the great student movement in defense of the autonomy of the universities, the threats of general strike on the part of the unions, and multiple urban struggles for the right to the city.

This boom in struggles was projected on the first government after the National Front, that of Alfonso López-Michelsen (1974–1978), cofounder of the Liberal Revolutionary Movement (MRL), who was not, for all that, a revolutionary, given that he had opposed the agrarian reform and the industrial model built on substitution of imports, anticipating the economic aperture and forging the nation's destiny as the "South American Japan." The high number of protests during his term stands out, as does the broad coverage of these, geographically and in terms of population, particularly in the case of the national civic stoppage of September 14, 1977 (Medina 1984, chapter 8).[9]

The decline of social struggles at the end of López-Michelsen's term was consolidated during that of his successor, Julio César Turbay (1978–1982), who adopted the doctrine of national security with the excuse of stopping the action of urban guerrillas, particularly that of the Movement of 19th of

April (M-19). Close to the first anniversary of the civic stoppage of '77 he promulgated an exceptional norm, the Security Statute, thanks to which a repressive wave was unleashed that wound up hitting social actors and politicians of the opposition.[10] In this way, in the context of a nearly permanent state of siege, the Military Courts of Justice were used to condemn supposed guerrilla members, many of whom were in reality social and political leaders. In parallel, the violation of human rights intensified, particularly torture and disappearances (Villegas and Moreno 1980).

But Turbay also saw himself obligated to open the door to an amnesty to acclimate the peace dialogues with the insurgency, which would be the signal accomplishment of the following president, Belisario Betancur (1982–1986). About halfway through his term, the government conducted negotiations with the primary guerrilla forces, save for the ELN, which opposed itself in that moment to a political end to the armed conflict. A timid political and fiscal decentralization resulted from these negotiations, due in part to pressure from social movements, particularly those on civic issues.[11] In that context, the social, political, and armed left favored unity processes in social organizations and created political fronts such as A Luchar, the Unión Patriótica, and the Frente Popular, which propelled large mobilizations like those of 1986–1988 in the center and northeast of the country, because of which these areas were badly attacked.

In this way, the second period of peak-to-peak pendulum of protest began. It occurred halfway through the government of Virgilio Barco (1986–1990), which was marked by growing pressure for a structural solution to the national crisis, made evident not only by the eruption of narcotrafficking but also by the increase in urban crime, the emergence of multiple vigilante groups, and the paramilitary overflow that gave rise to the second wave of violence from the end of the 1980s through the present (Grupo de Memoria Histórica 2013). It also coincides with what Arce and Wada (see introduction) consider the period of economic liberalization under the Washington consensus in addition to the wave of democratization in the continent. In this critical moment, popular mobilization, particularly among students, opened the door for the convocation of a Constitutional Assembly, which in six months produced a new political constitution for the country.

This event took place during the government of César Gaviria (1990–1994), together with the implementation of the Constitution, which from the beginning fed the tension between social democratic and neoliberal policies, as noted above. During this four-year term, Colombia's commercial opening was broadened, which affected internal economic activity and labor relations in both rural and urban contexts. Protests dropped during these years, due perhaps to the reformist expectations that the new Constitution brought and the negative impact of this trade opening, which weakened the traditional actors of social struggle, wage earners and peasants. This trend continued during the term of Ernesto Samper (1994–1998), who strove in vain to offer a "human face" to economic liberalization: his reformist desires were frustrated by the allegations of narcotraffickers funding his campaign, which came to be known as the "8.000 Process," and which undermined the legitimacy of his mandate.

This second period closed with the first year of the administration of Andrés Pastrana (1998–2002), who took up again the dialogues with the FARC, for which he created the demilitarized zone of El Caguan. This included five municipalities that together made up an area the size of Switzerland, from which the national military removed its forces. When these dialogues began in 1999, a new peak of struggles appears in the dataset, in part because of the expectations of forthcoming peace accords and humanitarian exchanges and in part because it was the first time that a National Development Plan was debated publicly. In parallel, another mobilization began, this one successful, against a demilitarized zone for the ELN in the south of the department of Bolivar. Then Colombia also began a period in which, according to Arce and Wada (see introduction), Latin America would experience a commodity boom.

The dialogues with the FARC failed, because neither party was determined to end the war, which favored the bellicose proposal of Álvaro Uribe-Vélez (2002–2010). Uribe-Vélez governed for two presidential terms, being reelected contrary to the Constitution of '91. His double term of office had three pillars: citizen security, investor confidence, and social cohesion. Of these, the need to "recover order and security" stood out (Archila Neira 2012, 164). At the start of his unusually long administration, protests dropped, due to his authoritarian behavior, but beginning in 2006 they began to grow until they reached a peak in 2007; this was due to an unusual boom in mobilizations of victims of the armed conflict and broad manifestations by social actors regarding transfers of public expenditure and the pension system in public universities. Uribe-Vélez succeeded in controlling the guerrillas without defeating them, while negotiating with much greater generosity for the demobilization of the paramilitaries. This latter may have allowed people to feel less frightened when taking to the streets to protest, which may partially explain the increase in struggles of this next-to-last period in our study.

The new peace dialogues with the insurgency, the signing of the Peace Accord with the FARC, and the continuation of the war marked the last period of peak-to-peak pendulum we observe, which covers the government of Juan Manuel Santos (2010–2018), who also won reelection, and the first sixteen months of Iván Duque Márquez's government (2018–2022). Santos was Uribe-Vélez's heir with regard to economic policies, particularly the deepening of extractivism—one of the four "locomotives" he used to metaphorically frame the axes of his first term—but he took a different turn with regard to peace, opening dialogues with the FARC in Havana in 2013 and signing accords in 2016, whereupon he started unsuccessful conversations with the ELN. So Santos was characterized by trying to reconcile two divergent political outlooks: negotiation with the insurgency and reformism on the one hand and the preservation of an economic model rooted in neoliberalism on the other. His former patron, Uribe-Vélez, distanced himself to the point of forming an opposition bloc against peace accords, managing to defeat by a narrow margin (0.42 percent) the plebiscite to approve these in October of 2016. In this context we observe an upturn of protest in 2013, related to the agreements in Havana, particularly around agrarian issues, together with the refusal of Santos to consider even a light modification to the development model and poor public relations management of the situation (Archila, García et al. 2014). Following this peak, the indicators of social protests dropped, but continued to be high when compared to the historical trend outlined by the BDLS.

A good part of that mobilization is due to: i) the backsliding of both the limited democratic opening achieved during Santos's government and the rights guarantees earned by political participation through social mobilization in the streets; ii) the weak implementation of the agreements made in Havana;[12] iii) the importance conceded to the extractive economy during the administrations of Uribe-Vélez and Santos, which resulted in an assault on the agroindustrial and industrial apparatuses; and iv) the terrible management of the commodities boom, which did not reduce poverty or socioeconomic inequalities.

We saw high-density social mobilizations, of both reactive and proactive types, during Duque's term, despite the bad portents for protest represented by public declarations adverse to it, made by both the first defense minister and the president himself.[13] These included a national strike in which universities and technological public education institutions demanded that the government attend to the immense budgetary deficit that threatened their existence in 2018. The following year saw an indigenous and peasant *minga* that demanded guarantees for ethnic, peasant, and land rights. There were also a national strike of government workers challenging the tax reform and arising from breach of agreements, as well as mobilizations of rural inhabitants against the exploitation of hydrocarbons through fracking. To this we add the social struggles of coca-growing peasants against forced eradication of illicit crops in violation of the first point of the Peace Accord and, above all, the national strike that began on the 21st of November 2019, over a wide list of demands made by diverse social actors (Archila, García, et al. 2019).

Actors (Who)

Figure 4.2 shows some interesting changes in the dynamics of Colombia's popular protest. We see a clear diminishing of the historical weight of class actors, particularly wage earners and peasants, as a result of economic liberalization policies, among other aspects that we will address below. The struggles of wage earners, which stood out during the first two periods, track the incremental dismantling of the manufacturing industry and evidence the impact on state employment of both the administrative reforms attendant to decentralization and the privatization of state public services, transport, and industries where the primary owner had been the state.

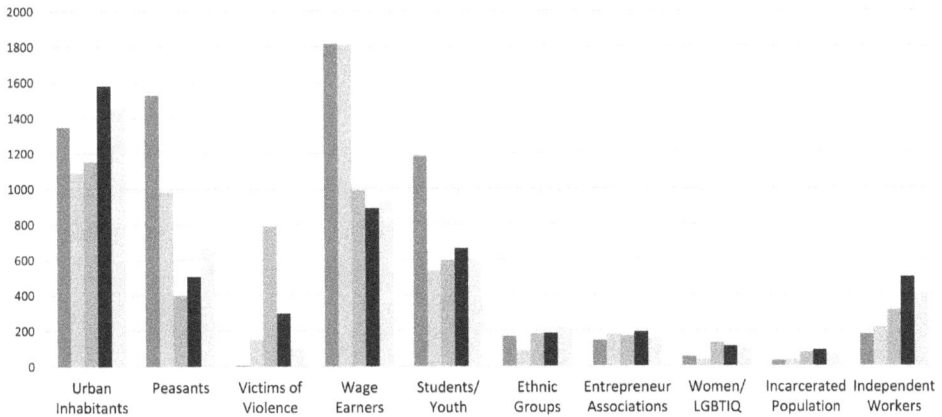

Figure 4.2. Actors, 1975–2019. BDLS (2022).

From the beginning of the period under study, the defense of public patrimony was central to the agenda of the mobilization of wage earners, along with the struggle against the diminishing of the quantity and quality of formal employment and the defense of the rights of association and collective bargaining over working conditions. The protests of wage earners of the first periods denounced state repression and the subsequent degrading of the armed conflict from the middle of the '80s, the violence stemming from which was also directed against labor organizations and made Colombia the country with the greatest rate of murders of trade unionists in the world (Archila et al. 2012).

Multinational corporations have opted for widespread labor outsourcing, which has facilitated the violation of labor laws, first by prohibiting the organization of workers, which assaults freedom of association, and second, by hiring labor through associated labor cooperatives that are nothing more than disguised temporary work agencies, which feeds the spurious notion that "members of a cooperative" cannot demand payment of social security because they are not classified as workers. After years of social mobilization, wage earners succeeded in suppressing this form of contracting, based on its harm to rights already won.

In the more recent periods, the mobilization of government employees has been significant. Among these, the education sector stands out, followed by health workers, who have taken up the banner against both delaborization and the *enclosure of the commons*, that is, the privatization of common goods such as education and health, which should be subject to public or collective control. Labor actors affiliated with mining and oil extraction have also gained greater visibility. They have not only fought for the betterment of working conditions, but also have participated in social mobilization against the socioenvironmental impacts of activities related to their jobs, and over the failure to deliver on economic development promised to surrounding communities.

The vertiginous fall of peasant mobilization followed the impact of the commercial opening and political violence. At the beginning of the period, this group fought for land and in defense of their economies, given the challenge of an agrarian counterreform in response to the massive occupations and squatting in rural lands of the early 1970s, and which was expressed in the paralysis of agrarian reform, legislation that favored large landowners, the regulation of the state of siege, and the militarization of rural areas. To all this we can add the fragmentation of peasant organizations, a product of the repression, the violence, and the spotlights on the various actors of the Left (Prada 2002, 126–27).

During the second subperiod, half of the peasant struggles continued to demand access to land, but other struggles gained salience, particularly fights against the dismantling of state institutions for credit, agricultural markets, technical assistance, and price controls; protests against human rights violations and grave violations of international humanitarian law against the peasantry; and demands for a negotiated end to the armed conflict. In the third subperiod, land struggles can be seen to diminish notably, and we see a rise in those questioning fumigation of illicit crops, the import of food, the impact on the peasant economy of Colombia's free trade agreement (TLC), and the abandonment by the state of any policy that favored that economy.

Note in figure 4.2 that, while peasant struggles drop in the first three subperiods, the struggles of victims of the armed conflict rise. During this time the majority of these victims were displaced peasants. Despite the relative drop in peasant protest, in 2013 we see an upturn of it, owing to a confluence of factors, including the visibility of the agrarian issue at the negotiations in Havana, traditional failures of the state to deliver, environmental and labor resistance to the deepening of the extractive model, the poor management of agrarian conflicts (to the degree of denying their existence), and the search for recognition (Archila, García et al. 2014).

In their turn, urban inhabitants—an elusive category, which includes both those who fight for the right to the city and also those who act within it for different motives—increased their participation in protest, eventually taking first place at the beginning of the twenty-first century. These actors seek, through their struggles, to confront the precarity of conditions of urban life and the local, regional, and national public policies that affect them. These actors played a relevant role in the constitution of regional civic movements in the 1980s by placing at the center of the public debate the expectation of regional development. To them is owed, in part, the politico-administrative and fiscal decentralization that took place. More than a class identity, this group presents a polyclassism, or the convergence of many social strata with an explicit spatial reference.

For their part, students maintain relatively stable visibility throughout the studied years, although the entries in the BDLS show a growing presence of secondary-education students in public spaces, without outshining entirely those at the university level. Although this group is moved by issues that affect it, in particular the quality of education and the defense of the public sector, they also tend to exhibit much solidarity with other social and political struggles. We should highlight the dominant political role played by student social actions in the making visible of the 8.000 Process against President Samper, as well as the Student Movement of the Seventh Pamphlet in the National Constituent Assembly that drafted the Constitution of '91.[14]

Although the four analyzed sectors account for the bulk of protests in Colombia in the second half of the twentieth century and beginning of the twenty-first, in the latest periods we see emerging "new" actors such as independent workers and victims of violence, the latter of whom are mostly women. In the first case, their formation is related to the recent destructuring of the world of labor and the growth of informality in the cities, which in turn produces friction with relevant authorities around the management of public space. As for the second group, the growth of violence has brought victims to carry out symbolic mobilizations seeking truth, justice, and reparations, which have great impact on public opinion. But in this case, their identity is less centered on their gender than on their status as victims. Something similar occurs in the case of low-income women heads of household, who prioritize challenging the austere effects of the economic opening over gender-specific struggles.

The primary form of visibility for social movements around gender issues—to which we add LGBTI issues—is not protest, and for this reason they do not show high numbers in figure 4.2. These groups prefer other, less confrontational means, such as lobbying and political alliances, to achieve victories that wind up being longer-lasting than those of other social actors. Among other methods, they also fall back on cultural and academic activities to achieve visibility (Gómez 2011). Nevertheless, the protests of women in the LGBTI population have placed in the public arena issues that generate intense debate: abortion, marriage equality, adoption by homosexual couples, multiplicity of family types, state and religious infringement on bodies, gender violations, and the killing of women (*feminicidio*).

Ethnic groups, particularly indigenous ones, also do not show high indicators of protest, and instead mark a participation that corresponds to their population size, which is close to 3 percent. All in all, the indigenous movement has been indefatigable in fighting for land—now redefined in terms of territory—identity, culture, and autonomy. They have confronted diverse adversaries: first the landowners allied to agents of the state, then the paramilitaries, and at times also the guerrillas. The symbolic weight and courage of these struggles is significant, with acts of civil disobedience against armed actors standing out in particular (Peñaranda 2006). The same is not the case for Black actors, Afro-Colombians, palenqueros, and raizales, who are part of the multitudes who protest, but may be subsumed within peasant identities or those of inhabitants of the urban–rural frontier. Recently, they have emerged as social actors in the Pacific Coast, products of the persistent violence looming over them in addition to the traditional abandonment of the state. Their leaders tend to privilege institutional lobbying mechanisms over protest.

Indigenous and Afro-descendant protests bare the racism that is present in large parts of Colombian society, which is expressed both in a disdain for ethnic groups and a lack of awareness of their existence, or in actions that do not account for the fact that they put at risk these groups' survival. Such is the case of struggles to obtain cultural recognition, to recover and pre-serve ancestral lands, and to guarantee prior consultation, all of them placed at risk by the clash with extractivism.

Transport and commercial entrepreneurs and business associations may have effective mechanisms to pressure the state to obtain what they wish, but on occasion they turn to social mobilization in order to push for policies in their favor and, in some instances, to join with other social actors in rejecting violence that has found in them a target.

Incarcerated populations, for their part, advance few protests, but these are notorious when they do happen because they uncover human rights violations: the inhumane carceral conditions among which stand out over-crowding (related to the excessive penalization of Colombian judicial system and the slowness with which it operates), together with the precarity of medical attention and resocialization programs.

In summary, although there is an oscillation in the proportion of historical actors in the protests—workers, peasants, students, and urban inhabitants—class identities have been weakened.[15] This is due to factors that are material, political, and cultural, such as the twenty-first-century neoliberal offensive that decreases the material bases of existence: formal employment, access to land, and dignified habitat. The weakening of organizational forms of redress such as labor unions and peasant associations also counts greatly, in addition to the darkening of utopic horizons due to the crisis of critical thinking and the collapse of truly constituted social-ism. These factors, in turn, support the arrival of new actors who tend to be more and more visible. Even within more traditional social movements, we see emerging revamped forms of visibility on issues of gender, ethnicity, and age. Such is the case of collectives of women victims, workers, or peas-ants, of youth in these same sectors, and even of Black and indigenous peo-ple in the world of labor. For this reason, we believe that, at least in the Colombian case, rather than contrasting "old" and "new" social move-ments, we observe a permanent reconfiguration of identities emerging within historically significant sectors.

Another sign of the greater weight of actors who struggle for and within cities is the clear tendency toward "urbanization" of protest in Colombia. If, in historical times, the peasants, the indigenous groups, and other agrarian social groups were very visible in protests and at times were their protagonists—for example, in the 1920's and '30s and, above all, in the '70s—beginning with the end of the twentieth century the largest share of struggles took place in urban spaces without that necessarily meaning they were over the right to the city (Torres 1993).

Claims (Why)

The categories we have applied to the BDLS distinguish motives or claims with a material flavor from those that are more political or cultural in nature. In this sense, there is a notable change between 1975 and 2019, as demands primarily around labor, land, or housing moved to claiming human rights in a holistic sense and properly political motivations (those involving the absences of the state or inadequate official solutions) (figure 4.3). Nevertheless, we do not have to go very far with this transformation. On the one hand, struggles for better conditions of material existence (such as disputes over housing, public services, or social services or against extractivism) do not go away; indeed, there are some that incorporate certain demands from the world of labor. On the other hand, many of these "material" demands imply "cultural" dimensions, as with land for indigenous people and even for the peasantry: that is not considered only as a means of production, but also as a place of recreation and culture and of the preservation of autonomy. Because of this, today we speak of the more complex concept of "territory." In addition, the persistence of "material" motives became evident in the boom of 2013. This was not a crude awakening of the "struggle of classes," but a way to articulate those motives with political and cultural dimensions of autonomy and dignity (Archila, García et al. 2014).

Continuing the historical trends of the nation's social struggles, during part of the 1980s land and urban areas took the lead. We can add to these demands for dignified housing, together with the labor demands.[16] Their relative decline in the 1990s does not mean that these material concerns were resolved, but rather that other issues acquired priority in the face of overflowing political violence. Moreover, the effects of the economic

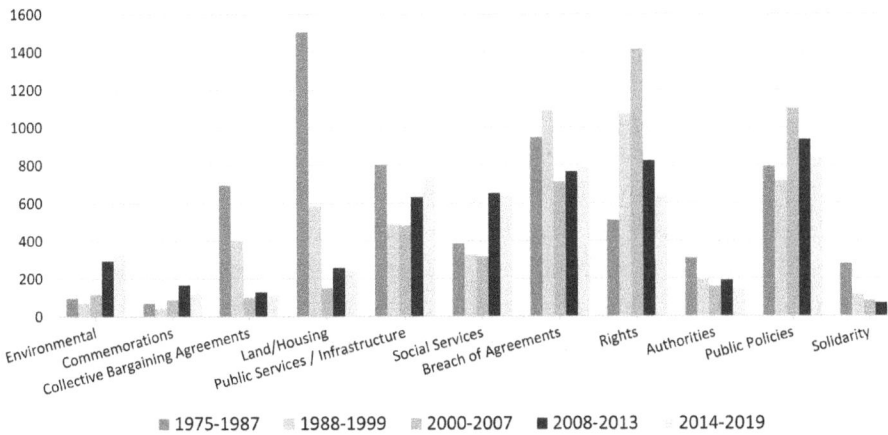

Figure 4.3. Claims, 1975–2019. BDLS (2022).

Legend: ■ 1975-1987 1988-1999 2000-2007 ■ 2008-2013 2014-2019

X-axis categories: Environmental, Commemorations, Collective Bargaining Agreements, Land/Housing, Public Services / Infrastructure, Social Services, Breach of Agreements, Rights, Authorities, Public Policies, Solidarity

opening have meant a great deterioration in labor and living conditions in cities and the countryside, which has resulted in the relative impoverishment of the urban and rural middle classes. In addition, public services and infrastructure, together with social services such as education, health, and security, have continued to occupy a high-profile role in popular demands. Meanwhile, many of those captured in the category of "breaches" clearly show that public and private entities violate agreements with diverse social movements and sometimes even laws that protect them or regulate their activities.

However, from the perspective of Protest Event Analysis, it is undeniable that since the 1990s we have seen a turn toward a greater share of demands we designate as political or cultural. The demands for the guarantee and enjoyment of human rights—not just civil and political, but socioeconomic, cultural, environmental, and collective—exhibit geometric growth beginning in that decade, with the exception of the last subperiod. The degraded war and the effects of the economic opening motivated people to reclaim their rights, particularly after the Constitution of 1991. In turn, properly political demands also grew over the years. If we add demands related to the authorities—both in favor of and against—we have a dynamic where social actors intrude increasingly into issues beyond their immediate sphere of action, to launch themselves into ever-broader public arenas.

There are claims that maintain low levels of participation, like those related to commemorations—typical of student movements—and solidarity. Although it would be ideal for them to have higher numbers, their existence itself speaks to the dimensions of solidarity of social movements with actors of the present and the past (which are the backdrop for commemorations). Finally, properly environmental demands show an important upward trend that corresponds to global concerns for the planet in the face of the nation's economic turn to extractivism. But it also supports the linkage between the material, the cultural, and the political in the dynamics of social struggles in Colombia. Now, environmental struggles tend to mutate in their orientation over time: from a conservationist ecologism that seeks to attenuate developmentalism there is increasingly a shift to an environmentalism that questions the development model, even that designated as "sustainable."

All in all, we can speak of a growing politicization of social actors, not only because of the issues that are increasingly debated in public arenas—human rights, public policies, and authorities—but because of the way in which these claims and others, such as the denouncing of broken agreements or the violation of rights, are directed increasingly at the state. Material deficiencies do not disappear, but they are formulated in a different way, as rights that can be demanded of the state, linking the material with the political and cultural. This finding, which can be called "proactivization of reactive claims," contributes to our understanding of the overarching hypothesis of this volume (see introduction) by showing a concrete process through the shift from reactive to proactive protests.

Decades of neoliberalism that, beyond the economy, have also strongly impregnated individual and collective subjectivities, have propelled multiple social actors to embark on the search for a new citizenship that, in addition to defending equality and liberty, proclaims respect for differences of all kinds—primarily regional, racial, ethnic, gender, sexual orientation, generational, religious, and linguistic—while also demanding dignity and autonomy. In this way, the growing politicization and proactivization that we observe does not mean that before there was no profound "political" dimension to social struggles, but rather that protest was not formulated explicitly as rights that could be demanded or as forms of a new citizenship.

Targets (Whom)

The trend toward politicization of social movements is ratified when we consider the adversaries or the targets of the protests we studied (figure 4.4).[17] While the greater share in the first cycles corresponded to the national executive, municipal governments have increasingly faced protests, unlike the departmental ones, which diminished relatively as targets beginning in the 1990s, albeit with a small recent uptick. (No doubt due to budgetary reasons associated with fiscal decentralization and the distribution of public royalties, the political game in 2019 centers on national and local levels.) State enterprises in different arenas and ownership composition comprised a considerable proportion of social struggles. In turn, private enterprises show a relative drop as adversaries, although they continue to be a powerful presence, particularly in the last subperiod.

The drop in the share of armed forces and police as targets is also noteworthy, contrasting with the growing role of irregular armed groups, particularly the paramilitaries, up until their supposed demobilization. This means that the official strategy of ceding the "dirty work" of containing protest to paramilitaries bore fruit. Meanwhile, the insurgency increasingly delegitimized itself in the eyes of social movements until the demobilization of the FARC. While it is true that the ELN and small but very

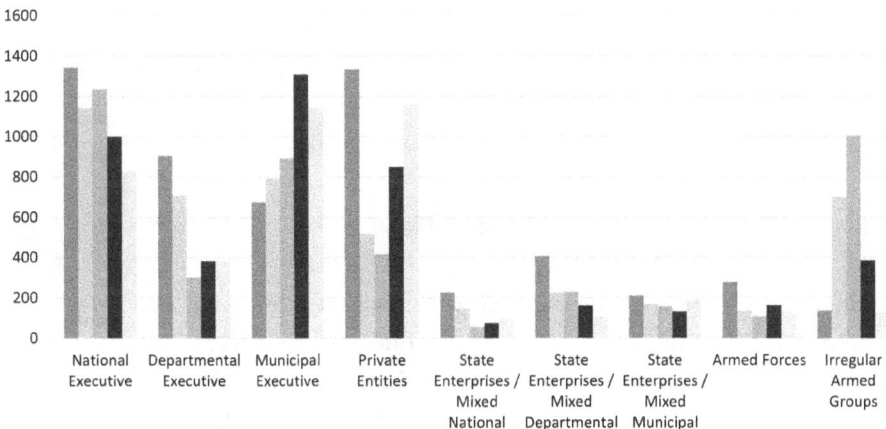

Figure 4.4. Targets, 1975–2019. BDLS (2022).

active splinter elements of the former Popular Liberation Army (EPL) and the selfsame FARC still exist, their role as adversaries has diminished in recent social struggles.

All of the above suggests a reflection that is not necessarily visible in the graphs, although it comes from the Protests Event Analysis, and that is the possibility that during the course of these forty-five years, and especially since the Constitution of 1991, the Colombian populace formed a new relationship with the state, one that moved it from being considered an enemy to an adversary.[18] This change has been incremental, and is more a medium-term tendency that began to insinuate itself before 1991 and deepened with the promulgation of the Constitution. Worryingly, despite the peace process, the stigmatization of protest to the point of penalizing it persists, together with the recourse to repression when dominant sectors feel their interests threatened. This type of state violence, particularly contentious when the Mobile Anti-Disturbances Squad (ESMAD) is deployed,[19] is not entirely separate from the Cold War logic that still persists, despite the fact that the Berlin Wall fell thirty-one years ago.

Also worrying, in addition to the unmeasured use of force, is the weak institutionality of the state to mediate social conflicts, particularly in rural areas; this has weakened democracy in recent times, as shown in figure 1.4. Because of this, violent measures continue to be employed to resolve social conflicts, especially by powerful landowning and cattle-ranching powers, and even some multinational corporations, resulting in the eruption of new cycles of violence on the national landscape. The growing polarization in the country on issues that should be unifying, such as the consolidation of peace, stokes even further the blaze of sociopolitical violence that does not abate.

Actions (How)

In figure 4.5 we see a drop in the historic modes of protest or actions in the terminology of this book: stoppages—which include strikes—and squatting in rural lands and urban areas. The former was crucial for collective actions of worker, peasant, civic, and student movements. It is possible that

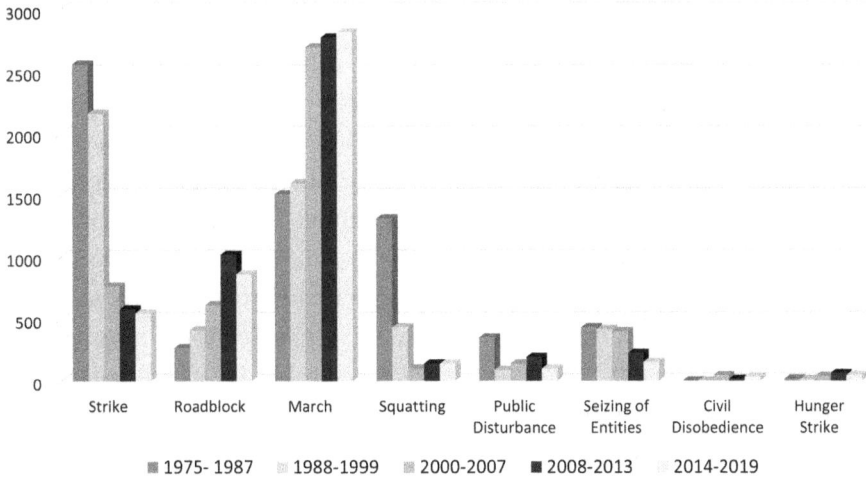

Figure 4.5. Actions, 1975–2019. BDLS (2022).

the weakness of some of these translated into the drop in this type of struggle; at least this is what Álvaro Delgado (2013) proposes with regard to the worker class. As for squatting, these modes were penalized shortly after the start of the period we analyze, which had an impact on their downward trend, although at the start of this century we saw an uptick, especially on the part of the indigenous movement of Cauca, which sought the land promised by the state, framed by what they called the "liberation of mother earth."

By contrast, we see an upward trend in mobilizations of various stripes—marches, rallies, public meetings, parades, demonstrations, pot-bangings (*cacerolazos*)—and roadblocks. The former are the least contentious collective social actions, and perhaps the least costly in every sense for social actors, contrasted with the other modality, which has the opposite character. Though we cannot speak of a radical change in repertoire, like that observed by Charles Tilly (2004) in recent centuries, there are signs of a tendency toward less confrontation in the dynamics of social struggle in Colombia, although some contentious forms of protest remain, such as disturbances, which are sharpened by the repressive intervention of the state, especially when the ESMAD is present.

There are other types of actions, less visible in the entries of the BDLS, but with great impact on public opinion. Hunger strikes, for example, are an extreme form of protest because of the implied self-punishment of those who resort to it, above all incarcerated people. Acts of civil disobedience also fall into this category, particularly as deployed by indigenous groups against armed actors, where the bravery implicit in confronting violence with only a traditional stick of authority leaves an impression. This, together with the cohesion of their movement, has led other actors to incorporate ethnic practices in their own mobilizations. In this way, one speaks of *mingas*,[20] peasants, and *cimarronas* guards,[21] and even of *territories* as applied to spaces that had previously not been considered as such, for instance universities or factories.

We offer one last consideration regarding the importance of virtual networks in recent mobilizations, as noted by Manuel Castells (2012) and Julie Massal (2014) regarding the Arab Spring and the global uprisings of the beginnings of the 2010s. Rather than being new modalities of protest, in our view virtual networks are new forms of convening to protest (Tilly 2004), which continue to demand a physical presence in public spaces.

Places (Where)

In spatial terms, the territorial entities with the greatest number of protests historically—over one thousand—have been the capital of the nation, Bogotá DC, and the departments of Antioquia, Santander, Valle, Atlántico, and Bolivar (figure 4.6 and map 4.1). This was not always the ranking, but in broad strokes the primacy of these five departments and the capital district are consistent.

During these forty-five years 1,009 municipalities participated at least once in a social struggle, the equivalent of 91.5 percent of the total (DANE 2018). The majority of the departmental capitals—and particularly the four largest cities in the country—account for a good part of the social struggles that have to do with departmental jurisdiction. Bogotá, as the nation's capital and seat of the executive agencies at a national level, was the setting for the largest number of social manifestations. It was followed, in order, by Medellin, Barranquilla, Cali, Cartagena, and Bucaramanga, followed by another fourteen departmental capitals.

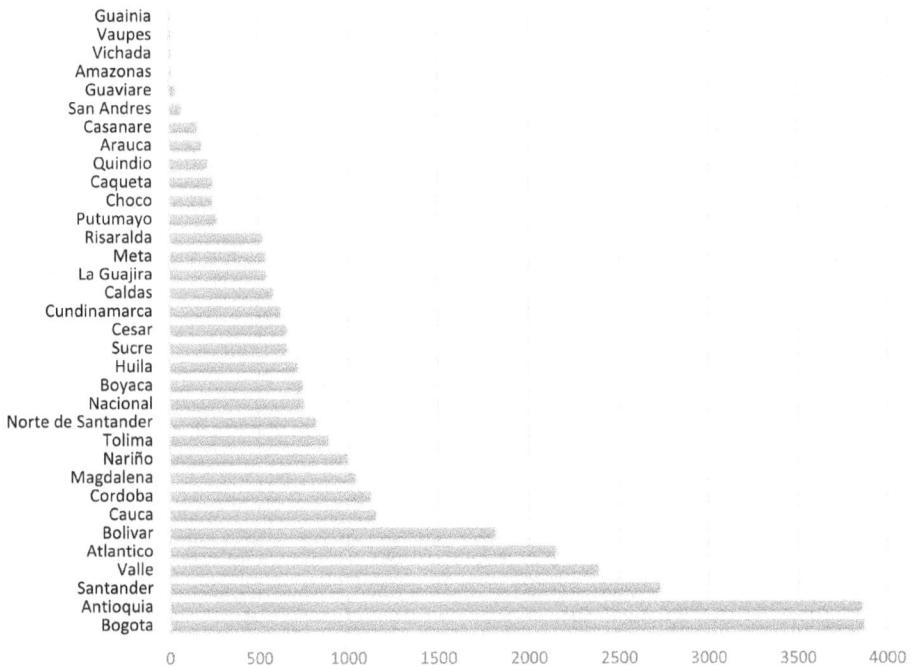

Figure 4.6. Departmental Participation in Social Struggles, 1975–2019. BDLS (2022).

That spatial distribution of the protests is related to two dynamics that can be deduced from a Protest Event Analysis. On the one hand, there is a strong showing of the richest departments, in social and economic terms, and their capitals carry the bulk of the numbers. On the other hand, there are also areas where new sources of wealth were opened, particularly through extractivism. In the first set of areas—primarily Bogotá/Cundinamarca, Antioquia, Valle, and Atlántico—there is a conventional logic to the protests, as in general one can expect greater concentration of demographic, economic, social, and cultural resources to correspond to more social struggles (Archila 2003).

In the second set of areas, we see the formation of vicious cycles that over time threaten the possibility of protest, if not those who exercise their right to protest. These tend to be as follows: openings of new sources of wealth; migration; appearances of social organizations; the presence of armed groups—insurgency, military, and paramilitary—and violence, protests, more violence, and so on successively until leaders and social

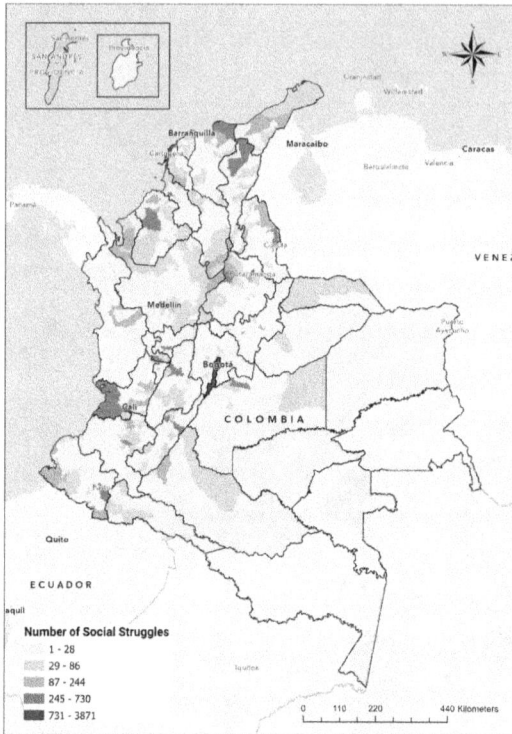

Map 4.1. Social Struggles in Colombia, 1975-2019. BDLS (2022).

organizations are annihilated.[22] These vicious circles became more visible with the commodities boom. In the former set, we see more state presence, not through the armed forces but through other institutions. In the second set, the state tends to be more absent, except for extreme issues of public order that attract the proliferation of other armed groups, which, in the name of skirting the vacuum left by the state or by appealing to its illegitimacy, generate the vicious cycles noted above. In this way, the violence unleashed since the 1980s, especially with the expansion of the paramilitary project, practically "pacified" by blood and fire regions that had been considered socially conflictive, such as the Middle Magdalena and the Uraba Antioquia. Because of this, in recent years these areas have had low numbers of social struggles, as evidenced by the geospatial elements of our database.[23]

In summary, we believe that the dynamic of social struggles tends to be

framed within the dispute over the inequitable distribution of the economic resources produced by the large urban centers or in extractive areas.
However, it is also, as noted by Barrington Moore (1989), a political matter
related to the perception of an unjust authority that does not attend to these
inequalities and fails to effectively protect the vulnerable. Because of this,
we have long considered protest not to be a mere spasmodic reaction in the
face of shortages of all kinds, but rather a rational and emotional response
to perceptions of injustice. This grants it an emancipatory character, associated with the search for a more egalitarian and just society (Archila 2003,
chapter 8). This is nothing less than the construction of a new, more inclusive citizenship, defensive of liberty and equality but respectful of differences in every sense—a citizenship that, when mobilized, claims with
growing autonomy recognition on the part of its adversaries.

Conclusions

After reviewing the trends of social protests in Colombia based on the BDLS
and using the Protest Event Analysis, we can confirm that the country was
also affected by the dual process that is central to this book: economic liberalization and democratization. Although the evolution of Colombia was
close to the Latin American average (see figures 1.1 and 1.4), especially economically and politically, due to the effects of the persistent violence and
the precarious institutional framework of the state, it lagged behind when
the rest of the continent was leaving dictatorships. The neoliberal opening,
as in other countries in the region, meant the loss of visibility of class actors
(workers and peasants), while urban dwellers, independent workers, and
victims became more visible. In terms of claims, not only was there a historical mutation from material needs to more political and cultural
demands, but issues of gender, ethnicity, and generation gained relevance
in the public agenda. The violence, which has not ceased despite the 2016
peace accords, partly explains this persistent demand for public policies
and respect for human rights and against breaches by the state. This same
violence is present in places where natural resources have recently been
extracted in the search for commodities. In terms of targets, the weight of

the state in all its levels as the main antagonist of the struggles in Colombia is immense.

This makes us consider the growing politicization of social protests in the country as a major trend, with the consequent demand for greater democracy and more state institutionality. This is what we indicated in the title of this chapter: a new agenda before the state's historical debt in terms of democracy and living conditions.

In this, Colombia echoes what has taken place in the rest of the continent, as we can see in this book. In effect, social movements in Latin America after the democratic transitions of the 1990s demanded more democracy not only internally, but above all from society. They have not limited themselves, however, to demanding a return to representative democracy, but rather desire a new, more active and participatory citizenship. With this they redefine their power relations not only with the state but also with the leftist movements that themselves are overcoming their traditional contempt for democracy. For that new citizenship, the issue of rights is key, not as mere concessions from above but also as victories and expansions from below. The formula of the "right to have rights" captures that attitude of demanding new rights proactively: for sexualities, ethnicities, races, generations, for territory, for autonomy, for the free development of personhood, for a dignified life, and more (Dagnino 1998, 46–52).

Notes

1. This article is based on a chapter written by Mauricio Archila titled "Trayectorias de las luchas sociales 1975–2015," from the book *Cuando la copa se rebosa: Luchas sociales en Colombia, 1975–2015* (Bogotá: CINEP, 2019). Given the similarity with the general framing of this project on popular protest in Latin America, we have updated the information to 2019 and made some adjustments to the text.
2. See figures 1.1 and 1.2 in the introduction of this volume.
3. This is attributed by some economists to the macroeconomic effects of the narcotics trade (Rocha 2001) and by others to the enormous international loans the country obtained between 1985 and 1989 (Suárez Montoya 2015).
4. This implies the segmentation of the productive process, placing part of the production chain in regions with lower costs without generating significant integration with the local economy and with little value addition,

as in the case of the *maquilas* and extractive activities (Alayza and Sotelo 2012, 16).

5. Colombia has free trade agreements in effect with Mexico (1995), the Caribbean Community (1999), Cuba (2001), the Southern Common Market/Mercosur (2005), El Salvador, Guatemala, Honduras (2009), the European Free Trade Association (2011), the United States (2011), Canada (2011), Venezuela (2012), the Pacific Alliance (2012), the European Union (2013), South Korea (2016), Costa Rica (2016), and Israel (2020). Consequently, Colombia entered the commodity boom stage mentioned by Arce and Wada in the introduction.

6. We take up again that which was already expressed in prior publications of the Social Movements Team with regard to what the BDLS measures, how it does so, and with what categories and by what criteria have they been constructed (Archila et al. 2002; Archila 2003, 2019; García 2019).

7. The denominations of black, Afro-Colombian, and palenquero follow the self-denominations of the respective groups, according to complex constructions of identity. Palenquero refers to slaves who, during colonial times, fled and formed communities protected by "palenques" or defense fences. In Brazil these communities were called "quilombos."

8. Raizal is the self-denomination of the native population of the archipelago of San Andres, Providencia, and Santa Catalina, located off the coast of Nicaragua in the Caribbean.

9. This was only outdone by the national stoppage that began on the 21st of November of 2019, continued with various manifestations of protest during the first months of 2020, and was suspended during the Coronavirus pandemic, together with the "national conversation" proposed by the Duque administration to attend to some of the demands of this protest.

10. "This decree crystallized a long process of creating and refining extraordinary measures against the expressions of unarmed protest, amalgamated to others emerging from fear of the guerrilla escalation and the nascent political terrorism" (Orozco 1992, 172).

11. This process was an attempt to make the state more efficient, bringing it closer to the individual citizen, stimulating the participation of the citizenry, democratizing politics, and, along the way, diminishing social conflict. In addition to the direct election of mayors and later of governors, central resources were transferred to municipal administrations. The result was unexpected: not only did social conflict and disengagement not decrease, but institutional disorder manifested among many public entities, if not higher degrees of clientelism and corruption (García and Zamudio 1997).

12. The many obstacles to the fulfillment of what was agreed in Havana included the defunding of several of the programs designed to

reincorporate the guerrillas into society; the government's refusal to restore legal rights to those who laid down arms and to reactivate various mechanisms for monitoring the implementation of the accord; clashes between the prosecutorial arm of the state and the Special Peace Jurisdiction; the resistance by diverse sectors to the Truth Commission; and the lack of education about the accords among wide swaths of the population (Taborda 2018).

13. We propose to understand density in collective social actions as the networks of solidarity that allow the transfer of capacities and efforts from some organizations to others; the legitimization of demands; the capacity to mobilize broad segments of the population; the duration of the event; the possibility of structuring effects over the long term; and the scale achieved by the protests in question (García 2006, 281).

14. According to one member of this student movement, the origin of the Colombian Constitution of 1991 cannot be separated from the "Silent Student March" to the central cemetery on August 25, 1989, a week after the high-profile assassination of Luis Carlos Galán, nor from the indignation evoked by the assassinations of two other presidential hopefuls, Bernardo Jaramillo and Carlos Pizarro (Carrillo 2010).

15. Collective identities are historical constructs that, while seeking to be naturalized, will always be contingent, due to this constructionist process (Archila 2003, chapter 7). Without collective identity, it is not possible to speak of the existence of social movements, because they define "us" as different from "them" (Touraine 1989). Class identity, marked since Marxism by its relation to the means of production, is one of the most primordial and encompassing identities, but it is not the only one raised by social movements. They also exist in cultural, ethnic, gender, sexuality-based, and generational dimensions, according to spatial-temporal contexts, and some gain greater visibility than others.

16. According to the census of 2018, 18.2 million people in Colombia lack dignified housing, 96.3 percent of homes have electricity, 86.4 percent have access to potable water, 76.6 percent are connected to sewer systems, 81.6 percent have sanitation services, 43.3 percent have access to the internet, and seven out of ten households have natural gas (DANE 2018).

17. In recent years we see an increase in the percentage of entries "without specific adversary," which, let us recall, refers to the intention of those protesting to address society as a whole rather than a specific antagonist.

18. According to the Mexican philosopher Enrique Serrano Gómez (1997, 31–39)—leaning on Karl Schmitt— to the "absolute enemies" all reason, and therefore all humanity, is denied. On the other hand, those he calls "just enemies" are recognized as humans who are other, but who have the same rights. We call the former enemies and the latter adversaries.

19. On ESMAD, see Archila (2019), and Lalinde (2019).
20. "Mingas" refers to collective work or activities.
21. "Cimarrón" literally means someone who individually escapes from slavery. Currently it refers to Colombia's black population.
22. We analyzed these vicious cycles for trade unionism, especially in the cases of banana growers, African palm laborers, and petroleum workers (Archila Neira et al. 2012).
23. In the case of the Middle Magdalena, see Archila Neira et al. 2006.

CHAPTER FIVE

Protesting in Good and Bad Times: Peru, 1980–2015

MOISÉS ARCE AND RENZO AURAZO

Introduction

The 1990s was a watershed period of realignment in Peruvian politics. The onset of economic liberalization can be traced to this decade, and while the country had already made important democratic gains in previous years, the 1990s became a period of autocratization and distinct from wider regional democratic trends. Threats to livelihoods emerged from economic liberalization but limited advantages to challenge market policies because of autocratization; these placed actors in a very difficult position. Economic liberalization policies in Peru would remain unchallenged until the early 2000s, when democratic rule was finally restored.

As is commonly acknowledged, the quality of political representation in Peru is very poor. Soon after the country's return to democracy in the 1980s, two sweeping crises—hyperinflation and political violence—took a toll on the party system, and since 1990 the political landscape has been occupied by a broad swath of political outsiders with little or no experience in government. These politicians are not supported by stable party organizations or institutions, and new parties or political movements are created in almost every electoral cycle. Scholars increasingly view the country as a democracy without parties (Levitsky and Cameron 2003).

The persistent low quality of political representation in the country makes protest politics a recurrent and fragmented phenomenon. Protests ebb and flow in different regions and times around the country. Prior research has examined the mobilization dynamics of specific sets of actors, such as labor (Parodi 1985), the peasantry (Quijano 1979; Starn 1991), and coca farmers or *cocaleros* (Castillo and Durand 2008), as well as popular resistance to privatization (Arce 2008), authoritarianism (Burt 2007), and mining (Bebbington et al. 2007; Arce 2014). In this chapter, and building on these contributions, we examine the protest landscape nationwide between 1980 and 2015 using the Base de Protestas Sociales del Perú (Arce 2023). The decades covered by this dataset overlap with a wide range of economic and political developments, such as the economic hard times and growing insurgency of the 1980s, the decline of democracy and progress toward pacification of the 1990s, and the commodity boom of the 2000s. The longitudinal nature of the data allows us to sort out protest waves and see how protests co-vary with changes in the environment (see Hutter 2014), such as the onset of economic liberalization and the decline of democracy in the 1990s. Our central argument is that both economic liberalization policies and changes in the country's democratic trajectory—the "hybrid political-economic environment" alluded to in the introductory chapter—realigned popular politics in Peru. While existing research has identified the emergence of new actors and new types of mobilization no longer centered on labor, the impact of economic liberalization on popular politics has been much deeper than previously documented. In fact, important changes can also be discerned in the claims and geographic places of collective action, yet the target of mobilization has remained surprisingly the same.

We begin this chapter by highlighting major events that took place in the country since the return to democracy.[1] Here, we distinguish three major periods of economic change, which also overlap with waves of mobilization and demobilization as a result of changes in the political environment. After describing our methods, we disaggregate the components of collective action (who, whom, why, how, and where) to show major shifts and continuities in popular politics. We exemplify these changes by comparing protest campaigns typical of the 1980s with those of the 2000s. The conclusion summarizes our findings and identifies areas of future research.

Globalization and Democratization

Figure 1.4 in the introductory chapter situates Peru's "hybrid political-economic environment" in the wider context of democracy and globalization across Latin America. The country's level of globalization closely followed the regional average. It did not move much during the 1970s and 1980s, but began to rise in the 1990s and, starting in the early 2000s, when Alejandro Toledo was president, the country became slightly more globalized than the region itself. Its level of democracy is a different story. In the 1970s, democracy was absent in much of the region, including Peru. The country became more democratic during the 1980s and the 2000s and beyond, but significantly less so than the Latin American region during the 1990s, when Alberto Fujimori was president. The period following the 1992 self-coup or *autogolpe* is seen as one of the few reversals from the wider trend of democratization in Latin America.

To analyze the ebbs and flows of Peruvian protests, we introduce three different periods of economic change since the return to democracy in 1980: crisis during the 1980s, market adjustment during the 1990s, and market expansion after the 2000s and beyond. These periods also overlap with decades of democratization and autocratization. Both the crisis and market expansion periods are associated with levels of democracy that are greater than the Latin American average. But the market adjustment period under Fujimori during the 1990s shows a significant drop in the country's level of democracy compared to the region (see figure 1.4).

During the 1980s, coinciding with Latin America's "lost decade," we talk about a "crisis" period. Throughout this decade, the country faced a severe economic crisis marked by hyperinflation, as well as an internal armed conflict unleashed by the Shining Path and other insurgency groups (McClintock 1998). The economic crisis proved particularly harsh on labor actors and contributed to the growing informalization of the work force. Yet against all odds, in 1985 one democratically elected president (Fernando Belaúnde) made a peaceful transition of power to another democratically elected president (Alan García). During the 1980s, the country's level of economic globalization remained flat, starting with a score of 43.1 in 1980 and ending at 43.3 in 1989, but its level of democracy rose considerably, from a value of 16.5 in 1979 to 67.9 in 1989 (see figure 1.4).[2]

The 1990s can be characterized as the "market adjustment" period, as the country embraced sweeping economic liberalization reforms introduced by President Fujimori (Arce 2005). The reforms were in line with the Washington consensus, which guided the transition to free markets across Latin America (Williamson 1990). During this period, the government reined in high inflation, numerous state-owned companies were privatized, and the country became open to trade and foreign direct investment, among other economic changes. Massive layoffs because of privatization and new labor flexibility laws contributed to the precarization of the workforce. The internal armed conflict ended, but Fujimori imposed a top-down authoritarian government after the 1992 self-coup (McClintock 2006). Despite Fujimori's popularity, which led to his reelection in 1995, the quality of democracy deteriorated due to fluidity of political institutions and the rule of law. The level of economic globalization increased from 43.1 in 1990 to 53.9 in 1999, but the country's level of democracy declined from 63.3 in 1990 to 38.9 in 2000 (see figure 1.4).

Finally, for the period of the 2000s and onward, we talk about the "market expansion" period, where the main characteristics were the recovery of democracy, economic growth fueled by a commodity boom (2002–2014), and the surprising continuity of the economic liberalization model (Vergara and Encinas 2016). During this period, President Toledo (2001–2006) began a long-awaited process of political and fiscal decentralization by allowing for the creation of regional governments (McNulty 2011). President García (2006–2011) consolidated the economic liberalization model by implementing free trade agreements with the United States and China. President Ollanta Humala (2011–2016) initially embraced a center-left political agenda, but once in office continued with the same market-oriented policies that Fujimori had started. The country's level of globalization increased further, from 58.8 in 2000 to 70.4 in 2017, and the level of democracy rose from 35.3 in 2000 to 78.4 in 2019 (see figure 1.4).

Peru's "hybrid political-economic environment" is characterized by a gradual rise of economic globalization, but a zig-zag pattern toward democracy. This hybrid environment affected popular politics in the country in important ways and confirmed the expectations of political opportunity theory insofar as more open political environments are associated with greater levels of mobilization (Tarrow 2011). In the 1980s, for instance, high inflation imposed severe economic hardships on the population, but the political environment was conducive for actors to challenge the rising cost of living. In the 1990s, following the prescribed austerity reforms of the Washington consensus, deep cuts in government magnified the severity of the economic crisis, but the autocratization period of this decade meant that political opportunities to challenge these reforms were limited. But when democracy was restored in the 2000s, the country no longer experienced a crisis, but rather an unprecedented economic expansion associated with a commodity boom. The percentage of the population living in poverty declined from 48.5 percent in 2004 to 27.7 percent in 2017. In the same period, those living in extreme poverty dropped from 17.4 percent to 3.8 percent (García and Pantigoso 2019). Peru's gross domestic product per capita more than doubled between 1990 (the start of the Fujimori government) and 2019, from $2,650 to $6,480 (constant 2010 US$) (Arce and Incio 2018). With these changes in the environment because of economic liberalization and democracy, popular politics also changed.

Methods

The Base de Protestas Sociales del Perú reports thirty-six years of contentious activities from January 1980 to December 2015, covering the governments of seven presidents: Fernando Belaúnde (1980–1985), Alan García (1985–1990), Alberto Fujimori (1990–2000), Valentín Paniagua (2000–2001), Alejandro Toledo (2001–2006), Alan García (2006–2011), and Ollanta Humala (2011–2016) (Arce 2023). It records 20,468 events that were collected from three of the newspapers with the highest circulation in the country (*La República*, *El Expreso*, and *El Comercio*), making it possible to indicate the date (day, month, year) and place (district, province, department, or region) of five collective action components: actor (who), target (whom), claim (why), action (how), and place (where).

As Hutter (2014) writes, protest event analysis is a form of content analysis that allows researchers to systematically compile and quantify information on political protests at different temporal (day, month, year) and spatial units (district, province, department, or region). The unit of analysis reported here is the event per year (see figure 1.3 of the introductory chapter). These events provide fine-grained information on the major components of collective action, but our analysis disaggregates this only to reveal "big picture" changes and continuities across these components.

Before moving forward, a brief note about this method's limitations is warranted. Protest event analysis only captures a segment of the events taking place in a given time and place. Ortiz et al. (2005) document four different types of biases in media coverage of these events: event characteristics, contextual factors, media structure, and research process. The first three types are associated with the size and intensity of the event, its proximity to a news agency, the issue attention cycle, and the profit motives and corporate interests of media outlets. Research on protest event analysis has shown that these biases tend to stabilize over time, and in most cases, information about the goals of the movements is incomplete (Earl et al. 2004). Our review shows that protest events in Lima are overrepresented compared to those in other regions, likely due to newspaper proximity to these events. Reflecting different corporate motives, the right-leaning newspaper *El Comercio* (19 percent) also reported fewer protest events than the left-leaning *La República* (32.3 percent).

Popular Politics in Peru

Since the return to democracy in 1980, Peru has experienced a broad cycle of protest, with rising and falling waves of mobilization. The three periods described earlier are analytically distinct because they coincide with different waves of greater or lesser protests. As figure 5.1 shows, and consistent with political opportunity theory emphasizing favorable political conditions (Tarrow 2011), an upward wave of mobilizations in the 1980s coincides with the "crisis" period and greater democratization, followed by a wave of demobilization in the '90s during the "market adjustment" and autocratization

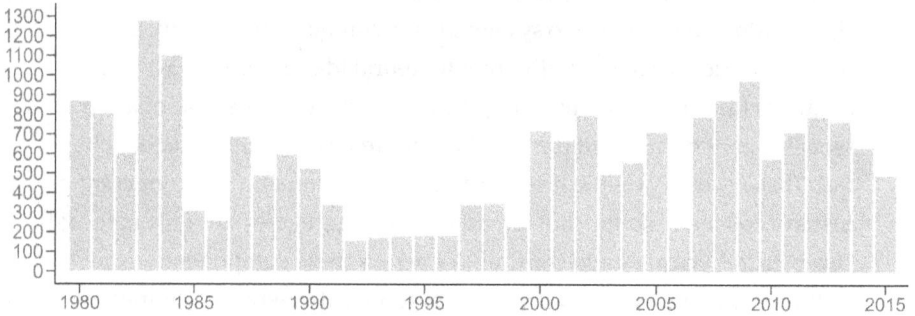

Figure 5.1. Popular Politics, Peru, 1980–2015. Arce (2023).

periods and, subsequently, a new upward wave of mobilization in the 2000s that converges with the "market expansion" period and the return of democracy.

The crisis period includes 6,995 protest events, a number that falls to 2,657 in the market adjustment period and then increases to 6,835 during the first ten years of the market expansion period.[3] In the thirty-six years covered by this study, the year 1983 was the one with the greatest conflict (with a monthly average of 107 protests), and 1992—the year of Fujimori's self-coup—was the one with the least (with a monthly average of thirteen protests). In 1983, the economy declined by 10 percent of GDP and inflation reached 125 percent for the first time in the economic history of the country. This year also marked the beginning of the external debt crisis in Latin America and the arrival of the El Niño phenomenon, which had devastating consequences on agricultural production and physical infrastructure.

These periods have similarities and differences across the five collective action components of interest. While the levels of mobilization declined during the market adjustment period, starting in the late 1990s and continuing throughout the market expansion period, in particular, the actors, the actions, the claims, and the places of collective action began to change, but the overall target of popular politics remained the same. These changes

support the coexistence of reactive and proactive mobilizations (see introduction). The actors became less centered on labor and labor organizations,
opening the doors to other actors who came mostly from civil society at
large (e.g., students, traditional communities). The actions moved away
from strikes to marches and stoppages. The claims also became less centered on labor (e.g., wage increases) and moved to a wide range of political
claims (e.g., accountability of elected officials). With regard to place, Lima
remained the epicenter of popular politics, but several regions outside the
capital began to experience greater levels of mobilization. Notwithstanding these changes, the target of protest remains the same. The executive
branch of government, in particular, the ministries that provide social services, such as health and education, were and are one of the main targets
of collective action. These components are thus codependent: a change in
actors is associated with a change in actions and claims, and so on.

Actors (Who)

We analyze actors by creating two broad clusters: labor and social actors.
Labor actors include groups of individuals who execute remunerative func-
tions. Examples include construction workers, teachers, doctors, miners,
public servants, and other workers in general, as well as their labor unions.
Labor actors include workers from both the private and public sectors. By
contrast, societal actors are individuals who are not connected to a given
market activity. These actors are best described by their position in society.
Examples include students, traditional communities, the unemployed,
retired citizens, and citizens in general.

   Glossing over the thirty-six years of this study, labor and social actors
reveal important changes during the three major periods of economic
change (figure 5.2). In the crisis period, for instance, protests were carried
out mainly by labor actors. In the market adjustment period, however, particularly in the first half of the 1990s, their involvement in protests dropped
significantly, to the point of almost matching the performance of social
actors. Starting in the late 1990s and continuing in the market expansion
period, labor and social actors displayed interchangeable performances, as

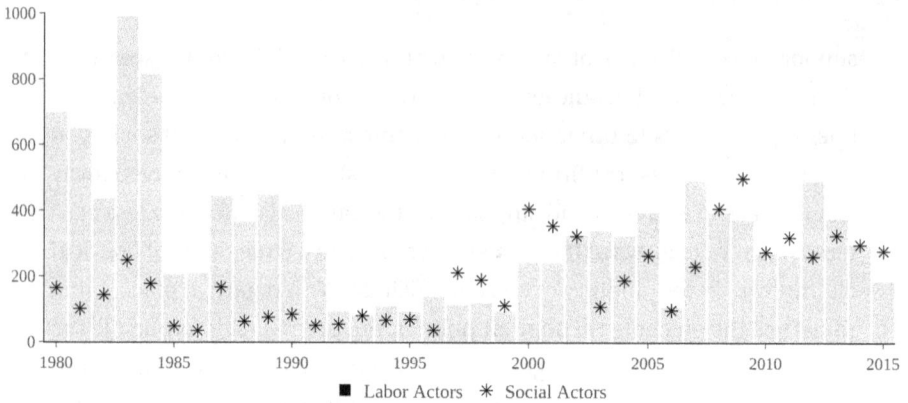

Figure 5.2. Actors, Peru, 1980–2015. Arce (2023).

neither of them appeared to stand out the most. While the performance of labor actors reemerged in the market expansion period, it was also significantly lower than that in the crisis period. Conversely, social actors become more visible in the 1990s and continuing throughout the market expansion period. Overall, the actors participating in protests became less centered on labor and labor-based organizations, providing space to other actors, who came mostly from civil society.

To gain a better understanding of who these actors are, we now disaggregate these two broad clusters. Over the period of study, and based on their percentage frequency of protest participation, we split up social actors into nine main categories: citizens (44.2 percent), students (21.2 percent), traditional communities (9.9 percent), political party supporters and affiliates (6.96 percent), prisoners (5.98 percent), retired citizens (4.41 percent), unemployed (3.36 percent), victims of violence (3.32 percent), and others (0.58 percent). When we plot these frequencies by year, we observe that the darkest densities correspond to citizens, and this recurrence stays relatively constant beginning in the early 2000s (see figure 5.3). No other social actors match the participation frequency of citizens. Some actors were engaged in intermittent popular contention, while others exclusively present peaks in specific years. Students had an active participation in the early 1980s, and their participation reemerges for a period of six years (1997–2002) and then again after 2010.

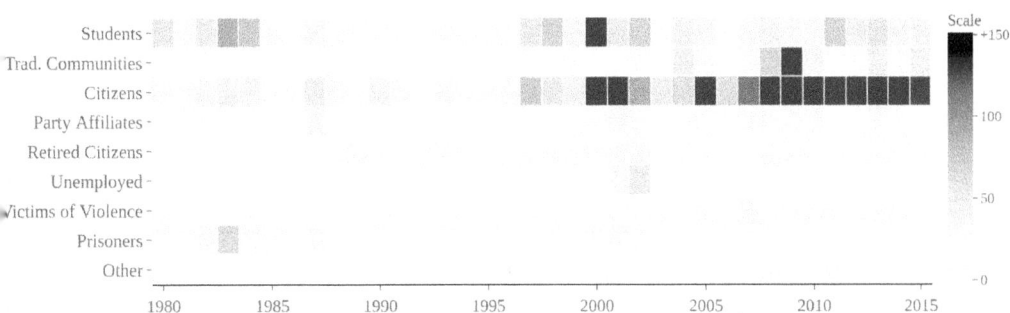

Figure 5.3. Social Actors, Peru, 1980–2015 (Annual Frequency). Arce (2023).

Next, we disaggregate labor actors based on economic sectors: primary (agriculture and mining), secondary (manufacturing), and tertiary (service). Their percentage frequency of protest participation over the period of study was 24.8 percent, 7.5 percent, and 67.7 percent, respectively (graph not shown). These numbers suggest that the bulk of labor protests are tied to the service sector. This sector engaged in significant popular contention in the crisis and market expansion periods. The manufacturing sector, by contrast, did not present any significant participation in the entire period. Several industries collapsed during the economic downturn of the 1980s, and those that remained faced intense market competition during the market adjustment period and beyond.[4] The growing informalization of the economy also explains the decline of the manufacturing sector.

Because the bulk of labor protests are associated with the tertiary (service) sector, figure 5.4 breaks up this sector into eight categories based on their percentage frequencies: transportation, health, education, public administration, municipal, judiciary, banking, and others. During the crisis period, several service actors had active performances, such as health, education, public administration, municipal, and to some degree, transportation. However, during the market expansion period, only education and health service actors exhibit significant peak years. Service actors related to country's bureaucracy (public administration, judiciary, and municipal) took part in popular contention mostly in the early 1980s. The banking sector displays the same pattern.

Summarizing the collective action component actor, our main finding is the emergence of social actors starting in the late 1990s and early 2000s.

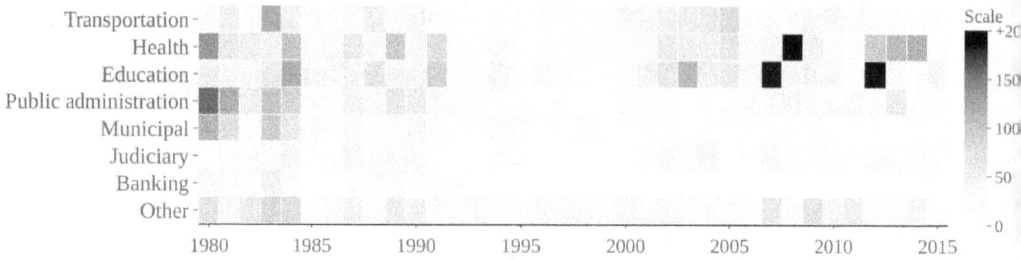

Figure 5.4. Labor Actors, Peru, 1980–2015 (Annual Frequency by Sector). Arce (2023).

These actors are primarily citizens (44.2 percent of protest participation) and they have occupied the space left by labor actors, whose political clout diminished because of the economic crisis and the implementation of economic liberalization policies. Our study also reveals that labor actors are mostly connected to the public sector, and that while there were several service sector actors with active performances in the 1980s, only those from health and education are active in the current period.

Actions (How)

We identify eight major actions of protest: marches, stoppages, strikes, hunger strikes, roadblocks, sit-ins, takeovers, and others. Based on their frequency over the period of study, strikes (29.4 percent), marches (22.3 percent), and stoppages (21.8 percent) are the most common actions of protest. In addition, while takeovers (5.5 percent) and hunger strikes (3.7 percent) were common in the crisis period, sit-ins (8.2 percent) and roadblocks (4.5 percent) gained more visibility in the market expansion period.[5] When we break up their frequencies by year (figure 5.5), we observe darker densities in the crisis and market expansion periods, with a remarkable position shift between strikes and marches (see figure 5.6).

Strikes dominated popular politics during the entire crisis period and the beginning of the market adjustment period. For instance, 68.3 percent of protests involving strikes were performed between 1980 and 1991. In those twelve years, an average of 342 labor protests were channeled through strikes per year, with the highest peaks in 1980 (539), 1981 (493), 1983 (739),

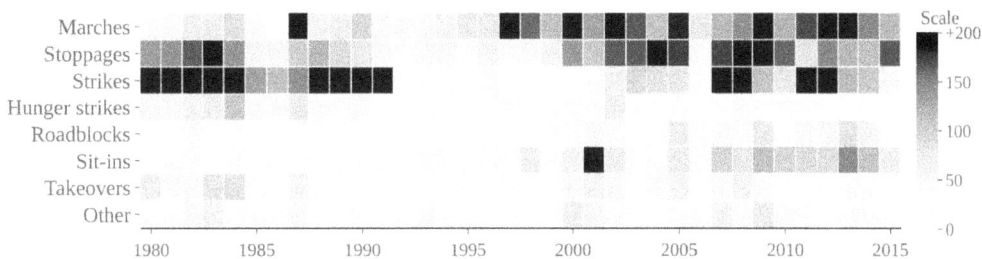

Figure 5.5. Actions, Peru, 1980–2015 (Annual Frequency). Arce (2023).

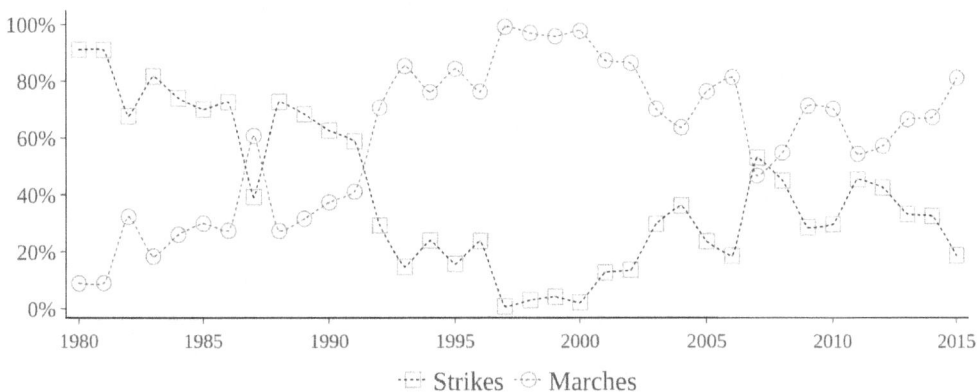

Figure 5.6. Strikes and Marches, Peru, 1980–2015. Arce (2023).

and 1984 (594).[6] As figure 5.6 shows, while there is a significant reduction in the number of strikes beginning with the adjustment period, small peaks appear in the market expansion period.

Marches became the primary action of protest starting in the mid-1990s, and this trend has continued during the market expansion period. When we consider the total number of marches executed in the thirty-six years studied (4,562), 75.7 percent of them took place between 1997 and 2015. While the frequency of marches does not have the intensity that strikes had in the 1980s, figure 5.6 shows how marches were performed continuously since the mid-1990s. On average, 181 marches per year took place from 2000 to 2015. Looking at the darkest densities in figure 5.5, these include 1997, 2000, and 2002, corresponding to 256, 343, and 339 marches, respectively.

Besides strikes and marches, stoppages are also present in both the crisis and the market expansion periods (figure 5.5).[7] Stoppages imply the control of certain geographic areas for short periods of time and the likely presence of a variety of actors with broader claims. The frequency of stoppages reflects a legacy of economic liberalization. In the crisis period, before the arrival of market policies and when labor laws strongly favored unions, strikes were preferred and arguably politically safer. But after economic liberalization, as labor laws changed to accommodate open markets, short-term stoppages became politically safer compared to indefinite strikes. Labor actors embraced this action during the market expansion period.[8]

Summarizing the collective action component action, our central finding is that marches and stoppages have replaced strikes in the configuration of popular politics. Strikes were dominant in the crisis period, but the frequency of marches and stoppages increased starting in the mid-1990s and the market expansion period. The strikes we observe in the market expansion period come mostly from the mining and transportation sectors on the private sector side and health and education on the public sector side. The frequency of stoppages in the current period reveals that workers' ability to mobilize changed in the aftermath of economic liberalization, as labor laws sought to accommodate competition and open markets, not unions.

Claims (Why)

We present six broad categories to compare the claims that motivated actors to protest: labor (labor conditions), political (the accountability of elected officials), service (public goods provision), economic (taxes, budget adjustments), environment (protection of the environment), and territorial (demarcation of territories, property rights). Based on their percentage frequency, labor (41.5 percent) and political (33.2 percent) claims concentrate the most protests.[9] When looking at their frequencies by year (figure 5.7), labor claims dominated popular politics throughout the crisis period—with remarkable peaks in the early 1980s—and regained some significance in the mid-2000s, albeit intermittently. In the opposite direction, protests with political claims had some visibility in the crisis period, but they

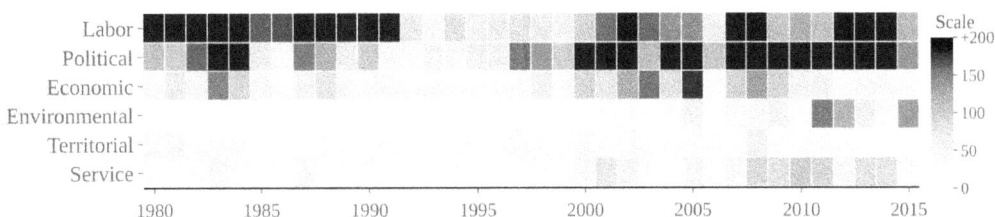

Figure 5.7. Claims, Peru, 1980–2015 (Annual Frequency). Arce (2023).

became more common during the market expansion period, with peaks in 2000 and 2009. Protests with economic, environmental, and service claims also had some visibility in the market expansion period vis-à-vis the other periods. The environmental claims are related to the commodity boom and resource extraction.

Because labor and political claims represent most claims, we disaggregate them next. Labor claims were broken up into seven categories: wage increases (57.6 percent), better labor conditions (11.9 percent), payments of salaries (9.9 percent), work reinstatement (6.8 percent), labor stability (3.1 percent), gratifications (3.4 percent), and other (7.3 percent). When these percentages are plotted by year, the darkest densities correspond to protests demanding wage increases, a trend that remains constant during the crisis period (figure 5.8). Wage increase claims represent 62 percent of total labor claims from 1980 to 1990. These eleven years have an average of 272 protests, with the highest peaks in 1980 (395 protests), 1981 (392 protests), and 1983 (467 protests). In the market expansion period, two small peaks related to wage increases are noticeable in 2008 (164 protests) and 2012 (290 protests).

Work reinstatement claims found small peaks of protest in 2001 (43 protests) and 2002 (90 protests). In those years, in response to campaign promises made by Toledo, workers laid off from privatized state-owned companies demanded their immediate reinstatement. Large national labor unions, such as CGTP (Central General de Trabajadores del Perú), CITE (Confederación Intersectorial de Trabajadores Estatales), CUT (Confederación Unitaria de Trabajadores), and CTP (Confederación de Trabajadores del Perú) reemerged into the political scene in support of this claim.[10]

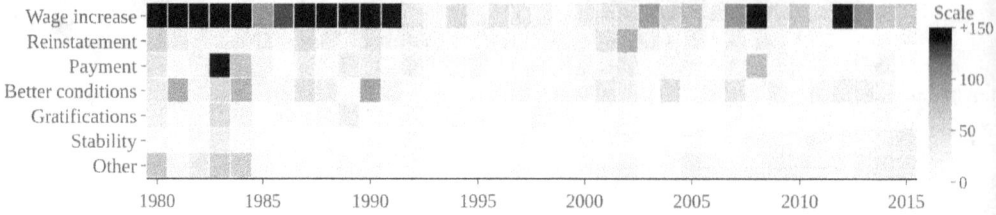

Figure 5.8. Labor Claims, Peru, 1980–2015 (Annual Frequency). Arce (2023).

Next, we disaggregate political claims into nine categories: rejection of mandates (31.3 percent), execution of duties (21.5 percent), disapproval of norms (18.1 percent), dismissal of authorities (9.3 percent), passing of laws (6 percent), compliance of agreements (5.3 percent), rejection of privatization (3.9 percent), execution of reforms (2.3 percent), and rejection of coca leaf eradication program (2.2 percent). When these frequencies are shown annually (see figure 5.9), claims related to the rejection of mandates began to surface in the mid-1990s and remained steady during the market expansion period. Other political claims with visibility during this period include the execution of duties, disapproval of norms, and, to some degree, the dismissal of authorities.

The highest peaks over political claims correspond to the rejection of mandates (257 protests in 2000) and the disapproval of norms (264 protests in 2009). We return to these two peaks at the end of this chapter. The rejection of privatization displays a unique dark density in 2002 (84 protests). It accounts for the regional mobilizations against the privatization of electric companies in southern Peru. Initially launched in Arequipa, protests rapidly diffused across other southern regions, such as Puno, Moquegua, and Tacna. Interestingly, the rejection of privatization does not show any visibility during the heyday of this policy (the 1990s), reflecting perhaps the precarious conditions of most public companies.

To wrap up the collective action component claim, our main finding is the interchangeable role played between labor and political claims in the crisis and market expansion periods, respectively. With rising inflation during the crisis period, the desire for better wages dominated labor claims in particular and popular politics in general. But with an improved

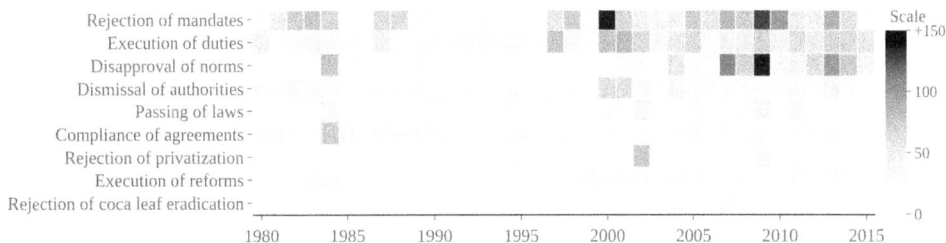

Figure 5.9. Political Claims, Peru, 1980–2015 (Annual Frequency). Arce (2023).

economy, political claims gradually gained more visibility. Protests with demands calling for the rejection of mandates, the execution of duties, and the disapproval of norms were far more common during the market expansion period. Overall, as the country moved from the hard times of the 1980s to the good times of the 2000s, protest claims became less centered on material issues (e.g., wage increases) and moved to a wide range of political claims (e.g., the accountability of elected officials).

Up until now, we can observe the interactivity of actors (who), actions (how), and claims (why). Labor actors pursued material claims (wage increases) by engaging in strikes, and social actors took up political claims related to governance through marches. The "hybrid political-economic environment" of democracy and globalization both demobilized (Roberts 2002; Aidi 2009) and repoliticized (Almeida 2007; Arce 2008; Silva 2009) contentious activity. To the extent that the emergence of traditional communities during the market expansion period favors a political cleavage based on ethnicity (see figure 5.3), the arguments of power of identity theory over the appearance of new social actors are also supported (Escobar and Alvarez 1992; Fuchs 2006).

Targets (Whom)

A question remains whether the target (whom) of collective action may have also changed as a consequence of globalization and democracy. One argument suggests that it shouldn't because in the end, the state is both the problem and the solution to collective demands. Another argument suggests that we should observe lower tiers of government as targets of collective action because of ongoing political and fiscal decentralization.

To explore these arguments, we create six main categories to identify to whom protests are directed: executive, legislative/judiciary, subnational governments, autonomous organizations, companies, and others. Over the 36 years of this study, and based on their percentage frequency, the executive (56 percent), companies (both public and private) (16.2 percent) and subnational governments (11.5 percent) received the most protests.[11] Looking at these frequencies by year (figure 5.10), the executive was the target of many protests during the crisis and market expansion periods, with peak years in 1983 (701 protests) and again in 2012 (670 protests). Companies, the second most common target of protest, had some visibility during the crisis period, but this dissipated quickly in the 1990s and reemerged slightly during the market expansion period.

When we disaggregate the executive, we observe that ministries are the most common target of protest during both the crisis and market expansion periods (see figure 5.11).[12] Nineteen ministries were selected as targets of protests; however, we only present the ones with the highest frequencies: Health (19.8 percent), Education (19.7 percent), Labor (14 percent), Economy (12.3 percent), Agriculture (6.9 percent), Justice (6.1 percent), Transportation (6.1 percent), Energy (4.3 percent), and Fishing (2.5 percent).[13] The first four of these account for two-thirds of the total number of protests directed to ministries in the whole series.

When these frequencies are broken up further by year, figure 5.11 shows that certain ministries concentrate significant popular contention in specific periods and years. In the crisis period, for instance, the targets of protest were more widespread across several ministries, including Economy,

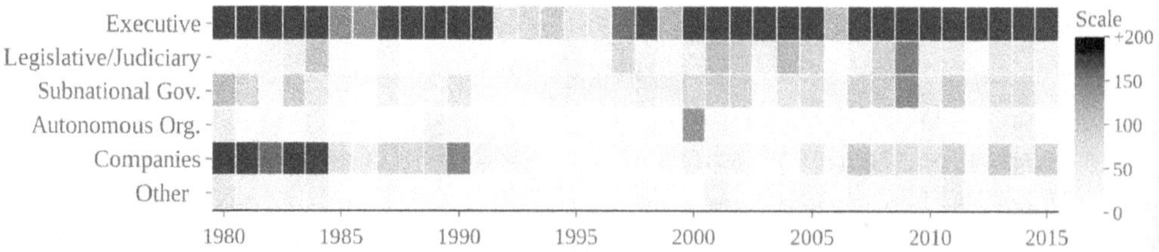

Figure 5.10. Targets, Peru, 1980–2015 (Annual Frequency). Arce (2023).

Figure 5.11. Ministries, Peru, 1980–2015 (Annual Frequency). Arce (2023).

Education, Justice, Health, and Labor. But in the market expansion period, only the Education and Health ministries stand out. The Ministry of Education, for example, faced three waves of demonstrations in 2003 (113 protests), 2007 (131), and 2012 (196). The Ministry of Health endured two waves, one in 2008 (182 protests) and the other in 2013 (114 protests). It goes without saying that the frequency of these ministries as targets of protests overlaps with the participation of labor actors in the service sector (see figure 5.4).

Companies were the second most common target of protest, particularly during the crisis period (see figure 5.10). When we split up these companies into private and public entities (see figure 5.12), we can see that during the crisis period both types faced several protests. This situation changed in the early 1990s as the presence of public companies as targets of protest dropped considerably, and this trend continued during the market expansion period. The absence of public companies as a protest target follows their privatization, one of the signature policies of Fujimori's economic reform program. By contrast, the presence of private companies as targets of protest slowly reemerges in the late 1990s and increases during the market expansion period. As mentioned earlier, these companies are associated with the mining and transportation sectors.

To summarize, the major finding of the collective action component target revolves around the role of the state in popular politics. The executive branch and, in particular, the ministries that provide social services, such as health and education, were and remain the main target of collective action since the return of civilian rule. The arrival of economic liberalization

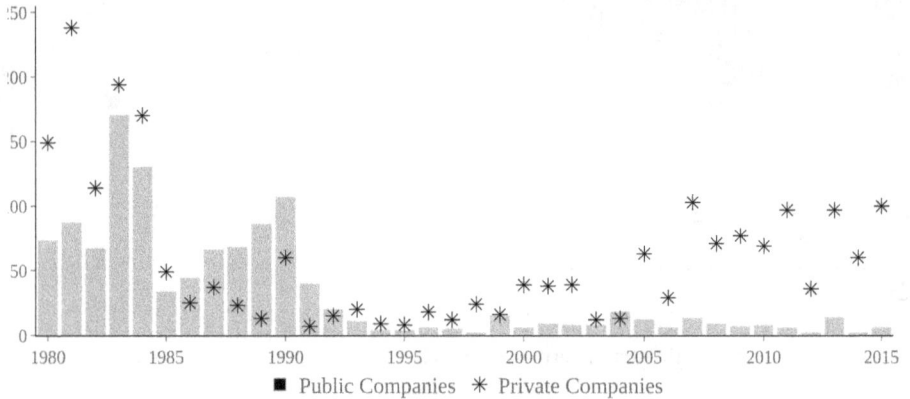

Figure 5.12. Public and Private Companies, Peru, 1980–2015 (Annual Frequency). Arce (2023).

policies in the 1990s and the expansion of these policies after Fujimori has not changed the centrality of the state as both the problem and the solution to collective demands. Moreover, both public and private sector companies were common targets of protest in the early 1980s but, following the privatization of state-owned companies during the market adjustment period, only private companies emerged as a target of protest in the current period. Finally, it appears that subnational governments also became target of protests because of political and fiscal decentralization, particularly during the market expansion period (see figure 5.10).

Places (Where)

Peru's territory is divided into twenty-four regions and one constitutional province (El Callao). In demographic terms, most of the Peruvian population lives along the coast (north and center) and in the highlands (south and central). More than nine million people reside in the region of Lima, representing 32.3 percent of the population. Of this figure, 91 percent live in one of the forty-three districts of the province of Lima. Considering these demographic and geographic characteristics, we first compare Lima with the rest of the regions (hereafter, peripheral regions). Then we disaggregate the frequency of regional performances across the periods of interest.

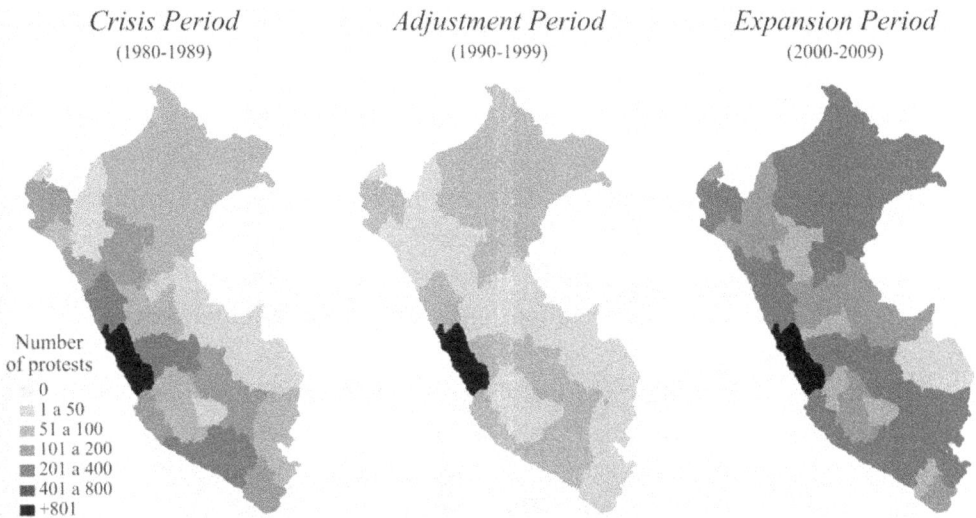

Crisis Period
(1980-1989)

Adjustment Period
(1990-1999)

Expansion Period
(2000-2009)

Number
of protests
    0
▨ 1 a 50
▨ 51 a 100
▨ 101 a 200
▨ 201 a 400
▨ 401 a 800
■ +801

Map 5.1. Actions by Region, Peru. The crisis, adjustment and expansion periods are ten years each: 1980–1989, 1990–1999 and 2000–2009, respectively. Arce (2023).

The region of Lima is the country's epicenter of popular politics, but as mentioned earlier, we should be aware of potential biases due to newspaper proximity to these events. In the thirty-six years of this study, this region accumulates 10,349 protests, that is, 50.6 percent of the total. On average, 287 protests take place in Lima every year. Peripheral regions account for 49.4 percent of protests, with an annual average of 281 protests distributed across the twenty-four remaining regions. The years with the highest peaks of mobilization in Lima were 1980 (637 protests), 1983 (760), and 1984 (624). By contrast, the years with greater mobilizations in peripheral regions are 2007 (532 protests), 2008 (584), and 2009 (690).

This initial comparison suggests a growth in mobilizations in peripheral regions in recent years. To capture this trend, we disaggregate the percentage frequencies by region over the periods of interest (see map 5.1). We observe darker densities in different regions, particularly during the market expansion period. For instance, when we compare the number of protests in that period with the crisis and market adjustment periods, the increase is substantial in northern coastal regions (e.g., Ancash, Piura, and Lambayeque), southern regions (e.g., Arequipa, Puno, and Cusco), and the northeast region of Loreto.

In peripheral regions, most protests are found during the market expansion period (64.6 percent). Lima, by contrast, exhibits a different pattern. Most protests are actually observed during the crisis and market adjustment periods (58.7 percent). These figures, however, do not suggest that Lima is losing its epicenter status of protest to peripheral regions. Lima still averages more than two hundred protests per year.[14] Outside Lima, the highest peak of protest corresponds to Puno, with almost ninety-seven mobilizations requesting the suspension of mining concessions in 2011.

Because more than 50 percent of protests are performed in Lima, we disaggregated the province of Lima to better understand where exactly mobilizations take place (graph not shown). Between 2003 and 2015, protests were largely concentrated in three districts (75.2 percent of protests): Lima Cercado (1,634 protests), Jesus María (480 protests), and San Isidro (127 protests). The main government buildings are in the Lima Cercado district, including the Presidential Palace, Congress, several ministries, and other government agencies. Traditional plazas, such as Dos de Mayo, San Martín, and Bolognesi, are common gathering points to initiate marches through downtown Lima. The Jesus María district holds two of the most targeted ministries: Health and Labor. Additionally, major avenues, such as Salaverry and Arequipa, connect these ministries to other nearby potential targets, including embassies and public sector hospitals. The San Isidro district houses one of the most sought-out targets of protest: the Ministry of Education. Several public sector and private company headquarters are also located in San Isidro.

To summarize, the analysis of the collective action component place suggests an increasing tendency for popular politics across peripheral regions, particularly during the market expansion period. This growth overlaps with the rise of subnational governments as targets of protests because of political and fiscal decentralization (see figure 5.10). Lima remains the epicenter of protest because of its population size and because it houses the major buildings that collectively make up the executive branch. Actors from peripheral regions often travel to Lima to make their claims known; thus, popular politics are likely to remain active in the capital city.

Protest Campaigns in the 1980s and the 2000s

During the 1980s, in the context of an imploding economy and rising inflation, workers from the ministries that provide social services, such as
Health and Education, exemplify the dominance of labor actors pursuing
material, reactive claims (wage increases). On the health side, the Peruvian
government failed to implement previous agreements on wage increases
made in 1981 and 1983, and in early April 1984, doctors associated with the
Instituto Peruano de Seguridad Social (IPSS) abandoned their hospitals,
effectively closing them down. They performed marches, sit-ins, and takeovers, initially in Lima but later spreading to the southern regions of Arequipa and Cusco. In June of the same year, when the mobilization by IPSS
doctors ended, workers associated with the Health Ministry went on strike,
too. The strike turned violent when the police arrested approximately thirty
doctors to prevent a takeover attempt. On the education side, in June 1988,
teachers from the public sector led a nationwide strike, closing schools for
about a month. Seeking to repel protest actions, the police detained about
150 teachers in Lima. Teachers only returned to their classrooms after
national union leaders and government officials agreed on salary increases.
In 1991, teachers organized another strike that lasted about four months
and almost triggered the loss of the academic year, which is nine months.
Looking back, despite the recent unprecedented economic expansion associated with the commodity boom, the labor conditions of health and education workers have lagged. Teachers went on strike in 2007 and 2012 and
health workers in 2008; in both cases, they mobilized to demand better
wages (figure 5.4). Reactive protests remain, but they are clearly less widespread than in the 1980s.

Two proactive protest campaigns exemplify the rise of social actors
demanding better governance. Shortly after staging a self-coup in April 1992,
Alberto Fujimori convoked a constitutional assembly to rewrite the country's
constitution. The new constitution centralized executive authority and
enabled him to run for reelection. In 1997, Fujimori's party dismantled the
Constitutional Tribunal because it opposed his plans to seek a second reelection. This event marked the beginning of a long-run and widespread political

opposition to Fujimori. In May of that year, over fifteen thousand people marched in the streets to defend the rule of law. In June, students, labor unions, journalists, political authorities, and civil construction workers organized demonstrations paired with sit-ins and sporadic one- or two-day work stoppages to express their disapproval of this measure. The early demands against reelection transitioned to a more encompassing political frame: the defense of democratic values, the respect of the rule of law, and, finally, a wholesale rejection of his regime. Demonstrators began to label the government as a dictatorship. In 2000, following allegations of voter fraud, hundreds of thousands of protesters in Lima rejected Fujimori's second reelection and demanded his resignation. The campaign was called the "March of the Four Suyos" (*Marcha de los Cuatro Suyos*).[15] Because of police repression, six people died and several were injured or went missing. In our analysis, the darker densities for students and citizens (figure 5.3) expressing the rejection of mandates (figure 5.9) through marches and stoppages (figure 5.5) capture these events well.

The protest campaign in opposition to the decrees that opened the Amazon region for development in 2008–2009 is another example of a proactive mobilization demanding better governance. In the context of the commodity boom, the government of García sought to expand extractive activities in the Amazon region. Indigenous organizations demanded the repeal of the decrees as well as the implementation of consulting rights over development projects that had an impact on their livelihoods. In the mobilization of June 5, 2009, in the province of Bagua, thirty-three people were killed in one day when the police were deployed to crack down on demonstrators. The unfortunate clash was known as the *Baguazo*. It sparked multiple demonstrations throughout the country in solidarity with the aggrieved communities of Bagua, and by mid-June 2009, the national Congress had suspended the decrees. Two years later, in August 2011, the government of Humala implemented the Law of Prior Consultation on behalf of indigenous communities. In our analysis, these events are summarized with the darker densities for traditional communities (figure 5.3) in northern Peru (map 5.1) expressing the disapproval of norms (figure 5.9) and targeting the executive branch, responsible for enacting the decrees, and later the legislative branch, calling for the repeal of these laws (figure 5.10).

Conclusions

Our review of the main collective action components in Peru suggests that there is a new configuration of popular politics, supporting the coexistence of reactive to proactive mobilizations (see introduction). During the crisis period, labor actors dominated the political scene, mostly in Lima. They organized strikes and petitioned for wage increases. Starting in the late 1990s and continuing through the market expansion period, by contrast, social actors began to emerge in peripheral regions and organized marches and stoppages to pursue a broad array of political claims. Thus, as the country moved from the hard times of the 1980s to the good times of the 2000s, popular politics changed. During the economic downturn, labor actors were at the forefront of social struggles and were chiefly concerned with their material well-being and survival. But with a growing economy, these economic concerns waned and new social actors began to demand better governance and hold elected officials accountable. In both instances, they targeted the state to make their demands known (table 5.1).

Even when market reforms have succeeded in diminishing the role of the state vis-à-vis the economy, the state is still the primary avenue to redress these claims. In the current context of economic expansion and stability following the commodity boom, the nature of claims has become more political, and includes several demands for better governance. This argument resonates with scholars who associate low-quality political institutions with surging popular contention (Moseley 2018). As mentioned earlier, political institutions in Peru are very weak, plagued by corruption and

Table 5.1. Summary of Collective Action Components

	HARD TIMES	GOOD TIMES
Actors (Who)	Labor actors	Social actors
Target (Whom)	Executive	Executive
Claims (Why)	Labor	Political
Actions (How)	Strikes	Marches and stoppages
Place (Where)	Lima	Peripheral regions

low levels of legitimacy, and, as our analysis shows, citizens are willing to take to the streets to make their political demands known. Protest remains a crucial mechanism for democratic accountability.

The economic periods of interest also allow us to revisit the relationship between economic liberalization and popular politics. As we have seen, the period of economic crisis was characterized by rising mobilizations, but there were limited reforms in the direction of open markets and competition at that time. When these reforms were finally launched—the period we called market adjustment—the country experienced a wave of widespread demobilization. One possible explanation behind this is related to the severity of the economic crisis of the 1980s, which led to the collapse of multiple industries and the growing informalization of the labor force. Another is related to the selective political repression that characterized the autocratization period of the 1990s under Fujimori. In the market expansion period, the country experienced levels of mobilization similar to the 1980s, but the claims of protesters were no longer about material concerns. There were important campaigns over economic liberalization policies in this period, such as protests over electricity privatization in the early 2000s and the opening of the Amazon for development in the late 2000s, but most noteworthy were the frequency of protests with political claims. Overall, both the bad times of the 1980s and the good times of the 2000s were tied to greater levels of mobilization. While a more open political environment conducive to protest was the common denominator across these two broad periods, the nature of claims shifted away from economic to political concerns. The high frequency of protests with political concerns reflects two persistent problems: a low quality of political representation and weak governance capacity.

Notes

1. This chapter draws on Arce (2023), which provides an extended account of protests in Peru for forty-one years, from 1980 through 2020.
2. The globalization scores reported in this section come from the KOF index of globalization (Gygli et al. 2019; Dreher 2006). The democracy scores are the electoral democracy indices from the Varieties of Democracy Project (V-Dem).
3. To make these periods comparable, the crisis, adjustment, and expansion

periods are kept at ten years each: 1980–1989, 1990–1999, and 2000–2009, respectively. However, the number of protest events for the entire market expansion period (2000–2015) is 10,815.

4. The highest number of protests led by the manufacturing sector was ninety-one in 1983.

5. Other actions represented 4.7 percent of all actions over the period of the study.

6. A strike often works as an umbrella protest action. Under a given strike, other actions such as marches, sit-ins, and takeovers can potentially be performed to maintain the strike or to increase its visibility.

7. Similar to strikes, stoppages allow for the performance of other actions.

8. The remaining actions present low-density frequencies. Even though roadblocks, sit-ins, and, to some degree, takeovers increased slightly in the market expansion period, their average frequency is lower than fifty protests in this period.

9. Protests related to economic, service, environmental, and territorial demands were 11.2 percent, 6.9 percent, 4.3 percent, and 3.0 percent, respectively.

10. In the same period, claims related to better labor conditions and payment of salaries present small peaks in 2004 (54 protests) and 2008 (81 protests).

11. The legislative/judiciary, autonomous organizations, and others accounted for 8.7 percent, 3.89 percent, and 3.79 percent of protest targets, respectively.

12. The president and the cabinet of ministers are two other categories we considered within the executive branch. Contentious actions targeting the president indicated a sporadic selection during the 1980s. However, the president showed a rising tendency as a target of protest after 2006, with peak years in 2009 (349 protests) and 2012 (335 protests). By contrast, the cabinet of ministers was not a recurrent target. The cabinet accounted for sixty protests at its major peak in 2008.

13. The other category (8.3 percent) includes ministries such as Defense, Housing, Production, Commerce, and Foreign Relations.

14. Even during the lowest period of protest, the 1990s, that average did not drop significantly. It was about 178.

15. The reference to the administrative units of the Inca Empire called Suyos was meant to capture the nationwide rejection of this reelection.

CHAPTER SIX

Popular Protests, Deglobalization, and Authoritarianism in Venezuela, 1983–2012

MARGARITA LÓPEZ MAYA

Introduction

Popular protest in Venezuela, also known as the politics in the streets, has been a constant in defining the relationship between society and state.[1] There is a long history about this form of interplay between the common people and those who control political power in the country. However, depending on the socioeconomic and political context, the frequency and forms of these protests have varied, as well as the actors and their motivations. These differences are a response to ongoing societal transformations, processes that at the end of the twentieth century were linked to a changing international context marked by economic globalization.

This chapter is based on a lengthy investigation of protests in Venezuela in the twentieth century.[2] The empirical source comes from two digitized datasets: El Bravo Pueblo (BDEBP), and another compiled by the human rights organization PROVEA (Programa Venezolano de Educación Acción en Derechos Humanos).[3] The first records protest events from a newspaper with national coverage, *El Nacional*, starting in the 1980s and until the end of the century. The second compiles social demonstration events collected by PROVEA since 1989. The datasets, in addition to recording protest events that occurred in these years, have a set of components that allow us to investigate the actions, actors, claims, dates, and places of protest events. Although the two datasets are different, there are similar components that allow us to make cautious comparisons.

Analyzing the dynamics of popular protests sheds some lights on the institutional strengths and weaknesses of a given society. Public demonstrations are closely linked to grievances and deficits in citizens' rights—that is, the democratic quality of the regime—but their modalities (repertoires) and claims are influenced by protests in other countries, as well as by social movements of a global nature. Analyzing the politics in the streets always requires constant information and reflection. This chapter illustrates the characteristics of protests that occurred in Venezuela to understand the relationship between citizens and power-holders over three decades.

This chapter reviews the landscape of Venezuelan popular protest from the 1980s, when the first signs of the structural crisis of society were revealed, until the end of the last government of Hugo Chávez in 2013. The crisis, which is characterized here as structural, had its causes in national dynamics, and also in changes in the international sphere. After providing background information on Venezuela in the context of democracy and globalization, the chapter explains protest trends using the above datasets. Then, using information from BDEBP, it examines the last two decades of the twentieth century, highlighting the year 1989, when the Caracazo or "Sacudón" took place, an event that produced a profound change in the landscape of the protests. Next, drawing on PROVEA reports, the chapter reviews the politics in the streets during the presidential terms of Hugo Chávez, a charismatic and populist leader who opened a new political era in the country's history. During Chávez's rule, political polarization was constant and actors embraced discourses and strategies typical of a struggle for hegemony. The conclusion presents some reflections on the politics in the streets under the Nicolás Maduro regime.

Globalization and Democratization

In the Venezuelan case, the globalization processes in the last twenty-five years of the twentieth century contributed to the definite collapse of the CEPAL (Comisión Económica para América Latina y el Caribe) development model—the import-substitution industrialization model that was adopted in the aftermath of World War II and supported by oil income.[4] The stability and success of the representative democratic political regime and its multiclass party system, which went hand in hand with this model beginning in 1958, was also tied to the peculiarities of a rentier economy, providing the state windfall revenues from the sale of oil in international markets (Karl 1994). In line with arguments that relate the abundance of natural resources to a host of negative outcomes, oil rents enabled a zero-sum game among democratic actors for several decades. Organized sectors such as capital, labor, the middle classes, and multiclass political parties supported democracy without major sacrifices to their interests because they relied on the income distribution from the state they controlled (Rey 1991).

As oil prices dropped in international markets, first in the mid-1970s and then in the early 1980s, the relationships between these political actors deteriorated and distributional struggles over oil income intensified. While other countries in the region transitioned from dictatorships to democracies, following an international context that delegitimized the former, and other countries absorbed the costs of economic liberalization policies associated with the Washington consensus, the scenario in Venezuela was prone to the erosion of democracy. The existing political system and its actors did not have adequate responses to this crisis or the political will to carry out the economic and political transformations demanded by the new times.[5]

The empirical information provided by the BDEBP dataset and the annual reports from PROVEA reveal changes in the number and features of street demonstrations since the Caracazo of February 1989. The Caracazo was a massive social explosion that disrupted the status quo. It spread over several days in the main cities of the country and resulted in a high death toll at the hands of security forces. It altered the traditional channels through which politics in the streets had operated until then (López Maya 2003).

In addition, the Caracazo revealed and exacerbated the dysfunctionality of the political representation system based on multiclass parties, unions, and other organizations acting as intermediaries between society and state. The lack of response by the party system to the Caracazo ultimately unleashed a crisis of political representation, which was visible in the streets. And because this crisis was not resolved, it produced a new era in the Venezuelan sociopolitical process with the arrival of Hugo Chávez and his Bolivarian movement.

Since 1992, a year that witnessed two failed coups (February and October), a growing rupture between some groups in the armed forces and the democratic regime became more apparent. In this context, the impeachment trial of President Carlos Andrés Pérez was held in 1993 after he was accused by the attorney general's office of embezzlement of funds tied to the presidency. The presidential elections at the end of that year temporarily eased the political tension. The results supported an incumbent who broke the traditional alternation between the political parties Acción Democrática (AD) and COPEI (Comité de Organización Política Electoral Independiente). Rafael Caldera, founder of COPEI but running outside the party, won the presidency with a new coalition party—Convergencia National. This coalition incorporated a handful of small political organizations with distinct political orientations, also known as the "chiripero."

Caldera, like Carlos Andrés Pérez in his second presidential period (1989–1993), utilized an antineoliberal discourse on the campaign trail. Once in office, however, given the recurring economic crisis, which was aggravated by the collapse of the banking system, he had no other option than to reach out to international lending institutions. Thus, Caldera introduced a second macroeconomic adjustment package outlined by the International Monetary Fund (IMF). During his tenure, some economic indicators improved; however, the Venezuelan people perceived them as insufficient and the poor provision of public services and the dissatisfaction with political parties continued. In 1998, economic conditions worsened with the new collapse of international oil prices, triggering sentiments of disenchantment and despair among the electorate. With the election of Chávez and his Bolivarian movement, Venezuelan society ditched for good the old democracy and sought political representation in the hands of new political actors.

Methods

STREET POLITICS IN VENEZUELA

Both the BDEBP and PROVEA datasets show the emergence of actors who had previously maintained a low profile and whose appearance was contingent on adverse economic and political contexts.[6] For example, in the 1990s, organizations of retirees and pensioners from the public sector engaged in reactive protests to demand income stability as inflation eroded the real value of their earnings. Judicial employees and informal workers (*buhoneros*), in turn, mobilized to protest against the increased precarization of the workforce. Middle-class sectors focused their requests on the provision of public services (e.g., water and transportation). Human rights organizations, such as COFAVIC (Comité de Familiares de Víctimas del Caracazo) and PROVEA, also voiced their concerns against violations of human rights and physical integrity.

Figure 6.1 presents the number of protest events of the period under study. If we examine the five years prior to the Caracazo using the BDEBP dataset (figure 6.1), we find a total of 876 protest events in the newspaper *El Nacional*, an average of about 175 protests per year: that is, approximately one every two days. In the following ten years, including the Caracazo, the figures from *El Nacional* show 1,939 protest events, or 194 protests per year, thus increasing slightly the daily number of events. The compilation by PROVEA is more interesting as it records protest events starting in October 1989, just after the Caracazo. It identifies a total of 6,503 events before the rise of Hugo Chávez: an annual average of 723 events, two per day, including weekends and holidays. Considering that these protests tend to disrupt daily life and that almost all of them take place in Caracas, this record-keeping is relevant, as it reveals high political turbulence in the capital.

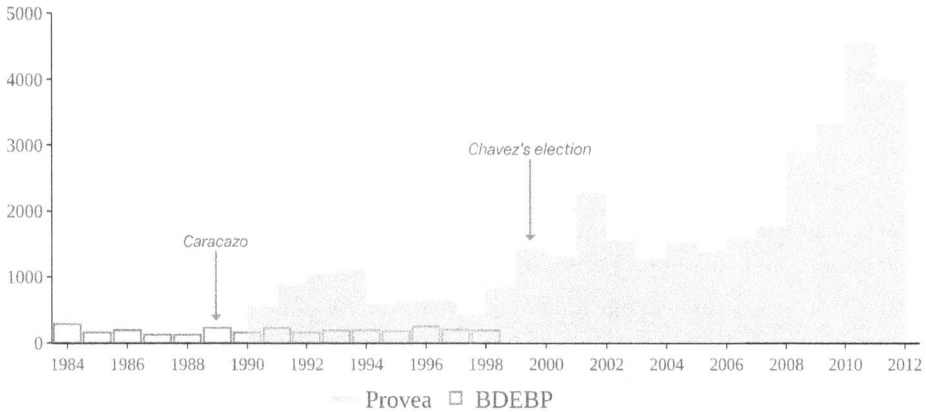

Figure 6.1. Number of Protests, 1983–2012. Protest figures begin in the month of October of each year and end in September of the following year, starting with October 1983. Beginning in 2012, the annual reports from PROVEA are prepared with information that goes from January to December. PROVEA, Situación de los derechos humanos (annual reports) and BDEBP dataset.

ACTIONS (HOW) AND CLAIMS (WHY)
BEFORE HUGO CHÁVEZ, 1983–1998

The BDEBP and PROVEA datasets also reveal new forms of protest, such as *cacerolazos* (pots-and-pans protests), power blackouts (*apagones de luz*), the taking over of public buildings (*encadenamientos a edificios públicos*), actions of public nudity (*desnudos*), whistles (*pitazos*), human chains (*cadenas humanas*), and vigils, among others. These protest performances sought to call attention to the disproportionate use of state repression. They were usually peaceful, but confrontational: that is, popular contention developed legally but was meant to cause displeasure and/or tension to power holders through actions such as road blockades (*cierres de vías*), public nudity, and the taking over of public buildings. Other protests were more violent. These were carried out by sectors tied to the student movement, as well as "unknown" actors wearing hoods to avoid face recognition. Their protest performances increased the intensity of violence as seen in the burnings of public and private transportation vehicles, garbage, and tires;

road blockades using trash bags, tires, and rods; and clashes with the police using stones, Molotov cocktails, and sticks.

The BDEBP dataset categorizes the types of routine actions as conventional, confrontational, and violent.[7] Whereas conventional protests were common in the years prior to the Caracazo, protests became more confrontational and violent post-Caracazo (see figure 6.2).

We observe an average of 12.5 percent of violent protests per year in the five years before the Caracazo. Violent protests, however, increased to 31.6 percent per year on average after the Caracazo. Popular contention reached significant violence spikes between 1992 and 1996, with estimates higher than this average in all of these years. The year 1992 stood out as the more violent in percentual terms: of the 159 protests recorded in the BDEBP dataset, 45.3 percent of them were violent. There were two failed coups in this year: one in February, led by Hugo Chávez, and one in October, directed by a group of military officers loyal to Chávez's Revolutionary Bolivarian Movement (MBR).

Violent contention diminished slightly in the late 1990s, to 23.4 percent in 1997 and 19.9 percent in 1998. Police repression had been a common response to the rise of violent interactions, and this reduction was related to a change in the state's response to public demonstrations. For instance, the first laws restricting the use of firearms against protesters and excessive force by the police in the Capital District of Caracas were enacted at around this time. In general, across the fifteen-year series of the BDEBP dataset, one out of four protest events were violent.

Turning to confrontational protests, these were on average 23.6 percent of all annual protest events before 1989. In these years, 1984 exhibits the highest spike (98 out of 283 protests were confrontational). In the ten years following the Caracazo (1989–1998), confrontational interactions experienced a

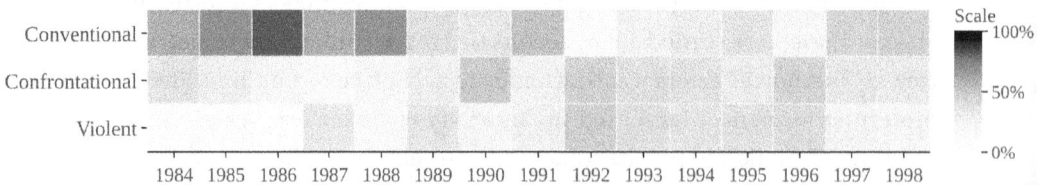

Figure 6.2. Actions, 1983–1998. El Bravo Pueblo Database (BDEBP).

significant increase; they averaged 35.6 percent of all yearly protest events. Moreover, between 1992 and 1996, almost half of protests acquired a confrontational tone. These numbers reveal that street demonstrations became more aggressive, and for Venezuela, a country that is not traditionally known for the visibility of its protests, these records reveal contradictory trends.

Turning to claims, and using the BDEBP dataset, figure 6.3 illustrates that the bulk of the protests involved socioeconomic claims. The trends, which are common across the period of study, suggest that the social convulsion of the Caracazo of 1989 did not substantially alter protest claim tendencies and support the arguments about the lack of response by powerholders. Protests with civil and political claims exceeded a third of the total of protest events only in certain years. Such were the cases of the periods 1986–1987 (46 percent), 1987–1988 (31.2 percent), 1991–1992 (40.8 percent) and 1998–1999 (34.9 percent). When exploring the context of these protests, between 1986 and 1988, for instance, actors mobilized proactively to request political reforms, especially regarding the decentralization of central authority.[8] These mobilizations contributed to the adoption of institutional reforms by the Presidential Commission for State Reform (Comisión Presidencial para la Reforma del Estado, or COPRE), which included the approval of decentralization laws.

In the period 1991–1992, the failed coup d'état of February 4, 1992 against the government of Carlos Andrés Pérez took place. This event influenced the emergence of violent protests in the following months in the form of

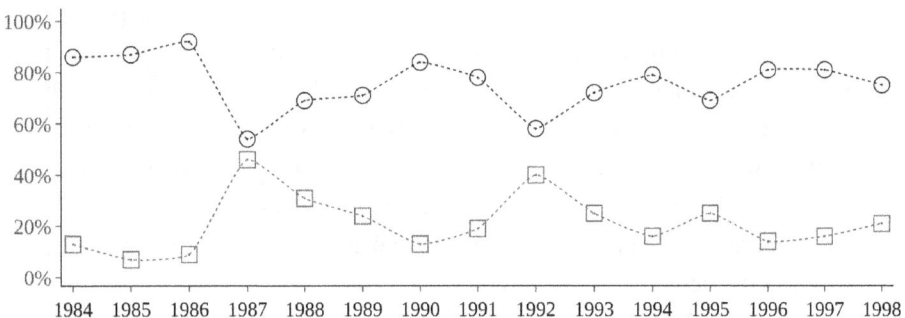

Figure 6.3 Claims, 1983–1998. The figure does not include the Other category. El Bravo Pueblo Database (BDEBP).

disturbances. According to the BDEBP dataset, some of these were carried out by students or "unknown" actors wearing hoods. Some examples of these disturbances include the invasion of rural lands in Acarigua (Portuguese state); the burning of the headquarters of Communist Party in that city; a general strike organized by the Federation of Teachers of Venezuela (Federación de Profesores de Venezuela, or FAPUCV); and mobilizations in support of the military insurgency of February 4th (BDEBP 2006). The 1998–1999 period overlaps with Chávez's first year in office. In this period, protests related to the election of the constituent assembly took masses to the streets.

To examine claims in greater detail, figure 6.4 disaggregates socioeconomic and civic-political claims into three subgroups each. The first subgroup (A) of socioeconomic demands incorporates protests related to conditions and rights to produce goods, such as requests for land and subsidies, protests against taxes, the extension of credit, and so on. The second subgroup (B) brings together claims related to the provision of public goods, such as access to health, education, water, and transportation. Subgroup (C), in turn, gathers demands related to income, such as increases of salaries, compliance with collective contracts, payments of retirement pensions, and payments related to labor debts. Collectively, these subgroups can be seen as examples of reactive mobilizations insofar as some of these claims were a response to the loss of economic and social benefits available to class-based actors during periods of state-led development (see chapter 1).

Turning to civic–political claims, the first subgroup (D) incorporates human rights demands relating to topics such as abuse, repression, and deaths. The second subgroup (E) includes civil rights petitions dealing with access to justice, free speech, and rejection or acceptance of laws and regulations, among other things. The third subgroup (F) aggregates claims that are distinctively political, including reports related to electoral fraud and calls for democratization and autonomy and against corruption. Figure 6.4 displays the density of these protests.[9]

Before the Caracazo, reactive demands related to income (subgroup C) were dominant. Almost two-thirds of popular contention observed in Venezuela (58.3 percent) sought to improve working conditions. Examples

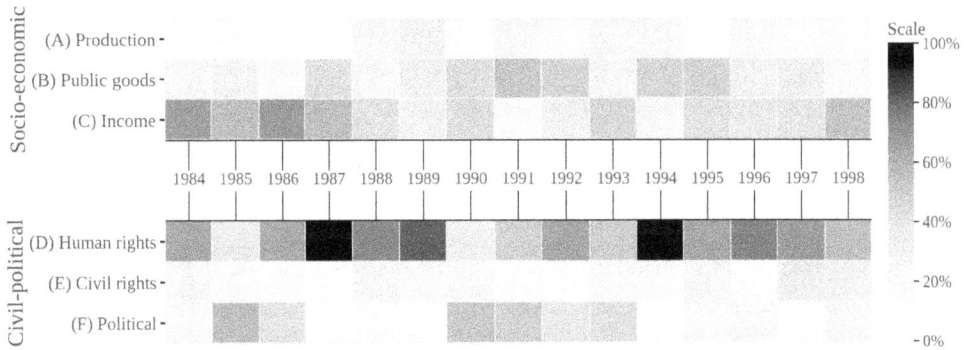

Figure 6.4. Subgroups of Protest Claims, 1983–1998.
El Bravo Pueblo Database (BDEBP).

include demands related to the erosion of real salaries, unfulfilled collective agreements or retirement pensions and, in general, the worsening of labor conditions. After the Caracazo, we observe a shift toward the deterioration of public services (subgroup B). In some years, subgroup B presents higher densities than claims related to income (subgroup C).

Turning to protests with civil-political claims, human right demands (subgroup D) have darker densities before and after the Caracazo. Popular contention related to repression, police brutality, raids, deaths, right to life, and violence continued throughout Chávez's period, as discussed in the next section. Claims in subgroup D constitute almost two-thirds of all civil–political protests. This finding reveals an important democratic deficit in the Venezuelan political order. After human right demands (subgroup D), the second most frequent sources of mobilization were violations of political rights, such as electoral fraud and calls for democratization and autonomy and against corruption (subgroup F). By contrast, civil rights petitions, such as requests for access to justice and free speech (subgroup E) were less common: between 16 percent to 18 percent of all protests before and after the Caracazo.

In all, amid an unsolved economic crisis—poverty rates went from 38.88 percent in 1986 to 48.3 percent in 1997—street demonstrations became a visible expression of a growing crisis of political representation. The streets became a sort of safety valve for citizen complaint. One of the consequences of this crisis was the arrival of populism.

ACTIONS (HOW) AND CLAIMS (WHY) UNDER HUGO CHÁVEZ, 1999–2012[10]

As in the previous period (1983–1998), popular contention remained in crescendo (see figure 6.1). According to the PROVEA dataset, throughout almost the entire fourteen years of the Chávez regime, protest events averaged five per day and the bulk of these demonstrations were cataloged as peaceful (92.6 percent of all protests) (figure 6.5). The repertoire of contention gained a more confrontational intensity; roadblocks, takeovers, marches, work stoppages, and hunger strikes surfaced as recurrent protest routines. Although PROVEA does not report the exact figures or the share of confrontational protests vis-à-vis conventional or violent performances (as reported by the BDEBP dataset in figure 6.2), the frequency of these protests and their confrontational nature reveal the turbulent atmosphere of daily life in Caracas and other Venezuelan cities.

In the first years of the Chávez era, the government embraced a discourse

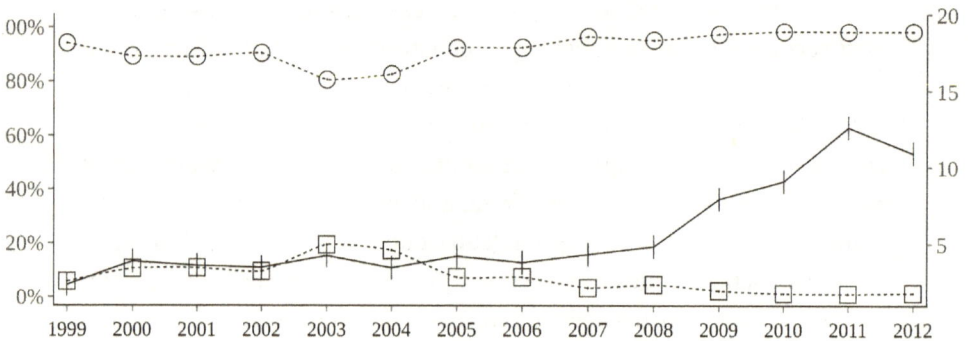

Figure 6.5. Actions, 1999–2012. Beginning in 2012, the annual reports from PROVEA are prepared with information that goes from January to December. There is limited quantitative information about protests starting in 2013. PROVEA, annual reports.

recognizing the right to protest peacefully and the prohibition on the use of firearms by security forces. Enacted in 1999, the new Bolivarian Constitution, in fact, reaffirmed the right to protest peacefully and went further by explicitly prohibiting security forces from "carrying firearms and deploying toxic substances to control peaceful demonstrations" (Article 68). Both the change of government and the new approach toward protests—in discourse and legality—reduced the incentives to use violent channels, a tendency that was also present during the last years of the Caldera government.

However, in 2005, as reported by the Observatorio Venezolano de la Conflictividad Social (Venezuelan Observatory of Social Conflict, or OVCS)[11], the Chávez regime gradually restricted the right to protest in public through the enactment of various legal actions, regulations, decrees, and state resolutions. The government thus returned to the criminalization of protest as seen in previous years. This change of course was a reaction to an emerging and widespread struggle for hegemony unfolding in Venezuela, with intense, polarized contention and peaks of violence, episodes that in the end were favorable to the Chávez regime. In all, the Chávez government returned to repression, a response that resembled the former democratic periods.

Violent protests have increased since 2000. They rose from 5.85 percent in 1999 to 10.68 percent in 2000, and then again to 19.44 percent in 2003 and 17.37 percent in 2004 (see PROVEA's annual reports). In other words, between late 2001 and 2004 violent protests doubled.[12] This increase is linked to the use of street protests as a political strategy by two major forces confronting each other: supporters of the Chávez government and the opposition to Chávez, the latter grouped into a catch-all political platform called Mesa de Unidad Democrática (Table for the Democratic Unity, or MUD). Both sides relied on polarization strategies; each presented the opposing force as the enemy and characterized the other group's plans for Venezuela as antagonistic and irreconcilable. In this zero-sum dynamic, the *chavismo* and MUD fought in diverse arenas—both legal and extralegal—seeking to destroy the other side and establish themselves as the dominant political force.

In this struggle for hegemony, street mobilizations played a continuous and essential role in sustaining the legitimacy of these political disputes. Some of them were extralegal and violent. In 2001, for example, anti-Chavistas gathered massively in the civic stoppage of December 10, a mobilization that was put together by business organizations and agrarian producers to raise their collective voice against laws enacted without consultation by the Chávez government. The stoppage took place in front of the union federation FEDECÁMARAS (Federación de Cámaras y Asociaciones de Comercio y Producción de Venezuela), and it was well-attended and impressive. Encouraged by these results, on April 8, 2002, MUD organized a civic stoppage, which preceded the April 11 coup attempt against Chávez. On that day, in the late hours of the stoppage, MUD asked citizens to take to the streets again. The call produced a massive demonstration in the east part of the city of Caracas, and later masses headed to the government palace in Miraflores to demand Chávez's resignation. This historic march ultimately unleashed violence near the government palace as anti-Chavistas clashed with official sympathizers. As it turned out, the government had also summoned its followers to guard the presidential palace and some of them carried firearms. In the months between the coup attempt of April and the oil strike of December, the city of Caracas saw its daily routines constantly interrupted with marches and countermarches called by both political sides. Protest became bidirectional. Marches interrupted traffic flows by blocking key road access points. Many of these mobilizations led to injuries and even fatalities. Organized by the managers of the state oil company PDVSA (Petróleos de Venezuela, S.A.), the oil strike sought to force Chávez's departure. Demonstrations by both political sides occurred almost daily. The oil strike lasted for two months, ending in February 2003.

The struggle for hegemony and mobilizations persisted throughout 2004 and 2005. The violent tendency of these confrontations decreased momentarily when the government of Chávez agreed to a recall presidential election to be held in August 2004 and congressional elections in 2005. These institutional channels were thus a safety valve, transforming previous violent episodes into a peaceful contention.

However, in 2006 and 2007, protests regained momentum, albeit not with the frequency of previous years. Some specific events intensified the struggle for political hegemony. Examples include the 2006 presidential elections, the shutdown of Radio Caracas Television (RCTV) by the government in 2007, and the launch of Chávez's XXI Century Socialism project to deepen his hold on power. The last two events unleashed a cycle of protest that year.[13] Street demonstrations reemerged in 2009; this time they were a response to Chávez's constitutional amendment project, via referendum, to support his indefinite reelection. This resulted again in marches and countermarches by both political sides. Violent protest decreased between October 2010 and September 2011, when the opposition participated in the congressional elections (which they had previously boycotted in 2005).

Figures 6.6 and 6.7 show protest claims during the Chávez period, though the data is incomplete. Figure 6.6 groups protests into socioeconomic and civic-political claims, and figure 6.7, in turn, breaks up these claims into subcategories. Overall, protests with socioeconomic claims were prevalent in the country as in previous years. But unlike the period before Chávez, protests with civic-political demands had higher densities in particular given years (for example, 45.6 percent in 2002, 42.7 percent in 2003, and 38.7 percent in 2010).

Disaggregating protests with socioeconomic claims, subgroup B consists of protests with claims related to access to better public services (similar to

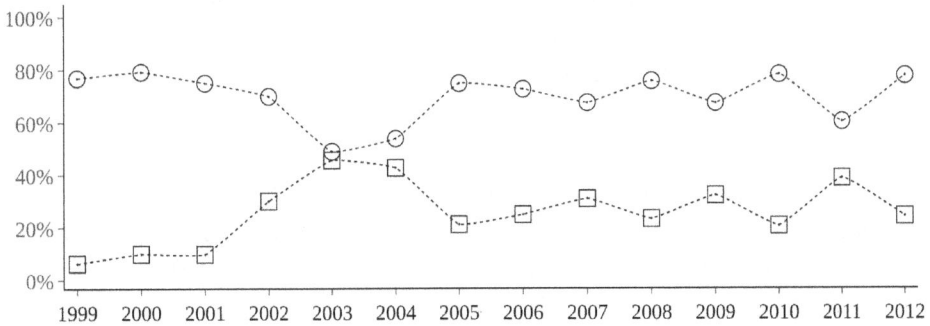

Figure 6.6. Protest Claims, 1999–2012. The figure does not include the Other category due to missing data. PROVEA, annual reports.

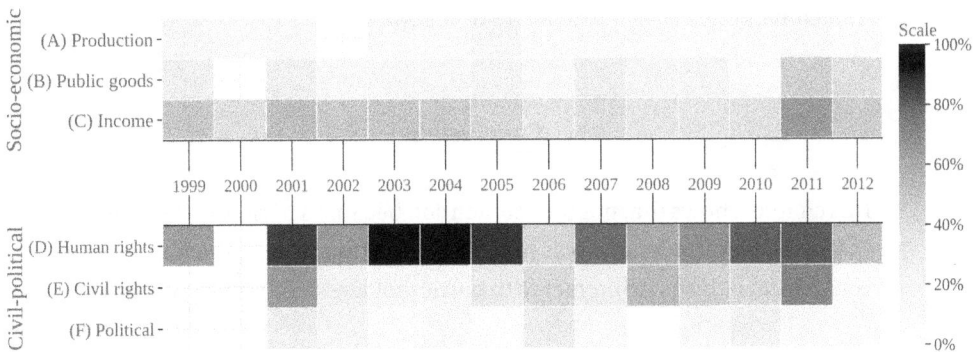

Figure 6.7. Subgroups of Protest Claims, 1999–2012. Years with the cross show missing data. PROVEA, annual reports.

subgroup B from the BDEBP dataset). This subgroup also mobilized societal actors. PROVEA describes the protests over improvements of water and
electricity services as taking place because of "poor services." Requests for
housing and better provision of health care also gained momentum late in
the Chávez era, and these claims persisted in crescendo during the government of Nicolás Maduro. Subgroup C, in turn, includes reactive protests
related to income conditions. (This is also comparable to subgroup C from
the BDEBP dataset.) Topics include calls for living wages and compliance
with collective agreements and disputes related to late payments of salaries
and retirement pensions. These protests were fairly common during the
Chávez era (see figure 6.7).

Turning to civil-political claims, subgroup A incorporates human rights
claims and subgroup B includes civil rights petitions. (Both subgroups are
comparable to the BDEBP dataset.) As figure 6.7 shows, protests with
human rights claims continued to be prevalent, followed by claims with
civil rights petitions. Among the latter, protests demanding free speech and
freedom of assembly were common. Subgroup C aggregates claims that are
distinctively political (similar to subgroup C from the BDEBP dataset).
Here, following PROVEA, the protests demanding better security or justice
display darker frequencies. In addition, protests by prisoners and their
families deploring the inhumane conditions to which the former were subjected and claims regarding the precariousness of the penitentiary and
judicial systems are noteworthy. Prisoners and their relatives often
embrace extreme protest routines, such as hunger strikes and "blood
strikes" (*huelgas de sangre*),[14] which goes to show the weakness of their
individual rights and political standing. This subgroup also includes citizen protests over criminal impunity at a time when the country began to
stand out as one of the most violent in the world.

Conclusions

This chapter shows that popular contention became a permanent phenomenon in these decades and was part of the traditional mechanisms used by
Venezuelan citizens to interact with power-holders. The timeline presented

indicates that starting in 1989, the year of the Caracazo, street demonstrations began to increase steadily, as did their intensity. In particular years, more actors took to the streets to make their voices heard. Protest performances also became more confrontational and violent. Confrontational tactics tend to rise when conventional forms lose effectiveness. Although these tactics tend to be peaceful, they attract attention and produce discomfort, challenge, or fear. Confrontational disputes raised both socioeconomic and civic–political claims. Violent performances, in turn, gained momentum during periods of political polarization, and actors embraced these performances strategically to achieve their goals. Violence protest routines were particularly evident between chavismo and the opposition in the period 2001–2004, with violence on both sides. Violent protests, however, were not unique to chavismo; the appearance in the 1990s of hooded collective actors cataloged as "unknown" and sectors of the student movement also produced high frequencies of violent protests. Many of these protests were initially peaceful but became violent because of heavy-handed police repression.

With few exceptions, reactive protests with socioeconomic claims are the ones that year after year move most Venezuelans to gather in public spaces to raise their complaints against the state. Labor complaints (e.g., demands for better working conditions and respect of labor rights) initially occupied most of the socioeconomic claims; however, as years progressed, requests for adequate public services (e.g., education, health, water, and electricity) also surfaced. This finding reveals the sustained deterioration of personal incomes and public services. Venezuelan citizens were ultimately experiencing a decline in access to these human rights.

Civic–political protests demanding respect for human dignity and human rights gained substantial visibility in this period. Similarly, demonstrations against social violence (e.g., repression, police aggression, break-ins) and those promoting the defense of life revealed deficits of human rights in the Venezuelan state. These protests were constant before and during the Chávez era. There were some years with peaks of protests with claims that were distinctively political. Before the Chavista era, actors took to the streets to press for political reforms and to support the failed coups of 1992 and also at the end of the Caldera government as the 1999 presidential elections became increasingly polarized. During the Chávez era, reactive protests over the defense of civil and political rights, as well as those denouncing the absence of freedom of speech and assembly, became prominent.

Politics in the streets sheds light on the relationship between the state and society in Venezuela. For one thing, it shows the precariousness of institutional channels to attend to citizens' demands for essential public services. Because government agencies are not effective in resolving conflicts or channeling social demands, as when collective contracts are neglected, water access is limited, or retirement pensions are paid late, actors such as unions, citizens, or retired workers will occupy public spaces time after time. They will engage in confrontational strategies such as road blockades to draw attention and thus secure a response from the government. Road blockades became a frequent protest performance in the 1980s and were especially common among retiree associations and neighborhood organizations. The rise to power of political elites representing chavismo did not improve the precariousness of institutional channels of communication. These actually worsened during the Chávez era and increased the presence of actors that traditionally did not embrace popular contention, such as the business sector and middle-class organizations. The target of these demonstrations was not the private sector. Instead, they targeted massively the public sector, which in the Venezuelan case is the most important employer, owner, and regulator of the provision of basic services—even in current times.

Chávez's death closed an era of political changes that began with his arrival in office in 1999. His successor, Nicolás Maduro, who remains in power at this writing, lacks Chávez's charismatic skills as well the high oil prices that Chávez had in previous years. Thus, Maduro inherited a weak government to sustain the legitimacy of the socialist economic model that Chávez sought to promote during his second government. In this context, starting in 2013 Maduro resorted to a mixed strategy to exercise social control. On the one hand, the regime pursued iron fist strategies to coerce and repress opposition groups; on the other, it advanced clientelistic and paternalistic relationships to keep the Chavista support base. He has not been able to advance Chávez's socialist model, producing a very complex humanitarian crisis. The authoritarian tendencies of Maduro have also immersed the country in an acute political crisis, which at this writing has no way out.

In this challenging context, politics in the streets continues, but it also faces various constraints. Repressive policing has been scaled up not only by different state security bodies, but also armed civilian groups—paramilitaries—and criminal organizations, sometimes acting in coordination with official security bodies. Maduro's government faced two protest cycles in 2014 and 2017, both of which ended in bloodshed. By 2021, Venezuela held about three hundred political prisoners and maintained a rigorous policy of criminalization and harassment toward civil society organizations (López Maya 2020). Furthermore, the COVID-19 pandemic deepened the regime's militaristic and repressive tendencies. This context has fragmented and weakened opposition political forces and contributes to a declining pattern of collective action, which could be a temporary trend. As long as the Venezuelan population faces numerous deficiencies in public goods provision and constant violations of their human rights, whether civil, political, social, economic, or cultural, the streets will remain the mechanism to reach power holders and push for social changes to advance inclusion, justice, and freedom.

Notes

1. For a historic perspective, see López Maya (2000). This chapter summarizes some of the data that are presented there.
2. This chapter draws on previous publications in journals and books, and these are cited to support the arguments of this chapter.
3. The El Bravo Pueblo Database (BDEBP) was the result of a research project of the Center for Development Studies (Centro de Estudios del Desarrollo, or CENDES) of the Central University of Venezuela. The coordinating researchers were Margarita López Maya and Luis E. Lander. The PROVEA dataset is a compilation of annual reports on human rights violations. These reports, in turn, are the result of efforts by joint civic organizations (e.g., Human Rights Center of the Catholic University Andres Bello [CDH-UCAB], the Venezuelan Observatory of Social Conflict [OVCS], and the Peace and Life Committee for human rights in the state of Barinas) to monitor protest control. These institutions have authorized PROVEA to

share much of their information to become critical inputs in elaborating human rights violation reports. PROVEA's annual reports, *Situación de los derechos humanos en Venezuela: informe anual*, are available online at provea.org/category/publicaciones/informes-anuales/.

4. For more information, see López Maya (2005).

5. Several works have explored the Venezuelan crisis. See, for instance, McCoy et al. (1995).

6. This information follows BDEBP in 2006 and PROVEA starting in 1989.

7. The BDEBP dataset classifies the intensity of protests based on three categories: Conventional: when protests are peaceful and do not arouse fear; Confrontational: while peaceful, they awaken fear among authorities, participants, or citizens, who may feel challenged by their novelty or aggressiveness; Violent: there is damage to property or physical integrity during the event; these protests are illegal.

8. The BDEBP dataset compiles the claim of a given protest and also provides a summary that contextualizes it. The information reported here comes from the BDEBP dataset as well as other reference sources.

9. In the BDEBP dataset, numbers do not necessarily round up to 100 percent because some mobilizations present multiple claims.

10. To describe this context, this section follows López Maya (2005).

11. OVCS reports are available from its website (www.observatoriodeconflictos.org.ve).

12. On average, 7.4 percent of popular contentions adopted a violent fashion in the period of study.

13. A protest cycle is understood as a period characterized by intense conflict and belligerence throughout the social system. It includes a rapid spread of collective action from more mobilized to less mobilized sectors; acceleration in the innovation of forms of belligerence; new or transformed frameworks for collective action; a combination of organized and disorganized participation; and intensive interaction sequences between challengers and authorities, which can lead to reform, repression, and sometimes revolution (Tarrow 2011). For the role of the student movement in the cycle of protests of 2007, see García Guadilla (2021).

14. Prisoners self-injure; they stitch their mouths to draw attention to their grievances.

PART II

A "MAGNIFYING GLASS" VIEW ON SPECIFIC PROTEST CAMPAIGNS

Local-Level Popular Protests in Central America at the Early Onset of Neoliberalism

PAUL ALMEIDA, LUIS RUBÉN GONZÁLEZ MÁRQUEZ,
AND MARÍA DE JESUS MORA

Introduction

The 2020–2021 nonviolent mass mobilizations of farmers in India, the 2019 austerity protests in Honduras, Iran, Iraq, Lebanon, Chile, South Africa, Haiti, France, Ecuador, and Colombia, and the upsurge in social movement activity throughout Latin America demonstrate that global economic processes (such as international food prices, debt/fiscal crisis of the state, mass unemployment, and public sector privatization policies) are associated with heightened levels of collective action and even regime change. At the same time, we know relatively little about how these "national revolts" against economic globalization vary at the local level within nations. This chapter explains the patterning of *subnational* opposition to economic liberalization—why some localities revolt while others remain demobilized.

Just as the South American nations of Argentina, Bolivia, Brazil, Chile,

Colombia, Ecuador, Paraguay, and Peru experienced massive demonstrations and protest activity in the first two decades of the twenty-first century, so too did the nations of Central America. The largest social movement campaigns have involved issues related to threats associated with economic globalization: economic liberalization, privatization, price increases, and regional free trade (Roberts 2008). In Costa Rica between 2003 and 2007, labor unions, universities, environmental groups, and nongovernmental organizations (NGOs) organized several mass street demonstrations and strikes in opposition to the Central American Free Trade Agreement (CAFTA). Some of the rallies reached up to one hundred and fifty thousand participants, making them the largest mobilizations in modern Costa Rican history (Raventós Vorst 2018). Similar large-scale actions erupted again over International Monetary Fund–advised reforms in 2018 and 2020 (Chase-Dunn and Almeida 2020 and Cordero 2022, respectively). In the October 2020 mobilizations, rural sectors in Costa Rica launched a disruptive campaign of roadblocks throughout the national territory against a new IMF loan program. In El Salvador in late 2002 and early 2003, doctors and health care workers joined in an alliance with NGOs to sustain a campaign against the privatization of the public hospital system. The campaign endured for nearly ten months and represented one of the largest campaigns against privatization in Latin America, with street demonstrations (the famous *marchas blancas*) mobilizing up to 3 percent of the entire Salvadoran population (Almeida 2008b).

Similar types of mass demonstrations have occurred in Guatemala, Honduras, Nicaragua, and Panama over the fifteen years before this chapter was written. In 2018, a mass movement against IMF-inspired social security reform in Nicaragua led to over two thousand protest events and three hundred deaths in the repressive response by the government (Cabrales Domínguez 2020; Cabrales Domínguez and Sánchez 2022). A year later, in 2019, Honduras erupted with large-scale national mobilizations against health care and education privatization (Sosa and Almeida 2019).

This chapter analyzes two early prototypical protest campaigns against threats from neoliberal globalization: the 1983 anti-IMF mobilizations against electricity price hikes in Costa Rica and the 1990 austerity package in Nicaragua. It offers a framework for understanding the conditions under which local communities in Central America mobilize against neoliberal forms of globalization. The combined processes of state-led development, democratization, economic threats, and building community and strategic capital are discussed to highlight the motivations and patterning of local resistance to threats from free market–oriented globalization. These conditions occurred early in Costa Rica and Nicaragua and provide exemplary cases whereby the structural antecedents stimulating collective action against neoliberalism replicate throughout the Global South in later decades.

Globalization and Democratization

Since the 1990s campaigns in the Global South against the threats associated with economic liberalization have led to major outbreaks of social unrest, including the toppling of governments via mass mobilization (Silva 2009; Goldstone 2011). As outlined in chapter 1, this trend of deepening globalization in the context of prolonged democratization is most pronounced in Latin America, creating the potential for reactive and proactive mobilizations. Moreover, oppositional political parties in democratic states have successfully converted the mass discontent and popular mobilizations against market reforms into electoral triumphs at the local and national levels of government (Macdonald and Ruckert 2009; Anria 2018). Yet even with dozens of journalistic and scholarly accounts of the major mobilizations, we know much less about the local variations in these social conflicts (Arce and Rice 2009; Mangonnet and Arce 2017; Barrie and Ketchley 2018; Leal 2020). In short, we examine how mobilizing agents build up these revolts from below at the local grassroots level into sustained national-level campaigns of opposition to globalization.

Increasingly, scholars recognize that analyzing how global processes impinge on local conditions within nation-states provides a promising new line of inquiry in the twenty-first century. Historical sociologists call for methodologies that allow for empirical studies of globalization penetrating down to the subnational level. For example, Saskia Sassen (2007, 4) contends,

"Conceiving of globalization not simply in terms of interdependence and global institutions but also as inhabiting the national opens up a vast and largely unaddressed research agenda." From this vantage point we can examine how globalization affects popular protest and social movement activity within nation-states, even down to the local level. Javier Auyero (2001) characterizes community-level battles over globalization as "glocal contention," whereby global economic conditions converge with local contexts to produce collective action unevenly across a national territory. Large-scale macroeconomic processes driving structural adjustment and social exclusion are interpreted at the community level by would-be collective actors as a "moral politics" (Auyero 2006). The study described here builds on the glocalization literature by demonstrating how the prolonged power of establishing state, administrative, and organizational infrastructures at the community level are used to resist unwanted changes brought about by deepening economic liberalization. When communities take advantage of democratization and benefit from state infrastructures and organizational assets in their localities, they can appropriate these structures and resources for a variety of mobilization tasks.

Protest campaigns in the Global South addressing threats from economic liberalization have erupted on the national political landscape from dozens of local actions at the community level combined with mass actions in capital cities. Localities vary in terms of the structural and organizational capital available to challengers and civic associations. Indeed, Edwards and McCarthy (2004) state in their review of the mobilizing structures literature that resources needed for collective action are unevenly distributed within national territories. A subnational perspective highlights key state, community, and strategic assets that are deposited across administrative subdivisions. These campaigns are more likely to be especially potent and sustained when coalitions emerge across civil society and the national territory and replicate at the local level.

Some of the most crucial elements determining the emergence of local resistance to threats from neoliberalism include structures left over from the development state and organizations operating at the community level. State structures include highways, administrative offices, and the expansion of public education and the public sector during the period of state-led development (Almeida, 2015, 2016). These structures create a situation whereby the earlier form of economic development (state-centered) faces off with the new form (neoliberalism). Highways provide strategic locations to apply pressure on the state. Most commonly, this takes the form of a roadblock or barricade by collective actors. In the case of Latin America, the most important highway running through the region is the Pan-American Highway, completed in 1963 at the height of state-led development. A strategic blockade there would prevent the transport of goods domestically and throughout Central America. The expansion of the public sector and the educational system also made collective action much easier to accomplish in dozens of localities across the national territory.

In the neoliberal era, community-based organizations and local chapters of left-oriented political parties have acted as some of the main place-based collectivities capable of launching a protest campaign. Some organizations are NGOs; others were created by the state in the previous development period and survived into the epoch of free-market reforms (Wada 2014). As neoliberal reforms weakened the social and associational power of traditional organizations such as peasant cooperatives and labor unions, oppositional political parties provided some of the only mass base for popular mobilization in a wide range of localities (Morris 1984). Under democratic conditions, oppositional parties have an interest in increasing voter turnout in the next election cycle. One pathway involves taking on a popular cause such as dissatisfaction with a particular neoliberal policy. Parties can begin with their militant affiliates and reach out to sympathizers in protest campaigns (Almeida 2010b). When opposition parties have some representation in local government, they also enjoy legitimacy to call nearby populations to participate in collective action.

In summary, we expect the local-level patterning of opposition to neoliberal reforms to be largely driven by state structures established in the state-led development era and community-level organizations active in the current period of economic globalization, especially local chapters of left-oriented parties. These are largely defensive struggles reacting to potential losses in economic and social benefits from the previous period of state intervention. We examine these propositions with more historical evidence below using the cases of Costa Rica and Nicaragua.

Popular Politics in Costa Rica and Nicaragua

Both Costa Rica and Nicaragua adjusted to the early globalization period in the 1980s and 1990s (see chapter 1). Even though the social sectors from state-led development, such as labor unions, the public sector, agrarian reform beneficiaries, and the educational sector, served as the main sources of organized opposition to specific neoliberal measures, they were also greatly weakened over time as global integration advanced. The social sectors benefiting from the process of intensified globalization tended to be those domestic groups tied to transnational capital and the new economic activities then emerging in the Caribbean Basin (Robinson 2003). In particular, the families and business groups that gained the most from globalization are tied to banking (especially with the upswing in remittances), nontraditional agribusiness and export crops (e.g., winter greens, pineapple, palm oil), export-processing zones of textiles and light assembly (*las maquiladoras*), and tourism (Robinson 2003; Chomsky 2021). Nonetheless, the oppositional coalitions born under state-led development attempted to slow down this process of accelerated globalization as well as find more equitable ways to distribute the material gains under the new economic model and under the rules of democratic politics using nonviolent mass mobilization as a central strategy.

COSTA RICA

Costa Rica entered into a debt crisis and democratized before most nations in Latin America (see chapter 1). Because of these early experiences with neoliberalism and democracy, Costa Rican mobilization offers an emblematic model of the forms and protagonists of collective action observed in subsequent decades throughout the Global South. The 1983 protests against IMF-imposed electricity price hikes represent one of the largest outbreaks of mass contention in modern Costa Rica (Alvarenga Venutolo 2005; Mora Solano 2011).

In our analysis, we give special attention to the organizations that make up the Dirección Nacional de Desarrollo de la Comunidad (DINADECO). DINADECO was established in 1967 as a state-led development attempt to organize community self-help associations throughout the national territory. It serves as a prime example of a state-created organization that can be also used for a variety of collective action purposes. The issue that began to organize multiple sectors (including community associations) by the end of the 1970s was the high cost of living. By 1980, there were over one thousand DINADECO community associations distributed across Costa Rica's eighty cantones as leftist militants attempted to unite them in a single confederation.

After marginal election results in 1970 and 1974, three leftist parties—the Partido Socialista, the Movimiento Revolucionario del Pueblo (MRP), and El Partido Vanguardia Popular (PVP)—decided to come together as a single leftist coalition called Pueblo Unido to compete in the 1978 elections. Pueblo Unido drew its base of support from popular movements and civil society associations, especially the university community, public sector workers, skilled workers, and the agricultural proletariat on the Caribbean and southern Pacific coasts, especially those on banana plantations. Upon taking representative seats in parliament and in their local governments in the late 1970s, the leftist parties increasingly engaged in issues that supported popular causes, such as price controls and infrastructure development in local communities.

A financial crisis deepened between 1978 and 1981. This led to several threat-induced mobilization campaigns, with mass marches against the high cost of living and transportation prices. The marches addressing the global financial crisis and its local effects on Costa Rica were the largest mobilizations in the late 1970s and early 1980s. In addition, the labor movement began holding major strikes in the public sector. The May Day marches also grew in size throughout the late 1970s; there, workers organized against price hikes and called for a single confederation uniting the country's labor unions. In mid-1980, left-leaning labor unions finally achieved the formation of the Confederación Unitaria de Trabajadores (CUT). The CUT held two one-day general strikes in 1981 against the high cost of living, with the highest participation rates in localities with labor associations affiliated with the confederation. The general strikes against austerity served to support Pueblo Unido in the 1982 elections, whereby the coalition won four national legislative representatives and twenty-two *regidores* to serve on municipal councils. This set the stage for Costa Rica's first major national mobilization against globalization—the 1983 popular campaign against IMF-imposed electricity price hikes. This represented the largest sustained mass action at the national level in the early 1980s.[1]

The International Monetary Fund had negotiated a price escalation on consumer electricity rates with the indebted Costa Rican government in November of 1982 as part of a letter of intent. As one of the first developing countries to default on its external debt (in July of 1981), Costa Rica was forced by the IMF to cut back on its subsidies for electricity consumption in order to secure future lines of credit and to reduce domestic budget deficits. By April and May of 1983, community-level committees sprang up to resist the rate increase, many emerging from preexisting DINADECO organizations with a leftist leadership from Pueblo Unido–affiliated political parties, especially the PVP (Alvarenga Venutolo 2005). For example, in February locally elected council representatives from Pueblo Unido began forming a committee with other popular organizations in Montes de Oca and nearby districts to protest the increasing prices.[2]

May Day demonstrations around the country in 1983 included an end to electricity price hikes as a central demand. Throughout the month of May demonstrations against escalating electricity bills erupted in working-class districts in San José and its surroundings, including Hatillo, Desamparados, Guadalupe, San Pedro, Tíbas, Alajuelita, and other, more distant towns such as Turrialba and Alajuela. On May 7 alone, a reported fifteen public gatherings against the price increases occurred in San José. The bulk of these demonstrations were by average citizens organized in community associations, but they also included known leftist leaders within the PVP and the CUT. In mid-May, five major women's associations issued a public statement denouncing the electricity price increases. By early June, local-level protests began surfacing in districts around the country, well beyond the capital. Community groups employed the novel tactic of the roadblock, which had proven to be successful just months before with small farmer groups (UPANACIONAL) demanding the renewal of subsidies for agricultural inputs (Edelman 1999). Even parliamentary and city council representatives of Pueblo Unido joined the protesters at the barricades—a clear sign of social movement–local political party alliances that characterized Costa

Rica in the late 1970s and early 1980s. The roadblock would become the favored tactic of multiple groups resisting neoliberal forms of capitalism throughout Central and South America in the twenty-first century (Silva 2009), including the *Gasolinazo* in Mexico in early 2017 and a protest by MAS party militants and indigenous communities in Bolivia in 2020.

At the peak of the movement, in the second week of June in 1983, Costa Rican citizens erected a reported thirty-six roadblocks around the country.[3] The government finally conceded to the community movement's demands to reduce electricity prices back to their December 1982 levels after days of barricades and street protests across the national territory. On June 9, leaders and legislative representatives of Pueblo Unido organized a street march to the National Assembly, where they celebrated the victorious outcome.[4] The tactic of the roadblock would be recommended by activists as strategic almost a generation later in the campaign against the privatization of telecommunications and electricity.

NICARAGUA

Nicaragua also transitioned to a neoliberal regime in early 1990 after the electoral defeat of the Sandinista party. The Sandinistas had been in power since the 1979 revolution that overthrew the dynastic dictatorship of the Somoza family. The Sandinista government enacted a series of social reforms that included land redistribution, mass-literacy campaigns, and substantial increases in health care access (Robinson 1996). Moreover, in spite of limitations—and internal tensions—under civil-war conditions, it also promoted an increase of organizational structures in civil society and improvement in the conditions for pluralist political competition without precedent in the history of the country. (See chapter 1 for the uptick in Nicaragua's Democracy Index following the 1984 elections.) This Third World revolutionary experiment culminated with a peaceful transition of power in the Executive branch from the Sandinistas to the opposition coalition, Unión Nacional Opositora (UNO). As a result, Violeta Chamorro became the new president of Nicaragua in 1990. This also permitted the demobilization and reincorporation of the counterrevolutionary army, the Contras (Torres-Rivas 2011).

Immediately upon taking power, the newly elected Chamorro government implemented severe austerity and privatization measures. The
decrees acted as a direct threat to the many social and economic gains of
the Sandinista Revolution. These included the annulment of the Civil Service Law, layoffs in public institutions, a monetary reform to reduce protec-
tions on consumer-goods prices, changes in the composition of judicial
power, and privatization of land redistributed to poor rural producers in
the 1980s (Decrees 10-90 and 11-90).[5]

Sandinista-based organizations responded quickly to the economic
threats with a series of strikes, barricades, roadblocks, and land occupations. The vanguard organizations included the National Workers Front
(FNT) (with many public sector unions), the Association of Rural Workers
(ATC), the Association of University Students (UNEN), the schoolteachers'
union (ANDEN), and a communal movement in popular neighborhoods
(*Movimiento Comunal*). Moreover, the Sandinista Central of Workers
(CST) became a central node among the different organizations and actors
participating in the protest campaign.[6] All of these popular organizations
had been created in the early years of the Sandinista Revolution. They represented a late attempt to promote popular democracy under state-led
development in the 1980s as the grassroots bases of the revolution. After
the Sandinista electoral defeat in 1990, these organizations immediately
converted into the main organized opposition to neoliberalism.

The social movement response in civil society centered on a series of
antiausterity protest events constituting the larger campaign, largely
between May and July of 1990. The mobilizations until early June centered
on a general strike and public workers' demands. By contrast, those at the
end of June and in July encompassed another general strike by public workers; an explosion of barricades throughout urban centers; land seizures and
work stoppages in rural areas; and occupation of workspaces, public enterprises (including transportation), universities, and radio stations. Besides
the organizations and actors, Nicaraguan popular organizations were
adapting and renovating their preexisting repertoires from the revolutionary and prerevolutionary insurrections (Torres-Rivas 2011; Guevara 2008)
for use in antineoliberal protest campaigns under democratization.

The peak moment of the protest campaign occurred in the second week of July. Newspaper reports estimated the number of workers complying with the strike as between 85,000 and 120,000.[7] By that time, the general strike had paralyzed the main government offices, the National Assembly, the major customs offices, and the national airport (Martí i Puig 1997). Rural workers had occupied farms and seized lands, mainly in the western regions (Chinandega, Leon, Estelí, Los Chontales, and Jinotega), which pushed back the start of the cotton cultivation season.[8] Street demonstrations had erupted in most of the major urban centers on the Pacific slope, the most densely populated section of the country (as demonstrated in map 7.2), from the *municipio* of Somoto (bordering Honduras) to Rivas (bordering Costa Rica). On July 9, the Movimiento Comunal mobilized "hundreds of thousands of capital city residents" to install "hundreds of barricades and ditches ... in almost all neighborhoods and streets of Managua."[9] During this culminating mass mobilization, the protest participants reportedly sang the Nicaraguan national anthem and one of the most popular protest songs in Latin America at the end of the state-led development era— "Venceremos" ("We Will Win").[10]

Methods

As Tarrow (2011, 191) states, "a campaign is a sustained, organized public effort making collective claims on targeted authorities." In our cases, both countries (Costa Rica and Nicaragua) experienced specific campaigns bounded in time and unified under the objective of preventing specific economic policies perceived as harmful to the popular sectors. The dependent variable is the count of protests at the local level. The unit of analysis is the municipality (*cantones* in Costa Rica and *municipios* in Nicaragua). Protest events were defined as three or more people engaging in social movement activities (e.g., street march, barricade, roadblock, rally, labor strike) connected to the larger campaigns against neoliberal measures. For such studies in collective action research, protest event analysis (PEA) was employed, using primarily newspapers (Wada 2004; Hutter 2014; Almeida 2019). In geographical and cross-sectional research of protest occurrence and distribution, scholars find it critical to document each protest event or the entire population of reported events. Using multiple sources is the best means to achieve this. For both campaigns, an original dataset was assembled and coded to the municipal level on community collective action using local newspapers and archival sources.

For the 1983 campaign in Costa Rica against consumer energy price increases, four hard-copy national newspapers were coded by protest event and geographical location for the entire period of the campaign (April to June 1983). The papers included *Prensa Libre, La Nación, La República*, and *Libertad*. We also coded documents and chronologies from the journal *Aportes*, Alvarenga Venutolo's (2005) study of Costa Rican citizen movements, and a chronology of social movements compiled by the Institute of Social Research (IIS) at the University of Costa Rica. For Nicaragua, we reviewed and coded austerity events from between May and October of 1990. Our data sources for Nicaraguan protest events included the country's three major newspapers, *La Prensa, Barricada*, and *El Nuevo Diario*. For Costa Rica, our PEA analysis yielded 122 protest events and in Nicaragua 642 distinct collective actions.

To examine subnational variation in the occurrence of threat-oriented protests in two countries, we employed multivariate count regression models of local antiausterity protests (measured as the total count of protests in a municipality) in both Costa Rica and Nicaragua. Independent variables represent measures of state-led development, community-level organizations, and structural controls. For the state infrastructure of highways variable, we use a dichotomous measure if the locality is intersected by one of the country's major transportation routes (coded as 0 for not intersected by a highway and 1 otherwise). Count regression models are appropriate when the dependent variable is a nonnegative integer (in this case, the count of municipal-level protest events). If linear regression models are used to analyze count data, it would likely lead to biased estimates. In both countries, the negative binomial regression models were chosen over standard Poisson regression models based on tests for overdispersion of the distribution of the count. (Overdispersion occurs if the variance of the count is larger than the mean.) The alpha values for all count models in both countries (which represent the actual amount of dispersion in the count-dependent variable) are significantly different from zero, indicating that the negative binomial count regression models are the more appropriate estimation procedure. Standard errors are estimated using Clustered Robust Standard Errors (CRSEs), with municipalities clustered by departments/provinces. Negative binomial regression coefficients of theoretical interest are interpreted using predicted probability measures of the count of protest events.

Empirical Results

COSTA RICA

Map 7.1 and table 7.1 present systematic empirical evidence on the correlates of those localities that resisted the 1983 IMF reforms in Costa Rica. Map 7.1 shows the geographical variation in local opposition. The map highlights the distributions of the DINADECO organizations, representation of leftist oppositional parties in local government, highways, and the association of protest events with the campaign. Data on protest events came from the coding of four national newspapers and chronological reports on the protest campaign discussed above. Thirty-six out of 81 (44.4 percent) Costa Rican municipalities (cantones) had at least one protest event against the IMF reforms.

Table 7.1 presents the results of two negative binomial regression models. One incorporates the impact of local leftist officials and the other the impact of local-level electoral support for leftist parties. In terms of state infrastructure and administrative offices, municipalities that serve as the provincial capital city experienced a higher rate of protest. In terms of community organizations, the number of DINADECO community organizations increased the rate of collectively resisting the IMF measures. Indeed, the anti–price hike movement first formed out of preexisting community development organizations where local *comités de lucha* were established. Figure 7.1 demonstrates that once a municipality reaches a threshold of twenty DINADECO organizations, one protest event is expected.

Table 7.1 also demonstrates that municipalities participating in the protest campaign tended to support left-wing oppositional political parties (the Pueblo Unido Coalition discussed above) more than nonparticipating

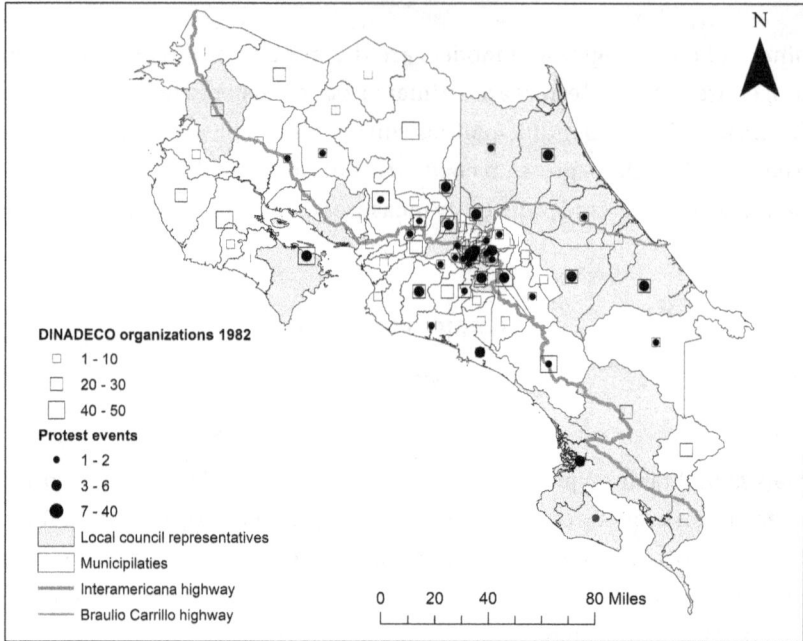

Map 7.1. 1983 Resistance to IMF Imposed Electricity Price Hikes in Costa Rica.

Table 7.1. Negative Binomial Regression Models of Municipalities in Costa Rica's May–June 1983 Anti-IMF Electricity Protests

INDEPENDENT VARIABLES	MODEL 1	MODEL 2
Administrative Infrastructure (Provincial Capital)	.489** (.194)	.799* (.190)
Transportation Infrastructure (Highway in Municipality)	−.285 (.309)	−.568 (.426)
Public University	.322 (.538)	.330 (.463)
Population Density	.0003*** (.000)	.0004*** (.000)
DINADECO	.034* (.017)	.047** (.017)
Local Pueblo Unido Council Members	.987*** (.196)	—
% Vote for Pueblo Unido in Legislature	—	.105*** (.021)
Log Likelihood	−104.678	−104.560
Pseudo R²	.18	.18
N	81	81

*p < .05 **p < .01 ***p < .001

Note: Clustered robust standard errors are in parentheses

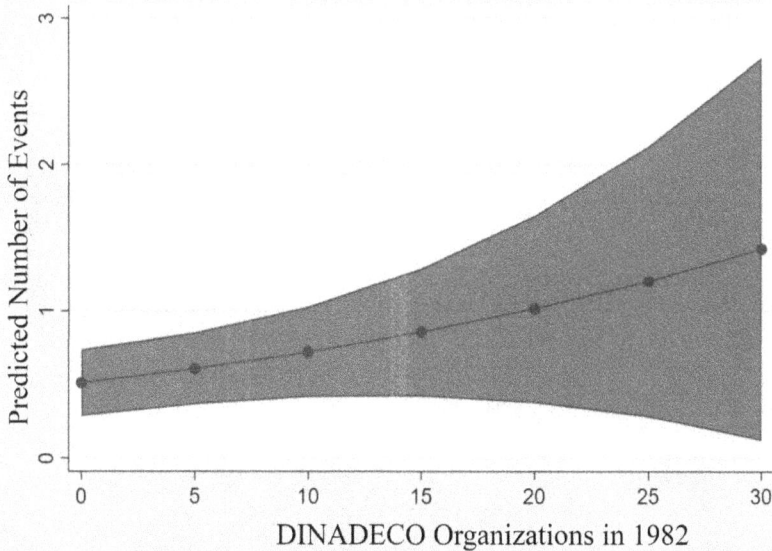

Figure 7.1. Predicted Count of Protest Events in Costa Rica Campaign by Number of DINADECO Organizations. Adjusted predictions with 95 percent confidence intervals.

communities. Those cantones with a member of Pueblo Unido on the local governing council (regidor) showed greater levels of resistance. As figure 7.2 illustrates, having a local leftist representative increases the predicted number of protest events to nearly two, and two local elected officials more than double the number of predicted protest events against IMF reforms in Costa Rica. Similar results are found in table 7.1 (Model 2) for the percentage votes for the leftist party for parliament. Receiving just 10 percent of the vote increases the likelihood of one protest event, and 15 percent of the vote for the leftist Pueblo Unido Party doubles the predicted rate of protest to two events. This is consistent with a "social movement partyism" perspective whereby in the late twentieth and early twenty-first centuries oppositional political parties played a major role in protest campaigns against globalization (Mangonnet and Arce 2017; Almeida et al. 2021).

Costa Rica legalized leftist parties before other developing countries with its early efforts at democratization. In the 1983 campaign against IMF

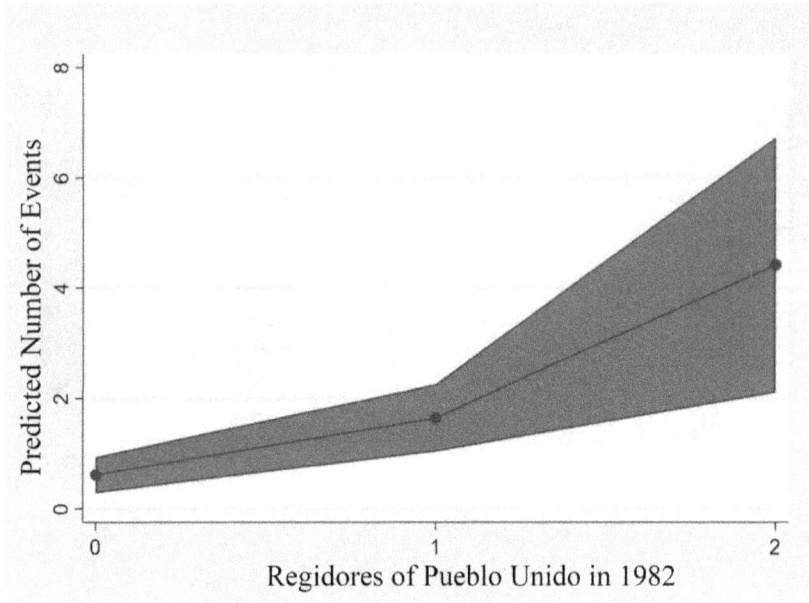

Figure 7.2. Predicted Probability of Local Left Party Officials on Protest Events. Adjusted predictions with 95 percent confidence intervals.

price hikes, socialist and communist parties, labor, and community organizers played a pivotal role in coordinating the protests in the jurisdictions under their influence.[11] This included participation by local leftist politicians in the actual roadblocks. From the indigenous mobilizations against agricultural reforms to the major austerity battles in South America in the late 2010s, scholars are increasingly recognizing the crucial role of oppositional political parties in providing a nationally coordinated mechanism to sustain collective action in the neoliberal era. Traditional large organizations such as trade unions and peasant associations have weakened over the past four decades with the debt crisis, and political parties partially fill the void. Finally, active districts in the collective action campaign were much more densely populated than lower and nonparticipating communities. Other scholars have viewed urban density as a proxy for urban labor unions and other mobilizing infrastructures, making protest much more likely in "over-urbanized" regions (Walton and Seddon 1994, 44).

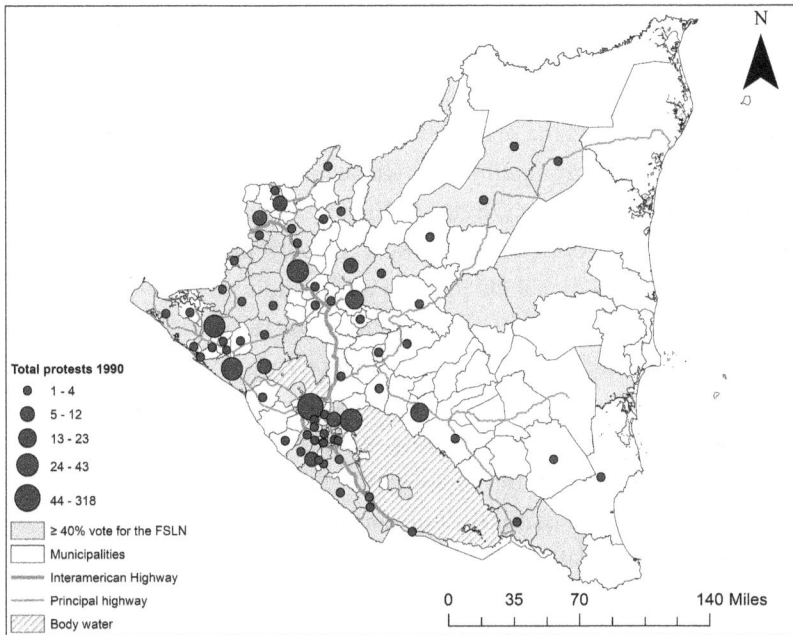

Map 7.2 1990 Austerity and Privatization Protests in Nicaragua.

NICARAGUA

As in Costa Rica, the popular resistance in Nicaragua relied heavily on the state infrastructure and community-level organizations, such as leftist parties. Map 7.2 shows the distribution of the antiausterity protest events, along with major highways and the distribution of electoral support. Slightly over half (51.4 percent) of Nicaragua's 144 municipalities reported a protest event, and 642 protest events were observed in total.

Table 7.2 reports the results of negative binomial count regression models predicting antiausterity protests at the municipal level. As in Costa Rica, the impact of leftist political parties is analyzed in two separate models. Provincial capitals again experienced a higher incidence of antiausterity contention. In contrast with Costa Rica, having a Sandinista in local power (as a mayor) did not have an impact on the rate of protest. In addition, models 1 and 2 find that highways maintain a significant positive influence on the rate of protest. Where a major highway runs through a municipality, the probability of protest increases from .58 to 1.8 (see figure 7.3). Hence state infrastructures of provincial capitals and major transportation corridors that expanded during the period of state-led development enabled collective protest in the early neoliberal era in Nicaragua.

Model 2 in table 7.2 analyzes the influence of local party strength on the rate of antiausterity protest. Increases in the percentage of the vote for the FSLN (Sandinista National Liberation Front) candidate for president in the February 1990 elections had a positive impact on the count of antiausterity events. Figure 7.4 shows the increase of preference for the leftist party on the expected count of antineoliberal protest. As the percentage of votes reaches 50 percent or higher in a municipality, an antiausterity collective action is more likely to take place. By late 1990, the Chamorro government entered negotiations with the Sandinista unions and pulled back from the most extreme austerity measures, including mass layoffs and salary decreases.

Table 7.2. Negative Binomial Regression Models Predicting Protests 1990 in Nicaragua

INDEPENDENT VARIABLES	MODEL 1	MODEL 2
Administrative Infrastructure (Provincial Capital)	2.12*** (.314)	2.08*** (.342)
Transportation Infrastructure (Highway in Municipality)	1.14*** (.175)	1.15*** (.191)
University 1990	.578 (.396)	.559 (.406)
Population Density	.004*** (.001)	.004*** (.001)
FSLN Mayor 1990	.261 (.216)	—
% Vote FSLN President	—	.024** (.009)
LR X²	780.41***	971.51***
Log Likelihood	−198.781	−196.078
Pseudo R²	0.27	.28
N	144	144

*p < .05 **p < .01 ***p < .001

Note: Clustered robust standard errors are in parentheses

Figure 7.3. Predicted Probability of Highway Penetration on Protest Events.

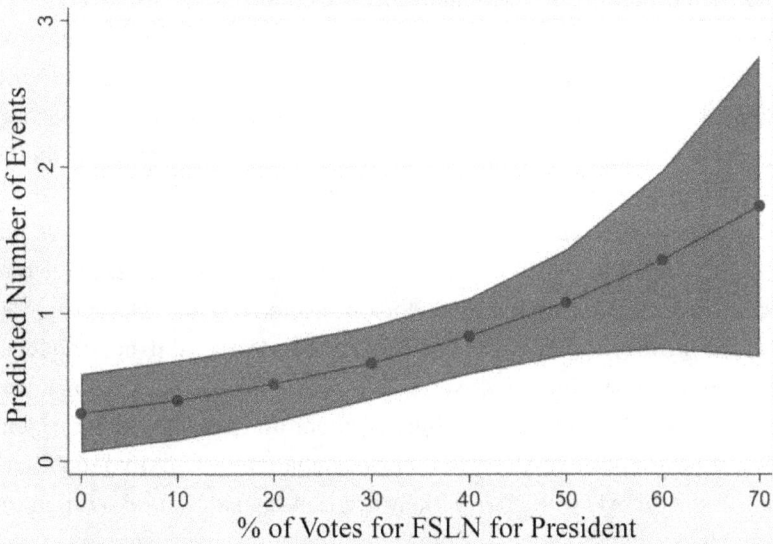

Figure 7.4. Predicted Probability of the Percentage Vote for FSLN President on
Anti-Austerity Protest. Adjusted predictions with 95 percent confidence intervals.

The close-knit alliance between antineoliberal protests and the leftist party appeared during the celebration of what was considered a major triumph of the mobilization campaigns. This context also expressed the adaptations of the party and the movements to the new neoliberal juncture. The end date of the major mobilizations occurred close to the anniversary of the Sandinista Revolution, on July 19th. On that occasion, in addition to party leaders, some of the main speakers were labor movement leaders of the recently concluded protest campaigns. The tone of the celebration—in spite of the revolutionary rhetoric—was of overall satisfaction because of the lack of a generalized violent escalation,[12] the establishment of channels of social dialogue with the Chamorro government, and the role of the National Army (loyal to the government yet nonrepressive toward protesters). The resolution signaled that opposition to neoliberalism would come from the streets in alliance with leftist parties in the legislature.[13]

In terms of differences, the two countries diverge slightly on the question of highways and oppositional parties in producing collective action. In Costa Rica, there was no statistically significant relationship between a locality with highways and the count of protest. Even though roadblocks were used widely in both campaigns in both countries as part of a core repertoire of contention, many of the events in Costa Rica occurred in working-class cantones just outside the capital city and in rural regions (with strong labor unions) that are not transected by a major highway. In Nicaragua, labor activists erected dozens of barricades in the largest cities on the major highways crossing through their localities.

In Nicaragua, having locally elected leftist party representation did not result in heightened levels of protest. In Costa Rica, it did increase the rate of collective action. In some cases, locally elected city council representatives from the leftist Pueblo Unido party coalition established the local committee of resistance against the IMF price hikes. In Nicaragua, it was less locally elected officials pushing resistance and more the historic identification with the FSLN party that moved subaltern groups into mobilization. That support for the party likely originated in affiliation with one of the mass organizations such as the communal movement, women's movement, rural worker associations, youth movement, or urban labor unions.

Those regions with greater electoral support for the FSLN showed more resistance to the new austerity measures as beneficiaries of the revolution perceived the erosion of hard-fought economic gains and social rights under the new austerity regime.

Conclusions

The "neoliberal battles" in Costa Rica and Nicaragua provide powerful lessons and trends shown in other struggles decades later. Perceived threatening conditions generated by international financial institutions sparked the largest mobilizations in these Central American countries, as in other Latin American states (similar to how Arce and Wada characterize reactive or defensive protests in chapter 1). The antineoliberal campaigns were sustained by oppositional political parties, social organizations, and structures established during the state-led development era. The role of oppositional political parties in supporting mobilization efforts is especially noteworthy. In chapter 1, emphasis was placed on the convergence of traditional left- and right-wing parties both pushing for neoliberalism. In our cases, left-wing parties mobilized social movement activities in resistance to the market model.

Costa Rica and Nicaragua offer a template for mass opposition to neoliberalism in the Global South under deepening neoliberalism. Early democratization combined with different transnational economic threats (the foreign debt crisis and structural adjustment) produced major campaigns of popular resistance. Costa Rican and Nicaraguan activists drew on oppositional political parties, the labor movement, students, and the public sector to defend themselves from unfavorable economic changes. Local opposition emerged in localities with a well-established state and community infrastructure. As chapter 1 outlines, these types of struggles against the market model tend to proliferate as other states democratize and face similar threatening economic conditions with the homogeneous nature of global economic integration and change, as vividly witnessed in 2019 and the early 2020s in Latin America.

Notes

1. Several mobilizations by small farmers linked to economic liberalization also took place in the early 1980s. These protests were largely contained in the agricultural sector alone (Edelman 1999).
2. "Constituyen comité contra costa de vida en Montes de Oca," *La Libertad*, February 3, 1983.
3. See "Bajarán las tarifas eléctricas," *La Nación*, June 10, 1983, 4a.
4. See "Gobierno revisará actitud ante problemas nacionales," *La Prensa Libre*, June 10, 1983.
5. As extra grievances: the intended new landowners were producers formerly identified with the Somoza dictatorship and the extinct national guard, and the Contras had not yet completed their military demobilization. *Barricada: Órgano oficial del Frente Sandinista de Liberación Nacional*, July 6, 1990, 6.
6. *Barricada*, May 1 and July 25, 1990, 6.
7. *Barricada*, July 10, 1990, 4.
8. *Barricada*, July 10, 1990, 4.
9. *Barricada*, July 10, 1990, 7.
10. This is similar to how protesters in Chile made Victor Jara's "El Derecho de Vivir en Paz" the unofficial anthem during the massive October 2019 campaign against transportation price hikes and other economic grievances. Once again, citizens resurrected the symbols of struggles from state-led development in the early 1970s to resist neoliberalism several decades later.
11. "Bloqueo eléctrico tiende a extenderse," *La Prensa Libre*, June 9, 1983.
12. The campaign did involve a few sporadic violent episodes that led to four deaths.
13. *Barricada*, July 20, 1990, 1, 12.

CHAPTER EIGHT

A Group-Based Approach to Analyze the Protest Landscape in Chile at the Height of Neoliberalism and Democracy

NICOLÁS M. SOMMA AND RODRIGO M. MEDEL

Introduction

This chapter explores Chile's protest landscape using a protest events data-set that covers the entire country between 2009 and 2019. We develop a group-based approach, which takes protest groups as the center of the analysis and examines how groups behave in terms of claims, tactics, targets, place of protests, and alliances. We use "groups" in a loose sense, closer to an abstract social category than to a clearly demarcated set of people with a common identity and social ties. Previous studies using protest event datasets show that the protest landscape is populated by diverse groups such as "workers," "students," and "environmentalists." This literature also reveals differences in different groups' protest behavior (Minkoff 1995, 1997; Wang and Soule 2012; Meyer and Minkoff 2004; Soule and King 2008). Protest groups cannot be automatically equated with social movements or social movement organizations (McCarthy and Zald 1977).

However, a group-based approach provides a clear link between the social movements literature and protest event dataset findings.

We show that students and workers are the two key groups protesting in contemporary Chile and argue that this is not causal. These two movements emerged as reactions to or by-products of the two main institutional developments in Chilean society in the last century—the development of capitalism and the nation-state. Thus, during the twentieth century, students and workers invested in organizational accumulation and territorial expansion that exceeded those of other movements. They have a distinctive feature that proved central for their endurance: "by default" meeting places and regular interaction sites for their members (e.g., schools and workplaces). Such contexts facilitated the creation of broad-scale organizational structures (Edwards and McCarthy 2004) that these groups activated for mobilization more easily than could other groups that had to build them from scratch.

However, market reforms since the 1970s and democratization since the 1990s have transformed these movements. On the one hand, market reforms quickly led to the reactivation of old grievances or "reactive movements" (Arce and Wada, introductory chapter of this book), where the student and labor movements mainly mobilized against economic liberalization reforms and economic threats. On the other hand, democratization and expanding political opportunities led to the emergence or reinvigoration of "proactive movements" that interacted with workers and students. The emergence of indigenous, environmental, and sexual diversity movements are good examples of these newcomers.

Globalization and Democratization

SOCIAL MOVEMENTS BEFORE MARKET REFORMS (1900–1973)

During the twentieth century, the combined expansion of capitalism and the state created the backbone of Chilean social movements: the labor and the student movements. We conceptualize these as "by-product movements" because they resulted from the expansion of Chilean society's main institutions: capitalist markets and the nation-state. These institutions unintentionally provided the motivations, resources, and opportunities for the organization of workers and students.

The Chilean labor movement gained traction in the late nineteenth and early twentieth centuries among mining workers in the north and urban workers in cities such as Santiago and Valparaíso, who organized themselves to improve their miserable living conditions. During these early decades, the expansion of capitalism, with its growing numbers of mines, factories, and workshops across the territory, created masses of workers who nurtured the movement. Popular urban riots and disorganized violence did not completely disappear, but they were gradually replaced by organized strikes and labor unions (Grez 2000). Governments did not welcome this and brutally repressed striking workers, killing hundreds of them, most famously during the Santa María de Iquique strike in 1907. The oligarchic system, dominated by the political and economic elites, did not want to incorporate workers into the political game. In a context of still very marginal popular electoral turnout, workers created their own parties: the Democrat Party (1887) and later on the Worker's Socialist Party (1921), which became the Communist Party in 1922 (Angell 1974).

From the 1930s onward, the state's growth produced masses of public workers, which strengthened the labor movement. After the 1929 crisis, the new import-substitution model encouraged the state to expand its activities through schools, bureaucratic agencies, and state-sponsored industrial projects. All of this happened amid rapid urbanization and the growth of urban middle classes. Thus, during the 1940s, many unions were established grouping public employees, teachers, and workers from particular fields, such as the leather and shoe industry. In 1953 such a group founded the CUT (Unitary Workers' Central). Labor unions became political players with strikes and votes as their weapons. They approached leftist and centrist parties but were not co-opted by them and kept their disruptive power—as the massive 1955 CUT-organized strike showed. Thus, Chile did not develop populist multiclass movements like those that appeared in Argentina under Peronism (Collier and Collier 1991).

By the 1960s, the labor movement had become an important political player. It continued growing horizontally—i.e., expanding to new sectors of the economy—thanks to the creation of peasant unions by the Christian Democrat government in power since 1962 (Affonso et al. 1970). The number of unionized workers doubled between 1965 and 1970, as did the number of voters between 1958 and 1970, giving workers more power both in strikes and at the ballot box. The movement also strengthened vertically: it allied with the leftist Communist and Socialist Parties and the centrist Radical and Christian Democrat Parties. Yet this momentum led to internal divisions between communist and socialist worker leaders with different orientations in the reform–revolution continuum. The Popular Unity (UP) government (1970–1973) marked the peak in the horizontal strength of the labor movement, with 33.7 percent of the force unionized (Durán and Kremerman 2015). But it was also the peak in vertical strength, as the CUT became a partner in the UP government by supervising production in the new centralized economy (Ulloa 2003; Gaudichaud 2003).

The student movement was the other major movement that emerged during the twentieth century. For workers, it was capitalism first and state growth second, the institutional sequence that boosted the movement. For students it was the opposite. Their growth resulted from the state's expansion, but in recent decades they were energized by the creation of an educational market.

As everywhere else, beginning in the nineteenth century Chilean republican rulers developed a network of public schools where children learned civic values and literacy skills (Ponce de León et al. 2012). The University of Chile was founded in 1842, with its federation of university students (the FECH) dating from 1907. The Catholic University was founded in 1888, followed by six other universities between then and 1966. Throughout the twentieth century, only a small number of upper- and upper-middle-class youth accessed these universities. Centrist parties dominated student federations—Christian Democrats at the Catholic University and Radicals at the University of Chile (Thielemann 2016). This was different from the labor movement, which was closer to leftist parties and ideologies since its beginnings.

In the 1960s, during the university reform process, students caught up and the communists and other leftist organizations gained power within student organizations. The Leftist Revolutionary Movement (MIR) emerged at the University of Concepción. In a more politicized environment, the student movement became stronger and more diverse. By 1973 there were about eight universities in the main Chilean cities (Santiago, Valparaíso, Concepción, Valdivia, and Antofagasta). They formed networks of student centers and organizations for middle- and upper-class youths, many of whom also participated in leftist and centrist parties and organizations. A smaller number of students, especially in the more conservative Catholic University, converged in rightist forces such as the *gremialismo* movement (Thielemann 2016). Except for the latter, all such associational life was brutally repressed and disarticulated when dictator Augusto Pinochet came to power in 1973.

MARKET REFORMS AND DEMOCRATIZATION (1973 TO OUR DAY)

In many Latin American countries, the transition to market reforms took place during democracy or simultaneously with democratization (see introductory chapter). In Chile, it was different. Market reforms started early on, in the 1970s, under authoritarianism rather than democracy.[1] The "Chicago Boys," a group of economists formed by Milton Friedman at the University of Chicago, persuaded Pinochet to make Chile a laboratory for market reforms. Pinochet did not have to convince voters as market-oriented democratic leaders had needed to do. Democratization took place when Chile's economic model was already reformed and hard to change due to institutional constraints. Democratic governments made some adjustments, but the bases of "the model" remained in place. As a result of growing openness, especially during the 1990s, Chile is nowadays the most economically globalized country in Latin America.

From the 1990s through the 2020s, Chile also consolidated a liberal democratic political regime, to the point that by 2019 it had the region's highest degree of electoral democracy, according to the V-Dem project. But Chile's democracy has limitations. Political parties are encapsulated (Bargsted and Maldonado 2018) and increasingly disconnected from the citizenry and civil society groups (Luna and Altman 2011). Over time Chileans became less interested in institutional politics (PNUD 2015). Participation in and identification with political parties (Luna and Mardones 2010) and electoral turnout (Bargsted, Somma, and Muñoz-Rojas 2019) plummeted dramatically. At this writing, Chile has the lowest electoral participation level in Latin America and one of the lowest in Western democracies (Voter Turnout Database).

Despite these limitations, democratization created opportunities for contestation in the streets, more civil liberties, and the collective organization of new groups. The representation crisis encouraged the activation of social movements autonomous from institutional political players, and collective protest grew rapidly in the twenty-first century (PNUD 2015; Somma and Medel 2017). This growth has been boosted by the greater use of digital technologies (Valenzuela, Arriagada, and Scherman 2012). Actions such as raising petitions, demonstrating, making public performances, and conducting online activism, among others, have become widespread and produced deep cultural consequences. Beyond students and workers, other relevant movements include the pensioner movement (Bugueño and Maillet 2019), the feminist movement (Reyes-Housholder and Roque 2019), the Mapuche movement (Bidegain 2015; Tricot 2009), the environmental movement (Akchurin 2015) and the sexual diversity movement (Somma, Rossi, and Donoso 2020).

SOCIAL MOVEMENTS AFTER MARKET REFORMS
AND DEMOCRATIZATION

How did the student and labor movements fare after market reforms and democratization? One might expect that, since they date from the pre-reforms era, they would be eclipsed by newer movements more attuned with current times. But this was not the case. Our analysis below shows that they are the ones that mobilize more people to the streets, do so more frequently, and are at the center of protest networks. Thus, there is a story of continuity. But there are also discontinuities. Market reforms and democratization affected them in important ways.

The 1970s was a tough decade for the labor movement. The Pinochet dictatorship decimated its ranks, murdering or exiling most of its leaders and outlawing labor unions, which government-controlled ones replaced. But decades of organizational accumulation could not be completely erased.

Worker organizations were central during the 1980s for rearticulating the opposition to Pinochet. They acted as brokers of the church, youth, student, and squatter organizations. Workers contributed to defeating Pinochet but, as did all other movements, at the end left in the hands of political parties the negotiation for the democratic transition (Drake 2003).

The 1970s were challenging not only politically but also economically. Unemployment, informality, and the growth of part-time jobs and the services sector made unionization more difficult. Yet the long-term impact of these changes should not be exaggerated. The unionization rate declined across the 1990s from 18 percent to approximately 13 percent but remained stable afterward. The same happened for the proportion of workers under collective negotiation (Winn 2004).

Market reforms also affected the student movement decisively but in different ways from the labor movement. While the Labor Plan of 1979 weakened workers' organization, the market education system rather encouraged student organization and mobilization. Higher education became commodified after a 1981 law encouraged the creation of private universities. From eight universities in 1980, Chile went to sixty by 2012. Postsecondary technical education institutions, less expensive and providing shorter degree times, also boomed: about one hundred were created (Bidegain 2015, 190). New regulations (mainly impulsed by Socialist president Ricardo Lagos) allowed banks to provide credits for paying educational fees, which in Chile are very high compared to other OCDE countries. This broadened access to students from popular classes. The result was massification: the number of university students doubled between 1987 and 2000 (Thielemann 2016, 65).

Students also took advantage of democratization, as did workers. With democracy reinstated, they recreated autonomous student federations and confederations that replaced those controlled by Pinochet. Thus, during the 2000s growing numbers of students met regularly on campuses in private and public universities across the country and elected their leaders. This created a mass of aggrieved students buried under heavy debts and ready to protest (Donoso and Somma 2019).

However, democratization did not reconnect the student movement with political parties. Rather, students became increasingly independent

(Somma and Medel 2017), with two exceptions: the *gremialista* student wing, which was always close to the Democratic Independent Union party, and some leftist student wings that were founding partners of the Broad Front coalition in 2017. Democratization also meant the proliferation of different wings within the student movement and new issues that overflowed preexisting student organizations. For instance, university campuses were privileged sites of feminist activism in the late 2010s and early 2020s. This created tensions within student organizations, which were still dominated by men.

Methods

We use the protest events dataset developed by the Observatory of Conflicts (Observatorio de Conflictos)[2] of the Centre for Social Conflict and Cohesion Studies (COES), a Chilean interuniversity research center. The unit of analysis is the "contentious action" or protest event—defined as an expression of collective unrest at a specific time and place (Garretón et al. 2018, 6). The dataset contains 23,398 events from 2009 to 2019 and more than thirty variables, including the place and date in which the event occurred, the estimated number of participants, the tactics adopted, the participating groups, and the demands raised.

As is commonly the case for protest events datasets, ours allows a systematic mapping of large numbers of protests across time and place and their connection to national events and local contexts. But our dataset has an additional strength. A recurrent criticism of protest datasets is the selection bias in their sources (Hutter 2014). Protest datasets often resort to one or two national newspapers and therefore underreport the protest activity outside, especially far away from capitals. To address this common problem, the Observatory daily reviews a wide variety of press media, five of which are national in scope and thirteen of regional scope. This captures many protests beyond the Región Metropolitana, which contains Chile's capital.

Because our dataset comprises only eleven years (2009–2019), we cannot directly study the impact of market reforms and democratization on popular politics as do the chapters in Part I of this book. As shown in figure 1.5 of the introductory chapter, our study period takes place in a country with already very high levels of economic globalization and democratization. Therefore, we give less attention to changes over time and provide an averaged, static picture of the Chilean protest landscape.

Popular Politics in Chile

We begin by offering a general overview of the changes during the last decade. Figure 8.1 shows the evolution of the number of protests in Chile throughout the period covered. There is a mild nonlinear growth across the decade with a strong jump in 2019, which results from the October outbreak (Somma et al. 2020). If we consider that during 2000–2012, there was also a growing trend in the number of protests (see Somma and Medel 2017, which uses a similar protest events dataset), we conclude that between 2009 and 2019, collective protest became pervasive in Chile. Moreover, we can speculate that, although reactive social movements were undoubtedly present, the October 2019 outbreak would have been unlikely without an expansion of feminist, environmental, urban dweller, cultural, and other proactive movements. The diversity of demands and groups in the streets during the 2019 outbreak resembles a "social movement society protest cycle" (Meyer and Tarrow 1998) rather than a singular social movement mobilization.

ACTORS (WHO)

In the previous discussion, we talked about "movements." However, protest datasets capture protest "groups"—which may be taken as a proxy of movements. We begin the analysis by characterizing seven important protest groups for the 2009–2019 period. Beyond workers and students, we add five groups representing other key movements in Chile during this period: feminists/sexual diversity groups,[3] residents/settlers, consumers/debtors, environmentalists/animal rights supporters,[4] and indigenous groups. Table 8.1 shows key "protest demography" indicators for these groups, ordered from more to less "mobilization power," or the estimated number

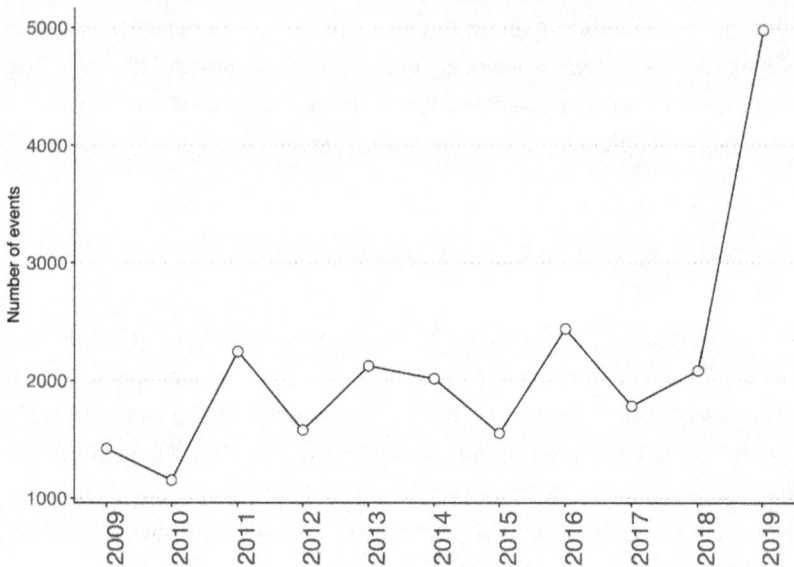

Figure 8.1. Number of Protest Events in Chile, 2009–2019. Observatorio de Conflictos.

of participants in the events with each group's presence during the period.

According to their mobilization power, workers and students are by far the main actors in the Chilean protest landscape. Each of them mobilized more than twelve million protesters during the 2009–2019 period (though obviously, some individuals may have participated more than once).

Workers and students reach these figures differently: workers are present in almost half of the events reported (49.5 percent), but these are not particularly large (1,330 participants on average). Students have a lower presence (21.3 percent), but their events are larger (average size = 3,530). The remaining groups are well below these figures: their mobilization power is several times less than that of students and workers. This is consistent with our argument that by-product movements—such as students and workers—have more favorable conditions to mobilize than other movements. It is noteworthy that workers appear in half of all protest events. This

Table 8.1. The "Demography" of Key Protest Groups (2009–2019)

GROUP	PRESENCE[1]	SIZE[2]	NUMBER OF EVENTS[3]	MOBILIZATION POWER[4]
Students	21.3%	3,530	3,970	14,014,100
Workers	49.5%	1,330	9,240	12,289,200
Feminist/Sexual Diversity	2.8%	7,710	514	3,962,940
Residents/Settlers	15.0%	1,190	2,800	3,332,000
Environment/Animal Rights	1.9%	1,490	353	525,970
Indigenous	4.6%	403	853	343,759
Consumers/Debtors	1.1%	1,460	196	286,160

1. Percentage of events where the group is present.
2. Average number of estimated participants for the events with the presence of the group. It is very difficult to get a precise estimate of protest participants (see Somma and Medel 2019). The numbers reported in news articles stem from rough estimations by protest leaders, the police, and/or journalists, or (when that information was not available) from the coders.
3. Number of events with the presence of the group.
4. Estimated number of people attending events with the presence of each group across the whole 2009–2019 period (computation: number of events times size).

Source: Observatorio de Conflictos, Centre for Social Conflict and Cohesion Studies (COES).

challenges any claim about the weakness of the workers movement. Although proactive movements have gained an important presence in democratic Chile, the mobilizing power continues to be stronger in historical by-product movements. These two broad patterns of mobilization (reactive and proactive) are not mutually exclusive paths. On the contrary: they coexist and mutually enhance each other, as we will see later in this chapter.

Let us look at the remaining groups. Feminist/sexual diversity groups take to an extreme the pattern of low presence (2.8 percent) but very massive size (7,710, the largest across all groups), which accounts for about 3.9 million people mobilized during the period. They protest sporadically, but when they do so, they carry many people to the streets, which is consistent with massive sexual diversity parades or Women's Day marches, the latter being especially large since 2018. Residents/settlers show the opposite pattern: a frequent presence (15 percent) but comparatively small events (1,190). This may be explained by the numerous cases of local grievances of an atomized nature. Given their territorial anchor, local residents have problems coordinating protests across the country or forming a national-level movement as other groups do. Indigenous groups have a relatively low presence (4.6 percent) and their events are relatively small (403 participants on average).

Consumers and debtors have an average event size (1,460) but are still very marginal in terms of presence (1.1 percent), giving them the lowest mobilization power across the seven groups studied. These two groups have emerged in recent decades due to economic and cultural modernization in Chile. The environmentalist and animal rights groups have a low presence (1.9 percent) and close-to-average size (about 1,490 for all events in our dataset).

Because these are very general categories, we often look at the subgroups composing them and the claims they voice in their protests. For the sake of brevity, we do not show figures or tables for many of the results reported.

CLAIMS (WHY) BY ACTOR

Workers/Labor

Half of the Chilean protests during the 2009–2019 period had worker presence, with this proportion ranging from 35 percent to 62 percent, and with a range between 561 and 1,130 yearly protest events of this type recorded in our dataset. This suggests, of course, that factors other than the by-product status of worker organizations affect its protest dynamics. Worker protests tend to concentrate outside the Metropolitan Region (89 percent), to a larger degree than the rest of the protests (76 percent).

The "workers" category is very general: it lumps together different subgroups. Our dataset allows disaggregating it into five: public workers, private workers, self-employed or small- or medium-sized firm workers, unemployed workers, and pensioners. Even though public workers represent only about 10 percent of Chile's labor force (Servicio Civil 2017, 15), they are the worker subgroup with more presence (27 percent in all protest events). This contrasts with workers employed in private companies and self-employed workers. Despite representing a larger share in the labor force, their presence is considerably lower (15 percent and 6 percent comparatively). This attests to the impressive organizational power of public labor unions.

Unemployed groups appear very little in protest events (1 percent), in contrast with Argentina, in which they formed the important *Piquetero* movement (Rossi 2017). One explanation of this difference is the stronger territorial organization of Argentinean civil society (Rossi 2019), which provides venues for organizing unemployed workers that are absent in Chile. Pensioners participate even less, but they have staged massive demonstrations in the No+AFP movement in recent years along with other groups. Pensioner movements are rare in Latin America, but they have occasionally pushed successfully for better pensions, as happened in Uruguay after democratic restoration.

The demands appearing in worker protests are mostly related to labor issues, as expected, but not all issues carry equal weight. Considering only those events with worker presence, the three most recurrent claims refer to classical labor issues such as wages (47 percent), working conditions (29 percent), and employment stability (23 percent). Collective negotiation is less frequent (9 percent), likely because only a small portion of workers have access to it, and pensions are even less frequent (6 percent).

Interestingly, workers occasionally voice nonlabor claims. These mostly refer to education (given the support of teacher unions to the student movement, as shown in the network analysis below) and health. Our dataset also allows identifying the economic sector to which protests relate (if any). When it comes to worker protests, the most frequent sector is education, again pointing to teacher unions' relevance. Also quantitatively relevant are health (health workers unions are strong in Chile), transportation, mining, commerce, and fishing.

Students

Table 8.1 shows that students were the other group that, along with workers, mobilized more people in Chile. We conceptualized both as by-product movements. But student protests are highly cyclical. Our dataset reports below 200 student protests in 2009 and 2010, a peak of 1,129 events in 2011, and a sustained decrease between 2012 and 2015 (with a low of 213 events), with a slight recovery for the more recent years. Despite persistently higher levels of protest presence compared to other groups, such presence varies notably across time. During 2011 about half of all protest events had student presence, but in 2009 that amounted to only 9 percent of the total. This is a huge variation (almost a 10:1 ratio) compared to worker protests (about 2:1).

Why this difference? One possible answer is the rapid cohort-replacement nature of student movements. Gifted leaders or strongly politicized student generations can promote massive mobilizations, but other cohorts or leaders may not match these. Because labor movements have more enduring leaders and constituencies, their composition (and hence mobilization power) is more stable across time. Another difference is that student protests are more likely to occur in the Metropolitan Region than nonstudent events. This may be partially explained by the concentration of university campuses and high schools with a strong mobilization tradition in the Metropolitan Region.

The student movement has two sectors: high-school students and tertiary (mostly university) students. They have different organizations and carry out protest campaigns in an independent fashion for their specific demands. However, in recent years—particularly in 2006 and 2011—they have coordinated actions under common demands such as increasing public education resources and reforming the market educational system. In such circumstances, their mobilization capacity has been huge, and they have pressed governments successfully. The presence of high-school and university students in the protest landscape is similar: while the former appear in 13 percent of all protest events in Chile, the latter appear in 11 percent.

Most of the claims displayed in student protests are related to educational issues. While this may seem obvious, it may not be so if we consider that the student movement has often pressed for noneducational issues such as a new constitution, tax reform, the environment, women's rights, and mental health. Considering all protests, however, student protests show a strong "claim specialization" in educational issues. Within these, the most frequent claims relate to specific educational institutions (e.g., infrastructure problems in buildings) and demands for free and public education (each present in 32 percent of events with student presence). The demand for free and public education was central in the 2011–2012 student protest wave. Also relevant, although less frequent, are claims related to ethical or legal infringements in education (including profiting from education, an important issue in the 2011 protests), as well as problems of educational inequality and quality. While both university and high-school students tend to display these claims, the former emphasize more frequently than the latter claims about educational debts and ethical issues. The most frequent noneducational claims of student protests are related to labor issues, violence against women, and the environment.

Residents/Settlers

By "residents/settlers" (or residents for short), we mean urban dwellers, but also residents of territorially bounded neighborhoods, localities, or communities. In recent decades, environmental damage in Chile motivated the formation of local groups of neighbors and environmental activist organizations that often engage in collective protest (Ossandón 2005).

Table 8.1 shows that residents have a considerable presence in the protest landscape (15 percent), although their events convoke fewer participants than most other groups. Residents are not articulated in an organic, national-level movement as most students and workers are. Theirs are local reactions to local problems that often recede once activists reach a solution with authorities or are defeated. Given their local nature, residents are relatively insulated from international protest waves or even from national issues. Interestingly, one peak of resident protests—in absolute numbers—was during 2012, 2013, and 2014: that is, in the years following the student movement's peak. One could speculate about a "demonstration effect" from students to residents with a lag of one or two years.

The relative presence of resident protests varies across regions, and such presence seems to be inversely related to the region's geographic centrality. The region of Aysén, in the south of Chile, has the highest percentage of resident protests considering all kinds of protests in the region—33 percent.

Aysén has developed a historically strong local identity driven by its relative isolation from national circuits. Conversely, the smaller relative presence of resident protests is for the Metropolitan Region (7 percent), which concentrates much of Chile's political, economic, and administrative power. Consistent with Davis (1999), this suggests that distance from power centers creates certain types of grievances that fuel resident protests. But what do residents aim at when taking to the streets?

Above, we noted that worker and student protests show a strong "claim specialization": that workers mostly protest for labor demands and students for educational demands. Specialization seems lower for residents, who display demands of quite different sorts. For instance, 15 percent of their protests are linked to transportation (highways, airports). This includes calls for improving connectivity as well as reactions against the negative consequences of these developments. But residents also protest against local pollution (13 percent), demand more resources and better legislation for local communities (11 percent), engage in NIMBY-style protests against nearby energy infrastructure projects (9 percent), and struggle to address housing and health needs, including undersupply of housing and hospitals and scarcity of physicians. Because each resident group tries to address its own specific needs, the aggregate pattern is variegated protest demands.

Indigenous Groups

Indigenous movements are rooted in the centuries-long struggle between the Chilean state and the pre-Columbian populations (mostly the Mapuche peoples). During the late nineteenth century, republican state-builders aggressively attempted to impose their law system, language, and culture. Indigenous resistance provided the basis for the oldest social movement in Chile today. While there are many Mapuche organizations, given their strongly territorial and fragmented nature, it is difficult to speak of a national-level Mapuche movement. Mapuche communities are anchored to ancestral territories imbued with religious and cultural values. They lack a tradition of political centralization.

As noted in table 8.1, indigenous presence in the protest landscape is relatively infrequent, and its events are comparatively small. Over the decade before this chapter was written, the indigenous protest cycle seems at odds with that of students: we have recorded a larger number of indigenous protests during 2016, 2017, and 2018, and during 2010, which were years of low student protest. In 2010, for instance, about 10 percent of all protest events had an indigenous presence (the highest in our timeframe). Most indigenous protests are performed by Mapuche groups, the largest indigenous group in Chile.

Indigenous protests vary widely across the territory. They are more pervasive in three south central contiguous regions: Araucanía (where 24 percent of all protests have an indigenous presence), Los Ríos (9 percent), and Bíobio (6 percent). In fact, 74 percent of all indigenous protests in Chile are concentrated in these regions, which historically concentrated much of the Mapuche population after the Spanish conquest in the sixteenth century. Conversely, indigenous protest is rare in the rest of the country. For instance, only forty-eight of such events took place in the Metropolitan region—about 1 percent of all protests there.

Indigenous groups have a considerable demand-specialization in their protests: most demands relate to indigenous issues. These include the devolution of ancestral lands (32 percent of all indigenous protests), the opposition to judicial sentences against indigenous peoples (29 percent), police repression (13 percent), and threats to cultural identities and lifestyles (1 percent). However, indigenous groups have also occasionally protested against energy projects threatening their environments, such as dams (5 percent) and other infrastructure projects (4 percent).

Environmentalist and Animal Rights Groups

As just seen, in Chile, residents and indigenous groups often protest against threats to their natural environments resulting from infrastructure projects and the like. However, there are other groups that are explicitly motivated by the protection of the environment and animal species and self-identify as such rather than as residents of certain localities or indigenous groups. As noted in table 8.1, they infrequently appear in the protest landscape—perhaps a sign of the difficulties of forming strong environmental movements in the Global South.

Environmental and animal rights protests peaked in 2011, along with student protests. This was perhaps the most active year of the Patagonia Against Dams campaign, which opposed building several dams in the Aysén region. This helps explain why these protests have the largest presence in the region of Aysén (6 percent of all protests there). Countrywide, the number of environmental protests almost doubled during 2017 and 2018 compared to 2015 and 2016, possibly resulting from the upsurge of environmental protests globally.

The most prevalent demands in environmental and animal rights protests are related to the building of energy projects, bridges, and highways (appearing in 40 percent of such protests), animal rights and vegetarianism (29 percent), followed by environmental NIMBY-style protests (13 percent), waste disposal (9 percent), and local pollution (6 percent). These results suggest that there could be links between residents' groups and environmental groups because their claims partially overlap, and figure 8.4 below confirms this. Finally, these groups occasionally participate in protests displaying nonenvironmental demands, especially educational ones, which suggests ties to student movements.

Feminist and Sexual Diversity Groups

Chilean society is structured around not only the nation-state and capitalism but also cultural norms that incarnate in different institutions and organizations. Two of them are patriarchy and heteronormativity. Movements advancing women's rights and sexual dissidence, while different from each other, can be conceptualized as organized reactions to the oppression resulting from patriarchy and heteronormativity, respectively.

Our dataset identifies a group labeled "homosexuals/sexual minorities/ feminists," which is present in 2.8 percent of all events and which unfortunately cannot be disaggregated into subgroups. Events staged by these groups, while rare, peaked in 2019, numbering 144, and then in 2018 with 61, versus a 7-to-21 range in previous years. This is clearly linked to the recent global upsurge of feminist protests. Feminist/sexual diversity events are more likely to take place in the Metropolitan Region than other events do, and as noted in table 8.1, they are the largest on average (about 7,710 participants). Their most frequent demands are related to violence against women (present in 31 percent of such events), the rights of gays (28 percent), lesbians (26 percent), and transsexuals (25 percent), and abortion (12 percent). In late 2019 a Chilean feminist group called Lastesis staged a choreography expressing opposition to male violence against women. It quickly spread across the world.

Consumers and Debtors

The consumption and acquisition of goods have expanded enormously in Chile in recent decades. The protests of consumers and debtors are not massive, either in participants or in frequency, but they have been persistent rather than sporadic. These protests are important not because of their quantity but because they express the costs that economic modernization has had on citizens, especially former higher-education students. In Chile in the last three decades, nearly one million students entered higher education. However, this access went hand in hand with the massive indebtedness of young people. The Nonpayment Movement, which groups together indebted former students, estimates that by 2017, more than eight hundred thousand students had defaulted on education loans (Labbé Yáñez 2017).

Other important sectors beyond students have organized around debt grievances. One example is motorists, who have mobilized against gasoline taxes and expressed discontent at the excessive charges of toll roads. Recently, the No + TAG movement has gained visibility acting upon the latter grievance, demanding a remission of 80 percent of toll-road use debts. Other small movements associated with retail houses and bank debts also belong to this group. Although they are not coordinated in large organizations, they recurrently engage in protests.

ACTIONS (HOW)

The Chilean protest landscape shows a wide array of tactics. Following the literature (Taylor and Van Dyke 2004; Medel and Somma 2016), we group them into four types: conventional (mostly marches and demonstrations), which take place in 37 percent of all protest events; cultural (mostly symbolic rituals and artistic performances: 8 percent); nonviolent disruptive (mostly strikes, roadblocks, or building takeovers: 40 percent); and violent (mostly setting vehicles, buildings, or lands on fire, hunger strikes, self-destructive actions, attacking security forces, or destroying public or private property: 14 percent). The predominance of nonviolent tactics—either pacific (conventional, cultural) or disruptive—is consistent with other studies for capitalist democracies (Soule and Earl 2005; Meyer and Tarrow 1998).

There are no appreciable changes across time in the prevalence of these types of tactics. Most protest events (78 percent) show only one type of tactic. Events with two or three types are rare (20 percent and 2 percent, respectively). Consistent with this, the tetrachoric correlations among three dummy variables indicating the presence (1) or absence (0) of each type are negative and significant, indicating a sort of "tactical specialization": protesters tend to use pacific *or* disruptive *or* violent tactics. This sort of "repulsion" is more notable among pacific and disruptive tactics (correlation = –.84).

Are there differences across groups in their tactical repertoires? Figure 8.2 shows the distribution of the four types of tactics in the events with each protest group's participation.[5] While there are notable variations across groups, one can roughly identify three profiles: a heavy and relatively even reliance on pacific and disruptive tactics (students, workers, and residents/settlers); a very heavy reliance on pacific tactics, with outstanding use of cultural tactics and little reliance on the other two (feminist and sexual diversity, and environmentalists and animal rights supporters); and a comparatively larger resort to violent tactics, in combination with the other two (indigenous groups). As we have explored in other research, the reasons behind the use of a certain type of tactics are closely related to the differential capacities of groups, especially their ability to convene adherents and the position they occupy in the political and productive structure of society (Medel and Somma 2016).

TARGETS (WHOM)

The most recurrent target of Chilean protests is the national government, which appears in 54 percent of all events, followed by local governments (20 percent), private companies (15 percent), and educational institutions (9

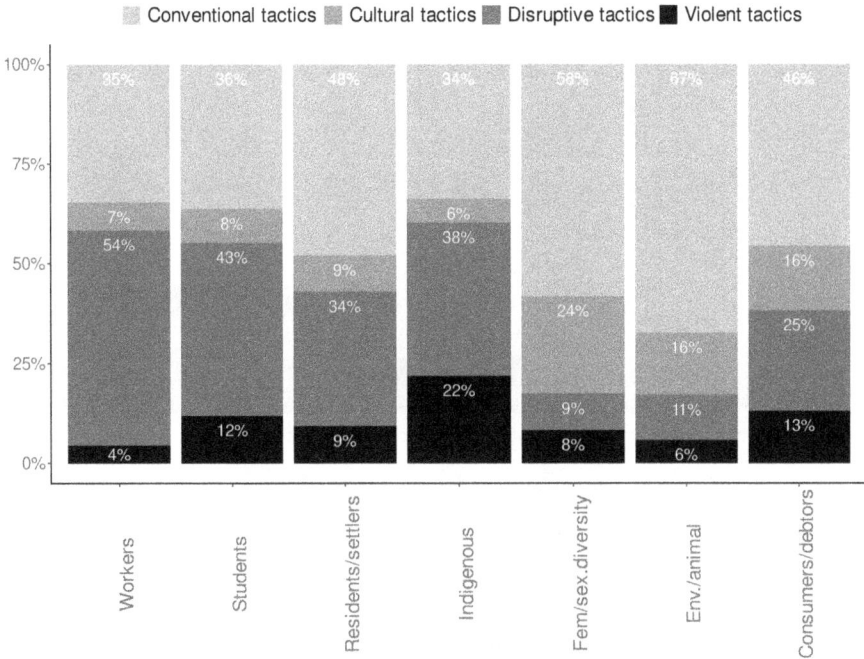

Conventional tactics ▨ Cultural tactics ▨ Disruptive tactics ■ Violent tactics

	Workers	Students	Residents/settlers	Indigenous	Fem/sex.diversity	Env./animal	Consumers/debtors
Conventional	35%	36%	48%	34%	58%	67%	46%
Cultural	7%	8%	9%	6%	9%	16%	16%
Disruptive	54%	43%	34%	38%	24%	11%	25%
Violent	4%	12%	9%	22%	8%	6%	13%

Figure 8.2. Protest Tactics Used by Selected Groups in Chile, 2009–2019.
Observatorio de Conflictos.

percent). Other targets, such as health institutions, foreign governments, or civil society organizations, are less frequent.[6] The importance of governments—and especially the national government—as protest targets is broadly consistent with Tilly (2015). National governments in modern states concentrate an impressive array of power resources and legal attributions. It makes sense for organized groups to direct their protest claims to them. This is especially the case in Chile, a centralized polity with a presidential system. It is not surprising that local governments are comparatively less targeted. This picture remains without major changes across time.

Figure 8.3 shows the distribution of the four most frequent targets for each of the selected groups. As with tactics, there is considerable variation. The national government is the single most frequent target for all groups. Local governments are a prominent target for some protest groups, notably residents. This is reasonable given the local nature of many of their demands. Local governments are also relatively salient in indigenous

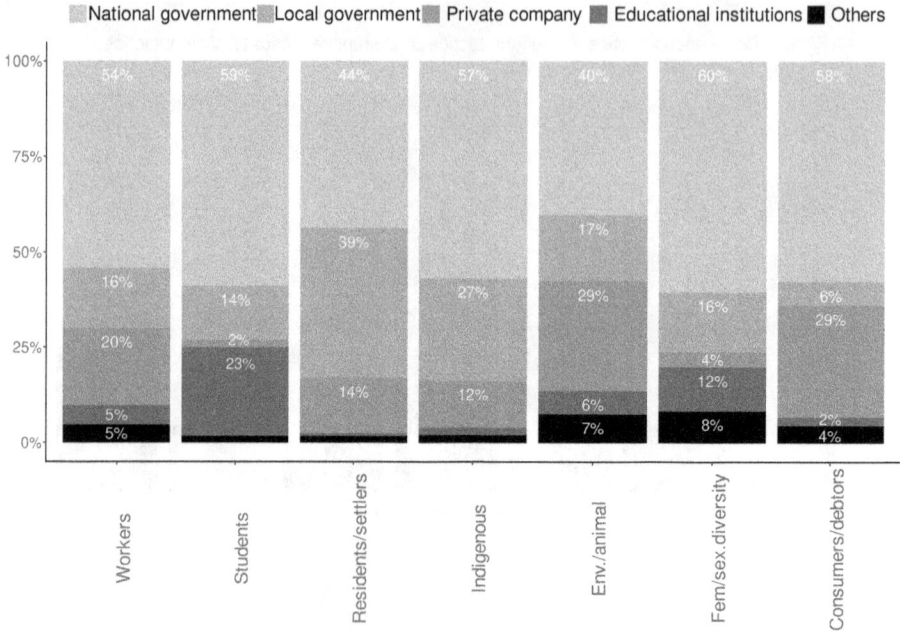

National government ■ Local government ■ Private company ■ Educational institutions ■ Others

Figure 8.3. Targets of Main Protesting Groups in Chile, 2009–2019.
Observatorio de Conflictos.

protests, which often have a territorial nature and are triggered by issues concerning local authorities. Private companies are often targeted by environmental groups, which protest against the environmental consequences of private economic activities; consumers and debtors, which mobilize against abusive charges or poorly rendered services; and workers, who often voice grievances against the companies that employ them. Finally, educational institutions are frequent targets of student protests and feminist and sexual diversity groups.

PLACES (WHERE)

To examine the distribution of protest activity across space, map 8.1 zooms in on the Metropolitan Region. Chile's capital, Santiago, is located there. The Metropolitan Region is the economic, administrative, demographic, and cultural center of Chile. It also has the largest number of protests across all regions.

Map 8.1. Distribution of Protests in the Metropolitan Region's Municipalities, 2009–2019. Observatorio de Conflictos. Municipalities colored in white had no protests recorded in the dataset.

The heat map in map 8.1 shows the number of protests in each municipality (*comuna*) of the Metropolitan Region during the 2009–2019 period. Darker tones indicate more protests. The municipality of Santiago concentrates many protests. This is a highly symbolic municipality because it harbors the presidential building and the main executive offices. In fact, the largest marches in Chile take place in the *Alameda* street, the central avenue of Santiago. Thus, the highest political authorities in Chile may listen and watch in person the passing of protesters. Such authorities are the most frequent targets of protest activity, as noted in figure 8.3.

Our group-based approach raises the question of whether the spatial distribution of protests varies across groups. Map 8.2 shows this for the municipalities of the Metropolitan Region.[7] The common pattern is that all six groups concentrate their protests in the municipality of Santiago. But

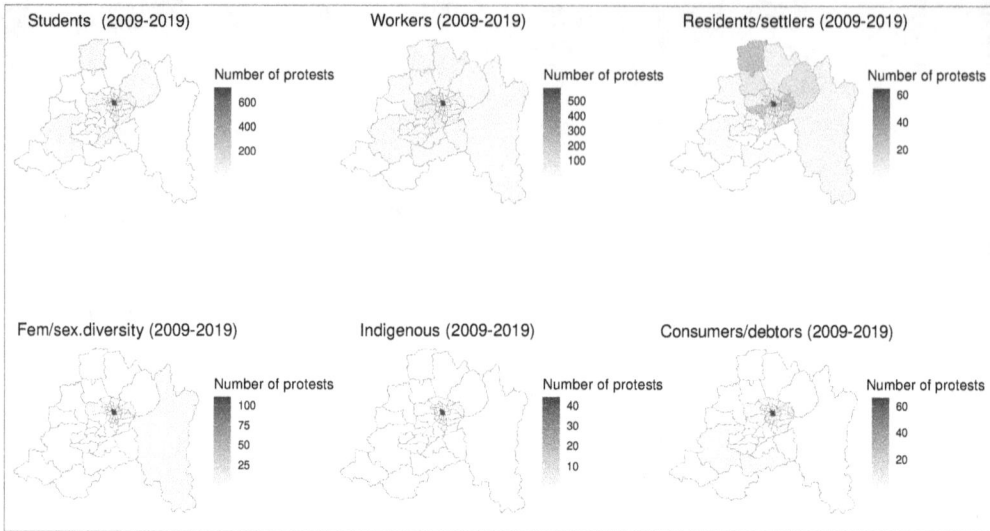

Map 8.2. Distribution of Protests in the Metropolitan Region's Municipalities, by Group. Observatorio de Conflictos. Municipalities colored in white had no protests recorded in the dataset.

there are some noteworthy departures from this pattern. Worker protests take place all over the region. This is because all municipalities have workplaces where workers may eventually strike or organize a picket. Student protests are more concentrated in a diagonal line running from southwest to northeast, perhaps reflecting the territorial concentration of educational institutions. Students rarely protest in the periphery of the Metropolitan Region.

Resident protests are the most evenly distributed ones, with considerable numbers in the northern, eastern, and central south municipalities. Environmental/animal rights and feminist/sexual diversity groups are comparatively tilted toward eastern municipalities, which tend to be richer. Such groups do not protest in the poorest neighborhoods. This seems in line with Ronald Inglehart's (1997) postmaterialist thesis. Finally, consumer/debtor protests sometimes take place in the southwestern municipalities—perhaps due to the presence of highways that disgruntled drivers block to raise their claims. We leave to the future an explanation of these differences.

THE NETWORKS OF PROTEST GROUPS

So far, we have treated social movements—as reflected empirically in protest groups—as independent units. But social movements are the result of
relational processes (Diani 2007). These relationships operate at different
levels. They work at the level of individuals who exchange resources and
frame definitions and values. But they also work at the level of organizations that create cooperative ties. In fact, social movement organizations
are often embedded in fields populated by other organizations with which
they form social movement "industries" and "sectors" (McCarthy and Zald
1977). To understand the relational nature of movements, we must understand the relational structure of protest events—in other words, the networks of alliances that different movements build for staging protests.

Which is the structure of alliances among protest groups in Chile?
Which groups protest together recurrently, and which ones do not protest
together at all? If two or more groups happen to protest in the same event
according to media accounts, the Observatory of Conflicts dataset indicates which groups these are. This is done in up to four groups. We thus take
co-participation in protest events as an indicator of an underlying alliance.
This is not perfect, of course. A group may be at a protest and not engage in
substantive collaboration with others. Or two groups may collaborate without necessarily showing up together at the protest site. However, previous
studies (e.g., Krinsky and Crossley 2014) suggest that two groups active in
the same demonstration have organizational closeness. To the seven
groups studied so far, we add political parties to explore the claim about
their distancing from social movements (Somma and Medel 2017; Bidegain
2015). If movements and parties are away from each other, this should be
represented in network visualizations.

Figure 8.4 shows the graphic representation of these alliances.[8] Each
node represents a protest group. Each line represents a protest in which two
groups collaborated. The figure takes into account the spatial distribution
of the nodes: nodes closest to each other maintain closer relationships than
those further away. Figure 8.4 shows the distribution of alliances for the
entire period (2009–2019).[9] We can see that there are strong alliances, for
example, between workers and students, and very feeble or nonexistent

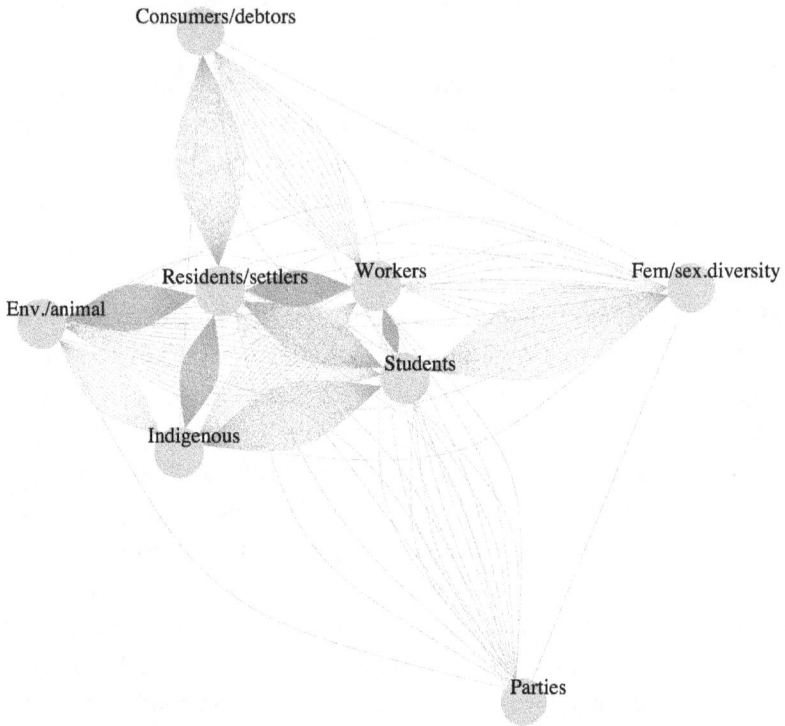

Figure 8.4. Protest Networks in Chile, 2009–2019. Observatorio de Conflictos.

alliances between political parties and residents or between indigenous and feminists/sexual diversity groups. Finally, the figure highlights groups very disconnected or isolated from the rest, mainly political parties and debtors/consumers.

Next, we evaluate the centrality of the nodes in the network. Centrality has to do with the ability of a node (or protest group) to connect with other actors in the network as a whole. In this case, we used the notion of centrality as closeness. The question is not whether a node has many links (since it can have many alliances with only one node), but rather how many connections it has with a wide array of other nodes. That is why centrality is often taken as a measure of prestige. A group closely connected to many others indicates something about its importance and, potentially, about its power (Krinsky and Crossley 2014; Wada 2014).

Figure 8.5 shows that the group with the highest degree of centrality is workers, followed by students. The centrality of Chilean workers stands in sharp contrast with a study about the United States (Cornwell and Harrison 2004), in which (using different data and methods) labor unions appear as very isolated from other civil society organizations. At the other extreme, in Chile, the most isolated node corresponds to political parties. This is consistent with the notion that parties are detached from other civil society groups.

Networks are not static structures. They change according to the political context or the transformations of social movements. To explore this point, we compare the alliance networks by separating our time period into five waves, where each wave represents two years of mobilization. We compare two-year networks mainly for practical reasons: they correspond to

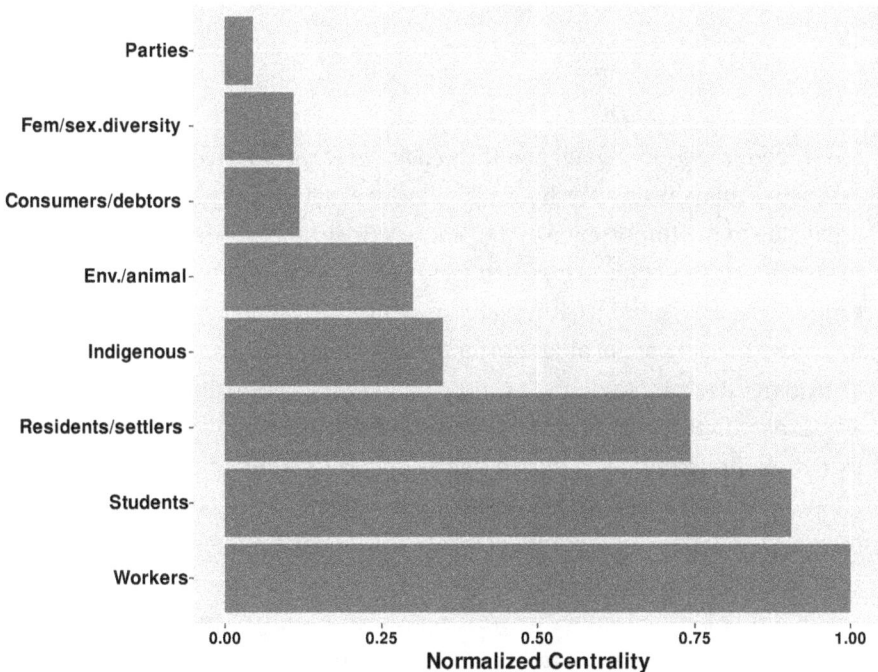

Figure 8.5. Standardized Centrality of Groups Protesting in Chile, 2009–2019. Observatorio de Conflictos.

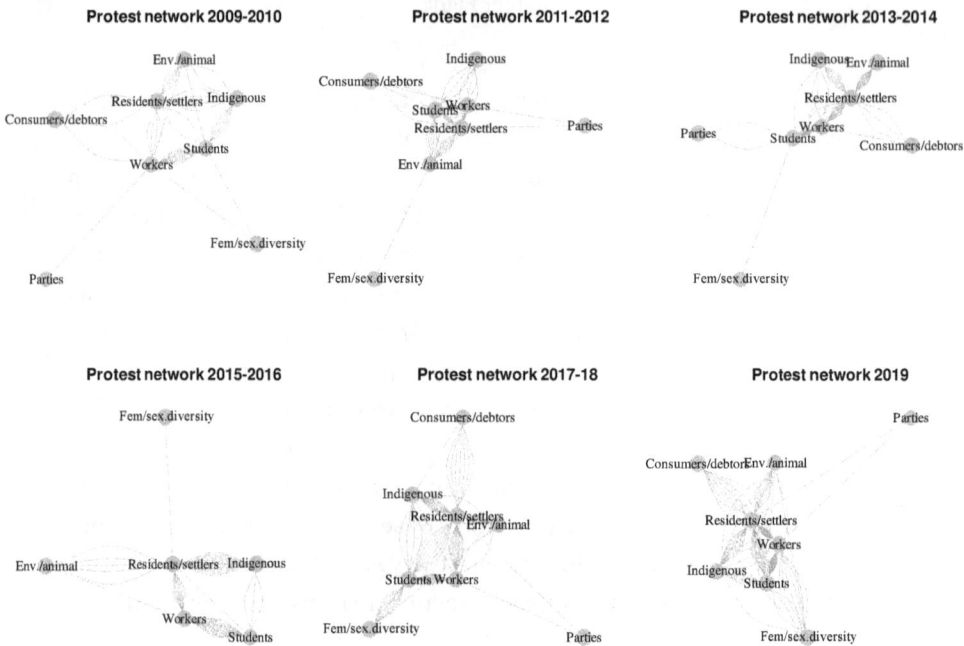

Figure 8.6. Protest Networks in Chile across Time. Observatorio de Conflictos.

the student wave (2011–2012) and the pensioner wave (2017–2018), the period's two primary protest cycles. In addition, we include the year 2019 separately due to the importance of the "social uprising" of the last months of that year (Somma et al. 2020). Therefore, we have five protest waves representing ten years, plus an extra year representing a wave on its own. Figure 8.6 shows the network of alliances for these six time periods.

In general terms, students, a central actor of the period, maintain relationships with three other central nodes: workers, residents, and, to a lesser extent, environmentalists/animal rights supporters. The workers–students alliance is the strongest and closest one throughout all periods in terms of proximity and density. Another constant is that parties remain relatively isolated from the main groups in all waves.

But figure 8.6 also shows interesting variations. First, residents, who started the first waves with rather moderate networks, became more central and strengthened their relationships with students, workers, debtors, and, especially, indigenous groups. In fact, along with students and workers, residents are a central group in the last two waves. Second, indigenous groups maintained relatively moderate relations with students during the first two waves and stayed far away from the other central nodes. In subsequent waves, their relationships with the other groups became stronger, especially with residents. For the last wave, they were much more connected also with students and environmentalists. Third, feminist groups, which also started quite isolated, generated closer relationships with students for the wave 2017–2018 and, for 2019, also with workers. Other groups with a weak presence in the first waves, such as environmentalists and consumers/debtors, were generally more connected in the last waves.

All protest groups, except for political parties, were much connected during the last wave of protest in 2019. This evolution shows that the network of alliances contains stable and changing relationships. In addition to the strong alliances that persist over time (mainly workers and students), new relationships take center stage according to the context of social protest. The figures reveal varied alliances between movements resorting to the two broad patterns of mobilization hypothesized in this book (reactive and proactive). There is a "reactive triangle" of alliances among workers, residents/settlers, and consumers/debtors (figure 8.4). But workers often ally with students, who in turn cooperate with environmental, feminist, and sexual diversity groups, which have greatly benefited from democratization.

Conclusions

Our approach provides a tentative answer to why different groups vary in their presence and intensity in the protest landscape. The literature on protest cycles has evidenced variations across time in the protest activity of different groups. It has tied such variations to shifting political opportunities, repression, and other factors that often change considerably across time (Tarrow 1993; McAdam 2010; Carey 2006). We consider this view useful but believe it is not the whole story. Beyond protest cycles, we speculate that there are sustained differences in the "basal" level of protest that are anchored in more enduring characteristics of protest groups.

Specifically, by-product movements such as worker and student movements developed early in the transition to "modern" society. The development of capitalism and the nation-state, two central institutions in this transition, provided the grievances, opportunities, and infrastructural conditions for students and workers to develop formal organizations and informal networks that could be activated for protest. Thus, historically both movements resulted from a combination of "proactive" political opportunities, but—especially in the case of workers—"reactive" pushes related to economic crises and state repression. In this way, the chapter speaks to the central questions of this book. Also, processes of collective learning and organizational accumulation across the twentieth century granted workers and students a strong basis for becoming leading actors in the contemporary protest landscape despite the deactivation and repression produced by the dictatorship in the 1970s and 1980s.

Market reforms beginning in the 1970s and democratization beginning in the late 1980s had complex and often contradictory effects on worker and student movements and favored the emergence of other "non-by-product" movements during the current century. Yet workers and students remain as central actors across time, as reflected in protest networks. However, the emergence of new issues—such as feminism—and the transitory decline of other ones—such as education—brought changes to protest networks and increased the centrality of groups with a weaker presence in the protest landscape, such as feminist, indigenous, and resident groups. We can relate these new groups with proactive movements because they raise demands more linked to cultural and political change. Despite this important emergence of new movements, the most important reactive movements, mainly workers, maintain an indisputable centrality in the Chilean protest landscape. However, network analyses show that both reactive and proactive movements interact with each other in dense—albeit fickle—alliances. Therefore, instead of a replacement or a transition from one type of mobilization to another, what has taken place in Chile is a coexistence between reactive and proactive movements that strengthen and diversify the protest landscape.

Also, student and worker movements have adapted to political and economic changes. In the workers movement, recently outsourced workers have taken distance from leftist parties and centralized labor unions and mobilized independently. Students have severed their links with political parties and became mobilized by new issues such as indebtedness and feminist claims. Groups mobilized around sexual diversity, local environmental grievances, and consumption hazards have gained a new space and are routinely recognized by political authorities. The social uprising in late 2019 illustrated the convergence of various groups with little formal organization and a notorious lack of centralized coordination. This anticipates a revamping of the Chilean protest landscape, which may be reflected in data about the decade of the 2020s.

Notes

1. Although the KOF Index suggests that economic globalization in Chile took off in democracy (from 1993 onward, see figure 1.5 of the introductory chapter), market reforms began in the 1970s. They did not immediately result in economic globalization.
2. See coes.cl/observatorio-de-conflictos/.
3. Unfortunately, the dataset does not differentiate among feminists and sexual diversity groups.
4. The dataset does not differentiate between environmentalists and animal rights supporters.
5. The figures consider all tactics adopted in such events, as reported by several variables indicating protest tactics. One event may contain more than one tactic.
6. As with tactics, our dataset allows recording more than one target for each protest event.
7. We exclude indigenous protests from this map because most of them take place in the Araucanía Region, in the south of Chile. In map 8.2, the colors indicate the relative number of protests within each group. Thus, the yellow mark for a group with few protests represents a smaller number of protests than the yellow mark for a group with many more protests.
8. To represent the networks visually, we used the R 3.5 software and the igraph package.
9. It is important to emphasize that this network does not represent the totality of the protests in Chile for the period, but only the protests where more than one group appeared.

CHAPTER NINE

Protests and Citizens' Revolution in Ecuador under Post-Neoliberalism

SANTIAGO ORTIZ

Introduction

In the conflict cycle that began in 1990, the social movements in Ecuador played an instrumental role in weakening the neoliberal governments that had dominated the political scene. This cycle went into decline at the beginning of the new century, but there were moments of reactivation later on. In the period of the Citizens' Revolution (2007–2017) under Rafael Correa, who served three consecutive presidential terms, several actors found answers to claims that had been repressed during the neoliberal period and decided to demobilize; others continued to protest as they disagreed with the Citizens' Revolution.[1] This occurred in the context of a "return of the state" economic expansion associated with the commodity boom and the deployment of redistribution policies fostered by the post-neoliberal regime. Correa also embraced a "permanent" electoral strategy to connect citizens with the state, and this strategy weakened and fragmented social organizations into pro- and anti-Correa camps.

Protest is a visible action in public spaces, which attracts the attention of the population and the authorities and produces uncertainty in the activities of others (Tilly 1998). This involves using a range of performances or forms of action that result in a response from the state or its opponents. A conflict cycle has dimensions that expand and become more complex in time and space. This chapter focuses on protest events and campaigns, understood as a series of actions that the same actors carry out in pursuit of the same demands and objectives. Conflicts and campaigns depend on the degree of organization of the actors, which provides them with a degree of connectivity, solidarity, and information, allowing them to sustain protest actions. The progress of the cycle depends on the capacity of the catalytic movements to "modulate" performances, in addition to the capacity of challengers to take advantage of the structure of political opportunities (Tarrow 1997).

The actors can employ moderate or conventional forms of action (marches, petitions, strikes) or radical forms (protests, blockades, confrontations with the police). The combination of performances has been a characteristic of social movements in Ecuador. The state plays a key role not only because it is an objective of collective action, but also because it fulfills a normative, institutional, and material role, aspects that were key in the "return of the state" during the Citizens' Revolution.

This chapter poses questions about the character of the 2007–2017 cycle of conflicts, its actors, claims, and actions, and the resolution of conflicts in the context of globalization and democratization, as well as the involvement of the state established by the Citizens' Revolution. To answer them, it draws on the dataset of the Centro Andino de Acción Popular (CAAP), existing literature on protest cycles, the relational theory of social movements (Tilly 1998; Tarrow 1997), and previous research on social movements in Ecuador (Ortiz Crespo 2016, 2018, 2021).[2]

The chapter starts with background information on the political crisis that preceded the Citizens' Revolution; then it presents an overview of the main characteristics of this revolution. Next, it analyzes the context and the cycle of conflicts during this period with two approaches: the quantitative, based on the examination of the CAAP dataset,[3] and the qualitative, examining the evolution of the cycle in relation to other contextual factors. The conclusion revisits the importance of this critical moment of democratization and globalization in Ecuador.

Globalization and Democratization

LIBERAL DEMOCRACY AND NEOLIBERAL
GLOBALIZATION (1990–2006)

The levels of conflict in Ecuador rose at the end of the twentieth century, but at the beginning of the twenty-first conflict declined and the indigenous movement—which played a catalytic role in several conflicts—became weaker (Sánchez Parga 2010). This decline occurred amid a triple crisis: political instability, with the fall of three presidents; economic recession; and a wide social crisis that led to greater inequality and the migration resulting from the financial crisis known as the Bank Holiday of 2000.

Ecuador, like other Latin American countries, established a liberal democratic regime in the early 1980s, with the end of the dictatorships and the return to the rule of law. Social movements took advantage of this favorable framework of political opportunities to strengthen social mobilization and political advocacy processes (Tarrow 1997). However, the democratic regimes faced a debt crisis in 1982 that made governments implement neoliberal policies. These policies had several effects: economic stagnation, deindustrialization, more flexible labor conditions, reduced social investment, and deeper inequality. By the mid-1980s, the collapse of the industrial workers' base was already evident. This eroded the power of the unions and the trade union federations grouped in the Workers' United Front (Frente Unitario de Trabajadores), actors who were protagonists of the social struggle against military governments. In addition, in the 1990s there was a new generation of structural reforms in line with the Washington consensus: trade liberalization, elimination of tariff restrictions, financial market deregulation, capital account liberalization, and privatization attempts (Ramírez Gallegos 2011).

This dual transition to liberal democracy and neoliberal globalization is depicted in figure 1.5 of the introductory chapter, which shows the increases in both the democratization and the globalization index. Although the democratic regime continued, the dual transition caused a conflictive situation for the country. The deeper inequality thwarted the expectations raised by the advent of democracy. The right and center-left parties were not sensitive to the claims made by the population. This led to frustration that eventually caused a crisis of representation of the political system and government instability in the midst of a struggle of powers and elites that became chronic.

Although the agrarian reform was halted by the military, the economic reforms promoted the participation of peasants in the market. However, the recession prevented peasants and indigenous people from finding a market and good prices for their products and restricted their employment opportunities in the cities to which they migrated in search of work. Both of these created contradictory political opportunity structures: while the economy affected the living conditions of peasants and indigenous people, politics maintained the conditions for participation, an opportunity that was taken by the indigenous people to mobilize in several uprisings.[4] Reforms to reduce the state represented threats and generated conditions for the mobilization of public employees, who carried out strikes against privatization.

The dual transition with austerity and deregulation policies deepened inequality and reduced the possibility either for conflicts to have tangible results or for the actors to achieve concrete benefits; this made the struggle for claims less effective. Consequently, social unrest declined. After 1998, as recorded by the CAAP (see figure 9.2, shown later), the number of conflicts became lower: from 689 in 1998 to 399 in 2006, a reduction of 42 percent.

The decline of social conflicts occurred when there was a shift in mobilization toward political contestation processes (Sánchez Parga 2010). This was a process of politicization in which the indigenous people affiliated with the Confederation of Indigenous Nationalities (Confederación de Nacionalidades Indígenas, or CONAIE) and the workers of public state-owned companies grouped in the Coordination of Social Movements resisted privatization. For example, the "No" vote triumphed in the 1995 referendum when the government tried to transfer social security to the private sector. One year later, the indigenous people formed the Pachakutik movement, which participated in the elections beginning in 1996 and played important roles in both the congress and local governments.

In 1998, the government felt compelled to convene a Constituent Assembly, which recognized collective and participatory rights while maintaining neoliberal economic regulations. However, this did not resolve the political crisis. The struggle between the elites continued, in addition to the crisis of the political parties and the massive popular mobilizations led in some cases by indigenous people and in others by urban movements. This, apart from the moderating role of the armed forces, was the framework that explains the fall of three presidents in a decade (Abdalá Bucaram in 1997, Jamil Mahuad in 2000, Lucio Gutiérrez in 2005). CONIAE and Pachakutik participated in the government of Gutiérrez (2003–2005), but they soon had to abandon him when he implemented the recommendations of the International Monetary Fund (IMF). While these falls did not produce a breakdown of formal democracy, it was evident that the population's distrust of the political system had deepened.

In short, the dual transition of democracy and economic liberalization tended to undermine the social struggle and to propose its transformation into political contestation. A shift from conflicts for equality to protests against inequality took place (Sánchez Parga 2010). In addition to this, the indigenous movement tried but failed to maintain its advocacy (Ospina 2009). As a result, the indigenous movement was neither able to lead the popular coalition nor to present an alternative to the regime's crisis. The internal struggle of the elites also prevented the achievement of governability.

Given the negative result of the two previous options, a third alternative paved the way. An unexpected actor came to power in 2007: a reformist coalition, encouraged by the rebellion of the *Forajidos* (outlaws) who dismissed Gutiérrez and supported by the urban middle classes sympathizing with the Citizens' Revolution. The revolution was spearheaded by Alianza País under the leadership of Rafael Correa.

POST-NEOLIBERALISM AND THE CITIZENS' REVOLUTION (2007–2017)

The transition from a neoliberal to a post-neoliberal regime resolved the crisis of the political system and transformed society–state relations. A previous study on the Citizens' Revolution highlighted several of its elements: a regime based on strong state capacities, social justice policies, and legitimacy reinforced by ten electoral processes (Ortiz Crespo 2018).

The "return of the state" was a relevant element. The globalization process continued to set the new context, not through austerity or neoliberal deregulation policies, but through Keynesian-inspired policies that needed a strong state. This was possible because of the commodity boom, remittances from migrants, and increased trade with China. Ecuador witnessed a combination of globalization with sovereignty and a boom in oil investments, agribusiness, hydroelectricity, and mining, with a consequent increase in exports and an expansion of the economy with growth rates of more than 4 percent in the 2007–2017 period.

The expansion of the economy and the active role of the state brought more jobs, higher income, and growth of the consumer market. The government prioritized social investment and expanded education and health coverage, reducing poverty and improving equity. The Gini Index measuring inequality declined from 53.3 in 2007 to 44.7 in 2017.[5] These changes also led to important social mobility as the middle class and the vulnerable sectors that emerged from poverty became larger. In 2003, these two social strata accounted for 44 percent of the total population, increasing in 2012 to 73 percent, while the percentage of the population living in poverty dropped from 55 percent to 26 percent (see figure 9.1). In some instances, these numbers were better than the Latin American averages.

Upward mobility and changes in social composition were the conditioning factors that explain the formation of the Citizens' Revolution bloc. It

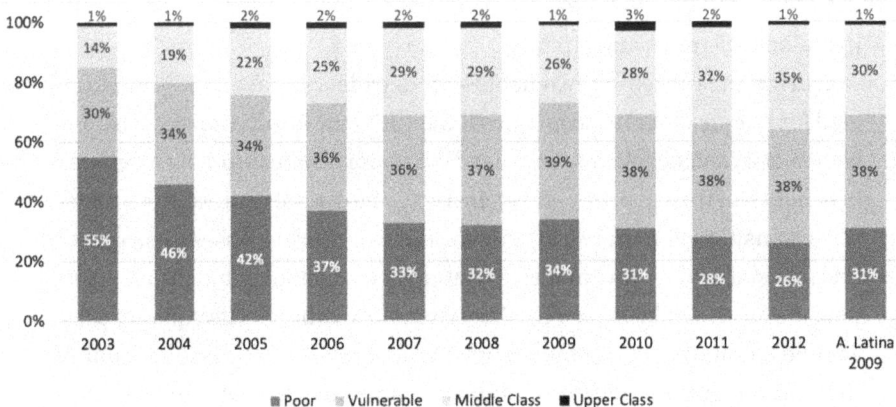

Figure 9.1. Changes in Social Mobility, 2003–2012. Habitus (2013).

was a polyclassist (*policlasista*) and heterogeneous bloc focused on the middle social strata, supported by popular sectors, and allied with business sectors benefiting from the expansion of the domestic market. This coalition secured the hegemony of Alianza País, Correa's governing party, but came into conflict with the financial elites, parties, and media that had dominated the country during the previous twenty-five years of neoliberalism.

The 2007–2008 Constituent Assembly designed the new form of the state. The 2008 Magna Carta recognized a plurinational state, multiple individual and collective rights, freedom of organization (Asamblea Constituyente, 2008, Art. 326, No. 7), collective bargaining (Art. 13), and the right to strike (Art. 14). The Constituent Assembly declared an amnesty for social leaders who had challenged the previous regimes and resolved that the National Assembly enact various laws to regulate participation; in doing so, it designed a broad institutional framework open to civil society at all levels of government. It also entrusted a national council to promote participation, accountability, and social control.

The "return of the state" had a material base resulting from an expanded economy, a stronger tax system, and channeled oil revenues, one that made it possible to implement infrastructure and public services in the territory. This material base set up a new institutional arena for social actors to interact with the state. Whereas previously the state had a weak role in conflicts, the new state expanded its capacity to intervene with resources, public policies, and conflict negotiation mechanisms. In addition, it established units in regions, districts, and circuits.

During the preceding two neoliberal decades, social actors had struggled for equality, but in the period of the Citizens' Revolution their claims were met by social policies, increased job opportunities, and the extension of benefits for the most vulnerable. In a way, the overall context of mobilizations transitioned from being reactive and centered on losses to proactive and focused on new advantages, as described in chapter 1, but the Citizens' Revolution also held its own contradictions. To elaborate, its equality project had a homogenizing content, with a universalist proposal of equality that did not consider ethnic claims. It is paradoxical that after the Constituent Assembly recognized the demand for plurinationality, in subsequent years collective rights were ignored; this prevented indigenous people from participating in the management of bilingual schools and providing prior consultation for environmental projects.

The process of democratization of the country during the period of the Citizens' Revolution was centered on elections, so Alianza País was able to assert itself as the leader of a broad coalition. The area of confrontation was the electoral arena through ten elections, which polarized the conflict between the Citizens' Revolution bloc and the right-wing opposition. This strategy made the main scenario of participation the ballot box and channeled the political mobilization of important sectors of the population. In spite of its efficient operation, Alianza País committed the "original sin" of coming to power hastily, which made it a movement closely connected to the state.

Another aspect that restricted opportunities for social movements was the access to institutions. While in the initial phase of the Constituent Assembly, participation channels had been opened, but these were closed in the second phase of government (2009–2013).[6] This occurred because individual participation at the ballot box was prioritized and the doors on collective advocacy for public policies were closed. The government implemented a series of measures to control the organizations and a systematic policy of decorporatization of the state, which eliminated the channels of direct presence of organized actors in the institutional framework, decision-making, and policy management.[7]

Rafael Correa considered suffrage the means of political participation and that therefore the elected officials were responsible for managing politics; for him, universal policies and the objective of "good living" (*buen vivir*) were the appropriate policies, so he could not yield to particular interests of social organizations. As a result, indigenous groups, the teachers' organization, and the unions that were part of the executive or management bodies of the ministries were excluded from the policy decision-making and management channels.

Other measures were taken to discourage popular organization: the nonobligatory nature of the hitherto compulsory membership in trade unions; the control of groups through the Registry of Social Organizations (Presidencia de la República PR 2013; Decreto 016), which discouraged a variety of social groups from obtaining or maintaining legal status; and the prohibition on public employees' unions. Besides those measures, the government implemented policies on control and prosecution of protest participants after the 30-S of 2010, a failed coup against Rafael Correa (Ortiz Crespo 2011).[8] These policies were aimed at raising the cost of collective action by the contenders (Tilly 2010b).

More than two decades of neoliberalism had weakened the social base of organizations, but the dismantling of corporativism and multiculturalism by the Citizens' Revolution, as well as the new policies of control on groups, eroded the organizational framework and the mobilizing potential of social movements.[9] The main tool of Alianza País to channel the popular participation of a broad "disorganized" and fragmented social current was its "permanent" electoral strategy, which helped it to maintain the support of more than 50 percent of the electorate for a decade.

The secondary positioning of social organizations and movements occurred once the government had consolidated during its first phase (2007–2009), as the former's contribution was necessary within the framework of the hegemony dispute with the elites but not necessary afterward. When the second phase started (2009–2013) and the "Keynesian moment" of the Citizens' Revolution took place, the state played an important role by proposing a policy that discouraged social organization. It was a strong state in the context of a weak civil society. The democratization dynamics of the first phase came to halt when the state's role over civil society became stronger. In the third and final phase (2014–2017), the government implemented policies of prosecution of protest participants, so organizations were deterred from recruiting, participating in policies, demonstrating, and making claims. This was reinforced by the media strategy and the inclusive and nationalist discourse of the Citizens' Revolution, which used a wide range of communication resources. The strategy also encouraged a direct relationship between the leader and the masses that undermined organizational mediations. Rafael Correa's leadership was essential to both his media role and his leading role in state management.

The scenario of democratization and economic growth changed during Correa's third presidential term. The economic crisis caused by the drop in oil prices made the state and its redistributive policies lose vitality. After 2014, the coalition suffered from disaffection among the urban middle social strata and high-poverty groups in the Andean region. Moreover, right-wing parties won the local elections in the main cities. The programmatic discourse shifted toward a pragmatic vision and left behind some of the environmentalist, nationalist, and utopian promises of the 2008 Constitution.

Although nationalist and redistributive politics strengthened the population's support for the regime, the establishment of a post-neoliberal model based on the extraction of natural resources and state modernization dispensing with corporate mediation and ignoring ethnic diversity alienated the radical organizations that considered the "state-centric" project of Alianza País a threat. This led to the emergence of two social currents in the organized popular world: for and against the government.

In terms of democratization, the Citizens' Revolution carried out its reforms within the framework of the rule of law and elections as a means of participation, in addition to promoting policies that improved equality; these dimensions affirmed democratic features, according to the concept of Tilly (2010a). However, there were factors that rolled back the democratization process: the justice referendum that concentrated power in the executive branch and the policies that discouraged social participation, violating the rights of organization and mobilization. Political participation tended to be individualized through the ballot box, and the provision of public services transformed the citizen into a customer. In this framework, direct government–population relations were established, and social mediation was discouraged. In all, the process moved from a phase with a highly capable state and a significant level of democratization to a final phase in which state and government capabilities as well as levels of democracy dropped.

Methods

This study uses the variables defined by the CAAP dataset: actors, claims, actions, places, state interventions, and outcomes of conflicts. *Actors* refers to groups that undertake the action, which may or may not assume a formal organizational expression. *Claims* refers to demands based on injustices or inequalities, whether they are material, political, or cultural. *Actions* refers to the form of struggle or performance of the conflicts, ranging from institutional to extrainstitutional; the most intense ones are those that result in confrontation. Unlike other datasets, CAAP includes the category of *state interventions*, placing the government and its institutions as "interlocutors" that intervene in the conflicts. Their actions may take the form of positive governance, such as negotiation, or negative governance, such as repression. These state interventions are recorded by CAAP as positive and negative *outcomes*.

As the dataset privileges the public nature of the conflict, the CAAP took the information from two print media sources with national circulation: *El Comercio* from Quito and the *Universo* from Guayaquil. Starting in August 2019, two other newspapers were included: *El Telégrafo* and the *Mercurio*.

The analysis of protest events in Ecuador registered by the CAAP dataset is an important source of information; it makes it possible to associate the cycle of conflicts with changes in certain contexts, with variations in democracy and the impact of globalization. One example of this is the Citizens' Revolution, which arose from a crisis in the political system, with the state mediating with the global economic context.

Popular Politics in Ecuador

There were 6,348 conflicts during the period of the Citizens' Revolution (2007–2017). As figure 9.2 shows, the downward trend of conflicts continued from 1999 to 2009. In other words, the level of conflicts decreased at the beginning of the Alianza País government, then increased in the middle of the decade, and decreased again at the end of the decade.

The social fabric was eroded with the migratory stampede produced by the Bank Holiday of 2000. Other factors weakened it further during this period. One of these was related to elections, as social struggle usually decreases at election time: there were annual electoral events in Ecuador, one after another, as a result of a political strategy employed by Alianza País to gain legitimacy. Economic expansion due to the commodity boom and the deployment of infrastructure and public services also made mobilization unnecessary as the population regained confidence in institutions.

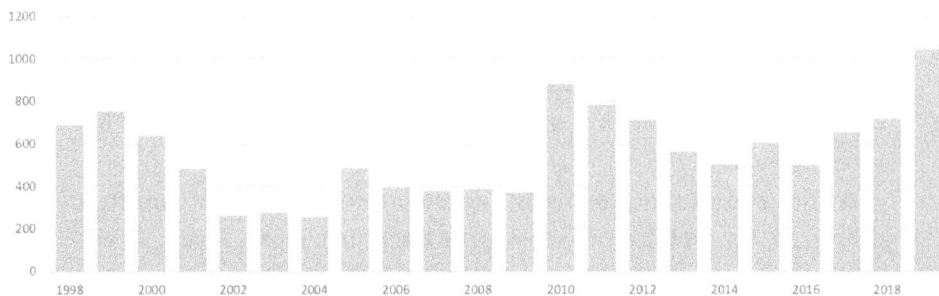

Figure 9.2. Conflicts, 1998–2019. CAAP conflict registry. Chart by author.

The downward trend suggested by Sánchez Parga for the neoliberal period was confirmed in the first term of Correa's government (2007–2009). There were moments when conflicts reemerged due to constitutional disputes, the pressure for the recognition of new provincial constituencies, or marches held by different sectors to demand that the Constituent Assembly include specific texts in the Constitution or take decisions such as amnesty for three hundred social-movement leaders. Environmental and indigenous movements also mobilized to support the Mining Mandate, a legal norm that annulled hundreds of contracts with mining companies.

Beginning in 2010, two phenomena had an impact on the reactivation of conflicts: the modernization of the state and the debate on the laws on natural resources. The former involved reforms that rationalized the labor relations of public employees and provoked the reaction of police and groups of state workers who participated in the 30-S failed coup. In this second phase (2009–2013), mobilization grew around the debate on mining, water resources, and land bills, through which the government would have determined the direction of economic development.

The government was also concerned that popular mobilization could destabilize it, and therefore needed actors to struggle on its behalf in public spaces.[10] It encouraged popular organizations of fishers, peasants, public employees, and teachers (Ortiz Campo 2021) and forged alliances with truck drivers and factions of the indigenous movement.

Correa's third term (2014–2017) was marked by the emergence of a new right-wing movement with an edge based on their electoral victory in 2014.

There were other factors that revealed the hegemonic dispute: the drop in oil prices, which jeopardized a dollarized economy, lower public opinion confidence, and the political weakness of Alianza País due to internal disagreements.

At the end of the progressive decade, the frequency of conflicts decreased, but mobilizations to oppose the state increased, such as the marches of the Black Flags (Banderas Negras). This movement representing the political right fought against the alleged electoral fraud that extended the dominance of Alianza País after Correa's departure.[11] In general, during Correa's third term, social organizations played a secondary role: those linked to the government did not manage to influence public policies, and opposition social movements did not manage to promote a sustained campaign that would allow them to create an alternative to the government or to right-wing parties.

Actors (Who)

In the period 2007–2017, workers were the most prominent actors, with 2,194 conflict events, a number that would be even larger if 984 conflicts by employee unions and 550 by trade unions were added (see figure 9.3). Workers were followed by local groups (1,591 events) and neighborhood organizations (1,466 events). Most events were of an urban nature. The category of heterogeneous groups—including environmentalists, human rights defenders, the sector of the middle class, and feminists—participated in 1,135 events. Comparatively, indigenous people and peasants added only 1,178 conflicts, supporting the notion of their secondary role throughout the period. These groups participated in relevant areas of contestation, such as education (for bilingual education), environment (for resistance to mining and oil projects), institutions and regulations (for the rejection of decorporatization and bills), and human rights (in relation to localized persecution). However, they lost the social and political leadership role they had in the antineoliberal struggle and were divided into various currents: in favor of or against the government. They also failed to achieve a successful electoral political expression of opposition to Correa's government.[12]

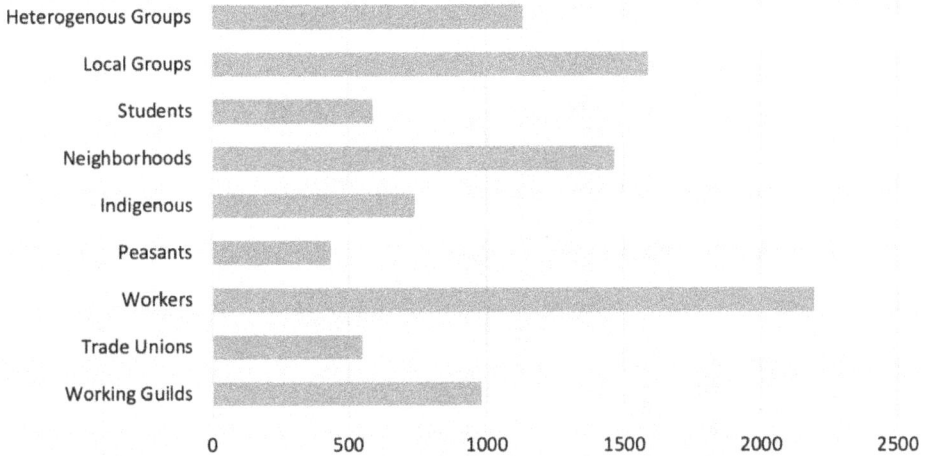

Figure 9.3. Actors, 2007–2017. CAAP conflict registry. Chart by author.

Claims (Why)

An examination of the claims shows that the most significant ones were the rejections of state policy (1,399 events) and labor policies (1,344) (see figure 9.4). The third place is occupied by claims against corruption (1,108) and in smaller numbers by wage claims (354). The gap between labor policies and wage claims was due to both the economic expansion that substantially improved incomes and the initiative to improve wages taken by the government; however, employers were reluctant to comply with mandates such as "outsourcing." There were 987 events related to claims for funding made by local and neighborhood actors to state and local governments as the latter had the budgets for public works. The "others" category is also important, with 1,117 conflict events with heterogeneous claims: housing, environment, human rights (especially due to the persecution of social leaders), and gender violence.

Environmental conflicts were directed at transnational companies and the state, which played an active role in the expansion of the oil and mining areas toward the south of the country and in the construction of several infrastructure megaprojects.[13] On this subject, and to identify specific data on environmental conflicts, the Environmental Justice Atlas reports

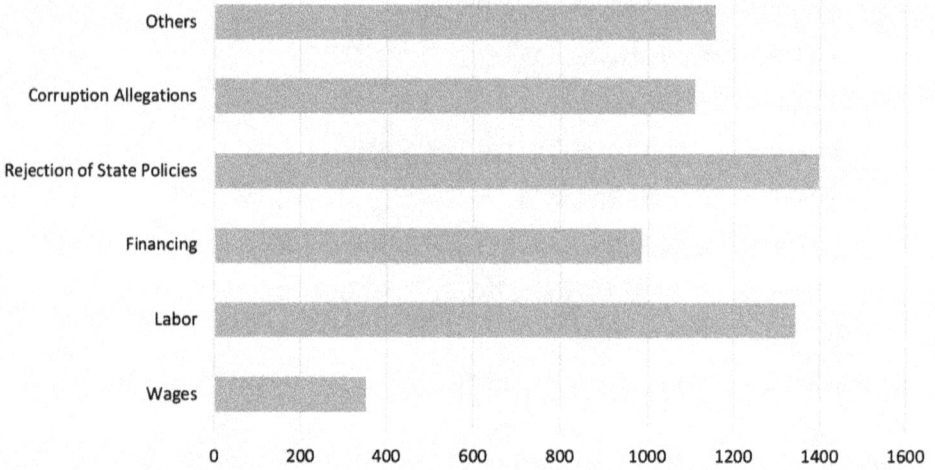

Figure 9.4. Claims, 2007–2017. CAAP conflict registry. Chart by author.

twenty-nine conflicts in 2021 dealing with mining (ten), oil (nine), water (six), and land (four).[14]

Most of these conflicts took place in indigenous and rural territories, had a medium or long duration, and employed highly conflictive performances. It is necessary to distinguish conflicts with local and regional incidence, the so-called eco-territorial conflicts (Svampa 2010), from those conflicts with national character. The former mobilized a variety of actors, such as antimining communities, irrigation boards, the indigenous movement, and environmental networks, to reject projects that they considered harmful to the rights of nature, as approved in the Constitution. The latter included actions around water, land, and mining bills (2009–2012). Examples include the March for Water, Life, and the Dignity of the Peoples (2012) and the mobilization around the Yasuní project (2014). The March for Water spread throughout the country and was supported by several local governments, CONAIE, teachers, and students, with the participation of nearly seventy thousand people; it was characterized by its great cultural and symbolic richness around the theme of water. However, this action failed to modify the government's intention to exploit natural resources or, more generally, the inclusion of the left-wing environmentalist pole in its platform.[15]

Another significant event was related to the Yasuní-ITT (Ispingo-Tiputini-Tambococha) initiative, aimed at keeping oil underground in the Amazon. The government led the proposal but later cancelled it, arguing that the international community had not supported it. In response, young environmentalists demanded a referendum to carry out the initiative, but the electoral authority denied it on the grounds of lack of signatures (Ortiz Crespo 2016, 2018). These conflicts revealed the tension caused by the primary export model, the leftist discourse of which alienated representative indigenous and environmental organizations, and the progressive government declaring itself to be leftist and organizing massive countermarches to counteract these mobilizations.[16]

In order to have a more precise idea of the weight of redistributive claims, we can separate them from those of a political nature. Redistributive claims comprised topics involving wages, labor, and financing, and political claims comprised protests against state policy and corruption. As figure 9.5 shows, conflicts over redistributive claims gradually declined, but in 2015, protests with political claims reached 55 percent. This means that struggles for political objectives increased during the third term of Correa's government, and that these were linked to right-wing parties increasing their political relevance.

Political claims were related to parties such as Sociedad Patriótica during the 30-S failed coup and the mobilizations led by conservative groups

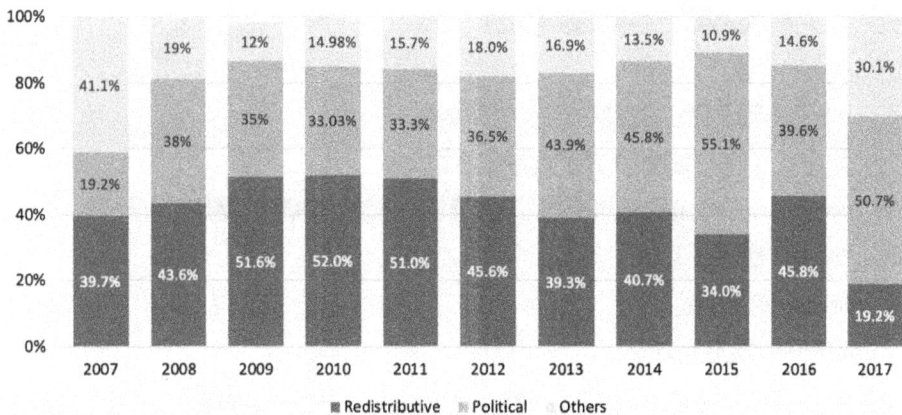

Figure 9.5. Redistributive and Political Claims, 2007–2017. CAAP conflict registry. Chart by author.

rejecting the tax bills of the inheritance and capital gains laws in 2015. These were moments when the opposition took to the streets to confront a government that ignored the property rights of Ecuadorians by accusing it of "authoritarianism" and "corruption." Then the dispute for hegemony restarted, which allowed right-wing parties to co-opt President Lenín Moreno to participate in their government.[17]

Actions (How)

Another variable in the conflict cycle is related to the forms of action or performances used by the contending actors. In general, during the Citizens' Revolution there was a high level of demonstrations (1,761 conflict events), followed by marches (834), threats (857), and suspended actions (704). Figure 9.6 reveals that less-confrontational forms of struggle generally took place during the Citizens' Revolution.

Differentiating between high-intensity (roadblocks, takeovers, protests, invasions) and low-intensity forms of action (marches, stoppages or strikes, threats) shows that the former had significant peaks, especially from 2011 to 2012, when they rose to 57 percent, and again in 2017, when they reached

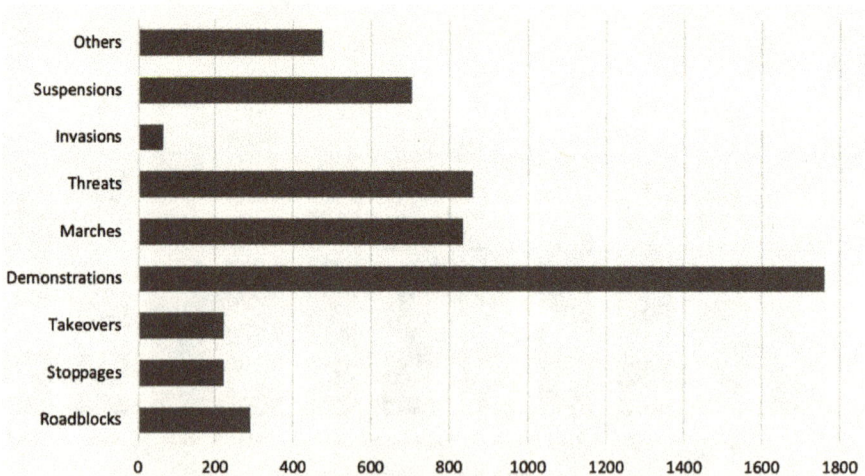

Figure 9.6. Actions, 2007–2017. CAAP conflict registry. Chart by author.

67 percent of all forms of action.[18] In the first case, the increase was related to the debate about natural resource laws. In the second, mobilizations against tax bills and alleged election fraud polarized the conflict.

There was also a difference between the intensity levels of the previous neoliberal period and that of the Citizens' Revolution: in the former, the mobilizations managed to destabilize the governments with more confrontational forms of struggle, which led to the fall of three presidents; this did not happen under Correa. The institutional framework of the state and the hegemony of the Citizens' Revolution were consistent during this period and social opposition did not succeed in overthrowing the president.

Targets (Whom)

Government ministries were a target of conflict in 969 events, followed by the president (829) and the judiciary (799) (see figure 9.7). While local governments played an important role before the Citizens' Revolution, the CAAP reports lower instances of municipalities (539 conflicts) and provincial councils (383 conflicts), and cantons or districts (107) as targets of protests. Overall, conflicts tended to take place at the national level, with a leading role of the executive, which had greater capacities and concentrated decision-making, and a secondary role of the legislature and the decentralized state.

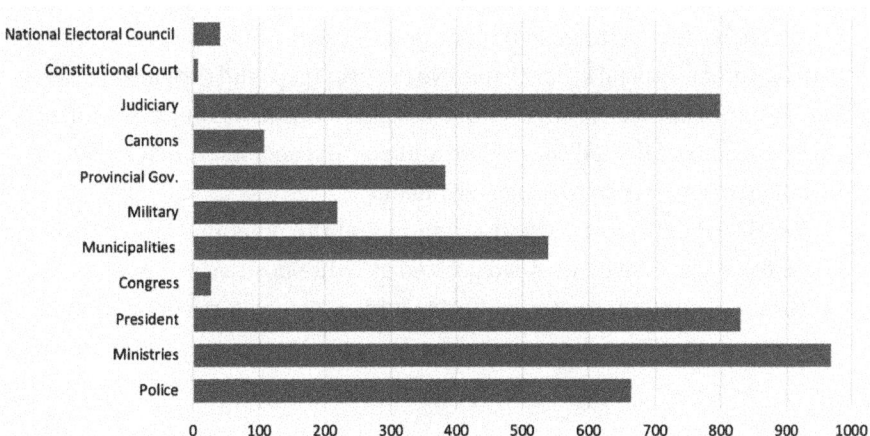

Figure 9.7 Targets, 2007–2017. CAAP conflict registry. Chart by author.

State Response and Outcomes of Conflict

In the neoliberal period, there was "an atrophy of institutional capacity for mediation" (Sánchez Parga 2010), while in the post-neoliberal period there was a growing capacity for state intervention by both the executive and the judiciary. CAAP reports higher frequencies of intervention in conflicts by the executive branch, government ministries, police, and judges compared to earlier periods.

While the "return of the state" was visible toward the end of the Citizens' Revolution, the government shifted toward mechanisms that discouraged organization through regulatory and administrative control systems, such as Decree 016 and accusations against social leaders, several of whom it imprisoned. The measures provoked claims for the defense of human rights. These disputes were associated with the discourse in defense of freedoms, banners promoted by NGOs, the mainstream media, and candidate and banker Guillermo Lasso. The defense of the social and collective rights of popular groups was, therefore, related to the struggle for freedom of expression and against authoritarianism, and this defense was led by right-wing parties. This discourse was the emblem that later justified Lenín Moreno's switch from Alianza País in 2017.

During the late years of the Citizens' Revolution, the government distanced itself from civil society and lost the political initiative. This lack of direction was evident in measures such as the Organic Criminal Law, which threatened health personnel for medical malpractice crimes and caused them to mobilize; entrance exams to universities, considered by young people to be a threat to their futures; the withdrawal of 40 percent of state support for social security to solve the fiscal gap; and the Family Plan, which, due to its conservative nature, alienated feminist groups. Several of these measures affected the middle and popular sectors, which began to distance themselves from the government.

The CAAP datasets record information on the outcomes of conflicts. These figures can be further categorized as either positive or negative. By outcomes of conflict, we mean the capacity to meet claims or to contain conflicts forcibly. Over the period of the Citizens' Revolution, 1,836 conflicts

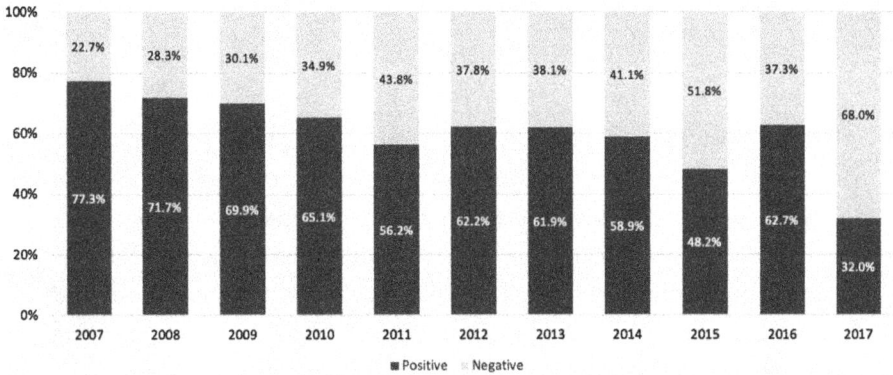

Figure 9.8. Positive and Negative Outcomes, 2007–2017.
CAAP conflict registry. Chart by author.

involved negotiation, and of this number, 1,399 had a positive or favorable resolution. Turning to negative outcomes, 1,058 conflicts were rejected, 927 had no resolution, and 288 were repressed. In general, the Citizens' Revolution was a phase of greater positive governance, with the mediating presence of the state. However, in 2015 and 2017, toward the end of Correa's third term in office, negative governance numbers grew (see figure 9.8).[19]

Places (Where)

In terms of location, the epicenter of the conflicts was the province of Pichincha (2,357 conflicts), where the capital and largest city, Quito, is located. After Pichincha, the second-largest number of conflicts (1,318) was concentrated in the province of Guayas, site of the city of Guayaquil. These places were followed by the provinces of Manabí (305), Azuay (251), and Esmeraldas (200). Conflicts in the southern provinces (Azuay, Loja, El Oro, Morona, and Zamora) reached 624 events, some of them related to mining conflicts that took place in those areas. Thinking about regions, during the Citizens' Revolution, the bulk of conflicts were concentrated in the Sierra (56 percent), followed by the Costa (34 percent) and the Amazon (5 percent).

Conclusions

Alianza País was born against a backdrop of a profound political crisis that started at the end of the twentieth century and the beginning of the twenty-first. Its actions relegitimized democratic institutions through a constitutional process and successive electoral victories, which stabilized the democratic regime. Consultations with the population and inclusive policies also responded to the redistributive claims coming from the neoliberal period; these gave an impression of greater democracy. However, a shift began to take place in the middle of the decade, with features that rolled back democracy, such as the reform of the justice system and the police, the prosecution of protest participants, and the distancing of the government from civil society.

The central factor that modified the conflict model was the state, whose stronger material base and institutional and media capacities made it the interlocutor, arbiter, and pivot of mobilization. Redistribution policies gained public support. State modernization affected corporate privileges and streamlined institutional processes, which provoked a backlash from various sectors. The pattern of accumulation based on oil and mining production led to the mobilization of peasant and indigenous actors, supported by the environmental movement. In addition, universal policies for "good living" were welcomed by the population but these did not recognize ethnic diversity.

The stronger capacities of the state allowed the Citizens' Revolution to confirm its hegemony, to subordinate social organizations through networks loyal to the government, and to exclude relevant social movements from the channels of access to the state. It was a regime that individualized the relationship with society by weakening social mediations and converting the population into voters, clients of public services, and the audience of the media and political spectacles made by the government. In general, the matrix of relationships between a state with strong capacities and civil society created a multipolar conflict, with several divided campaigns and without the leadership necessary to achieve a clear positioning of social movements.

Economic expansion and the "return of the state" formed a sui generis adaptation to globalization. In the preceding neoliberal period, austerity and deindustrialization policies made the trade union movement weak but produced the conditions for the emergence of the indigenous movement in the 1990s and popular mobilizations centered on the demand for equality. The second phase of neoliberal reforms provoked the mobilization of public workers against privatization. Consequently, the social struggle for economic and social claims shifted toward contestation against the democratic and neoliberal regime.

The economic boom that occurred after dollarization, the increase in commodity prices, and the post-neoliberal model allowed Correa's government to expand the domestic market; this gained the support of the population and reduced social conflict. However, the model also produced actions to oppose environmental policies and the decorporatization of the state by CONAIE and sectors of public employees, teachers, and the police. The oil price crisis in 2014–2015 halted expansion and state action, provoked an increase in redistributive conflicts, and undermined the social base of the Citizens' Revolution, which provided conditions for right-wing parties to reemerge.

In general, globalization weakened class actors organized in trade unions and peasant organizations; this revealed a social division resulting from twenty-five years of neoliberalism and a corrosive current that involved the market and caused a broad process of precariousness. The post-neoliberal model of the Citizens' Revolution improved equality and reduced poverty but failed to solve social and ethnic gaps; one of the consequences was precisely the distance between the poorest sectors of the population and the progressive pole. State-mediated globalization accentuated the conflict over natural resources, an area in which the indigenous movement remained an important actor.

Several trends can be noted in the 2007–2017 conflict cycle: in terms of protest frequency, the decline continued, but there was an increase in the second phase related to the new constitution, and a new reduction in the third phase. Paradoxically, workers remained active in conflicts and local and heterogeneous actors also gained relevance.[20] There was a significant occurrence of redistributive claims, which dropped in the third phase when political claims became more important. In terms of performances, there was lower intensity, but the 30-S failed coup, the March of the Black Flags, and environmental conflicts were moments of high confrontation. The majority of outcomes were positive, but the negative ones grew toward the end of the Citizens' Revolution. They had a greater territorial impact in the Sierra and cities such as Quito and Guayaquil remained the main localities of conflicts.

The decline in conflicts observed in the neoliberal period continued until 2009, but the cycle took on new faces. Multipolarity, or the division into at least two currents, one close to and the other distant from the government, took place with the emergence of local governments, environmental organizations, right-wing parties, the police, and, in the last stage, LGBT, feminist, and other groups with strong identity traits. In the midst of weaker organizational mediations, the citizen, reformist, and nationalist movement grouped by the state became stronger, while there was neither a significant sum of subjects organized for mobilization nor a catalyst movement, given the withdrawal of the indigenous movement. In addition, new forms of digital activism emerged, especially at the end of the progressive decade, when social networks became more popular.[21]

To sum up, while the expansion of democracy facilitated social mobilization and broadened the opportunity for conflict, the erosion of democracy limited organization and restricted mobilization and social conflict but accentuated political conflict. Globalization had a contradictory impact because it deterred conflict when the economy grew, but it also posed threats when policies that deepened inequality were imposed, as in the preceding neoliberal period. The model based on the exploitation of natural resources also caused conflicts but required a state with repressive and controlling policies that would threaten mobilization.

Notes

1. The left turn in Ecuador in 2007 is known as the Citizens' Revolution. The Alianza País coalition won the elections and came to power with the presidency of Rafael Correa and the call for a Constituent Assembly.
2. The conceptual approach used is the conflict cycle and the relational theory of social movements of Tilly (1998) and Tarrow (1997).

3. The quantitative dimension is based on the Conflict Registry of the Andean Center for Popular Action (CAAP) and the journal *Ecuador Debate*. The center has published analyses by José Sánchez Parga (1995, 1996, 2010) on certain stages of conflict, as well as periodic articles in *Ecuador Debate*. I acknowledge Francisco Rhon, executive director of the CAAP, and Lama Al Ibrahim, coordinator of the Registry, for sharing the dataset, and Jesús Tapia, who processed the dataset and prepared the tables and graphs. I also acknowledge colleagues who provided their comments: Pablo Ospina of UASB, Margarita Velasco of the Social Observatory of Ecuador, Nora Fernández of the Faculty of Economics at PUCE, Philip Altmann of the School of Sociology at Universidad Central, Stalin Herrera of IEE, and researcher David Suárez.

4. The First Indigenous Uprising (1990) occurred almost simultaneously with the Caracazo in Venezuela (1989).

5. The Gini Index for Ecuador can be viewed at https://datos.bancomundial.org/indicator/SI.POV.GINI?locations=EC.

6. In this chapter, we talked about three phases of government in 2007–2009, 2009–2013, and 2014–2017, which overlapped with the three consecutive presidential terms of Rafael Correa.

7. A study carried out in April 2009 by the National Secretariat of Planning and Development (SENPLADES) concluded that the Ecuadorian state suffered from a generalized phenomenon of corporatization and found that fifty-nine councils had civil society participation. Then the government dismantled the representation of trade union actors in state bodies and withdrew the management of bilingual education from CONAIE.

8. On September 30, the police, supported by the Sociedad Patriótica party and groups of workers linked to Movimiento Popular Democrático, held a national riot against the government that resulted in the temporary detention of President Rafael Correa in their Regiment Quito No. 1. The intervention of the army deterred the police, so the attempted coup failed. After an initial investigation that resulted in some prosecutions, a national court declared the case prescribed in 2019.

9. There is a phenomenon of organizational erosion, but no study offers a complete picture of the situation. According to surveys such as Latinbarometer, the union organization indexes of the Ministry of Labor, and studies on civil society, organizational levels have plummeted drastically since the beginning of the century (Andreetti, Bustamante, and Durán 2006).

10. The actors that formed Alianza País included electrical and social security unions as well as various trade unions, the United Workers Front (FUT), and Women for Life; peasant organizations such as the Eloy Alfaro Front, the National Federation of Agroindustrial Workers, Free Peasants of

Ecuador (Fenacle), the Ecuadorian Federation of Indigenous People (FEI), and the National Confederation of Peasant, Indigenous, and Black Women Organizations (Fenocin) (Harnecker 2011, 111). Several of these organizations were related to left-wing groups that became part of Alianza País.

11. The marches took place within the framework of the 2017 presidential elections in the surroundings of the National Electoral Court when Guillermo Lasso, candidate of the Creando Oportunidades movement (CREO), ignored the results that favored Lenín Moreno for Alianza País; months later, CREO supported Moreno's shift against Correa. The mobilizations promoted by right-wing sectors continued throughout the decade: first during the constituent phase in Guayaquil and then with the 30-S police riot; there were protests against abortion held by prolife groups, in addition to the March of the Black Flags and the pro-fraud mobilizations.

12. Pachakutik did not achieve significant electoral levels until 2000 when it allied with mestizo groups and Gutiérrez; however, these levels fell below 5 percent and remained so until the 2017 presidential elections, when they allied with Izquierda Democrática and registered 8 percent.

13. The CAAP Conflict Registry is limited because it does not distinguish between environmental claims and other types of claims that gained relevance in this century. Therefore, the data were drawn from the Environmental Justice Atlas.

14. For more information about the Environmental Justice Atlas (https://ejatlas.org/), refer to Temper, Bene, and Martinez-Alier (2015).

15. Various indigenous, environmentalist, popular, and left-wing actors formed a new coalition after the October 2019 strike.

16. The government managed to mobilize thousands of people against the March for Water through countermarches. In the following years, it called for massive rallies supported by social organizations that showed great logistical capacity as well as legitimization or electoral support devices; those rallies took place on May Day and other special occasions (Ortiz Crespo 2016).

17. During the Moreno government (2017–2021), a coalition of businessmen, military, media, and right-wing parties emerged. This was accompanied by a return to neoliberal policies and an authoritarian regime; evidence of this is the state repression in the October strike, which resulted in eleven dead, the declaration of a state of emergency, and a permanent curfew during the COVID-19 pandemic.

18. Evictions, detentions, and casualties reported in the CAAP registry were not included because these represent forms of state intervention, not forms of social struggle.

19. The categories "postponement of resolution" and "others" were not considered.
20. Since the 1980s, after the loss of class identity (worker and peasant), there have been changes in the social structure with the emergence of phenomena of urbanization, precariousness, and social differentiation, accompanied by new ethnic and gender identities.
21. Studies show that this activism was essential to the erosion of the progressive hegemony (see Ortiz Campo 2021).

CHAPTER TEN

Dynamics of Political Contention in Brazil

From Deepening to Debacle of Neo-Developmentalism

LUCIANA TATAGIBA AND ANDRÉIA GALVÃO

Introduction

The pattern of protests in Brazil changed significantly between 2011 and 2016. This shift is both quantitative, with the rise in the number of protests, and qualitative, with more heterogeneous social bases, claims, and repertoires of collective action being mobilized. In this chapter, we explore these features in the course of political contention and their relation to the economic and political crises faced by Brazilian society during this period.

The period when the Workers' Party (Partido dos Trabalhadores, or PT) took office (2003–2016) was characterized by a paradoxical combination of a neoliberal macroeconomic policy and the expansion of the state's role as a driver of economic development (Paulani 2016). The concept of neo-developmentalism seeks to grasp this singular economic and political landscape (Singer 2015). Brazilian literature has assessed the major impact of neo-developmentalist policy on distributive conflict over the appropriation of income and public resources (Boito 2018; Carvalho 2018). The distributive conflict, which is ordinarily intrinsic to capitalist societies, tends to escalate in contexts of economic crisis, such as that faced by the world as of 2008 and

Brazil after 2011. Moreover, unlike what was seen in other countries, the PT governments did not promote a "neoliberal shock" to tackle this crisis. On the contrary, the administrations of Lula da Silva chose to expand public spending, especially on social policies. Dilma Rousseff, in her turn, deepened the neo-developmentalist policy during her first term in office, exacerbating the disputes over the role of the state in the model of economic development and facing stiff opposition from the bourgeois sectors associated with international financial capital. To tackle the political and economic crises, Rousseff's second term adopted a neoliberal agenda, which caused widespread opposition along the political spectrum. Since then, Brazil has been quickly moving toward de-democratization and austerity reforms, according to figure 1.5 (see this book's introductory chapter).

This shifting context created new opportunities and threats for collective action and shaped the dynamics of social mobilization while, at the same time, it was being shaped by these dynamics.[1] In short, in this context of political contention, two opposing sides emerged: one seeking to advance political–economic reforms toward social justice, the other trying to restore the neoliberal agenda and promote austerity policies. Through the period covered by the dataset (from 2011 to 2016) organizations traditionally acting as mobilizers, such as labor unions and popular and student movements, remained important in organizing protests; however, their ability to recruit participants was undermined. Traditional forms of collective action, such as strikes and occupations, persisted and even increased in number. At any rate, what was new during this period was the emergence of a new right—or rather, new right-wing groups—supporting moral conservatism and austerity policies. The conflict playing out in the streets was framed in a way that associated the PT with corruption. As a result, the new right provoked a strong anti-PT sentiment in society known as *antipetismo*. In the midst of this political atmosphere, violence—in practice and discourse—became central to the new right's repertoire of action.

We observed two peaks of mobilization between 2011 and 2016. The first, in 2013, emerged when right- and left-wing groups competed for dominance on the streets, even in the same protest events held in June, which came to be known as *Jornadas de Junho*. The second peak occurred between 2015 and 2016, when the new right took the lead in organizing protest events calling for the impeachment of former president Rousseff[2] and the arrest of former president Lula.[3] A process of political instability took place between these two mobilization peaks, with the government gradually losing its support base, especially among the bourgeoisie and the middle classes, who began to express their growing dissatisfaction with the government's social policies and the state's intervention in the economy. These disputes redefined the Brazilian political landscape, contributing to the electoral victory of the extreme right in the presidential election of 2018.

Our analysis is guided by the integrated approach to protests (Tatagiba and Galvão 2019). With this approach, we intend to combine politics and economy into the understanding of the *context* in which protests emerge, drawing attention to the way in which class and other identity categories are integrated into the conformation of the *actors* who protest. This approach allows for an analysis of political contention across different social cleavages, as opposed to addressing them independently. In our analysis, we used data from a new database of protests in Brazil, created as part of our broader project named "Political contention from the rise to the crisis of the PT governments (2003–2016)."

This chapter is divided into three parts. First, we present our theoretical-methodological approach. Second, we address the political and economic factors shaping this context of contention. Third, we present the data on the protests, more specifically, an analysis of the actors who protest and their claims.

The Integrated Approach to Protests

We seek to contribute to the research agenda on the impacts of the global crisis of capitalism on national sociopolitical processes, particularly on the modeling of political contention (Barker et al. 2013; Della Porta 2015; Grasso & Giugni 2016). Drawing on different analytical approaches, these authors examine the relationships among the dynamics of the crisis of capitalism, class contradictions, and challenges to democracy.

Inspired by this debate, we offer an *integrated approach to protests*, based on a dialogue between the theory of political contention and Marxist theory. For this, we intend to combine economy and politics, class and other identity categories, and labor and social movements at the national and transnational levels. The integrated approach allows for the examination of the relationship between different social movements—those associated with labor issues, such as unions, or with other identities and goals—in order to explore their particularities and similarities, in addition to the connections between different movements and waves of mobilization.

In line with this perspective, by calling different subaltern conditions into question, we assume that movements that are seen as cultural and behavioral, fighting for changes in customs and values, are concurrently interfering with social positions, including class positions. These movements are fighting not only for symbolic but also material resources, and in doing so, they interfere with the distributive conflict, the conflict over the appropriation of income and public resources, which plays a central role in class conflict.

When analyzing the Global South, Della Porta (2015) recalls that economic tensions were historically important for the emergence of protests in peripheral countries and that a set of grievances can be identified as the result of the crisis of neoliberal capitalism that began in 2008 and the policy of commodification of rights. Current protests are calling into question not only the economic consequences emerging from this context, but also the legitimacy of the political system, its forms of participation, and the popularity of governments.

The resurgence of conservative movements and right-wing protests in the first decades of the twenty-first century has been commonly associated with economic and political crises (Davidson 2013; Zajak 2013; Shefner, Rowland, and Pasdirtz 2015; Caren, Gaby, and Herrold 2017). Although these movements express, to a great extent, the dissatisfactions of dominant social groups, they are not exclusively composed of these groups. Their social base mainly consists of middle-class groups aspiring to "appropriate part of the state for themselves" (Davidson 2013, 287). In general, these groups conceive of the poor as parasites draining the state's resources without contributing to the financing of the social policies from which they benefit. The middle class, however, does not have a cohesive political orientation, it "can be both liberal ('left-wing') on social issues and neoliberal on economic ones" (Davidson 2013, 286), possibly supporting far-right movements or reformist movements, especially in times of political polarization. This indeterminacy suggests that a social base can, under different circumstances and leadership, support different political projects. On the other hand, different social bases may engage in the same protest events and movements, even if they do so for different reasons. Tensions between classes and projects are thus present.

In view of this, we argue that the growing protests disrupting Brazil beginning in 2011 were driven by the impacts of the crisis of capitalism on the Brazilian economy, the contradictory legacies of the PT governments, and the different types of dissatisfactions they have caused (Singer and Loureiro 2016). The conflict around the appropriation of income and public resources was expressed on the streets in different political agendas, ranging from the defense of social policies to the fight against corruption. Different groups, movements, and social classes have been variously, irregularly, and even contradictorily connected by these agendas.

Methods

Our research uses the Protest Event Analysis (PEA) methodology, which was created in the field of social movement studies and involves the production of a catalog of protest events based on the definition of a set of variables linked to the research questions (Koopmans and Rucht 2002; Hutter 2014). As highlighted by Arce and Wada in the introduction to this book, the main advantage of this method is that it allows us to examine a varied set of themes and social movements and build historical series to identify variations in the patterns of protests over time and space, something not provided by traditional methods of social movement research, such as the case study and qualitative approaches (Hutter 2014).

Despite being a widely used method, PEA is not without problems. One of its disadvantages is the selectivity and bias of the sources. Because an event is more likely to be reported by the media the larger, more violent, and more long-lasting it is (Klandermans and Staggenborg 2002), any list of events in a period of time will inevitably be incomplete, so that only those events that managed to overcome the obstacles in becoming newsworthy are included. This inclusion is in itself an indicator of the contenders' success, even though the media do not always frame them favorably.

The source used to build our database was the newspaper *Folha de São Paulo* (FSP), one of the largest nationwide daily newspapers in Brazil, based in the state of São Paulo. The FSP was chosen because of its digital collection, in which all editions printed since 1921 are available.[4] The possibility of having regular access to the news, with national coverage, and a functional platform weighted favorably for choosing this source in view of our research goals. This source, however, also carries certain biases to our analysis. The first type of bias refers to the newspaper's editorial line. The FSP clearly adopted a position against the PT governments, especially after 2006 (Biroli and Mantovani 2014), following the coverage of the Mensalão and Lava Jato corruption scandals.[5] This bias may have affected the way in which the protests were reported, in the sense that events in defense of the government and/or the PT may have been underreported, while those organized by the opposition received greater coverage. The second type of bias relates to the fact that the southeast region is better represented in our sample (59.6 percent), particularly the state of São Paulo (40 percent).[6] Therefore, it is important to take this bias into account whenever we refer to national trends. Finally, the third problem is the quality of information. Two important variables that frequently appeared as missing information in our database are the organizations calling the protests and the number of participants.[7]

Due to our theoretical approach, we address contentious collective action broadly. This is one of the specificities of our database: it includes events that were called by social movement organizations and labor unions, as well as "spontaneous" demonstrations called by unorganized collectives or individuals, comprising various events such as strikes, occupations, marches, art intervention, depredation, derision against politicians, roadblocks, and rebellions. Our unit of analysis is the protest event. We understand a protest event as a collective action involving at least two people, initiated by groups in society, with an extrainstitutional nature (that is, a public event that disrupts routine and either causes some type of damage or threatens to do so), intended to support claims or grievances that, if redressed, would affect the interests of others (Tilly 1978). The most significant challenge in using this concept is to define whether what is reported by the news represents a single event or multiple events: in other words, to establish temporal and geographical boundaries (Olzak 1989). For the protest event to be defined as *one* event, all of the following characteristics must be present: actions must have the same start date, with no interruption, in response to the same "call" and sustaining the same claim/grievance, even if they are different and/or take place in different locations. In 2019, we made a version of the database available for public consultation with four of its original twenty-four variables.[8]

For this chapter, we focused our analysis on two variables: the actors at the protests and their claims. With these variables, we can highlight correlations between the political and the economic crises and characterize the dynamics of political contention during the period studied. Our database comprises 1,285 protest events organized between January 1, 2011 (Rousseff's first day in office) and August 31, 2016 (when she was definitively removed from office by the Senate), an average of 222.6 protests per year.

Crises of the Neo-Developmentalist Model and Political Instability

Brazil is a peripheral country integrated into the global economy, and thus vulnerable to shifts in the international context (Pochmann and Moraes 2017). So when the international economic crisis erupted in 2008, the dispute between groups defending different models of economic development became aggravated. While some groups supported adopting or deepening the neo-developmentalist approach, others expressed their critiques of the state's intervention in the economy, calling instead for the return to an orthodox neoliberal perspective. Yet other groups were critical of the social and environmental costs associated with a development model based on agribusiness and exploitation of natural resources. This dispute—which was an expression of the divisions between right- and left-wing social groups—intensified the distributive conflict between social classes, increasing the dissatisfaction with the PT governments and generating various forms of antipetismo.

The PT governments sought to tackle the crisis by expanding credit provision through state-owned banks, reducing interest rates, offering tax incentives to stimulate consumer spending and revitalize certain industries (such as construction), and devising measures to create more jobs. This policy rapidly led to economic growth between 2010 and 2013, low unemployment rates (until 2014),[9] and reduction of inequality (Pochmann 2014). Concurrently, the combination of three factors led to an external imbalance: the production structure had not been modernized, industrial production had been stagnant since 2010, and the price of commodities dropped as of mid-2012 (Mello and Rossi 2018). The appreciation of the *real* against the dollar kept inflation under control, but the disproportionate increase in imports led to a negative impact on the balance of trade (Carvalho 2018), affecting industrial production and investments in the country (Carneiro 2018).

The strategy to integrate the Brazilian economy into the world economy through the formation of large national groups in industries in which heavy engineering and agribusiness companies are competitive had impacts on the environment and labor because this generates lower-quality jobs. Transformations in the occupational structure—the decreasing of the industrial employment rate and expansion of the service sector—contributed to the dissemination of a new pattern of labor relations, one that is more flexible and individualized. New types of employment contracts and new approaches to managing the workforce resulted in the elimination of supervisory occupations and created more precarious labor relations, even for skilled workers with higher education.

Furthermore, as a result of the expansion of credit to families and rise in consumer spending, inflation was hitting services provided by less qualified workers (domestic workers, hairdressers, civil construction workers), affecting mainly those "workers whose wages increased less—those who found themselves in the middle of the [social] pyramid" (Carvalho 2018, 47). The ongoing international crisis and the slowdown in the flow of international capital toward peripheral economies in 2011 limited the expansion of credit and consumer spending.

During her first term in office (2011–2014), Dilma Rousseff adopted a series of measures that further deepened the neo-developmentalist model in place—interest rate reductions, payroll exemptions for businesses, tax incentives, control of energy and oil derivatives prices, additional financial support for the Brazilian Development Bank (BNDES), devaluation of the *real*—all in response to demands of the real sector. The incentives granted to the private sector by the government were not able "to reverse the trajectory of investment retraction" and stimulate industrial production (Mello and Rossi 2018, 270).

In 2013, investments started to decline. The process of upward social mobility was interrupted, as seen by a drop in the percentage of Brazilians whose living standards correspond to those of the upper-middle and middle classes (Quadros 2015). However, it should be noted that the weakening of the Brazilian economic foundations did not affect broad macroeconomic indicators such as GDP and the unemployment rate, nor was it noticed by ordinary citizens.[10] A Datafolha survey released in January 2012 indicated that during Dilma Rousseff's first term, the government had reached the highest approval rating since the reestablishment of democracy in 1988. Its approval ratings ("great" and "good") rose from 47 percent in March 2011 to 59 percent in January 2012 and reached a peak of 65 percent in March 2013, according to the Datafolha survey carried out that month. Approval ratings were higher among higher-income citizens (those earning more than ten times the minimum wage), a group in which the government's approval rating hit 70 percent. The March 2013 rating, just three months before the country was disrupted by the June protests, was equally distributed among all income strata. At that time Brazilians were optimistic about the economy: expectations regarding purchasing power were the highest since 1994 and job security rates peaked in a series of surveys that had been carried out since December 1998. (Seventy-five percent of respondents said they were not at risk of being fired.)

In sum, a diffuse dissatisfaction with the development model and defense of neoliberal measures by certain social groups did not translate into disapproval of the government or pessimism about the economy. It remains for us to explain the rising number of strikes and protests as of 2012.

It should be noted that the reduction in unemployment and informal employment rates and the integration of the working class into the

Table 10.1. The Main Problem Facing the Country (%)

CATEGORIES	2011	2012A	2012B	2013
Health	31	39	40	48
Education	12	8	11	13
Corruption	3	7	4	11
Violence/Security	16	14	20	10
Unemployment	11	9	6	4
Hunger/Extreme Poverty	7	5	3	2
Economy	1	1	1	2
Inflation	1	1	1	2
Salary	3	1	1	1
Abusive Taxes/Tax Reform	0	0	0	1
Drugs/Drug Trafficking	2	2	1	0
Housing	2	2	1	0
Income Distribution/Inequality	1	1	0	0
Land Reform	0	0	0	0
Floods	0	1	0	0
Other Issue	8	4	2	2
All	0	0	0	0
None	0	0	0	0
Do not know	4	4	4	2

Note: Question: "Considering the areas that are under the responsibility of the federal government, in your opinion, what is the main problem facing the country today?". The surveys were carried out on the following dates: March 15 and 16, 2011; January 18 and 19, 2012; December 13, 2012; and June 27 and 28, 2013. Spontaneous and single answer in %.

Source: DataFolha Institute of Research. 2021. Datafolha Surveys.

consumer market were not accompanied by an improvement in the access to and quality of public policies. Issues that have historically been top concerns among Brazilians—health, violence/safety, and education—stood out in public opinion surveys, with respondents from different occupations and income and education levels, as shown in table 10.1.

The conflicts and contradictions associated with the neo-developmentalist model adopted by the PT governments resulted in material and

ideological repercussions that affected social groups and classes differently. The popular sectors, organized in various social movements, many
of which were close to or allied with the PT governments, repeatedly
expressed their discontent with how limited the public policies were, while
also seeking to expand social rights, overcome setbacks, reduce harmful
impacts of government measures on the environment, and oppose land
expropriation and violence against traditional peoples (Galvão and Novelli
2020).

Sections of the bourgeoisie and middle classes, in turn, have opposed
those policies they see as undermining free competition, threatening representative democracy (due to the expansion of institutional arenas open
to popular participation), and constraining individual merit and compe-
tence. This is the case of affirmative action programs and benefits granted
to economically vulnerable populations, policies that directly or indirectly
disturb the meritocratic ideology and standards of social distinction trea-
sured by the middle classes (Cavalcante 2015; Saad-Filho and Boito 2016).
These social sectors gradually channeled their dissatisfaction into a diffuse
corruption charge that mostly targeted politicians linked to the PT.

Thus, the protest events follow an upward curve in a context of economic optimism (marked by high expectations about employment and
purchasing power) and political optimism (the government's approval
rating hitting a record high among all social classes). However, the economic slowdown and decline in social mobility not only aggravated the
distributive conflict but also led to a shift in political perceptions and
behaviors as of 2013, as shown in table 10.1. At the time, while the concern
about corruption, health, education, the economy, and inflation was
growing, people's interest in unemployment, poverty, wages, and income
distribution was declining, as will be highlighted in the detailed analysis
of the data. This shift in perception changed the pattern of protest participants' concerns and claims and created political instability.

As will be elaborated next, our data suggest that June 2013 played a key
role in this process. The left was unable to accommodate the various agendas revealed in those protests in a political project capable of overcoming
the limitations of the neo-developmentalist model and, at the same time,
resist the pressure to resume the neoliberal agenda. When the economy

stopped growing,[11] employers started to combat full employment and press for reductions in labor costs, paving the way for the flexibilization of labor legislation, as well as other items on the neoliberal agenda (Bastos 2017). The dominant sectors' attack on the neo-developmentalist model did not prevent the reelection of Dilma Rousseff in 2014. Nevertheless, the adoption of an austerity policy and growing political instability further weakened the government. Rousseff was accused of failing to keep her campaign promises and lost significant popular support early in her second term.

The shrinking economy was perceived in 2015 as a sign of the government's inability to manage a crisis whose very existence had been denied during Rousseff's presidential campaign. The opposition's challenge to the election result and Operation Lava Jato were factors in the loss of confidence in the political system and, above all, in PT politicians, fueling the political crisis.

Two topics have dominated the political scene since then: the tax burden (encapsulated in the "cost Brazil" thesis)[12] and corruption. The antitaxation discourse, which was increasingly evident after the implementation of a "taxmeter"[13] by the Commercial Association of São Paulo in 2005, was invigorated in 2015 and 2016 by a campaign known for the motto *"Não vou pagar o pato"* ("I will not pay the duck"—equivalent to the British "I will not carry the can") against the raise in taxes. Such a campaign—whose symbol, a yellow duck, was frequently seen in protests in favor of Dilma Rousseff's impeachment—was promoted by the Federation of Industries of the State of São Paulo. As taxes weigh more heavily on the middle-class and poorer strata of the population, members of the middle class tend to see themselves as victims of a heavy tax burden that exists to sustain social programs from which they do not benefit. Thus, "the conviction that distributive policies are made to their detriment develops in sections of the middle class" (Carneiro 2018, 21). The antitaxation discourse, together with accusations of misuse of public resources, fueled the anticorruption agenda setting the tone of the protests as of 2013. In this way, the distributive conflict is overshadowed by the theme of corruption, which is used instrumentally to put up a fight against the administrations that invested the most in policies to promote social inclusion and reduce inequality.

According to Martuscelli (2016), the fight against corruption is linked to the distributive conflict through a discourse that associates the granting of benefits to individuals and companies—which are seen as incapable of succeeding on their own efforts and thus in need of the state's intervention—with bribery and diversion of public funds. This discourse, based on the meritocratic ideology (Boito 2017), proclaims the importance of having equal opportunities, safeguarding equality before the law, and ensuring respect for the rules of the game; it distrusts any form of affirmative action or public incentive to production, which "creates privileges and distorts free competition" (Cavalcante 2018, 114). In this sense, what has been seen in the global cycle of protests, and also in the Brazilian case, is the fight against corruption being misappropriated by right-wing groups in order to delegitimize social welfare policies and promote austerity measures to solve the crisis (Bratsis 2017). Paradoxically, the theme of corruption—which was instrumental in challenging PT's policies against poverty and social inequality—was also taken up by popular sectors, demonstrating the measure of this theme's flexibility, its potential to be presented as a common interest to different social groups.

The scandals were treated selectively to associate the PT with corruption and create an environment favorable to impeachment. The fact that Dilma Rousseff's administration practiced accounting maneuvers to cover fiscal deficit was used as a pretext for impeaching the president, even though all of her predecessors had engaged in the same practice. The impeachment was the instrument used to overturn a legitimately elected government. In the face of the government's decreasing popularity, it was used as a form of recall, as well as a way to implement a political project that had been rejected in the presidential election.

Popular Politics in Brazil

As indicated in the previous section, the policies implemented by Lula and Rousseff's administrations induced positive changes in the labor market and achieved better distribution of income and reductions in unemployment, inequalities, and social hierarchies. Working-class and vulnerable groups interpreted the changes as an *opportunity* to achieve their goals. By contrast, economic elites and the middle and upper-middle classes perceived the changes as a *threat* to their economic interests and social positions. As discussed in the introductory chapter, Almeida (2010a) would characterize this as a "hybrid political-economic environment." Within this context, protests emerged among those who wanted to expand these policies and those who wished to restore the status quo. In this sense, with respect to actors and claims, one finds both continuities and changes when comparing to previous protests.

As the economy was shrinking, the distributive conflict escalated, creating a dynamic of intertwined economic and political crises feeding into each other. The protests, however, turned massive before the economic and political crises were evident.

As shown in figure 10.1, the protest events over this period followed a fluctuating trajectory. In 2012, they followed an upward curve, with an increase of 140 percent compared to 2011, surpassing the average for the period studied (222.6 protests per year). This suggests that all the accumulated dissatisfaction that exploded in 2013, with double the average number of events, had already been building pressure in the previous year. The June protests of 2013 marked the political history of Brazil by putting millions of people on the streets in almost daily protests throughout the month. These protests had a decentralized dynamic, with different organizations simultaneously calling for demonstrations in different cities. Although the protests were initially fueled by people expressing reactive opposition to the increase in public transport fares, they later incorporated a wide range of agendas and targets, exposing the different sources of tension and discontent with the PT governments in society. In terms of the overarching hypothesis of this edited volume, the Brazilian protest landscape in 2013 can be seen as the fullest expression of a combination of proactive and reactive protests.

These particular protests are also important because of their ramifications. As seen in figure 10.2, they had an immediate impact on the approval ratings of Dilma Rousseff's administration, even though the protesters initially targeted the subnational governments that were responsible for regulating public transport fares. The number of participants is an additional indicator of the political strength of these mobilizations: more than two million Brazilians were protesting in 450 cities.

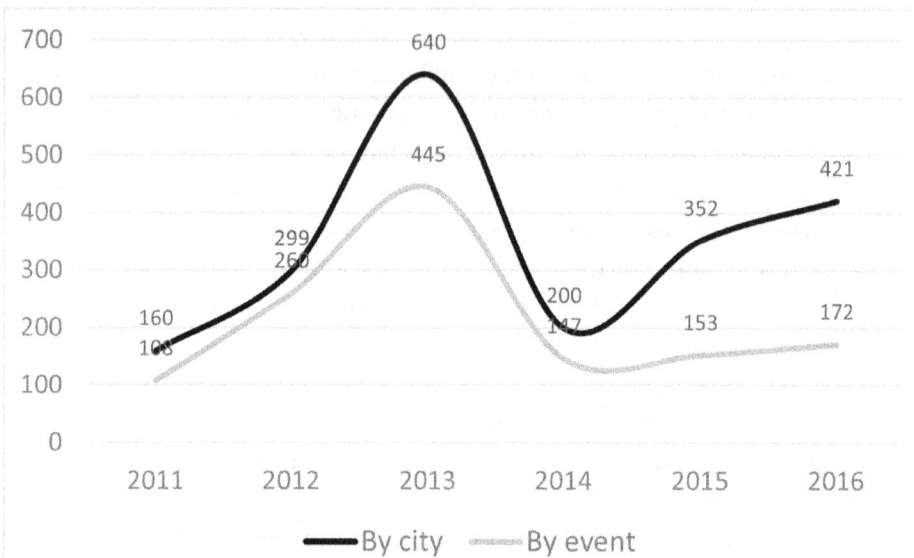

Figure 10.1. Total Number of Protests per Year. Year-to-year variations in the number of protest events from January 1, 2011, to August 31, 2016. The bottom line refers to the number of protest events per year. If a protest event was held in more than one location, it was still considered as one protest event. Total of 1,285 protest events. The top line corresponds to information on the coordinated protest events: those organized by the same set of actors, on the same day, with the same goals and targets but held in different locations. Data refer to the number of cities in which the protests were held. Total of 2,072 protest events. Tatagiba and Galvão, 2019.

After a period of decline in 2014, possibly due to the electoral process that took place that year, the protests gained new momentum during the campaign for the impeachment of Rousseff, who had just been reelected for a second term. This campaign, launched in 2015, was invigorated in 2016, although it did not reach, in numerical terms, the level observed in 2013. The year-to-year variation is subtle, lower than the average for the period studied, with 153 protests in 2015 and 172 in 2016. However, this decrease does not indicate that mobilization was receding, but rather that the organizations had reached a better level of coordination, setting the dates for demonstrations together according to the impeachment proceedings in the National Congress, with right- and left-wing organizations disputing the outcome of this process of mobilization (Tatagiba 2018).

Just as in the protests in 2013, the impeachment campaign stood out for

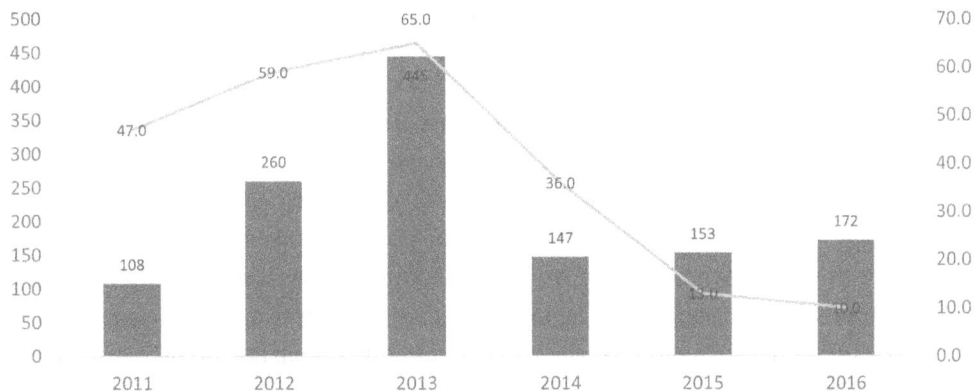

Figure 10.2. Number of Protest Events and the Approval Ratings of Dilma Rousseff's Administrations. Question: "In your opinion, is President Dilma's administration great, good, regular, bad, or terrible?" The surveys were carried out on the following dates: March 15 and 16, 2011; January 18 and 19, 2012; March 20 and 21, 2013; May 7 and 8, 2014; April 9 and 10, 2015; March 17 and 18, 2016. Columns correspond to the number of protest events per year. N=1,285. Datafolha Survey, 2021; Tatagiba and Galvão, 2019.

its numerical and symbolic strength. The campaign produced five major nationwide mobilizations, four of them in 2015 and one in early 2016. The first, held on March 15, 2015, saw 1,700,000 people take to the streets, a surprising number by Brazilian standards. The last massive mobilization, on March 13, 2016, brought together three million people across the country. Data on the scope of this protest event indicate that a right-wing wave had spread to all Brazilian states in cities of different population sizes. The most prominent avenue in the city of São Paulo, Avenida Paulista, was the central stage of the demonstrations calling for the impeachment of President Rousseff, placing the state of São Paulo at the heart of the protests. In March 2016, five hundred thousand people took over Avenida Paulista, the largest mobilization recorded in the city's history. Demonstrations against the impeachment did not show the same mobilization capacity.

Actors (Who)

We found continuities and innovations regarding the social groups protesting during the period studied. On the one hand were those social groups that form the backbone of the Brazilian left, such as popular/territorial, union, and student movements, who kept their leading role in the protests, although with lower recruitment capacity when compared to previous decades. On the other hand, there were new actors in contentious politics, created in the context of the political and economic crises: the anti-PT movements that we identify—albeit imprecisely—as "diffuse groups and individuals" and "ad hoc collectives." These actors proved to be very efficient in recruiting protesters, mainly through the intensive use of social media.

Figure 10.3 shows that social movements with a long history of mobilization, such as the *workers' movements* (31 percent) and the *popular movements and movements of residents* (19 percent),[14] are in the top two positions. Together, they represent 50 percent of the social groups organizing protest events in the period. Within these two groups, we identified formal organizations with a strong presence in civil society and a history of mobilization dating back to the transition to democracy, such as the Unified Workers' Central (CUT), the largest union federation in Brazil, and the Landless Workers Movement (MST), the largest movement organization fighting for access to rural land. Another was a newer movement organization fighting for housing, which has grown stronger as of 2013, the Homeless Workers Movement (MTST). Workers' and popular movements mobilized around their specific agendas: wages and working conditions and improvement of living conditions, respectively. Additionally, they presented their claims regarding social and economic policies, defended agrarian reform and the environment, and condemned police violence in urban peripheries. These actors were immersed in a politically polarized context and, amid the course of contention, decided to defend then-president Dilma Rousseff, despite their dissatisfaction with her administration.

However, the strength of their numbers did not necessarily translate into mobilization capacity. This was the case with several union organizations that, as discussed by Galvão (2019), lost prominence and legitimacy over this period and struggled to speak to society as a whole, mainly due to their proximity to the PT government.

Students (12 percent) take third place among the social groups protesting

Workers' movements	31.0
Popular movements and movements of residents	19.0
Students	11.9
Anti-PT groups	6.2
Diffuse groups and individuals	5.3
Identity groups	5.3
Collectives or ad hoc groups	5.1
Native peoples	3.5
Partisan activists	3.1
Environmentalists	1.9
Human Rights activists	1.8
Family and friends of victims	1.6
Religious people	1.4
Businessmen	1.2
Other	1.8

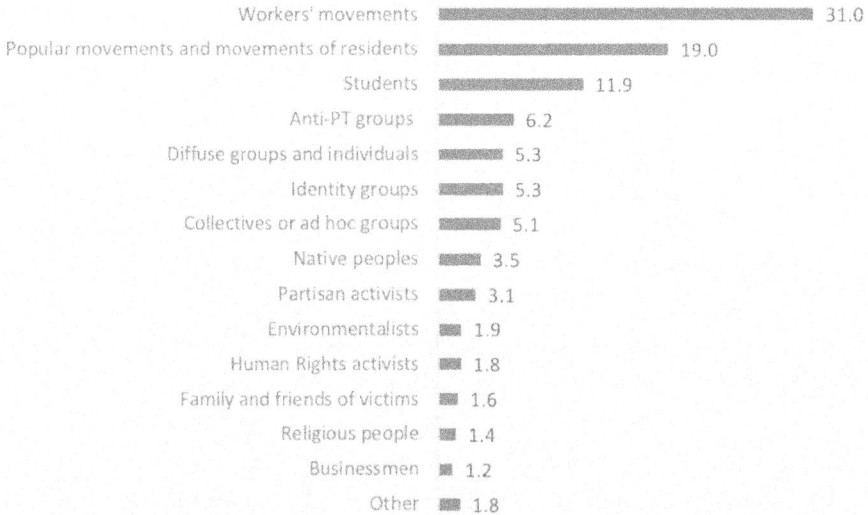

Figure 10.3. Social Groups at the Protests (%). The category "social groups protesting" was constructed based on information on the organizations calling the protests and social bases participating in the protest events. Multiple variable (N=1,469), with underreporting corresponding to 5.3% of the total. Tatagiba and Galvão, 2019.

the most. This social group has a long history of mobilization, having fought against the military dictatorship (1968–1984) and participated in the contentious episodes that culminated in the impeachment of former president Collor de Mello in 1992. Although traditional organizations such as the National Union of Students (UNE) are still organizing protests, new autonomist groups who refuse to be represented by student organizations or use their long-established strategies have grown stronger since 2011. Among these new groups are the Free Pass Movement (MPL)—responsible for organizing the demonstrations that triggered the June protests of 2013—and collectives of high-school students that emerged from the important cycle of school occupations in the states of São Paulo and Paraná, the first ramification of the June protests.

The *anti-PT groups* (6.2 percent) occupy the fourth position, a great innovation of social activism in the period studied. What makes antipetismo a sociopolitical phenomenon is not just rejection of the PT but *hatred for the PT*, a feeling with strong mobilizing potential. It was the *hatred for the PT*, performed in public contention, that allowed the demonstrators, most of them with no previous experience with protests, to build a sense of collective identity. This emotional engagement with the cause shaped the protest—images spread widely of protesters biting or burning PT flags or carrying posters depicting decapitated or hanged former presidents. Aggressiveness was fueled by a very particular use of social media (Dias 2017; Zanini and Tatagiba 2019) and empowered to pervade other realms of everyday life, such as family and friendship relations. This cognitive and emotional disposition had important implications for recruitment, shaping the features of the mobilization, which took the form of a moral crusade.

The challengers' target was not just the PT government, but also left-wing parties and unions and the leftist culture broadly. As pointed out by Tatagiba, Trindade, and Teixeira (2015), "This disposition is evidenced by the mottos repeated at the protests: 'Brazil will not be another Venezuela', 'My flag will never be red', 'I want my country back' or even, in a confrontational tone, 'Go to Cuba!'" From an electoral perspective, the spreading of antipetismo may suggest that center-right parties are empowered but still willing to defend the rules of democracy; however, from a sociopolitical perspective, antipetismo has an intrinsically antidemocratic nature (Tatagiba 2019).

The social base of the protests organized by anti-PT groups is formed by sections of the middle and upper-middle classes (Arias and Cavalcante 2019).[15] By briefly outlining the three main organizations behind the protests, we offer a sense of the innovation they represent on the political scene. These organizations were Vem pra Rua (Come to the Street), Movimento Brasil Livre (Brazil Free Movement or MBL) and, playing a lesser role, Revoltados Online (Outraged Online), alongside a myriad of small groups that took advantage of the political opportunities opened by the impeachment campaign. Revoltados Online, created in 2000 by a former evangelical pastor, is the closest to the far right. It articulated a highly radicalized discourse during the impeachment campaign, inciting physical violence and defending a military intervention in the country—demands that had already been marginally expressed in the protests of 2013 (Dias 2017, 54).[16] The MBL was created in 2013 to directly intervene in the cycles of mobilization in favor of the impeachment. This organization emerged in association with Estudantes pela Liberdade, the Brazilian branch of Students for Liberty, and based its activities at the universities to train young liberals. The MBL is made up of young leaders with the stated goal of "rejuvenating" the right-wing discourse in Brazil. They advocate for the reduction of the state's role in the economy, expansion of privatizations, and reduction of the age at which a criminal offender is treated as an adult, among other views. They are critics of the PT governments' social policies, especially the Bolsa Família program, and reparation measures, such as racial quotas in universities. Finally, the newest of these three organizations, Vem pra Rua, was created in 2014 to support the center-right candidate in the upcoming presidential election. Its leaders are businessmen with connections to São Paulo's economic and political elites. On their website, they claim to fight corruption and defend "ethics in politics," economic freedom, and tax cuts. Over the course of the events, and according to the circumstances, these organizations combined the defense of austerity policies with a conservative moral agenda (Rocha 2019). Deprived of significant political capital, they relied on the financial and logistical support of powerful organizations, such as the Federation of Industries of the State of São Paulo (FIESP), the hegemonic media, chiefly the Globo media conglomerate, evangelical religious networks, the Freemasonry, certain union federations, and even self-employed workers, mainly truck drivers.

Finally, we highlight one last innovation emerging from this period, which we identify with the categories *"diffuse groups and individuals"* and *"collectives or ad hoc groups."* The first category refers to disorganized groups or individuals participating in protest events, mainly in demonstrations held during the great peaks of mobilization in 2013. The second relates to innovations in the challengers' organizational form. It includes groups that identify themselves as "collectives," as opposed to the social movement organization format, and ad hoc groups, usually more goal-oriented and ephemeral when compared to the collectives, which die out once their goals are achieved and/or their focus shifts to other issues.[17]

Table 10.2 shows the growing importance of the diffuse groups and individuals, anti-PT groups, and ad hoc collectives after 2013. Although the same groups occupy the first three positions in both moments, the main novelty was the fact that the anti-PT groups moved from the eighth to the

Table 10.2. Changes in the Ranking of the Main Social Groups at the Protests before and after June 2013

BEFORE THE JUNE PROTESTS OF 2013	AFTER THE JUNE PROTESTS OF 2013
Workers' movements	Workers' movements
Popular movements and movements of residents	Popular movements and movements of residents
Students	Students
Identity groups	Anti-PT groups
Native peoples	Diffuse groups and individuals
Human rights activists	Collectives or ad hoc groups
Collectives or ad hoc groups	Identity groups
Anti-PT groups	Partisan activists
Environmentalists	Native peoples
Diffuse groups and individuals	Environmentalists
Family and friends of victims	Religious people
Partisan activists	Human rights activists
Religious people	Family and friends of victims
Businessmen	Businessmen
Other	Other

Note: Column 1 refers to the social groups protesting in events held between January 1, 2011 and June 5, 2013. Column 2 refers to the social groups protesting in events held between June 6, 2013 and August 31, 2016. Multiple variable (N = 1,393). Tatagiba and Galvão, 2019.

fourth position and the diffuse groups and individuals changed from the tenth to the fifth. Thus, our data suggest that the June protests of 2013 changed the political context and affected the dynamics of activism in two important ways: by empowering right-wing sectors in society and encouraging the participation of unorganized individuals.

Claims (Why)

As shown in figure 10.4, there were three large sets of issues driving the protest events between 2011 and 2016: *government and political system* (25.2

percent), *salary and working conditions* (17.6 percent), and *living conditions in cities* (16.5 percent). The category *"government and political system"* mainly covers issues associated with the (poor) workings of democracy, in addition to expressions—formulated along the lines of antipetismo— against the government and PT. The fact that, since 2015, this category has come to predominate is a new trait in political contention in Brazil. The category *"salary and working conditions"* covers a set of well-established, long-term claims usually made by formal and unionized workers in Brazil- ian mobilizations. The category *"living conditions in cities"* reflects the ways in which daily experiences of deprivation played out in the course of con- tention, especially the issue of public transportation and housing, demands highly associated with the class-based experience of workers, particularly those who have the most precarious jobs.

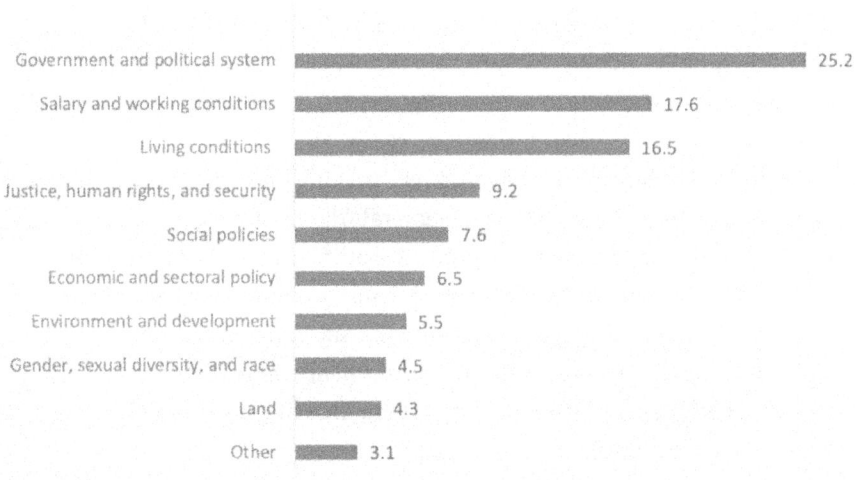

Category	Percent
Government and political system	25.2
Salary and working conditions	17.6
Living conditions	16.5
Justice, human rights, and security	9.2
Social policies	7.6
Economic and sectoral policy	6.5
Environment and development	5.5
Gender, sexual diversity, and race	4.5
Land	4.3
Other	3.1

Figure 10.4. Claims Made at the Protests (%). Multiple variable (N=1,373), with underreporting corresponding to 3.9% of the total. The category "government and political system" includes events against politicians and administrations of various political views and party affiliations, events in favor or against Rousseff's impeach- ment, against corruption, supporting or criticizing the workings of certain political institutions, events defending the freedom of expression, in favor of democracy or the dictatorship, and those supporting media regulation. Tatagiba and Galvão, 2019.

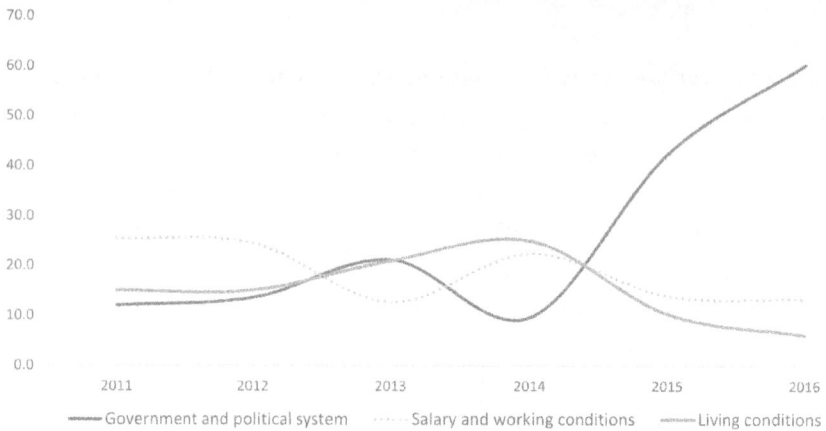

Figure 10.5. Main Claims per Year (%). Multiple variable (N=813), corresponding to 59% of the total claims. Tatagiba and Galvão, 2019.

Claims regarding the issues of *government and political system* were already present in 2011, albeit in a small number of protest events. Although these claims were on the rise in 2013, it was only after 2015 that they dominated the public agenda, reaching a point where they were present in 60 percent of protest events in 2016 (see figure 10.5), at the peak of the political crisis.

The presidential election of 2014 was a turning point, with the defeated candidate denouncing an alleged electoral fraud and triggering a serious political crisis. Since then, widespread dissatisfaction with the workings of the political system has been channeled into the sociopolitical phenomenon of antipetismo. As a way to measure the antipetismo phenomenon, we isolated those protest events in the *"government and political system"* category that had targeted the federal government, Lula, the PT, or PT leaders, as shown in figure 10.6.

Claims regarding *salary and working conditions* (17.6 percent) occupy the second position in figure 10.4. Our data contradict the views of scholars who argue that labor is no longer an important category for explaining collective action in contemporary societies, that it would have been replaced by post-material demands, such as those based on the recognition of identities. Our findings suggest that class-based conflicts remain important, alongside conflicts structured around other identity categories. In 2012,

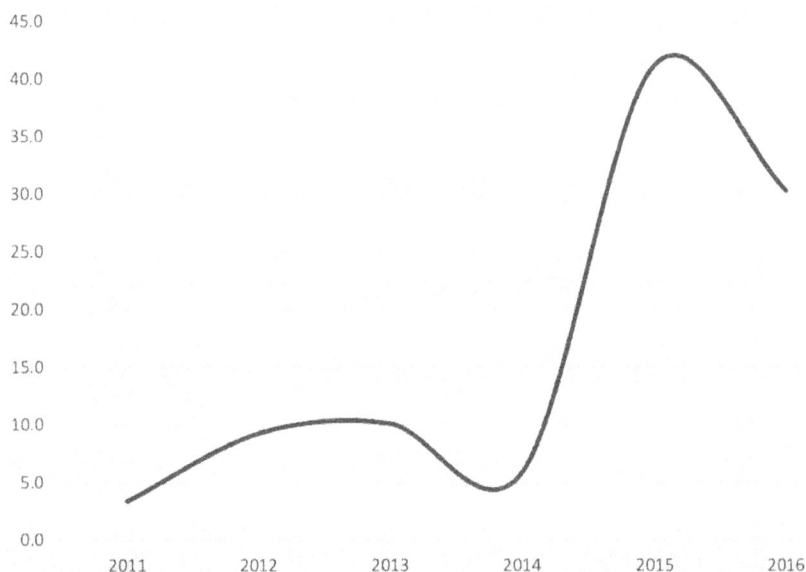

Figure 10.6. Evolution of Anti-PT Protests (%). Anti-PT protests encompasses the events included in the subcategory "government and political system" in "Claims made at the protests," events that targeted the administration of President Dilma Rousseff, the PT, PT representatives, or former president Lula and were called by organizations defined as antipetistas. N=121, which corresponds to 32% of the "government and political system" category. Tatagiba and Galvão, 2019.

there was a large wave of strikes involving more than thirty occupational groups, chiefly among federal civil servants. The federal universities—which had previously undergone a process of expansion—were affected by the strikes: forty-one of the fifty-nine institutions halted their activities, with workers acting in defense of salary, career, and improvements to education policy. Civil construction workers also joined the strikes, especially workers at hydroelectric plants and those working on construction sites of the stadiums for the 2014 Soccer World Cup. Finally, workers in more precarious sections of the service sector joined in the strikes, such as street cleaners in Rio de Janeiro, who halted their activities during the *Carnaval* of 2014 and achieved significant economic gains when the country's economy was already slowing down. It should be noted that many of these strikes occurred without the sanction of union leaders (Galvão 2019). The prospects of having labor rights restricted also stimulated significant mobilizations by trade union federations and popular movements. In response to employers' pressure for flexible legislation, members of Congress have since introduced bills designed to create new modalities of precarious employment contracts, expand outsourcing, derogate the law through negotiation, reduce social security benefits, and restrict retirement. In 2015, three days of struggle were organized to resist the expansion of outsourcing and oppose the proposed labor and pensions reforms (Galvão and Marcelino 2020).

In the third position are claims concerning *living conditions in cities*, which encompass the following issues: housing (40 percent of this category), transportation (38 percent), and urban policy and public services (which, together, make 23 percent).[18] At this juncture, housing and transportation took a central position, with the latter triggering the June protests of 2013. However, our data indicate that the issue of price and/or quality of public transportation had already been present in protests since 2011, mainly in Rio de Janeiro and São Paulo. Measures adopted by the federal government to tackle the housing deficit led to an exponential increase in the price of urban land; as a result, the country experienced a real-estate boom between 2009 and 2015. The pressure on land price had a direct impact on rent prices and urban mobility, pushing the poor more and more to the urban periphery. In the context of the mega-events, the tensions around this issue increased, given the constant violations of the right to housing and mobility in the host cities. In this context, the mobilization capacity of those movements organized around the issues of housing and transportation increased, especially between 2011 and 2014, resulting in vigorous mobilizations that united various groups to the left of the PT, many with an autonomist inclination. In 2014, while housing was the main claim in the protests, the occupations promoted by the MTST to press for housing projects in São Paulo were in evidence.

In the fourth position, *"Justice, human rights, and security"* (16.5 percent) refers to demands to solve crimes committed either by the state or by private individuals or groups (78 percent) and broad demands for more security and changes in the public security policy, including the issue of drugs. These claims were mostly made by residents of poor communities denouncing police brutality—violent police approaches, killings of residents, and, to a lesser degree, execution of social movement activists—and demanding a proper investigation of massacres.

The fifth category, *"social policies"* (7.6 percent), includes demands for better education (72 percent) and health. *"Economic and sectoral policy"* (6.5 percent) covers demands related to the interest rate policy, tax reduction, privatization of ports and airports, and oil field auctions, among others. The category *"environment and development"* (5.5 percent) includes claims related to natural resources (except for land, which is addressed in a separate category), environmental protection, and animal rights, and covers events held to oppose the construction of hydroelectric dams, transposition of the São Francisco River, and the hosting of mega-events. The campaigns *"Não vai ter copa"* (No cup) and *"Ocupação Copa do Povo"* (People's Cup Occupation) encapsulate the effort of bringing together movement organizations and issues related to housing and urban mobility. *"Gender, sexual diversity, and race"* (4.5 percent) comprises demands associated with the fight against sexism and violence against women, and those against or in favor of abortion and same-sex civil union. In 2011, LGBT issues sparked protests against the sex education proposals issued by the Ministry of Education, as well as against homophobia. Over the period, five protest events directly addressed the racial issue, mostly the matter of racial quotas in universities. The category *"land"* (4.0 percent) comprises demands for the demarcation of indigenous and *quilombola*[19] lands, agrarian reform, and settlement policy.

As shown in table 10.3, the June protests of 2013 had an impact on claims, altering the ranking of the main claims being made in protests since then. The comparison before and after June 2013 shows that the three categories at the top of the list in T1 (Before the June protests of 2013) and T2 (After the June protests of 2013) are the same, but they occupy different positions: in T2, *"government and political system"* and *"living conditions in cities"* become central, while claims related to *"salary and working conditions"* fall to the third place. Claims regarding *"social policies"* represent the most significant shift, moving from the eighth to the fourth position. The category *"gender, sexual diversity, and race"* loses centrality, albeit women's participation in the protests against Rousseff's impeachment was important. We can thus assume that the direction of the June protests of 2013 was under

Table 10.3: Changes in the Ranking of Claims before and after June 2013

BEFORE THE JUNE PROTESTS OF 2013	AFTER THE JUNE PROTESTS OF 2013
Salary and working conditions	Government and political system
Government and political system	Living conditions
Living conditions	Salary and working conditions
Justice, human rights, and security	Social policies
Economic and sectoral policy	Justice, human rights, and security
Gender, sexual diversity, and race	Economic and sectoral policy
Land	Environment and development
Social policies	No data
Environment and development	Other
No data	Land
Other	Gender, sexual diversity, and race

Note: Column 1 refers to the claims being made at the protest events held between January 1, 2011, and June 5, 2013. Column 2 refers to the claims being made in protest events held between June 6, 2013, and August 31, 2016. Multiple variable (N = 1,387).

Source: Tatagiba and Galvão, 2019.

dispute, but ultimately, in the context of increasing distributive conflict, the balance of power shifted in favor of the right and its agendas.

Conclusions

This chapter analyzed the features of the protests during the most troubled period in Brazilian history since the reestablishment of democracy in 1988. As demonstrated, changes in the features of protests over the period are associated, on the one hand, with the impacts of the contradictory economic, political, and cultural legacies of the PT governments on distinct social classes and groups and, on the other hand, with the intensification—due to the international financial crisis—of the distributive conflict, which was accompanied by growing political instability.

Our data show that, between 2011 and 2016, political contention in Brazil was marked by the combination of two distinct logics: the growing political polarization between the right and left and the increasing heterogeneity of actors and claims, as attested by the diversity in these areas that came to be central in the public sphere. These findings, in part, are resonant with this volume's overarching hypothesis, as the proactive protests were associated with the reactive ones. With regard to actors at the protests, the novelty lies in the emergence of social groups linked to the new right and the massive participation of the middle classes as of June 2013. With respect to claims, we stress the centrality of the issue of democracy, particularly its (poor) workings and the selective use of the theme of corruption, which ultimately empowered the phenomenon of antipetismo and delivered Rousseff's impeachment after the successful campaign of 2015 and 2016.

The fight against corruption was thus the gateway to the political radicalization that eroded Brazilian democracy, paving the way for the election of Jair Bolsonaro in 2018. It was also instrumental in solving the distributive conflict by advancing the neoliberal agenda and, in the years since the impeachment, systematically restricting social and labor rights. This dramatic outcome changes the conditions for social mobilization and creates a new scenario in which the dynamics of political contention are conditioned by the surging right and the rise to power of the far right.

Notes

1. This argument was previously developed in Tatagiba and Galvão (2019) and Tatagiba (2019).
2. Rousseff was president between January 2011 and April 2016. Her second term was interrupted by an impeachment process, completed in August of the same year.
3. After two consecutive terms in office (2003–2006 and 2007–2010), Lula was arrested in April 2018 and imprisoned until November 2019.
4. *Folha de São Paulo* is available at https://acervo.folha.com.br/index.do.
5. Mensalão was a corruption scheme revealed in 2005, in which money from public funds was used to pay off politicians and secure their support. The political repercussions of this scheme affected mostly the PT. The operation known as Lava Jato was launched by the Federal Police and the Judiciary in March 2014 to investigate bribery and embezzlement from

state-owned companies. This operation was controversial because it broke the law on the pretense of fighting corruption, in addition to disrupting civil construction companies and creating a crisis of political representation unprecedented in Brazilian democratic history. For an analysis of the interactions between the Lava Jato investigations and the campaign for Rousseff's impeachment, see Tatagiba (2018).

6. The representation of the other regions was the following: Northeast (13.7 percent), Midwest (11.9 percent), South (9.2 percent), and North (5.5 percent).

7. This problem is not limited to the FSP, as one can see in Olzak (1989).

8. Luciana Tatagiba and Andréia Galvão, "Banco de dados: os protestos no Brasil (2011–2016)," 2019, available at https://www.nepac.ifch.unicamp.br/banco-de-dados.

9. According to the Monthly Employment Survey of the Brazilian Institute of Geography and Statistics (IBGE), the unemployment rate declined from 6.8 percent to 4.3 percent between 2009 and 2013.

10. With respect to GDP, despite a downward trend from 7.6 percent in 2010 to 4.0 percent in 2011 and 1.9 percent in 2012, it later recovered slightly, reaching 3.0 percent in 2013.

11. The percentage of GDP growth was only 0.5 percent in 2014, reaching negative figures in the following years: –3.8 percent in 2015 and –3.6 percent in 2016.

12. "Cost Brazil" is an expression used by economic and political elites to defend changes in work legislation that aimed to reduce labor costs and, therefore, workers' rights.

13. The "taxmeter" aims to bring the problem of tax burden versus poor quality of education, health, and other social policies to the public sphere. It displays on big panels how much money citizens expend annually paying tax.

14. The category "popular movements and movements of residents" includes groups linked to neighborhood associations, landless and homeless organizations, community movements for the improvement of public service provision, and fronts articulating these different movements.

15. Studies on this topic, however, indicate that antipetismo has also infiltrated a morally conservative share of the popular sectors, which took on the fight against "gender ideology" and in favor of the traditional family while the government was pursuing policies to ensure sexual and reproductive rights (Biroli 2019). At the same time, the spread of the theology of prosperity, based on the valuing of entrepreneurship and individual effort (Almeida 2017), made it difficult to acknowledge the role of the state—and the importance of public policies—in reducing inequalities and poverty. The expansion of neo-Pentecostal doctrines reinforced conservative

discourses not only morally and behaviorally, but also from a sociopolitical perspective. Such development is well-illustrated by the intense discussions that took place regarding the reduction of the legal age as a way to tackle the public safety issue and by the initiative known as *escola sem partido* (nonpartisan school), which aims to prevent sex education and programs deemed to be "left-wing" and contrary to Christian thought.

16. Although the protest events organized by this group are not numerically relevant, they matter because they call into question the consensus around democracy. It is also important to stress that the establishment in Congress of the Comissão da Verdade (Truth Committee) on May 16, 2012, played a key role in reinforcing the protesters' inclination toward military intervention. As a result of its investigations into the crimes committed by the military during the dictatorship (1964-1985), this committee caused deep dissatisfaction among the military—which subsequently distanced itself from the government—and stimulated episodes of confrontation between opponents and supporters of the military dictatorship (1964-1985).

17. As an example, we highlight the collectives acting against Brazil's hosting the World Cup and Olympic Games.

18. "Urban policy" refers to disputes over urban legislation in São Paulo, while "public services" concerns the definition of areas for informal trading activities and demands for services such as lighting, covering of manholes, replacement of traffic lights, and tree pruning.

19. Quilombos are communities of descendants of runaway slaves who settled in remote areas.

CHAPTER ELEVEN

Conclusion

Protest, Politics, and Event Count
Analysis in Latin America

MARÍA INCLÁN

Since its beginning, the study of social movements has been dominated by case-study analyses. The main reason has been the labor intensity of the endeavor. Empirical evidence of social mobilization, by necessity, needs to be collected by the interested researchers, as this type of collective action always begins outside of official registries and institutional politics. Collecting information on protest activity requires extended fieldwork seasons, even if these are to be devoted only to the archival research of protest events. Over the years students of social movements have made great strides in systematically collecting standardized protest event data following "hard news" media reports of specific contentious activity (Earl, Martin, McCarthy, and Soule 2004). There have also been significant efforts for the collection of comparable protest event data, like the one launched by the Armed Conflict Location & Event Data Project.[1] However, as Moisés Arce and Takeshi Wada point out in the introductory chapter to this volume, not even these impressively large and detailed data sources can easily avoid the selection bias problem that all protest event analyses face because of their need to rely on media reports of the events. More important to this volume is recognizing that all protest event data sources and analyses tend to provide only partial or country-specific answers to research questions of contextualized protest activity. This volume breaks new ground in putting together country-specific protest event analyses to construct the big puzzle of contentious politics in Latin America. In doing so, the contributing authors, who compiled their datasets with specific and diverse research questions in mind, have rehighlighted the importance of contextualizing contestation—namely the effects of the dual process of political and economic liberalization on the region's protest activity. This volume presents multiple datasets based on local sources—both Spanish and Portuguese media reports that allow the contributing authors to take one more step against potential selection biases.

This volume presents a historical analysis of contentious politics over fifty years in Latin America. The different country-specific protest event datasets allow contributors to follow the reactions of mobilized civil society as they faced political and economic regime changes. The authors of this volume address a common research interest: that is, the consequences of globalization and democratization on protest in ten different countries in the continent: Bolivia, Brazil, Chile, Colombia, Costa Rica, Ecuador, Mexico, Nicaragua, Peru, and Venezuela. Each dataset was collected for the authors' specific research objectives and to analyze a country's protest activity during different periods. Still, all of them include the core information needed to offer comparable findings on key collective action components, namely: actors (who), place (where), time (when), targets (whom), actions (how), and claims (why). Each country's protest event analysis, then, contributes to building the big picture of how processes of economic and political liberalization affected contentious politics in the region during at least the last half of the twentieth century and the first two decades of the twenty-first. The analyses in the different chapters address the consequences of the dual process of liberalization by showing how popular politics changed as globalization and democratization took hold on the continent. They allow researchers to better understand the processes by which contentious politics was normalized as conventional political participation, and contentious repertoires were normalized into conventional channels of interest articulation. First, as political liberalization from dictatorial regimes to more democratic ones advanced in the continent, state elites changed their views of protest activities and increasingly perceived them as an integral part of ordinary politics rather than as threats. Second, as economic liberalization moved toward globalization, protest actors, claims, and actions also changed over time. Contentious politics transformed from being dominated by unionized workers, peasants, and other traditional social-movement actors to being led by a more diverse mobilized civil society. Their protest repertoires changed from strikes, sit-ins, and land seizures to include marches, road and building blockades, and artistic performances. Protest claims moved from seeking economic compensation and defending labor rights to demanding political rights in its different expressions (women, indigenous, LGBTQ+, environmental rights). Nevertheless, as table 11.1 shows, there are certain commonalities across cases, not only in terms of actors, but also in relation to their protest claims, actions, and targets. This summarized comparison already points at the effects of the dual process of liberalization in the region—to be specific, that the processes of democratization and globalization generated grievances but also opened opportunities for mobilized actors to defend their political rights, civil liberties, and socioeconomic prerogatives.

The principal contribution of this volume is accomplishing broad comparisons of collective action components across time and space using country-specific protest event datasets. Its relevance lies in highlighting how generalizable country-specific quantitative studies can be when pointing at regional trends of political and economic liberalization on protest tactics, actors, targets, and claims. This volume's findings are also important because the long-term ("bird's-eye") and short-term ("magnifying glass") analyses of the causes of popular mobilization point the causal arrows in the same direction, providing theoretical and methodological consistency to each chapter.

This volume shows how country-specific studies can offer generalizable findings, despite the fact that not all Latin American countries are included. While the inclusion of Cuba or Nicaragua during their current authoritarian periods would prove very difficult, these cases could offer interesting tests to the book's argument of the effects of the dual process of political and economic liberalization on popular politics. More important is the fact that the analyses in this volume do not include transnational dimensions of

Table 11.1. Popular Protests in Latin America in the Age of Globalization and Democracy

Collective Action Component	Broad Categories of Collective Action Component	COUNTRY								
		"Bird's-Eye"					"Magnifying-Glass"			
		Mexico	Bolivia	Colombia	Peru	Venezuela	Costa Rica and Nicaragua	Chile	Ecuador	Brazil
Main Protesting ACTORS	Workers/Labor Unions					X	X	X	X	X
	Public Sector Employees		X							
	Teachers/Univ. Employees		X							
	Wage Earners			X						
	Middle Class Sectors					X				
	Citizens/Civic Orgs.	X			X					
	Students		X	X	X			X		X
	Peasants			X						
	Traditional Communities				X					
	Urban Dwellers/Residents	X		X				X	X	X
	Informal Sector Workers					X				
	Popular Organizations	X							X	
Prominent ACTIONS	Marches	X		X	X	X	X	X	X	X
	Demonstrations	X								
	Sit-Ins	X								
	Roadblocks		X	X	X		X	X		X
	Blockages					X			X	
	Occupations								X	
	Strikes		X	X	X			X		
Dominating CLAIMS	Socioeconomic	X	X	X	X	X	X	X		
	Living Conditions									X
	Labor					X			X	X
	Political	X	X	X	X	X		X	X	X
	Programmatic			X						
Salient TARGETS	Executive Authorities	X	X	X	X	X	X	X	X	X
	Judicial Authorities							X		
	Political Parties									X
	Businesses	X		X				X		
	Armed Groups			X						

contentious politics when globalized economic liberalization is one of the main explanations of popular politics development in the continent. Still, I do not believe that including such variables would change the theoretical arguments of the book, namely that the dual process of liberalization allowed for the emergence of new popular politics actors and confirmed the central role of the state in contentious politics.

The long-term analyses are illustrated in Part I. These chapters go beyond the overall level of mobilization, which is common in cross-national analyses, to examine the major components of collective action. They allow us to observe that, while the dual transformation processes of economic and political liberalization affected popular protest actors, claims, and actions over time, protest targets (state authorities) and places (prominent political and economic centers) remained central recipients of protest groups' disruption and responsibility attribution. Economic and political liberalization processes transformed popular politics from being dominated by class-based organizations, such as unionized workers and peasants, to a more plural mobilized civil society comprising students, women, indigenous peoples, LGBTQ+ organizations, urban dwellers, and environmentalist organizations. Popular claims transmuted from seeking more concrete economic compensations and prerogatives to defending a plurality of political rights as well as a second and third generation of human rights. Contentious repertoires went from more radical actions such as physical attacks and property invasions to marches, rallies, and other more conventional demonstrations.

Chapters in Part II of the book examine critical moments of globalization or democracy, such as the onset of neoliberalism and the emergence of and backlash against post-neoliberal regimes. Chapters 7 and 8 zoom in on the inferential analysis of subnational political contexts and the organizational factors and mobilizing networks driving protest activity, while chapters 9 and 10 provide short-term analyses of protest activity in the post-neoliberal period. The latter two chapters are essential to testing the volume's claim that popular contention triggered by socioeconomic grievances generated by market-oriented policies was further facilitated by the political liberalization process of the continent.

Together, this volume's chapters offer sensitivity tests for the analysis of popular politics in Latin America during the dual process of economic and political liberalization. The long-term trend studies (Part I) provide the historic analysis of the development of popular politics in the continent in the last seventy years. By tracing the path of actors, actions, claims, and targets over time, the authors identify the effects that processes of regime change and global integration have had in the citizenry's demands, who has articulated them, and how have they presented them to the authorities. The short-term studies (Part II) allow for comparative analyses over subnational factors and mobilizing networks triggering contention during crucial periods of economic shocks and political crises. The wealth of analytic possibilities shown by these chapters is impressive.

Summary of the Book

In chapter 2, the lasting effects of Mexican corporatism and one-party regime become evident when we observe how long it has taken for a more plural and mobilized civil society to emerge. It also becomes evident when we consider the interest co-optation and the demobilization of organized labor through stabilization pacts implemented during the economic liberalization period. Nowadays, social mobilization in Mexico faces a dual challenge: on the one hand, a populist government claiming to fight neoliberalism while focalizing popular politics among sectors of the population, whose labor rights and socioeconomic prerogatives are at risk of being taken away, and on the other, the increasing threat of criminal violence. Takeshi Wada points out the possibility of popular contention turning violent following the organized crime pattern of protesting. Recent violent protests organized by the different cartels operating in the country prove him right. However, my take is that these events are only increasing the costs of protesting to popular politics actors, as they have to weigh the costs not only of state repression when planning dissenting collective action, but also those that violent nonstate actors pose on their mobilizing efforts and on politics in general.

In chapter 3, Roberto Laserna identifies three different periods in which popular politics developed in Bolivia: (1) state authoritarianism (1970–1985),

(2) open markets and democracy (1985–2003), and (3) state populism (2003–2019). During the period of state authoritarianism, protest activity remained low given the violent state repression used to control popular contention by military and civilian governments alike. During the transition to open markets and democracy, however, popular protest increased again, following the traditional pattern of mobilization during democratic transitions: an initial effervescent peak of activity triggered by more open and tolerant scenarios for contentious politics and a natural decay of protest as democracy settles in and dissenting interests are funneled through institutional channels. Nevertheless, incipient institutions proved insufficient to deal with further political pressures of social participation and political inclusion. Consequently, during state populism, institutional channels of interest representation weakened further and popular contention became the main mechanism for accessing public resources.

While Colombia has always been considered one of the oldest Latin American democracies, chapter 4 illustrates how its institutional framework remained relatively precarious when it came to the political incorporation of dissident and excluded groups. Still, it shows that popular politics in Colombia have always aimed to strengthen state institutions and expand democracy. This trend of the institutionalization of political rights is reflected in the evolution of protest activity over time. More contentious forms of protest characterized the first analyzed periods, while more conventional demonstrations are dominating current contention. Claims have also passed from seeking land and collective bargaining compensations to demanding the protection of political rights, the respect of binding agreements, and the provision of public and social services. Urban dissident actors have never lost their centrality in Colombian popular politics. Still, the participation of peasants and unionized workers has decreased, making room for students, independent workers, ethnic groups, and victims of violence to raise their voices. Thus, over time, a more active and participatory citizenry has been articulating new political rights. By strengthening institutions protecting the right-to-have-rights formula, organized civil society has been proactively pressing for the recognition of sexual diversity rights, ethnic and racial rights, and the rights to a clean environment and a dignified life.

Chapter 5 shows how protest politics has evolved during democratic progress and democratic decay in Peru. The 1980s was a period of economic and political liberalization coupled with economic and political crises driven by the presence of hyperinflation, the informalization of the economy, and an armed conflict led by the Shining Path and other groups, all of which threatened to destabilize the political regime. This political and economic instability opened opportunities for mobilization. During the 1990s, however, as democracy decayed during Fujimori's regime, labor rights were not protected as the economy underwent a major market reorientation. Popular politics suffered a significant decrease not only because of Fujimori's dictatorial management of social dissent, but also because the further informalization of the economy caused a demobilization of the organized labor sector. Since the 2000s, democracy in the country has been strengthened, while the market economy has expanded. This second dual process of economic and political liberalization appears to be conducive to further democratization: economic globalization has generated a relatively prosperous period of economic growth driven by a commodity boom, and political liberalization has allowed a more diverse mobilized civil society to flourish. As in the case of Colombia, over time, popular politics has passed from being dominated by unionized sectors advocating for labor rights and socioeconomic prerogatives to include students, popular organizations, and citizens in general with more political and policy-oriented claims toward different state authorities and representatives. Popular politics has changed from reactive to proactive mobilization, expanding the dissenting actors' repertoire of claims, targets, and protest forms. This goes along the lines of the complex growth of civil society as democracy deepens and the market economy affects different interests.

Chapter 6, on Venezuela, makes an additional contribution to the long-term analyses in this volume by not only analyzing the effects of economic and political liberalization on popular politics in the 1980s, but also pointing at the effects of democratic decay and deglobalization on dissenting popular politics since the 1990s. The long period of analysis allows for the identification of a watershed moment: the Caracazo in 1989, which marked a clear before-and-after change in the way in which protest activity influenced politics in the country. Additionally, the comparison of popular politics and its mobilizing characteristics surrounding the Caracazo is further

justified, as the "before" period coincides with the last politically and economically liberal period in the country, while the "after" period overlaps
with dictatorial rule focused on the deglobalization of its economy. Within
this comparison, however, Margarita López Maya identifies not only significant differences in protest repertoires and interactions between movement and countermovement actors, but also important similarities among
dissenting claims. In my view, the most striking finding is the fact that protest movement claims have remained dominated by socioeconomic grievances (income and labor conditions), poor provision of public services, and
human rights abuses. This is striking not only because it signals that these
socioeconomic grievances, generated during periods of economic liberalization, were not resolved by the implemented deglobalizing policies, especially during the second Chávez administration. Moreover, the fact that
protest activity continued to denounce the precarity of labor, public services, and human rights speaks loudly to the failures of the so-called Bolivarian revolution to alleviate living conditions of the most disadvantaged
sectors of the population. Another surprising finding was that the state's
response to dissent remained relatively unchanged between the periods. I
believe this speaks not only to the prevailing incipient institutional framework to incorporate popular claims despite Venezuela's long history of
democracy, but also to the unexpected similar tendency to criminalize dissent by both democratic and authoritarian authorities and their disinterest
in representing popular interests. Among the differences between democratic and authoritarian authorities, López Maya finds that protest activity
has turned more confrontational over time. However, this confrontation
does not occur exclusively between protesters and state authorities, but
also between movement and countermovement actors. Organizations in
favor of and against Chávez took to the streets to express their grievances
against one another as much as to articulate their interests to state authorities, often resulting in violent clashes, especially during periods of political
polarization.

Chapters 7 and 8 offer interesting cross-sectional analyses that zoom in
on the inferential analysis of subnational political contexts and the organizational factors and mobilizing networks driving protest activity. In chapter 7, the authors contextualize their study across two specific protest

campaigns against the implementation of market-oriented policies, which was perceived as harmful by popular sectors in Costa Rica and Nicaragua in 1983 and 1990, respectively. Their results further add to the arguments of this volume: because in both countries mobilizing campaigns occurred in relatively democratic periods, the analysis shows that it was the political liberalization process and not democratic decay that allowed popular politics against economic liberalizing policies to flourish. Hence, more and not less democracy better protects labor and citizens' rights threatened by neoliberal politics.

Chapter 8 details a network analysis of actors and organizations leading popular politics in Chile at the height of both economic and political liberalization. Students and workers appear to be the main protest actors. The authors argue that this finding is not a coincidence; it is well-grounded in the processes that established the market economy and the political system in the country. They consider that organizations of students and workers in Chile are the by-product of the development of capitalism and the nation-state. These actors protesting together contest the grievances generated during economic liberalizing periods. Their traditions allowed these actors to endure the repressive response of authoritarian authorities and, at the same time, become the remnants over which democratizing organizations built their mobilizing networks to push for further political liberalization. As the mobilizing networks became more diverse, students and workers became nodal points for incoming indigenous, feminist, LGBTQ+, urban settler, consumer, and environmentalist organizations. Students and workers dominated the more disruptive actions within the repertoire of contention, while incoming organizations during and after the initial political liberalizing period opted for more conventional forms of protest. While students and workers will always have their specific demands to defend labor rights and socioeconomic prerogatives (reactive claims), these will become more sophisticated (proactive) as political liberalization deepens and these actors interact with other groups' claims.

Chapter 9 makes two relevant contributions to this volume's theme. First, Santiago Ortiz's study shows that, while redistribution policies may help governments to mitigate contention, they are certainly insufficient to address the socioeconomic grievances attributed to neoliberal policies.

Although the expansion of the economy and the active role of the state significantly reduced inequality in Ecuador by providing more jobs, higher
income, market growth, and investment in education and health, the labor
rights bases over which industries and markets expanded during the commodity boom were the same on which market economies of the neoliberal
period were built. Thus, although the state expanded its capacity to intervene and negotiate conflicts, it is no surprise that workers are still aggrieved
and that the social security of a multiethnic citizenry calling for universal
rights and benefits has yet to materialize. As previous liberalizing policies
did not contemplate the negative effects on labor and debtor rights, the
redistributive policies of today do little to repair them. Second, deciphering
the explanatory factors of popular politics in democracies of the post-
neoliberal era offers interesting insights into the democratic nature of
Ecuador's left-leaning leaders, who promote the need to bring the state
back in to implement a social justice platform while restricting social participation and attacking autonomous civil society organizations and the
very same democratic practices that allowed them to gain popular support.
It seems that the political liberalization that previously empowered peasants and workers to protest against the negative consequences of neoliberalism are now an inconvenience to authorities who brand themselves as
left-leaning, who lack either the political will or the know-how to address
the interests of a pluri-ethnic, diverse, and sophisticated citizenry now
accustomed to living in a democracy.

Chapter 10, on Brazil, closes the analysis of popular politics within post-
neoliberalism by showing that the establishment of political and economic
liberalization is not a panacea. Not only are social justice movements
demanding further redistributive policies still prevalent there, but right-
wing groups supporting austerity measures and moral conservatism are
emerging. At first, popular protests concentrated on pressing for the expansion of redistributive policies set in place by the leftist administrations of
Presidents Luiz Inácio Lula da Silva and Dilma Rousseff. These produced
relatively successful results in improving income distribution as well as
reducing unemployment and socioeconomic inequalities. However, as the
economy shrank, countermovement groups began demanding the return
to status quo austere policies. Countermovement mobilization has been

smaller in size and has a shorter history and contention tradition, but its composition is more diverse and its agenda more vocal and confrontational, particularly in online media. It includes anti-PT (Workers' Party) groups, religious leaders, businesspeople, partisan activists, and unaffiliated groups and individuals. Their grievances are directed toward not only state authorities, but also mobilizing rivals. Corruption denunciations launched against Lula and Rousseff by right-wing politicians further fueled the antagonism between pro- and anti-PT protesters. As movement–countermovement dynamics evolved, the groups' discourse over the appropriation of income and public resources began to radicalize. We now know that while the social justice movement in Brazil was fighting against what we recognize as structural racism and demanding universal social rights, the right-wing movement covered their exclusionary agenda with an anticorruption façade.

Reexamining Reactive and Proactive Contention

In the introduction, Moisés Arce and Takeshi Wada argue that the dual but asynchronous process of liberalization led to the airing of socioeconomic and political grievances by popular politics actors who took advantage of the political opportunities opened in a hybrid political–economic environment (Almeida 2010a). The different protest event analyses presented in this volume show how effective this empirical strategy is to test how contextual political and economic factors at different levels of analysis affect protest cycles. In this hybrid environment, Arce and Wada argue, reactive and proactive protests coexist and often overlap with each other. Globalization and democratization have brought in new actors, such as LGBTQ+, environmentalist, women's, indigenous peoples', and antiracist organizations, who are mostly engaging in proactive patterns of protest. However, as table 11.1 shows, workers, students, and popular organizations of, e.g., debtors, residents, and consumers are still central popular politics actors. These central actors are still leading reactive patterns of protest campaigns and cycles.

More important is the fact that the state has not lost its centrality as a protest target, widespread political decentralization reforms in the region notwithstanding. The results summarized in table 11.1 also confirm that state authorities—central governments in particular—remain identified as the source of the citizenry's problems and solutions (Jenkins and Klandermans 1995). Reactive protesters tend to demand that state authorities provide solutions to their grievances, while proactive protesters tend to attribute their grievances to the state. In either case, the state remains at the center for the resolution of popular politics conflicts.

This centrality should not come as a surprise. Even if we presume that the process of economic globalization reduced the state's role in economy and its ability to redistribute considerably, the state is still the guardian of the rule of law. To economic interests, this change translates into binding free-market and investing regulation and provisions. To political actors, guaranteeing the rule of law means that democracy is "the only game in town." To popular politics actors, the rule of law equates to maintaining the legal and even constitutional protection of their labor rights and socioeconomic prerogatives. To the general citizenry, it should represent not only the protection of their rights but also equal access to justice.

The overlapping and interactive patterns of reactive and proactive mobilization uncovered by this volume indicate that, although economic liberalization has generated more and new socioeconomic grievances, globalization and democracy have opened more opportunities for mobilization to both traditional and new popular politics actors. These actors have presented new claims or reframed their old ones by taking advantage of national contexts as well as transnational geopolitics and markets and mobilizing resources, networks, and trends. As proactive mobilization strengthens these popular politics actors, they may start to alter redistributive policies. Moreover, as this type of mobilization deepens and becomes more diverse, it may help to expand political rights and civil liberties to those sectors of the population still marginalized or excluded. Transnational feminist and antiracist movements are already fighting for these. Migrants' organizations are also making great strides to defend their rights. Thus, a more proactive mobilization may contribute to the definition of new social contracts across different Latin American countries.

New Research Opportunities for Protest Event Analysis

While I do not foresee that this type of mobilization will stop globalization in its tracks, I do believe that proactive organizations are already identifying niches in the globalized social movement society to advance their claims. Finding these niches has depended more on specific than structural political opportunities (Meyer and Minkoff 2004). Democratization processes in the region opened mobilizing structural political opportunities for all; now it is up to popular politics groups to identify and take advantage of specific political opportunities (SPOs) opened by the political system in which they operate. SPOs may open to different popular politics actors depending on whether their political allies gain office. This book and the recent episodes from the region it describes provide several examples of the emergence of these SPOs and how different popular actors can make use of them.

To illustrate, an SPO opened in Bolivia when Evo Morales won the presidency in 2006. As Laserna pointed out (chapter 3), the SPO triggered a sustained increase in contentious popular politics led by Evo Morales himself and produced important changes in economic policy as well as the political incorporation of a popular agenda. This process is very much along the lines of Silva and Rossi's (2018) and Rossi's (2017) arguments on the second wave of political incorporation of leftist interest and actors.

In Colombia, the June 2022 electoral victory of Gustavo Petro (the first leftist president in the history of the country), along with the election of the first Afro-descendant woman, Francia Márquez, to the vice-presidency, may open SPOs for popular politics actors to expand peace agreements as well as for Afro-Colombian organizations to advance their interests. In chapter 4, Mauricio Archila Neira and Martha García Velandia—who wrote well before the election and were thus unable to observe the electoral effects of the recent social outburst—were already highlighting an increasing trend of the politicization of social protest calling for greater democracy and the political incorporation of popular politics actors and interests. The SPO marked by the June 2022 elections clearly accelerated the trend they had found.

The 2021 electoral victory of Pedro Castillo in Peru is yet one more recent example of how SPOs could give popular politics actors increasing access to power. The constitutional limitations to the executive power and the fact that Castillo faced a divided government may have hindered his efforts to alter the social contract in the country. At this writing, his administration was only in its second year, and it was short-lived. Given his ousting from power, it will be of great interest to find out how this new SPO will enable popular groups to make their voices heard.

In Chile, an SPO suddenly opened when a wave of protest triggered by an increase in public transit fares ended in calling for a national plebiscite in October 2020; this in turn led to a convention to reform the country's constitution and allowed popular politics actors to gain a seat at the table. At this writing, we are still waiting for the eventual constitution to be drafted and approved, but I have no doubt that the emergent SPO at this political juncture in Chile will lead to the incorporation of popular politics' demands and that, as a result, the new constitution will likely represent a new political contract for the country. This is not a small accomplishment: before this, only the 1917 Mexican Constitution incorporated labor and land tenure rights that guaranteed land redistribution programs as well as the creation of the labor sector in the country. Popular politics in the age of globalization and democracy have the potential to bring about such an important institutionalization, and that is why we should continue to study popular protests in Latin America.[2]

Protest event data analysis remains the tool of choice in comparing, for example, the effects of state responses to popular politics (Inclán 2012). Students of protest activity may also deepen their analyses into looking at granted concessions, repressive measures, allies in power, elections, mobilizing media and networks, and protesting frames, to name a few. The bird's-eye and magnifying glass analyses in this volume already point toward more inferential possibilities based on protest event data, namely the effects of different political contexts as political opportunity providers for popular politics mobilization and success in achieving their goals. Contextualizing contestation may also enable protest activity students to better identify which campaigns attract different participants (Inclán and Almeida 2017; Inclán 2019; Inclán 2021; Somma, Rossi and Donoso 2020). Still, our analytical possibilities have expanded almost exponentially as methodological tools and data sources became more diverse and sophisticated. I believe that the protest event research frontier nowadays lies on the ethical use of big data, optical character recognition, and text analysis. The second and third of these may be used to analyze how protest activity is framed in the media and the effects of these framing processes on public attitudes toward popular politics. The analysis of political ads and mobilizing campaigns on social media may allow us to venture into the extent to which mis- and disinformation are being used as mobilizing tools and analyze their consequences on popular politics' mobilizing efforts.

Additionally, as organized civil societies in Latin America become more plural and sophisticated, we should observe not only that they are better equipped to deal with political and economic changes and shocks, but also that they become more regionally if not globally integrated. Transnational networks of mobilization across the continent should open new mobilizing resources, frames, and strategies. The integration of proactive mobilization may strengthen domestic popular politics campaigns fighting against similar socioeconomic and political challenges. We have already witnessed the global proliferation of #MeToo and antiracist movements with different successes depending on the domestic political contexts they have faced in each country. Protest event analysis and the systematic extraction of information may still prove useful to decipher the effects of global integration, transnational mobilizing networks, and democracy on proactive popular politics. We may need to add only one more level of information into our inferential analyses: transnational-level data on economic and informatic integration, solidarity networks, and political cooperation, which will uncover how well-adapted popular politics actors are to a global economy and how well-suited they are to respond to the prevailing autocrats and emerging populist threats to democracy in the region. Nevertheless, proactive popular politics will only flourish if democracy is to prevail in the continent and globalization continues to provide opportunities for mobilization.

Notes

1.   The Armed Conflict Location & Event Data Project (ACLED) can be accessed at https://acleddata.com/.

2. SPOs more generally may vary from one mobilizing campaign to another. Collecting this data may again prove to be labor-intensive. Janice Gallagher (2022), for instance, accounts for the legal opportunities and obstacles faced by relatives of the "disappeared" in Mexico who organized to demand justice for the victims of organized crime. Systematizing this ethnographic effort for other popular movements in the country or for similar movements in other countries seems ambitious, if not impossible.

Bibliography

Databases and Datasets

Base de Datos de Luchas Sociales (BDLS). Bogotá: Centro de Investigación y Educación Popular (CINEP). www.cinep.org.co/base-de-datos-luchas-sociales/.

Base de Datos El Bravo Pueblo (BDEBP). Caracas: Centro de Estudios del Desarrollo (CENDES)–Universidad Central de Venezuela. Unpublished.

Base de Protestas Sociales del Perú. Created by Moises Arce. New Orleans: Tulane University. Unpublished.

Bolivian database, untitled. Created by Centro de Estudios de la Realidad Económica y Social (CERES). Cochabamba, Bolivia: CERES. Unpublished.

Brazilian database, untitled. Created by Luciana Tatagiba and Andréia Galvão. São Paulo: State University of Campinas (UNICAMP). Unpublished.

Ecuadoran database, untitled. Created by Centro Andino de Acción Popular (CAAP). Quito: CAAP. Unpublished.

Mexican Popular Contention Database (MPCD), Version 2020.06. Created by Takeshi Wada. Tokyo: The University of Tokyo, 2020. Unpublished.

Observatorio de Conflictos (Observatory of Conflicts). Created by the Centre for Social Conflict and Cohesion Studies (COES). Santiago, Chile: COES.

Situación de los Derechos Humanos: Informe Anual. Created by Programa Educación-Acción en Derechos Humanos (PROVEA). Caracas: PROVEA. Unpublished.

V-Dem [Country–Year/Country–Date] Dataset v10. Edited by Varieties of Democracy (V-Dem) Project. Created by Michael Coppedge, John Gerring, Carl Henrik Knutsen, Staffan I. Lindberg, Jan Teorell, David Altman, Michael Bernhard, M. Steven Fish, Adam Glynn, Allen Hicken, Anna Luhrmann, Kyle L. Marquardt, Kelly McMann, Pamela Paxton, Daniel Pemstein, Brigitte Seim, Rachel Sigman, Svend-Erik Skaaning, Jeffrey Staton, Steven Wilson, Agnes Cornell, Nazifa Alizada, Lisa Gastaldi, Haakon Gjerløw, Garry Hindle, Nina Ilchenko, Laura Maxwell, Valeriya Mechkova, Juraj Medzihorsky, Johannes von Römer, Aksel Sundström, Eitan Tzelgov, Yi-ting Wang, Tore Wig, and Daniel Ziblatt. 2021.

Voter Turnout Database. Stockholm: International Institute for Democracy and Electoral Assistance (IDEA). www.idea.int/data-tools/data/voter-turnout.

World Bank DataBank. World Bank Group. http://databank.worldbank.org.
     Accessed March 13, 2021.

Print and Online Resources

ACNUR-UNHCR. 2018. *Tendencias globales: desplazamiento forzado en 2017.*
     Report. Geneva, Switzerland: Alto Comisionado de las Naciones Unidas
     para los Refugiados. www.acnur.org/stats/globaltrends/5b2956a04/.
Acosta, Mariclaire. 2012. "NGOs and Human Rights." In Camp, *Oxford Hand-*
     book of Mexican Politics, 423–45.
Affonso, Almino, Sergio Gómez, Emilio Klein, and Pablo Ramírez. 1970. *Movi-*
     miento campesino chileno. 3 vols. Santiago: ICIRA.
Agencia para la Reincorporación y la Normalización (ARN). 2020. "ARN en
     Cifras. Corte al 20 de febrero de 2020." Accessed April 30, 2020. https://
     www.reincorporacion.gov.co/es/agencia/Paginas/ARN-en-cifras.aspx.
Aidi, Hishaam D. 2009. *Redeploying the State: Corporatism, Neoliberalism, and*
     Coalition Politics. New York: Palgrave Macmillan.
Akchurin, Maria. 2015. "The Politics of Water: Privatizing Water and Sanitation
     Utilities in Argentina and Chile." PhD dissertation, University of Chicago.
Alayza, Alejandra, and Vicente Sotelo. 2012. *Revisión del impacto de los TLC en*
     América Latina: una mirada sobre las estrategias de desarrollo de la región
     y las industrias extractivas. Lima: OCMAL.
Almeida, Paul D. 2007. "Defensive Mobilization: Popular Movements against
     Economic Adjustment Policies in Latin America." *Latin American Per-*
     spectives 34, no. 3: 123–39.
———. 2008a. "The Sequencing of Success: Organizing Templates and Neolib-
     eral Policy Outcomes." *Mobilization* 13, no. 2: 165–87.
———. 2008b. *Waves of Protest: Popular Struggle in El Salvador, 1925–2005.* Min-
     neapolis: University of Minnesota Press.
———. 2010a. "Globalization and Collective Action." In *Handbook of Politics:*
     State and Society in Global Perspective, edited by Kevin T. Leicht and J.
     Craig Jenkins, 305–26. New York: Springer.
———. 2010b. "Social Movement Partyism: Collective Action and Oppositional
     Political Parties in Latin America." In *Strategic Alliances: Coalition Build-*
     ing and Social Movements, edited by Nella Van Dyke and Holly J. McCam-
     mon, 170–96. Minneapolis: University of Minnesota Press.
———. 2014. *Mobilizing Democracy: Globalization and Citizen Protest.* Balti-
     more: Johns Hopkins University Press.
———. 2015. "Unintended Consequences of State-Led Development: A Theory of
     Mobilized Opposition to Neoliberalism." *Sociology of Development* 1, no.
     2: 259–76.

———. 2016. "Social Movements and Economic Development." In *Sociology of Development Handbook*, edited by Gregory Hooks, 528–50. Berkeley: University of California Press.

———. 2018. "The Role of Threat in Collective Action." In Snow et al., *Wiley-Blackwell Companion to Social Movements*, 43–62.

———. 2019. *Social Movements: The Structure of Collective Mobilization*. Berkeley: University of California Press.

Almeida, Paul, and Chris Chase-Dunn. 2018. "Globalization and Social Movements." *Annual Review of Sociology* 44: 189–211.

Almeida, Paul, and Allen Cordero Ulate, eds. 2015. *Handbook of Social Movements across Latin America*. New York: Springer.

Almeida, Paul, and Hank Johnston. 2006. "Neoliberal Globalization and Popular Movements in Latin America." In Johnston and Almeida, *Latin American Social Movements*, 3–18.

Almeida, Paul, and Amalia Pérez Martín. 2020. "Economic Globalization and Social Movements in Latin America." In *The Oxford Handbook of the Sociology of Latin America*, edited by Xóchitl Bada and Liliana Rivera-Sánchez, 390–411. Oxford: Oxford University Press.

Almeida, Paul, Eugenio Sosa, Allen Cordero Ulate, and Ricardo Argueta. 2021. "Protest Waves and Social Movement Fields: The Micro Foundations of Campaigning for Subaltern Political Parties." *Social Problems* 68, no. 4: 831–51.

Almeida, Ronaldo de. 2017. "A onda quebrada: evangélicos e conservadorismo." *Cadernos Pagu* 50.

Alonso, Angela, and Ann Mische. 2017. "Changing Repertoires and Partisan Ambivalence in the New Brazilian Protests." *Bulletin of Latin American Research* 36, no. 2: 144–59.

Alvarenga Venutolo, Patricia. 2005. *De vecinos a ciudadanos: movimientos comunales y luchas cívicas en la historia contemporánea de Costa Rica*. San José, Costa Rica: Editorial de la Universidad de Costa Rica.

Andreetti, Cristina, Fernando Bustamante, and Lucía Durán. 2006. *La sociedad civil en el Ecuador: una sociedad civil eficaz más allá de sus debilidades*. Quito: Fundación Esquivel/Civicus.

Angell, Alan. 1974. *Partidos políticos y movimiento obrero en Chile*. Mexico City: Ediciones Era.

Anria, Santiago. 2018. *When Movements Become Parties: The Bolivian MAS in Comparative Perspective*. Cambridge, UK: Cambridge University Press.

Arce, Moisés. 2005. *Market Reform in Society: Post-Crisis Politics and Economic Change in Authoritarian Peru*. University Park: Pennsylvania State University Press.

———. 2008. "The Repoliticization of Collective Action after Neoliberalism in Peru." *Latin American Politics and Society* 50, no. 3: 37–62.

———. 2010. "Parties and Social Protest in Latin America's Neoliberal Era." *Party Politics* 16, no. 5: 669–86.

———. 2014. *Resource Extraction and Protest in Peru*. Pittsburgh: University of Pittsburgh Press.

———, ed. 2023. *Perú: Cuatro décadas de contienda popular*. Quito: FLACSO Ecuador.

Arce, Moisés, and José Incio. 2018. "Perú 2017: Un caso extremo de gobierno dividido." *Revista de Ciencia Política* 38, no. 2: 361–77.

Arce, Moisés, and Roberta Rice. 2009. "Societal Protest in Post-Stabilization Bolivia." *Latin American Research Review* 44, no. 1: 88–101.

Archila, Mauricio, Martha C. García, Santiago Garcés, and Ana M. Restrepo. 2019. "21N: ¡Y la copa se rebosó!" *Cien Días* 97: 1–10.

Archila, Mauricio, Martha Cecilia García, Ana María Restrepo, and Leonardo Parra. 2014. *Luchas sociales en Colombia, 2013: Informe especial*. Bogotá: CINEP.

Archila Neira, Mauricio. 1991. *Cultura e identidad obrera: Colombia 1910–1945*. Bogotá: CINEP.

———. 2003. *Idas y venidas, vueltas y revueltas: protestas sociales en Colombia, 1958–1990*. Bogotá: CINEP/ICANH.

———. 2012. "Luchas laborales y violencia contra el sindicalismo en Colombia, 2002–2010: ¿otro daño 'colateral' de la Seguridad Democrática?" *Controversia* 198: 161–213.

———. 2019. "Control de las protestas: una cara de la relación Estado y movimientos sociales, 1975–2015." In Archila Neira et al., *Cuando la copa se rebosa*, 95–151.

Archila Neira, Mauricio, Alejandro Angulo Novoa, Álvaro Delgado Guzmán, Martha Cecilia García Velandia, Luis Guillermo Guerrero Guevara, and Leonardo Parra. 2012. *Violencia contra el sindicalismo, 1984–2010*. Bogotá: CINEP.

Archila Neira, Mauricio, Ingrid Johanna Bolívar Ramírez, Álvaro Delgado Guzmán, Martha Cecilia García Velandia, Fernán E. González González, Patricia Madariaga Villegas, Esmeralda Prada Mantilla, and Teófilo Vásquez Delgado. 2006. *Conflictos, poderes e identidades en el Magdalena Medio, 1990–2001*. Bogotá: CINEP.

Archila Neira, Mauricio, Álvaro Delgado Guzmán, Martha Cecilia García Velandia, and Esmeralda Prada Mantilla. 2002. *25 años de luchas sociales en Colombia, 1975–2000*. Bogotá: CINEP.

Archila Neira, Mauricio, Santiago Garcés Correa, Martha Cecilia García Velandia, Javier Lautaro Medina Bernal, Ana María Restrepo Rodríguez, and Mauricio Torres Tovar. 2020. *La crisis de la salud es anterior al COVID-19*. Bogotá: CINEP.

Archila Neira, Mauricio, Martha Cecilia García Velandia, Leonardo Parra

Rojas, and Ana María Restrepo Rodríguez, eds. 2019. *Cuando la copa se rebosa: Luchas sociales en Colombia, 1975–2015*. Bogotá: CINEP.

Arias, Santiane, and Sávio Cavalcante. 2019. "A divisão da classe média na crise política brasileira (2015–2016)." In *O Brasil e a França na mundialização neoliberal: mudanças políticas e contestações sociais*, edited by Paul Bouffartigue, Armando Boito, Sophie Béroud, and Andréia Galvão, 97–125. São Paulo: Alameda.

Asamblea Constituyente 2007–2008. 2008. *Constitución de la República del Ecuador*. Registro Oficial 449 de 20 de octubre.

Auyero, Javier. 2001. "Glocal Riots." *International Sociology* 16, no. 1: 33–53.

———. 2006. "The Moral Politics of Argentine Crowds." In Johnston and Almeida, *Latin American Social Movements*, 147–62.

———. 2007. *Routine Politics and Violence in Argentina: The Gray Zone of State Power*. Cambridge, UK: Cambridge University Press.

Bailey, John. 2012. "Drug Traffickers as Political Actors in Mexico's Nascent Democracy." In Camp, *Oxford Handbook of Mexican Politics*, 466–94.

Barber, Benjamin R. 1992. "Jihad vs. McWorld." *Atlantic Monthly* March 1992, 53–65.

Bargsted, Matías, Nicolás M. Somma, and Benjamín Muñoz-Rojas. 2019. "Participación electoral en Chile: una aproximación de edad, período y cohorte." *Revista de ciencia política* (Santiago) 39, no. 1: 75–98.

Bargsted, Matías A., and Luis Maldonado. 2018. "Party Identification in an Encapsulated Party System: The Case of Postauthoritarian Chile." *Journal of Politics in Latin America* 10, no. 1: 29–68.

Barker, Colin, Laurence Cox, John Krinsky, and Alf Gunvald Nilsen. 2013. *Marxism and Social Movements*. Leiden: Brill.

Barrett, Philip, Maximiliano Appendino, Kate Nguyen, and Jorge de Leon Miranda. 2020. "Measuring Social Unrest using Media Reports." IMF Working Paper 2020/219. July 17.

Barrie, Christopher, and Neil Ketchley. 2018. "Opportunity without Organization: Labor Mobilization in Egypt after the 25th January Revolution." *Mobilization* 23, no. 2: 181–202.

Bastos, Pedro Paulo Zahluth. 2017. "Ascensão e crise do governo Dilma Rousseff e o golpe de 2016: poder estrutural, contradição e ideologia." *Revista de Economia Contemporánea* 21, no. 2: 1–63.

Bebbington, Anthony, M. Connarty, W. Coxshall, H. O'Shaughnessy, and M. Williams. 2007. *Mining and Development in Peru, with Special Reference to the Rio Blanco Project, Piura*. London: Peru Support Group.

Beer, Caroline C. 2003. *Electoral Competition and Institutional Change in Mexico*. Notre Dame, IN: University of Notre Dame Press.

———. 2012. "Invigorating Federalism: The Emergence of Governors and State Legislatures as Powerbrokers and Policy Innovators." In Camp, *Oxford Handbook of Mexican Politics*, 119–42.

Beissinger, Mark R. 1998. "Event Analysis in Transitional Societies: Protest Mobilization in the Former Soviet Union." In Rucht et al., *Acts of Dissent*, 284–316.

———. 2002. *Nationalist Mobilization and the Collapse of the Soviet State*. Cambridge, UK: Cambridge University Press.

Bensusán, Graciela, and Kevin J. Middlebrook. 2012. "Organized Labor and Politics in Mexico." In Camp, *Oxford Handbook of Mexican Politics*, 335–64.

Bermeo, Nancy. 2016. "On Democratic Backsliding." *Journal of Democracy* 27, no. 1: 5–19.

Bidegain, Germán. 2015. "Autonomización de los movimientos sociales e intensificación de la protesta: estudiantes y mapuches en Chile (1990–2013)." PhD dissertation, Pontificia Universidad Católica de Chile.

Bilello, Suzanne. 1996. "Mexico: The Rise of Civil Society." *Current History* 95, no. 598: 82–87.

Biroli, Flávia. 2019. "A reação contra o gênero e a democracia." *Nueva Sociedad*, especial em português: 76–87.

Biroli, Flávia, and Denise Mantovani. 2014. "A parte que me cabe nesse julgamento: a *Folha de S. Paulo* na cobertura ao processo do 'mensalão.'" *Opinião Pública* 20, no. 2: 204–18.

Bizberg, Ilán. 2010. "Una democracia vacía: sociedad civil, movimientos sociales y democracia." In Bizberg and Zapata, *Movimientos sociales*, 21–60.

Bizberg, Ilán, and Francisco Zapata, eds. 2010. *Movimientos sociales*. Vol. 4 of *Los grandes problemas de México*. 16 vols. Mexico City: Colegio de México.

Boito, Armando, Jr. 2017. "A corrupção como ideologia." *Crítica Marxista* 44: 9–19.

———. 2018. "Lava-Jato, classe média e burocracia de Estado." In *Reforma e crise política no Brasil*, edited by Armando Boito Jr., 253–64. Campinas: Editora da Unicamp.

Boulding, Carew. 2014. *NGOs, Political Protest, and Civil Society*. Cambridge, UK: Cambridge University Press.

Boulding, Carew, and Claudio A. Holzner. 2021. *Voice and Inequality: Poverty and Political Participation in Latin American Democracies*. New York: Oxford University Press.

Bratsis, Peter. 2017. "A corrupção política na era do capitalismo transnacional." *Crítica Marxista* 44: 21–42.

Brinegar, Adam, Scott Morgenstern, and Daniel Nielson. 2006. "The PRI's Choice: Balancing Democratic Reform and Its Own Salvation." *Party Politics* 12, no. 1: 77–97.

Brockett, Charles D. 2005. *Political Movements and Violence in Central America*. Cambridge, UK: Cambridge University Press.

Bruhn, Kathleen. 1997. *Taking on Goliath: The Emergence of a New Left Party and the Struggle for Democracy in Mexico*. University Park: Pennsylvania State University Press.

Bugueño, Joaquín Rozas, and Antoine Maillet. 2019. "Entre marchas, plebiscitos e iniciativas de ley: innovación en el repertorio de estrategias del movimiento No Más AFP en Chile (2014-2018)." *Izquierdas* 48: 1-21.

Burt, Jo-Marie. 2007. *Political Violence and the Authoritarian State in Peru: Silencing Civil Society*. New York: Palgrave Macmillan.

Cabrales Domínguez, Sergio. 2020. "La oleada de protestas del 2018 en Nicaragua: procesos, mecanismos y resultados." In *Anhelos de un nuevo horizonte: aportes para una Nicaragua democrática*, edited by Alberto Cortés Ramos, Umanzor López Baltodano, and Ludwing Moncada Bellorin, 79-96. San José, Costa Rica: FLACSO Costa Rica.

Cabrales Domínguez, Sergio, and Mario Sánchez. 2022. "Anti-Repression Protests in Nicaragua: An Authoritarian Transformation." In Snow et al., *Wiley-Blackwell Encyclopedia of Social and Political Movements*, 176-78.

Cadena-Roa, Jorge. 2016. *Las organizaciones de los movimientos sociales y los movimientos sociales en México, 2000-2014*. Mexico City: Friedrich Ebert Stiftung.

Calderón, Fernando, and Roberto Laserna. 1983. *El poder de las regiones*. Cochabamba, Bolivia: CERES.

Camp, Roderic Ai, ed. 2012. *The Oxford Handbook of Mexican Politics*. Oxford: Oxford University Press.

Caren, Neal, Sarah Gaby, and Catherine Herrold. 2017. "Economic Breakdown and Collective Action." *Social Problems* 64, no. 1: 133-55.

Carey, Sabine C. 2006. "The Dynamic Relationship between Protest and Repression." *Political Research Quarterly* 59, no. 1: 1-11.

Carneiro, Ricardo. 2018. "Navegando a contravento: Uma reflexão sobre o experimento desenvolvimentista de Dilma Rousseff." In *Para além da política económica*, edited by Ricardo Carneiro, Paulo Baltar, and Fernando Sarti, 11-54. São Paulo: Unesp Digital.

Carrillo, Fernando. 2010. "La Séptima Papeleta o el origen de la Constitución de 1991." In *La Séptima Papeleta: historia contada por algunos de sus protagonistas, con ocasión de los 20 años del Movimiento Estudiantil de la Séptima Papeleta*, edited by María Lucía Torres Villarreal, 23-64. Bogotá: Universidad del Rosario.

Carvalho, Laura. 2018. *Valsa brasileira: do boom ao caos económico*. São Paulo: Todavia.

Castells, Manuel. 2010. *The Power of Identity*. Malden, MA: Wiley-Blackwell.

———. 2012. *Redes de indignación y esperanza*. Translated by María Hernández. Madrid: Alianza.

Castillo, Mayari, and Anahí Durand. 2008. "Movimiento cocalero, política y representación: los casos boliviano y peruano." In *Identidades, etnicidad y racismo en América Latina*, edited by Fernando García, 47-72. Quito: FLACSO.

Cavalcante, Sávio. 2015. "Classe média e conservadorismo liberal." In *Direita, volver!: o retorno da direita e o ciclo político brasileiro*, edited by Sebastião Velasco e Cruz, André Kaysel, and Gustavo Codas, 177–96. São Paulo: Fundação Perseu Abramo.

———. 2018. "Classe média, meritocracia e corrupção." *Crítica Marxista* 46: 103–25.

Chase-Dunn, Christopher, and Paul Almeida. 2020. *Global Struggles and Social Change: From Prehistory to World Revolution in the Twenty-First Century.* Baltimore: Johns Hopkins University Press.

Chng, N. R. 2012. "Regulatory Mobilization and Service Delivery at the Edge of the Regulatory State." *Regulation and Governance* 6, no. 3: 344–61.

Chomsky, Aviva. 2021. *Central America's Forgotten History: Revolution, Violence, and the Roots of Migration.* Boston: Beacon Press.

Chong, Alberto, and Florencio López-de-Silanes. 2004. *Privatization in Mexico.* Research Department Working Paper 513. Washington, DC: Inter-American Development Bank.

Cleary, Matthew R. 2006. "A 'Left Turn' in Latin America? Explaining the Left's Resurgence." *Journal of Democracy* 17, no. 4: 35–49.

———. 2007. "Electoral Competition, Participation, and Government Responsiveness in Mexico." *American Journal of Political Science* 51, no. 2: 283–99.

Cohen, Jean L. 1985. "Strategy or Identity: New Theoretical Paradigms and Contemporary Social Movements." *Social Research* 52, no. 4: 663–716.

Cohen, Jean L., and Andrew Arato. 1992. *Civil Society and Political Theory.* Cambridge, MA: MIT Press.

Collier, David, and Ruth Berins Collier. 1991. *Shaping the Political Arena.* Princeton: Princeton University Press.

Collier, Ruth Berins, and Samuel Handlin, eds. 2009. *Reorganizing Popular Politics: Participation and the New Interest Regime in Latin America.* University Park: Pennsylvania State University Press.

Coppedge, Michael, et al. 2021. V-Dem. *See under* V-Dem in Databases and Datasets section.

Cordero, Allen. 2022. "Protests against the 2018 Fiscal Reform in Costa Rica." In Snow et al., *Wiley-Blackwell Encyclopedia of Social and Political Movements*, 505–7.

Cornelius, Wayne A. 2000. "Blind Spots in Democratization: Sub-National Politics as a Constraint on Mexico's Transition." *Democratization* 7, no. 3: 117–32.

Cornelius, Wayne A., Todd A. Eisenstadt, and Jane Hindley, eds. 1999. *Subnational Politics and Democratization in Mexico.* San Diego: Center for U.S.–Mexican Studies, University of California.

Cornwell, Benjamin, and Jill Ann Harrison. 2004. "Union Members and

Voluntary Associations: Membership Overlap as a Case of Organizational Embeddedness." *American Sociological Review* 69, no. 6: 862–81.

Correa-Cabrera, Guadalupe. 2013. *Democracy in "Two Mexicos": Political Institutions in Oaxaca and Nuevo León.* Basingstoke: Palgrave Macmillan.

Corredor, Consuelo, and Clara Ramírez. 2018. "¿Cuál será el ritmo de implementación del acuerdo de paz en el nuevo gobierno?" *Cien días vistos por CINEP* 94: 18–23.

Dagnino, Evelina. 1998. "Culture, Citizenship, and Democracy: Changing Discourses and Practices of the Latin American Left." In *Cultures of Politics, Politics of Culture: Re-visioning Latin American Social Movements*, edited by Sonia E. Alvarez, Evelina Dagnino, and Arturo Escobar, 33–63. Boulder, CO: Westview Press.

Davidson, Neil. 2013. "Right-Wing Social Movements: The Political Indeterminacy of Mass Mobilization." In *Marxism and Social Movements*, edited by Colin Barer, Laurence Cox, John Krinsky, and Alf Gunvald Nilsen, 277–97. Leiden: Brill.

Davis, Diane E. 1999. "The Power of Distance: Re-Theorizing Social Movements in Latin America." *Theory and Society* 28, no. 4: 585–638.

Delgado, Álvaro. 2013. *Auge y declinación de la huelga.* Bogotá: CINEP.

Della Porta, Donatella. 2015. *Social Movements in Times of Austerity: Bringing Capitalism Back into Protest Analysis.* Cambridge: Polity Press.

Departamento Administrativo Nacional de Estadística (DANE). 2018. *Censo Nacional de Población y Vivienda, 2018.* Gobierno de Colombia. www.dane.gov.co/index.php/estadisticas-por-tema/demografia-y-poblacion/censo-nacional-de-poblacion-y-vivenda-2018.

Diani, Mario. 2007. "The Relational Element in Charles Tilly's Recent (and Not So Recent) Work." *Social Networks* 29, no. 2: 316–23.

Dias, Tayrine dos Santos. 2017. " 'É uma batalha de narrativas': os enquadramentos de ação coletiva em torno do impeachment de Dilma Rousseff no Facebook." Master's thesis, Universidade de Brasília.

Domínguez, Jorge I., and Alejandro Poiré, eds. 1999. *Toward Mexico's Democratization: Parties, Campaigns, Elections, and Public Opinion.* New York: Routledge.

Donoso, Sofía, and Nicolás M. Somma. 2019. " 'You Taught Us to Give an Opinion, Now Learn How to Listen': The Manifold Political Consequences of Chile's Student Movement." In *Protest and Democracy*, edited by Moisés Arce and Roberta Rice, 145–72. Calgary: University of Calgary Press.

Drake, Paul W. 2003. "El movimiento obrero en Chile: de la Unidad Popular a la Concertación." *Revista de Ciencia Política (Santiago)* 23, no. 2: 148–58.

Dreher, Axel. 2006. "Does Globalization Affect Growth? Evidence from a New Index of Globalization." *Applied Economics* 38, no. 10: 1091–110.

Dunkerley, James. 1984. *Rebellion in the Veins: Political Struggle in Bolivia, 1952–82*. London: Verso.

Durán, Gonzalo, and Marco Kremerman. 2015. "Sindicatos y negociación colectiva: panorama estadístico nacional y evidencia comparada." Working Paper. Santiago: Fundación Sol.

Earl, Jennifer, Andrew Martin, John D. McCarthy, and Sarah A. Soule. 2004. "The Use of Newspaper Data in the Study of Collective Action." *Annual Review of Sociology* 30, no. 1: 65–80.

Eckstein, Susan Eva. 1977. *The Poverty of Revolution: The State and the Urban Poor in Mexico*. Princeton: Princeton University Press.

Edelman, Marc. 1999. *Peasants against Globalization: Rural Social Movements in Costa Rica*. Stanford, CA: Stanford University Press.

Edwards, Bob, and John D. McCarthy. 2004. "Resources and Social Movement Mobilization." In Snow et al., *Blackwell Companion to Social Movements*, 116–52.

Eisenstadt, Todd A. 2000. "Eddies in the Third Wave: Protracted Transitions and Theories of Democratization." *Democratization* 7, no. 3: 3–24.

———. 2007. "The Origins and Rationality of the 'Legal Versus Legitimate' Dichotomy Invoked in Mexico's 2006 Post-Electoral Conflict." *PS: Political Science & Politics* 40, no. 1: 39–43.

———. 2011. *Politics, Identity, and Mexico's Indigenous Rights Movements*. New York: Cambridge University Press.

Eisenstadt, Todd A., and Jennifer Yelle. 2012. "Ulysses, the Sirens, and Mexico's Judiciary: Increasing Precommitments to Strengthen the Rule of Law." In Camp, *Oxford Handbook of Mexican Politics*, 210–33.

Eisinger, Peter K. 1973. "The Conditions of Protest Behavior in American Cities." *American Political Science Review* 67, no. 1: 11–28.

Ekiert, Grzegorz, and Jan Kubik. 1999. *Rebellious Civil Society: Popular Protest and Democratic Consolidation in Poland, 1989–1993*. Ann Arbor: University of Michigan Press.

Ellis-Jones, Mark. 2003. "States of Unrest III: Resistance to IMF and World Bank Policies in Poor Countries." *World Development Movement Report*. London: World Development Movement.

Escobar, Arturo, and Sonia E. Alvarez. 1992. *The Making of Social Movements in Latin America*. Boulder, CO: Westview Press.

Farthing, Linda, and Ben Kohl. 2007. "Bolivia's New Wave of Protest." NACLA. September 25. nacla.org/article/bolivia's-new-wave-protest.

Favela, Margarita. 2010. "Sistema político y protesta social: del autoritarismo a la pluralidad." In Bizberg and Zapata, *Movimientos sociales*, 101–46.

Ferrero, Juan Pablo, Ana Natalucci, and Luciana Tatagiba, eds. 2019. *Socio-Political Dynamics within the Crisis of the Left: Argentina and Brazil*. New York: Rowman & Littlefield.

Fillieule, Olivier, and Manuel Jiménez. 2003. "Appendix A: The Methodology of Protest Event Analysis and the Media Politics of Reporting Environmental Protest Events." In *Environmental Protest in Western Europe*, edited by Christopher Rootes, 258–79. Oxford: Oxford University Press.

Fox, Jonathan. 1994. "The Difficult Transition from Clientelism to Citizenship: Lessons from Mexico." *World Politics* 46, no. 2: 151–84.

Fox, Vicente. 2001. *Primer Informe de Gobierno: Anexo*. Mexico City: Presidencia.

Foyer, Jean, and David Dumoulin Kervran. 2015. "The Environmentalism of NGOs versus Environmentalism of the Poor? Mexico's Social-Environmental Coalitions." In Almeida and Cordero Ulate, *Handbook of Social Movements across Latin America*, 223–35.

Fuchs, Christian. 2006. "The Self-Organization of Social Movements." *Systemic Practice and Action Research* 19, no. 1: 101–37.

Gaitán, Laura, Mario F. Martínez, Paulo A. Pérez, and Fabio E. Velásquez. 2011. *El sector extractivo en Colombia*. Bogotá: Foro Nacional por Colombia.

Gallagher, Janice. 2022. *Bootstrap Justice: The Search for Mexico's Disappeared*. New York: Oxford University Press.

Galvão, Andréia. 2019. "Labour Conflicts and Union Strategies in Dilma Rousseff's Governments." In Ferrero et al., *Socio-Political Dynamics within the Crisis of the Left*, 141–64.

Galvão, Andréia, and Paula Marcelino. 2020. "The Brazilian Union Movement in the Twenty-First Century: The PT Governments, the Coup, and the Counterreforms." *Latin American Perspectives* 47, no. 2: 1–17.

Galvão, Andréia, and José Marcos Nayme Novelli. 2020. "Neoliberalismo exacerbado: devastação ambiental e degradação social." Paper presented at the 12º Encontro da ABCP (Associação Brasileira de Ciência Política), online event, October 19-23. www.abcp2020.sinteseeventos.com.br/simposio/view?ID_SIMPOSIO=10.

García, Marcial, and Paulo Pantigoso. 2019. *Peru's Mining & Metals Investment Guide 2019/2020*. Lima: EY Peru. cdn.www.gob.pe/uploads/document/file/292934/EY_Perus_Mining_and_Metals_Business_and_Investment_Guide_2019-2020.pdf.

García, Martha Cecilia. 2006. "Barrancabermeja: ciudad en permanente disputa." In Archila Neira et al., *Conflictos, poderes e identidades en el Magdalena Medio, 1990–2001*, 243–312.

———. 2019. "Introducción." In Archila Neira et al., *Cuando la copa se rebosa*, 25–62.

García, Martha Cecilia, and José Vicente Zamudio. 1997. *Bajo la lupa: descentralización en Bogotá, 1992–1996*. Bogotá: CINEP.

García Guadilla, María Pilar. 2021. "Democracia participativa, protestas sociales y autoritarismo en el socialismo del siglo XXI: el movimiento estudiantil venezolano." *América Latina Hoy* 85: 73–89.

Garretón, Matías, Alfredo Joignant, Nicolás Somma, and Tomás Campos. 2018. "Informe Anual Observatorio de Conflictos." *Nota COES de Política Pública* 17. Report.

Gaudichaud, Franck. 2003. "La Central Única de Trabajadores, las luchas obreras y los Cordones Industriales en el periodo de la Unidad Popular en Chile (1970–1973): análisis histórico crítico y perspectiva." Translated by Oliver Alvarez Seco and Rocío Anguiano Pérez. Online document. Archivo Chile. www.archivochile.com/Ideas_Autores/gaudif/gaudif0001.pdf.

Gillingham, Paul. 2012. "Mexican Elections, 1910–1994: Voters, Violence, and Veto Power." In Camp, *Oxford Handbook of Mexican Politics*, 53–76.

Goldstone, Jack A. 2004. "More Social Movements or Fewer? Beyond Political Opportunity Structures to Relational Fields." *Theory and Society* 33: 333–65.

——. 2011. "Understanding the Revolutions of 2011: Weakness and Resilience in Middle Eastern Autocracies." *Foreign Affairs* 90, no. 3: 8–16.

Goldstone, Jack A., and Charles Tilly. 2001. "Threat (and Opportunity): Popular Action and State Response in the Dynamics of Contentious Action." In *Silence and Voice in the Study of Contentious Politics*, edited by Ronald R. Aminzade, Jack A. Goldstone, Doug McAdam, Elizabeth J. Perry, Sidney Tarrow, William H. Sewell, and Charles Tilley, 179–94. Cambridge: Cambridge University Press.

Gómez, Diana Marcela. 2011. *Dinámicas del movimiento feminista bogotano: historias de cuarto, salón y calle, historias de vida (1970–1991)*. Bogotá: Universidad Nacional de Colombia.

González, Fernán, Ingrid Bolívar, and Teófilo Vásquez. 2002. *Violencia política en Colombia*. Bogotá: CINEP.

Goodwin, Jeff, and James M. Jasper. 2003. "Caught in a Winding, Snarling Vine: The Structural Bias of Political Process Theory." In *Rethinking Social Movements: Structure, Meaning, and Emotion*, edited by Jeff Goodwin and James M. Jasper, 3–30. New York: Rowman & Littlefield.

Graham, Carol, and Moises Naím. 1998. "The Political Economy of Institutional Reform in Latin America." In *Beyond Trade-Offs: Market Reforms and Equitable Growth in Latin America*, edited by Nancy Birdsall, Carol L. Graham, and Richard H. Sabot, 321–62. Washington, DC: Inter-American Development Bank.

Grasso, Maria T, and Marco Giugni. 2016. "Protest Participation and Economic Crisis: The Conditioning Role of Political Opportunities." *European Journal of Political Research* 55, no. 4: 663–80.

Grayson, George W. 2004. "Mexico's Semicorporatist Regime." In *Authoritarianism and Corporatism in Latin America: Revisited*, edited by Howard J. Wiarda, 242–55. Gainesville: University Press of Florida.

Grebe, Horst. 1998. *Las reformas estructurales en Bolivia*. La Paz: Fundación Milenio.

Grez, Sergio. 2000. "Transición en las formas de lucha: motines personales y huelgas obreras en Chile (1891–1907)." *Historia* (Santiago) 33: 141–225.

Grindle, Merilee S. 2009. *Going Local: Decentralization, Democratization, and the Promise of Good Governance*. Princeton: Princeton University Press.

Grupo de Memoria Histórica. 2013. *¡Basta Ya! Colombia: memorias de guerra y dignidad*. Bogotá: Centro Nacional de Memoria Histórica.

Guevara, Onofré. 2008. *Cien años de movimiento social en Nicaragua: relato cronológico*. Managua: Instituto Nacional de Historia de Nicaragua y de Centroamérica.

Gurr, Ted Robert. 1970. *Why Men Rebel*. Princeton: Princeton University Press.

Gygli, Savina, Florian Haelg, Niklas Potrafke, and Jan-Egbert Sturm. 2019. "The KOF Globalisation Index: Revisited." *Review of International Organizations* 14, no. 3: 543–74.

Haber, Paul Lawrence. 1994. "The Art and Implications of Political Restructuring in Mexico: The Case of Urban Popular Movements." In *The Politics of Economic Restructuring: State-Society Relations and Regime Change in Mexico*, edited by Maria Lorena Cook, Kevin J. Middlebrook, and Juan Molinar Horcasitas, 277–303. San Diego: Center for U.S.-Mexican Studies, University of California.

Habermas, Jürgen. 1981. "New Social Movements." *Telos* 49: 33–37.

Habitus. 2013. *La evolución de la clase media en Ecuador, 2003–2012: Una aplicación preliminar del modelo del Banco Mundial a la serie de encuestas nacionales s de hogares*. Quito: Habitus.

Hanagan, Michael, and Charles Tilly, eds. 1999. *Extending Citizenship, Reconfiguring States*. Lanham, MD: Rowman & Littlefield.

Harnecker, Martha. 2011. *Ecuador: una nueva izquierda en busca de la vida en plenitud*. Quito: Universidad Politécnica Salesiana.

Herkenrath, Mark, and Alex Knoll. 2011. "Protest Events in International Press Coverage: An Empirical Critique of Cross-National Conflict Databases." *International Journal of Comparative Sociology* 52, no. 3: 163–80.

Hernández, Myriam. 2015. *Una nación desplazada: informe nacional del desplazamiento forzado en Colombia*. Bogotá: Centro Nacional de Memoria Histórica.

Hiskey, Jonathan. 2012. "The Return of 'the Local' to Mexican Politics." In Camp, *Oxford Handbook of Mexican Politics*, 545–68.

Hochstetler, Kathryn. 2006. "Rethinking Presidentialism: Challenges and Presidential Falls in South America." *Comparative Politics* 38, no. 4: 401–18.

———. 2012a. "Civil Society and the Regulatory State of the South: A Commentary." *Regulation and Governance* 6, no. 3: 362–70.

———. 2012b. "Social Movements in Latin America." In *Routledge Handbook of*

Latin American Politics, edited by Peter Kingstone and Deborah J. Yashar, 237–48. New York: Routledge.

Huntington, Samuel P. 1991. *The Third Wave: Democratization in the Late Twentieth Century.* Norman: University of Oklahoma Press.

Hutter, Swen. 2014. "Protest Event Analysis and Its Offspring." In *Methodological Practices in Social Movement Research,* edited by Donatella della Porta, 335–67. Oxford: Oxford University Press.

Inclán, María. 2008. "From the ¡Ya Basta! to the Caracoles: Zapatista Mobilization under Transitional Conditions." *American Journal of Sociology* 113, no. 5: 1316–50.

———. 2009. "Repressive Threats, Procedural Concessions, and the Zapatista Cycle of Protests, 1994–2003." *Journal of Conflict Resolution* 53, no. 5: 794–819.

———. 2012. "Zapatista and Counter-Zapatista Protests." *Journal of Peace Research* 49, no. 3: 459–72.

———. 2018. *The Zapatista Movement and Mexico's Democratic Transition: Mobilization, Success, and Survival.* New York: Oxford University Press.

———. 2019. "Mexican Movers and Shakers: Protest Mobilization and Political Attitudes in Mexico City." *Latin American Politics & Society* 61, no. 1: 78–100.

———. 2021. "What Moves Students? Ritual versus Reactive Student Demonstrations in Mexico City." In *Student Movements in Late Neoliberalism: Dynamics of Contention and Their Consequences,* edited by Lorenzo Cini, Donatella della Porta, and César Guzmán-Concha, 27–54. Cham: Palgrave Macmillan.

Inclán, María, and Paul D. Almeida. 2017. "Ritual Demonstrations versus Reactive Protests: Participation across Mobilizing Contexts in Mexico City." *Latin American Politics and Society* 59, no. 4: 47–74.

Inglehart, Ronald. 1997. *Modernization and Postmodernization: Cultural, Economic, and Political Change in 43 Societies.* Princeton: Princeton University Press.

———. 2008. "Changing Values among Western Publics from 1970 to 2006." *West European Politics* 31, no. 1–2: 130–46.

Jenkins, J. Craig, and Bert Klandermans. 1995. "The Politics of Social Protest." In *The Politics of Social Protest: Comparative Perspectives on States and Social Movements,* edited by J. Craig Jenkins and Bert Klandermans, 3–13. Minneapolis: University of Minnesota Press.

Jenkins, J. Craig, and Thomas V. Maher. 2016. "What Should We Do about Source Selection in Event Data? Challenges, Progress, and Possible Solutions." *International Journal of Sociology* 46, no. 1: 42–57.

Johnston, Hank. 2005. "Talking the Walk: Speech Acts and Resistance in Authoritarian Regimes." In *Repression and Mobilization,* edited by

Christian Davenport, Hank Johnston, and Carol Mueller, 108–37. Minneapolis: University of Minnesota Press.

Johnston, Hank, and Paul Almeida, eds. 2006. *Latin American Social Movements: Globalization, Democratization, and Transnational Networks*. Lanham, MD: Rowman & Littlefield.

Johnston, Hank, and Jozef Figa. 1988. "The Church and Political Opposition: Comparative Perspectives on Mobilization against Authoritarian Regimes." *Journal for the Scientific Study of Religion* 27, no. 1: 32–47.

Jones, Mark P. 2005. "The Role of Parties and Party Systems in the Policymaking Process." Paper prepared for the Workshop on State Reform, Public Policies, and Policymaking Processes, Inter-American Development Bank, Washington, DC. February 28–March 2.

Kane, Anne E. 1997. "Theorizing Meaning Construction in Social Movements: Symbolic Structures and Interpretation during the Irish Land War." *Sociological Theory* 15, no. 3: 249–76.

Karl, Terry Lynn. 1994. "The Venezuelan Petro-State and the Crisis of Its Democracy." In McCoy et al., *Venezuelan Democracy under Stress*, 33–55.

Klandermans, Bert, and Suzanne Staggenborg, eds. 2002. *Methods of Social Movements Research*. Minneapolis: University of Minnesota Press.

Kleinberg, Remonda Bensabat. 2000. "Economic Liberalization and Inequality in Mexico: Prospects for Democracy." In *Economic Liberalization, Democratization, and Civil Society in the Developing World*, edited by Remonda Bensabat Kleinberg and Janine A. Clark, 219–40. New York: St. Martin's Press.

Klesner, Joseph L. 2012. "Regionalism in Mexican Electoral Politics." In Camp, *Oxford Handbook of Mexican Politics*, 622–46.

Koopmans, Ruud, and Dieter Rucht. 2002. "Protest Event Analysis." In Klandermans and Staggenborg, *Methods of Social Movement Research*, 231–59.

Kriesi, Hanspeter, Ruud Koopmans, Jan Willem Duyvendak, and Marco G. Giugni. 1995. *New Social Movements in Western Europe: A Comparative Analysis*. London: University College London Press.

Krinsky, John, and Nick Crossley. 2014. "Social Movements and Social Networks: Introduction." *Social Movement Studies* 13, no. 1: 1–21.

Kurtz, Marcus J. 2004. "The Dilemmas of Democracy in the Open Economy: Lessons from Latin America." *World Politics* 56, no. 2: 262–302.

Labbé Yáñez, Daniel. 2017. "Movimiento de deudores universitarios advierte: 'Eliminar el CAE no garantiza nada.'" Elciudadano.com, April 17. www.elciudadano.com/organizacion-social/movimiento-de-deudores-universitarios-advierte-eliminar-el-cae-no-garantiza-nada/04/17/.

Lalinde, Sebastián. 2019. *Elogio a la bulla: protesta y democracia en Colombia*. Bogotá: Dejusticia.

Langston, Joy. 2006. "The Birth and Transformation of the Dedazo in Mexico." In *Informal Institutions and Democracy: Lessons from Latin America*, edited by Gretchen Helmke and Steven Levitsky, 143-59. Baltimore: Johns Hopkins University Press.

Laserna, Roberto. 1980. *El "estado" boliviano, 1971-1978: economía y poder.* Cochabamba: Universidad Mayor de San Simón, Instituto de Estudios Sociales y Económicos.

———. 1991. "La acción social en la coyuntura democrática." *Síntesis* 14: 213-62.

———. 1994. *La masacre del valle: el desencuentro militar-campesino.* Cochabamba: Centro de Estudios de la Realidad Económica y Social (CERES).

———. 2003. "Bolivia: entre populismo y democracia." *Nueva Sociedad* 188: 4-14.

———. 2009. "Decentralization, Local Initiatives, and Citizenship in Bolivia, 1994-2004." In *Participatory Innovation and Representative Democracy in Latin America*, edited by Andrew Selee and Enrique Peruzzotti, 126-55. Baltimore: Woodrow Wilson Center Press with Johns Hopkins University Press.

Laserna, Roberto, and René Mayorga. 1985. *Crisis, democracia y conficto social.* Cochabamba: CERES.

Leal, Diego F. 2020. "Mass Transit Shutdowns as a Tactical Innovation in Bogotá, Colombia." *Social Currents* 7, no. 2: 1-21.

Levitsky, Steven. 2018. "Latin America's Shifting Politics: Democratic Survival and Weakness." *Journal of Democracy* 29, no. 4: 102-13.

Levitsky, Steven, and Maxwell A. Cameron. 2003. "Democracy without Parties? Political Parties and Regime Change in Fujimori's Peru." *Latin American Politics and Society* 45, no. 3: 1-33.

Levitsky, Steven, and Kenneth M. Roberts, eds. 2011. *The Resurgence of the Latin American Left.* Baltimore: Johns Hopkins University Press.

Lindau, Juan D. 1998. "The Civil Society and Democratization in Mexico." In *Market Economics and Political Change: Comparing China and Mexico*, edited by Juan D. Lindau and Timothy Cheek, 187-218. Lanham, MD: Rowman & Littlefield.

Loaeza, Soledad. 2000. "Uncertainty in Mexico's Protracted Transition: The National Action Party and Its Aversion to Risk." *Democratization* 7, no. 3: 93-116.

López Maya, Margarita. 2000. "¡Se rompieron las fuentes! La política está en la calle." In *Venezuela siglo XX: visiones y testimonios*, vol. 3, edited by Asdrúbal Baptista, 73-132. Caracas: Fundación Polar.

———. 2003. "The Venezuelan 'Caracazo' of 1989: Popular Protest and Institutional Weakness." *Journal of Latin American Studies* 35, no. 1: 117-37.

———. 2005. *Del viernes negro al referendo revocatorio.* Caracas: Alfa Grupo Editorial.

———. 2020. "Política de la calle y sociedad civil." In *Elementos para una transición integral e incluyente en Venezuela: una visión desde lo local*, edited by Juan Carlos Rueda Azcuénaga, 360–413. Online document. Instituto para las Transiciones Integrales (IFIT). ifit-transitions.org/publications/building-an-inclusive-transition-in-venezuela-a-local-perspective/. Accessed June 3, 2021.

Lührmann, Anna, and Staffan I. Lindberg. 2019. "A Third Wave of Autocratization Is Here: What Is New About It?" *Democratization* 26, no. 7: 1095–1113.

Luna, Juan Pablo, and David Altman. 2011. "Uprooted but Stable: Chilean Parties and the Concept of Party System Institutionalization." *Latin American Politics and Society* 53, no. 2: 1–28.

Luna, Juan Pablo, and Rodrigo Mardones. 2010. "Chile: Are the Parties Over?" *Journal of Democracy* 21, no. 3: 107–21.

Lustig, Nora. 1992. *Mexico: The Remaking of an Economy*. Washington, DC: Brookings Institution.

Macdonald, Laura, and Arne Ruckert. 2009. "Post-Neoliberalism in the Americas: An Introduction." In *Post-Neoliberalism in the Americas*, edited by Laura Macdonald and Arne Ruckert, 1–18. London: Palgrave.

Magaloni, Beatriz. 2005. "The Demise of Mexico's One-Party Dominant Regime: Elite Choices and the Masses in the Establishment of Democracy." In *The Third Wave of Democratization in Latin America: Advances and Setbacks*, edited by Frances Hagopian and Scott P. Mainwaring, 121–46. Cambridge, UK: Cambridge University Press.

Mainwaring, Scott. 1999. "Latin America's Imperiled Progress: The Surprising Resilience of Elected Governments." *Journal of Democracy* 10, no. 3: 101–14.

Mangonnet, Jorge, and Moisés Arce. 2017. "Los determinantes electorales y partidarios de la beligerancia popular en las provincias argentinas, 1993–2007." *Revista SAAP: Sociedad Argentina de Análisis Político* 11, no. 1: 11–34.

Martí i Puig, Salvador. 1997. *La revolución enredada: Nicaragua 1977–1996*. Madrid: Los libros de la Catarata.

Martuscelli, Danilo Enrico. 2016. "As lutas contra a corrupção nas crises políticas brasileiras recentes." *Crítica e Sociedade: Revista de Cultura e Política* 6, no. 2: 4–35.

Massal, Julie. 2014. *Revueltas, insurrecciones y protestas: un panorama de las dinámicas de movilización en el siglo XXI*. Bogotá: IEPRI, Universidad Nacional de Colombia.

Mattiace, Shannan. 2012. "Social and Indigenous Movements in Mexico's Transition to Democracy." In Camp, *Oxford Handbook of Mexican Politics*, 398–422.

Mayorga, René Antonio. 1987. *Democracia a la deriva: dilemas de la participación y concertación social en Bolivia*. La Paz: CERES.

Mazzuca, Sebastián L. 2013. "Lessons from Latin America: The Rise of Rentier Populism." *Journal of Democracy* 24, no. 2: 108–22.

McAdam, Doug. 2010. *Political Process and the Development of Black Insurgency, 1930–1970*. 2nd edition. Chicago: University of Chicago Press.

McAdam, Doug, Sidney Tarrow, and Charles Tilly. 2001. *Dynamics of Contention*. Cambridge, UK: Cambridge University Press.

McCarthy, John D., and Mayer N. Zald. 1977. "Resource Mobilization and Social Movements: A Partial Theory." *American Journal of Sociology* 82, no. 6: 1212–41.

McClintock, Cynthia. 1998. *Revolutionary Movements in Latin America: El Salvador's FMLN and Peru's Shining Path*. Washington, DC: Institute of Peace Press.

———. 2006. "Electoral Authoritarian versus Partially Democratic Regimes: The Case of the Fujimori Government and the 2000 Elections." In *The Fujimori Legacy: The Rise of Electoral Authoritarianism in Peru*, edited by Julio F. Carrión, 242–67. University Park: Pennsylvania State University Press.

McCoy, Jennifer, Andrés Serbin, William C. Smith, and Andrés Stambouli, eds. 1995. *Venezuelan Democracy under Stress*. New Brunswick, NJ: Transaction.

McNulty, Stephanie. 2011. *Voice and Vote: Decentralization and Participation in Post-Fujimori Peru*. Stanford, CA: Stanford University Press.

McPhail, Clark, and David Schweingruber. 1998. "Unpacking Protest Events: A Description Bias Analysis of Media Records with Systematic Direct Observations of Collective Action—the 1995 March for Life in Washington, DC." In Rucht et al., *Acts of Dissent*, 164–95.

Mechkova, Valeriya, Anna Lührmann, and Staffan I. Lindberg. 2017. "How Much Democratic Backsliding?" *Journal of Democracy* 28, no. 4: 162–69.

Medel, Rodrigo Miguel, and Nicolás M. Somma. 2016. "¿Marchas, ocupaciones o barricadas? Explorando los determinantes de las tácticas de la protesta en Chile." *Política y Gobierno* 23, no. 1: 163–99.

Medina, Medofilo. 1984. *La protesta urbana en Colombia en el siglo veinte*. Bogotá: Aurora.

Mello, Guilherme, and Pedro Rossi. 2018. "Do industrialismo à austeridade: a política macro dos governos Dilma." In *Para além da política econômica*, edited by Ricardo Carneiro, Fernando Sarti, and Paulo Baltar, 245–82. São Paulo: Unesp Digital.

Melucci, Alberto. 1996. *Challenging Codes: Collective Action in the Information Age*. Cambridge, UK: Cambridge University Press.

Mercado, René Zavaleta. 1974. *El poder dual en América Latina: con un prefacio sobre los acontecimientos chilenos*. Mexico City: Siglo XXI.

Meyer, David S., and Debra C. Minkoff. 2004. "Conceptualizing Political Opportunity." *Social Forces* 82, no. 4: 1457–92.

Meyer, David S., and Sidney Tarrow, eds. 1998. *The Social Movement Society: Contentious Politics for a New Century*. Lanham, MD: Rowman & Littlefield.

Minkoff, Debra C. 1995. *Organizing for Equality: The Evolution of Women's and Racial-Ethnic Organizations in America, 1955–1985*. New Brunswick, NJ: Rutgers University Press.

———. 1997. "The Sequencing of Social Movements." *American Sociological Review* 62, no. 5: 779–99.

Monsiváis, Carlos. 1987. *Entrada libre: crónicas de la sociedad que se organiza*. Mexico City: Ediciones Era.

Moore, Barrington. 1989. *La injusticia: bases sociales de la obediencia y la rebelión*. Mexico City: UNAM.

Morales, Juan Antonio, and Jeffrey David Sachs. 1988. "Bolivia's Economic Crisis." In *Developing Country Debt and the World Economy*, edited by Jeffrey David Sachs, 57–80. Chicago: University of Chicago Press.

Mora Solano, Sindy. 2011. "Las disputas por los sentidos de lo político en Costa Rica: hacia un balance de las luchas populares de la presente década." In *Una década en movimiento: luchas populares en América Latina en el amanecer del siglo XXI*, edited by Massimo Modonesi, and Julián Rebón, 275–96. Buenos Aires: CLACSO.

Morris, Aldon D. 1984. *The Origins of the Civil Rights Movement: Black Communities Organizing for Change*. New York: Free Press.

Moseley, Mason W. 2018. *Protest State: The Rise of Everyday Contention in Latin America*. Oxford: Oxford University Press.

Moseley, Mason W., and Daniel Moreno. 2010. "The Normalization of Protest in Latin America." *AmericasBarometer Insights* 42. www.vanderbilt.edu/lapop/insights/I0842en.pdf.

Mouffe, Chantal. 1988. "Hegemony and New Political Subjects: Toward a New Concept of Democracy." In *Marxism and the Interpretation of Culture*, edited by Cary Nelson and Lawrence Grossberg, 89–104. Urbana: University of Illinois Press.

Naím, Moises. 1995. *Latin America's Journey to the Market: From Macroeconomic Shocks to Institutional Therapy*. San Francisco: Institute for Contemporary Studies.

Negrete, Rodrigo. 2013. "Derechos, minería y conflictos: aspectos normativos." In *Minería en Colombia: derechos, políticas públicas y gobernanza*, edited by Luis Jorge Garay Salamanca, 23–56. Bogotá: Contraloría General de la República.

O'Connell, T. J. 2008. "Repression and Protest: The Limitations of Aggregation." *Strategic Insights* 7, no. 2: 1–7.

O'Donnell, Guillermo. 1994. "Delegative Democracy." *Journal of Democracy* 5, no. 1: 55–69.

Offe, Claus. 1985. "New Social Movements: Challenging the Boundaries of Institutional Politics." *Social Research* 52, no. 4: 817–68.

Olson, Mancur. 1965. *The Logic of Collective Action: Public Goods and the Theory of Groups*. Cambridge, MA: Harvard University Press.

Olvera, Alberto J. 2010. "De la sociedad civil política y los límites y posibilidades de la política de la sociedad civil: el caso de Alianza Cívica y la transición democrática en México." In Bizberg and Zapata, *Movimientos sociales*, 181–225.

Olzak, Susan. 1989. "Analysis of Events in the Study of Collective Action." *Annual Review of Sociology* 15: 119–41.

Orbuch, Terri L. 1997. "People's Accounts Count: The Sociology of Accounts." *Annual Review of Sociology* 23: 455–78.

Orozco, Iván. 1992. *Combatientes, rebeldes y terroristas: guerra y derecho en Colombia*. Bogotá: Universidad Nacional de Colombia/Temis.

Ortega Ortíz, Reynaldo Yunuen. 2000. "Comparing Types of Transitions: Spain and Mexico." *Democratization* 7, no. 3: 65–92.

Ortiz, David, Daniel Myers, Eugene Walls, and María-Elena Díaz. 2005. "Where Do We Stand with Newspaper Data?" *Mobilization* 10, no. 3: 397–419.

Ortiz Crespo, Santiago. 2011. "30-S: la vulnerabilidad del liderazgo de la Revolución Ciudadana y de la institucionalidad en Ecuador." *Íconos* 39: 25–34.

———. 2016. "Marcha por el agua, la vida y la dignidad de los pueblos." *Letras Verdes* 19: 45–66.

———. 2018. "Revolución Ciudadana en Ecuador: de lo nacional popular a lo nacional estatal." In *Estados en disputa: auge y fractura del ciclo de impugnación al neoliberalismo en América Latina*, edited by Hernán Ouviña and Mabel Thwaites Rey, 234–65. Buenos Aires: El Colectivo/CLACSO/IEALC.

———. 2021. *La Revolución Ciudadana y las organizaciones sociales: el caso de la Red de Maestros, 2007–2017*. Quito: FLACSO Ecuador.

Ospina, Pablo. 2009. "Nos vino un huracán político, la crisis de la CONAIE." In *Los Andes en movimiento: identidad y poder en el nuevo paisaje político*, edited by Ospina Peralta, Olaf Kaltmeier, and Christian Büschges, 123–64. Quito: CEN.

Ossandón, Loreto. 2005. "Los nuevos movimientos sociales en Chile: el caso del movimiento ambiental." Bachelor's thesis, Universidad de Chile.

Ostria, Gustavo Rodríguez. 2006. *Teoponte: sin tiempo para las palabras, la otra guerrilla guevarista en Bolivia*. Cochabamba: Grupo Editorial Kipus.

Oxhorn, Philip D. 2009. "Beyond Neoliberalism? Latin America's New Crossroads." In *Beyond Neoliberalism in Latin America? Societies and Politics at the Crossroads*, edited by John Burdick, Philip Oxhorn, and Kenneth M. Roberts, 217–34. New York: Palgrave Macmillan.

Pacheco, Mario Napoleón. 2008. *Políticas de crecimiento en democracia*. La Paz: Fundación Milenio.

Parodi, Jorge. 1985. *La desmovilización del sindicalismo industrial peruano en el segundo belaundismo*. Lima: Instituto de Estudios Peruanos.

Paulani, Leda. 2016. "Uma ponte para o abismo." In *Por que gritamos golpe?: para entender o impeachment e a crise política no Brasil*, edited by Ivana Jinkings, Kim Doria, and Murito Cleto, 69–75. São Paulo: Boitempo.

Peña Nieto, Enrique. 2017. *El Quinto Informe de Gobierno: Anexo Estadístico*. Mexico City: Presidencia. www.presidencia.gob.mx/quintoinforme. Accessed February 12, 2018.

Peñaranda, Ricardo. 2006. "Resistencia civil y tradiciones de resistencia en el suroccidente colombiano." In *Nuestra guerra sin nombre: transformaciones del conflicto en Colombia*, edited by Francisco Gutiérrez, María Emma Wills, and Gonzalo Sánchez Gómez, 315–29. Bogotá: IEPRI, Universidad Nacional de Colombia/Norma.

Pérez Arce, Francisco. 1990. "The Enduring Union Struggle for Legality and Democracy." In *Popular Movements and Political Change in Mexico*, edited by Joe Foweraker and Ann L. Craig, 105–20. Boulder, CO: Lynne Rienner.

Pérez-Liñán, Aníbal. 2018. "Impeachment or Backsliding? Threats to Democracy in the Twenty-First Century." *Revista Brasileira de Ciências Sociais* 33, no. 98: 1–15.

Pérez-Liñán, Aníbal, and Scott Mainwaring. 2015. "Cross-Currents in Latin America." *Journal of Democracy* 26, no. 1: 114–27.

Pérez-Yarahuán, Gabriela, and David García-Junco. 1998. "¿Una ley para organizaciones no gubernamentales en México? Análisis de una propuesta." In *Organizaciones civiles y políticas públicas en México y Centroamérica*, edited by José Luis Méndez, 451–88. Mexico City: ISTR, M.A. Porrúa, Academia Mexicana de Investigación en Políticas Públicas.

Perreault, Thomas. 2006. "From the Guerra del Agua to the Guerra del Gas: Resource Governance, Neoliberalism and Popular Protest in Bolivia." *Antipode* 38, no. 1: 150–72.

Piven, Frances Fox, and Richard A. Cloward. 1977. *Poor People's Movements: Why They Succeed, How They Fail*. New York: Vintage.

PNUD. 2015. *Informe sobre desarrollo humano en Chile, 2015: los tiempos de la politización*. Santiago, Chile: PNUD.

Pochmann, Marcio. 2014. *O mito da grande classe média: capitalismo e estrutura social*. São Paulo: Boitempo.

Pochmann, Marcio, and Reginaldo Moraes. 2017. *Capitalismo, classe trabalhadora e luta política no início do século XXI: experiências no Brasil, Estados Unidos, Inglaterra e França*. São Paulo: Fundação Perseu Abramo.

Ponce de León, Macarena, Francisca Rengifo, and Sol Serrano. 2012. *Historia de la educación en Chile (1810-2010)*. Volume 2: *La educación nacional (1880-1930)*. Santiago: Taurus.

Prada, Esmeralda. 2002. "Luchas campesinas e indígenas." In Archila Neira et al., *25 años de luchas sociales en Colombia, 1975-2000*, 125-66. Bogotá: CINEP.

Presidencia de la República PR. 2013. Decreto Ejecutivo 016. Funcionamiento del Sistema Unificado de Información de las Organizaciones Sociales y Ciudadanas. Registro Oficial 19, Suplemento, de 20 de junio.

Przeworski, Adam. 1991. *Democracy and the Market: Political and Economic Reforms in Eastern Europe and Latin America*. Cambridge, UK: Cambridge University Press.

Quadros, Waldir. 2015. "Paralisia econômica, retrocesso social e eleições." *Texto para Discussão* 249: 1-12.

Quijano, Aníbal. 1979. *Problema agrario y movimientos campesinos*. Lima: Mosca Azul.

Ramírez Gallegos, Franklin. 2011. "El Estado en disputa: Ecuador 1990-2011." In *Estado de los derechos de la niñez y la adolescencia en Ecuador 1990-2011*, 52-64. Quito: Observatorio de los Derechos de la Niñez y Adolescencia, UNICEF.

Raventós Vorst, Ciska. 2018. *Mi corazón dice No: El movimiento de oposición del TLC en Costa Rica*. San José: Universidad de Costa Rica.

Remmer, Karen L. 1991. "New Wine or Old Bottlenecks? The Study of Latin American Democracy." *Comparative Politics* 23, no. 4: 479-95.

———. 2008. "The Politics of Institutional Change: Electoral Reform in Latin America, 1978-2002." *Party Politics* 14, no. 1: 5-30.

Restrepo, Ana María. 2019. "El espacio en movimiento: cómo pensar la producción del espacio en cuarenta años de luchas sociales en Colombia." In Archila Neira et al., *Cuando la copa se rebosa*, 241-66.

Rey, Juan Carlos. 1991. "La democracia venezolana y la crisis del sistema populista de conciliación." *Revista de Estudios Políticos* 74: 533-78.

Reyes-Housholder, Catherine, and Beatriz Roque. 2019. "Chile 2018: desafíos al poder de género desde la calle hasta La Moneda." *Revista de Ciencia Política* (Santiago) 39, no. 2: 191-216.

Rich, Jessica, Lindsay Mayka, and Alfred Montero. 2019. "The Politics of Participation in Latin America: New Actors and Institutions." *Latin American Politics and Society* 61, no. 2: 1-20.

Roberts, Kenneth. 2002. "Social Inequalities without Class Cleavages in Latin America's Neoliberal Era." *Studies in Comparative International Development* 36, no. 4: 3-33.

———. 2008. "The Mobilization of Opposition to Economic Liberalization." *Annual Review of Political Science* 11, no. 1: 327-49.

———. 2012. "Market Reform, Programmatic (De)alignment, and Party System

Stability in Latin America." *Comparative Political Studies* 46, no. 11:
1422–52.

———. 2016. "Democracy in the Developing World: Challenges of Survival and
Significance." *Studies in Comparative International Development* 51, no. 1:
32–49.

Robinson, William I. 1996. *Promoting Polyarchy: Globalization, US Intervention,
and Hegemony*. Cambridge, UK: Cambridge University Press.

———. 2003. *Transnational Conflicts: Central America, Social Change, and Globalization*. London: Verso.

Rocha, Camila. 2019. " 'Imposto é Roubo!' A formação de um contrapúblico
ultraliberal e os protestos pró-*impeachment* de Dilma Rousseff." *Dados*
62, no. 3: 1–42.

Rocha, Ricardo. 2001. "El narcotráfico en la economía de Colombia: una mirada
a las políticas." *Planeación y Desarrollo* 32, no. 3: 93–136.

Rossi, Federico M. 2017. *The Poor's Struggle for Political Incorporation: The Piquetero Movement in Argentina*. Cambridge, UK: Cambridge University Press.

———. 2019. "Conceptualising and Tracing the Increased Territorialisation of
Politics: Insights from Argentina." *Third World Quarterly* 40, no. 4: 815–37.

Rubin, Jeffrey W. 1996. "Decentering the Regime: Culture and Regional Politics
in Mexico." *Latin American Research Review* 31, no. 3: 85–126.

Rucht, Dieter, Ruud Koopmans, and Friedhelm Neidhardt, eds. 1998. *Acts of
Dissent: New Developments in the Study of Protest*. Berlin: Edition Sigma.

Ruiz, Nubia. 2011. "El desplazamiento forzado en Colombia: una revisión
histórica y demográfica." *Estudios Demográficos Urbanos* 26, no. 1: 141–77.

Saad-Filho, Alfredo, and Armando Boito. 2016. "Brazil: The Failure of the PT
and the Rise of the 'New Right.'" *Socialist Register* 52: 213–30.

Sabet, Daniel. 2008. "Thickening Civil Society: Explaining the Development of
Associational Life in Mexico." *Democratization* 15, no. 2: 410–32.

Sánchez Parga, José. 1995. *Conflicto y democracia en Ecuador*. Quito: Centro
Andino de Acción Popular (CAAP).

———. 1996. *Las cifras del Conflicto social en el Ecuador, 1980–1995*. Quito: CAAP.

———. 2010. *Decline de los conflictos y auge de las violencias: Ecuador, 1998–2008*.
Quito: CAAP.

Santa María, Mauricio, Mauricio Perfetti, Gabriel Piraquive, Víctor Nieto, Jennifer Timote, and Erick Céspedes. 2013. "Evolución de la industria en
Colombia." Bogota: Archivos de Economía Documento 402, Departamento Nacional de Planeación.

Sassen, Saskia. 2007. *A Sociology of Globalization*. New York: W. W. Norton.

Selee, Andrew. 2012. "Municipalities and Policymaking." In Camp, *Oxford
Handbook of Mexican Politics*, 101–18.

———. 2015. *Decentralization, Democratization, and Informal Power in Mexico*.
University Park: Pennsylvania State University Press.

Serrano Gómez, Enrique. 1997. "Las figuras del 'otro' en la dinámica política." *Cultura y Trabajo* 42: 31–39.

Servicio Civil. 2017. "Empleo público en Chile: nudos críticos, desafíos y líneas de desarrollo para una agenda 2030." Online report. Dirección Nacional del Servicio Civil. biblioteca.digital.gob.cl/handle/123456789/3659.

Sewell, William H. 1999. "The Concept(s) of Culture." In *Beyond the Cultural Turn: New Directions in the Study of Society and Culture*, edited by Victoria E. Bonnel and Lynn Hunt, 35–60. Berkeley: University of California Press.

Shefner, Jon, Aaron Rowland, and George Pasdirtz. 2015. "Austerity and Anti-Systemic Protest: Bringing Hardships Back." *Journal of World-Systems Research* 21, no. 2: 459–94.

Shefner, Jon, and Julie Stewart. 2011. "Neoliberalism, Grievances, and Democratization: An Exploration of the Role of Material Hardships in Shaping Mexico's Democratic Transition." *Journal of World-Systems Research* 17, no. 2: 353–78.

Silva, Eduardo. 2009. *Challenging Neoliberalism in Latin America*. New York: Cambridge University Press.

Silva, Eduardo, and Federico Rossi, eds. 2018. *Reshaping the Political Arena in Latin America: From Resisting Neoliberalism to the Second Incorporation*. Pittsburgh: University of Pittsburgh Press.

Simmons, Erica S. 2016. *Meaningful Resistance: Market Reforms and the Roots of Social Protest in Latin America*. Cambridge, UK: Cambridge University Press.

Singer, André. 2015. "Cutucando onças com varas curtas: o ensaio desenvolvimentista no primeiro mandato de Dilma Rousseff (2011–2014)." *Novos Estudos: CEBRAP* 102: 42–71.

Singer, André, and Isabel Loureiro. 2016. *As contradições do lulismo. A que ponto chegamos?* São Paulo: Boitempo.

Smelser, Neil J. 1962. *Theory of Collective Behavior*. New York: Free Press.

Smith, Peter H., and James N. Green. 2019. *Modern Latin America*. 9th edition. New York: Oxford University Press.

Snow, David A., Donatella della Porta, and Doug McAdam, eds. 2022. *The Wiley-Blackwell Encyclopedia of Social and Political Movements*. Oxford: Wiley-Blackwell.

Snow, David A., Sarah A. Soule, and Hanspeter Kriesi, eds. 2004. *The Blackwell Companion to Social Movements*. Oxford: Blackwell.

Snow, David A., Sarah A. Soule, Hanspeter Kriesi, and Holly J. McCammon, eds. 2018. *The Wiley-Blackwell Companion to Social Movements*. 2nd edition. Oxford: Wiley-Blackwell.

Somma, Nicolás M., and Rodrigo Medel. 2017. "Shifting Relationships between Social Movements and Institutional Politics." In *Social Movements in Chile: Organization, Trajectories, and Political Consequences*, edited by

Sofía Donoso and Marisa von Bülow, 29–61. New York: Palgrave Macmillan.

———. 2019. "What Makes a Big Demonstration? Exploring the Impact of Mobilization Strategies on the Size of Demonstrations." *Social Movement Studies* 18, no. 2: 233–51.

Somma, Nicolás M., Federico M. Rossi, and Sofía Donoso. 2020. "The Attachment of Demonstrators to Institutional Politics: Comparing LGBTIQ Pride Marches in Argentina and Chile." *Bulletin of Latin American Research* 39, no. 3: 380–97.

Sosa, Eugenio, and Paul Almeida. 2019. "Honduras: A Decade of Popular Resistance." *NACLA Report on the Americas* 51, no. 4: 323–27.

Soule, Sarah A. 2013. "Protest Event Research." In Snow et al., *Wiley-Blackwell Encyclopedia of Social and Political Movements*, 1019–22.

Soule, Sarah A., and Jennifer Earl. 2005. "A Movement Society Evaluated: Collective Protest in the United States, 1960–1986." *Mobilization* 10, no. 3: 345–64.

Soule, Sarah A., and Brayden G. King. 2008. "Competition and Resource Partitioning in Three Social Movement Industries." *American Journal of Sociology* 113, no. 6: 1568–610.

Spalding, Rose J. 2014. *Contesting Trade in Central America: Market Reform and Resistance.* Austin: University of Texas Press.

Stahler-Sholk, Richard, Harry E. Vanden, and Glen David Kuecker. 2008. "Introduction." In *Latin American Social Movements in the Twenty-First Century: Resistance, Power, and Democracy*, edited by Richard Stahler-Sholk, Harry E. Vanden, and Glen David Kuecker, 1–15. Boulder, CO: Rowman & Littlefield.

Starn, Orin. 1991. *"Con los llanques todo barro": reflexiones sobre rondas campesinas, protesta rural y nuevos movimientos sociales.* Lima: DESCO.

Strawn, Kelly D. 2008. "Validity and Media-Derived Protest Event Data: Examining Relative Coverage Tendencies in Mexican News Media." *Mobilization* 13, no. 2: 147–64.

Suárez Montoya, Aurelio. 2015. "La tercera oleada neoliberal o quién pagará la crisis." *El Tiempo*, March 2, 2015. www.eltiempo.com/archivo/documento/CMS-15327296.

Svampa, Maristella. 2010. "Movimientos sociales, matrices sociopolíticas y nuevos escenarios en América Latina." Working Paper. Universität Kassel. https://biblioteca.clacso.edu.ar/Alemania/unikassel/20161117033216/pdf_1110.pdf.

Swidler, Ann. 1986. "Culture in Action: Symbols and Strategies." *American Sociological Review* 51, no. 2: 273–86.

Taborda, Francisco. 2018. "Vientos de retroceso en la implementación del acuerdo de paz con las FARC-EP." *Cien días vistos por CINEP* 94: 2–8.

Tamayo Flores-Alatorre, Sergio. 1999. *Los veinte octubres mexicanos: la transición a la modernización y la democracia, 1968-1988*. Mexico City: Universidad Autónoma Metropolitana-Azcapotzalco.

Tarrow, Sidney. 1989. *Democracy and Disorder: Politics and Protest in Italy, 1965-1975*. Oxford: Oxford University Press.

———. 1993. "Cycles of Collective Action: Between Moments of Madness and the Repertoire of Contention." *Social Science History* 17, no. 2: 281-307.

———. 1997. *El poder en movimiento: Los movimientos sociales, la acción colectiva y la política*, translated by Herminia Bavia and Antonio Resines. Madrid: Alianza.

———. 1998. "Studying Contentious Politics: From Event-ful History to Cycles of Collective Action." In Rucht et al., *Acts of Dissent*, 33-64.

———. 2011. *Power in Movement: Social Movements and Contentious Politics*. 3rd edition. Cambridge, UK: Cambridge University Press.

———. 2012. *Strangers at the Gates: Movements and States in Contentious Politics*. Cambridge, UK: Cambridge University Press.

Tatagiba, Luciana. 2018. "Entre as ruas e as instituições: os protestos e o *impeachment* de Dilma Rousseff." *Lusotopie* 17, no. 1: 112-35.

———. 2019. "Crossroads of Brazilian Democracy: Dynamics of Social Mobilization during the Left Turn Cycle." In Ferrero et al., *Socio-Political Dynamics within the Crisis of the Left*, 37-64.

Tatagiba, Luciana, and Andreia Galvão. 2019. "Os protestos no Brasil em tempos de crise (2011-2016)." *Opinião Pública* 25, no. 1: 63-97.

Tatagiba, Luciana, Thiago Trindade, and Ana Claudia Teixeira. 2015. "Protestos à direita no Brasil (1997-2015)." In *Direita, volver!: o retorno da direita e o ciclo político brasileiro*, edited by Sebastião Velasco e Cruz, André Kaysel, and Gustavo Codas, 197-212. São Paulo: Fundação Perseu Abramo.

Taylor, Verta, and Nella Van Dyke. 2004. "'Get Up, Stand Up': Tactical Repertoires of Social Movements." In Snow et al., *Blackwell Companion to Social Movements*, 262-93.

Teichman, Judith. 1996. "Economic Restructuring, State-Labor Relations, and the Transformation of Mexican Corporatism." In *Neoliberalism Revisited: Economic Restructuring and Mexico's Political Future*, edited by Gerardo Otero, 149-66. Boulder, CO: Westview Press.

Temper, Leah, Daniela del Bene, and Joan Martinez-Alier. 2015. "Mapping the Frontiers and Front Lines of Global Environmental Justice: The EJAtlas." *Journal of Political Ecology* 22, no. 1: 255-78.

Thielemann, Luis. 2016. *La anomalía social de la transición: movimiento estudiantil e izquierda universitaria en el Chile de los noventa (1987-2000)*. Santiago de Chile: Tiempo Robado Editoras.

Tilly, Charles. 1977. "Getting It Together in Burgundy, 1675-1975." *Theory and Society* 4, no. 4: 479-504.

———. 1978. *From Mobilization to Revolution*. New York: Random House.

———. 1986. *The Contentious French*. Cambridge, MA: Belknap Press.

———. 1993. "Contentious Repertories in Great Britain, 1758-1834." *Social Science History* 17, no. 2: 253-80.

———. 1998. "Conflicto político y cambio social." In *Los movimientos sociales: Transformaciones políticas y cambio cultural*, edited by Benjamín Tejerina and Pedro Ibarra Güell, 25-42. Madrid: Trotta.

———. 2004. *Social Movements, 1768-2004*. Boulder, CO: Paradigm.

———. 2005. "Introduction to Part II: Invention, Diffusion, and Transformation of the Social Movement Repertoire." *European Review of History* 12, no. 2: 307-20.

———. 2008. *Contentious Performances*. Cambridge: Cambridge University Press.

———. 2010a. *Democracia*. Translated by Raimundo Viejo Viñas. Madrid: Acal.

———. 2010b. *Regimes and Repertoires*. Chicago: University of Chicago Press.

———. 2015. *Popular Contention in Great Britain, 1758-1834*. London: Routledge.

Torres, Alfonso. 1993. *La ciudad en la sombra*. Bogotá: CINEP.

Torres-Rivas, Edelberto. 2011. *Revoluciones sin cambios revolucionarios: ensayos sobre la crisis en Centroamérica*. Guatemala City: F&G Editores.

Touraine, Alain. 1988. *Return of the Actor: Social Theory in Postindustrial Society*. Minneapolis: University of Minnesota Press.

———. 1989. *América Latina: política y sociedad*. Madrid: Espasa/Calpe.

Trejo, Guillermo. 2012. *Popular Movements in Autocracies: Religion, Repression, and Indigenous Collective Action in Mexico*. New York: Cambridge University Press.

———. 2014. "The Ballot and the Street: An Electoral Theory of Social Protest in Autocracies." *Perspectives on Politics* 12, no. 2: 332-52.

Trejo, Guillermo, and Sandra Ley. 2021. "High-Profile Criminal Violence: Why Drug Cartels Murder Government Officials and Party Candidates in Mexico." *British Journal of Political Science* 51, no. 1: 203-29.

Trevizo, Dolores. 2011. *Rural Protest and the Making of Democracy in Mexico, 1968-2000*. University Park: Pennsylvania State University Press.

Tricot, Tito. 2009. "El nuevo movimiento mapuche: hacia la (re)construcción del mundo y país mapuche." *Polis* (Santiago) 8, no. 24: 175-96.

Ulloa, Víctor. 2003. *El movimiento sindical chileno: del siglo XX hasta nuestros días*. Santiago: Oficina Internacional del Trabajo.

Valenzuela, Sebastián, Arturo Arriagada, and Andrés Scherman. 2012. "The Social Media Basis of Youth Protest Behavior: The Case of Chile." *Journal of Communication* 62, no. 2: 299-314.

Velázquez García, Mario Alberto. 2010. "Los movimientos ambientales en México." In Bizberg and Zapata, *Movimientos sociales*, 275-335.

Vergara, Alberto, and Daniel Encinas. 2016. "Continuity by Surprise:

Explaining Institutional Stability in Contemporary Peru." *Latin American Research Review* 51, no. 1: 159–80.

Villegas, Jorge, and Geraldo Rivas Moreno. 1980. *Libro negro de la represión, 1958–1980.* 2nd edition. Bogotá: FICA.

Wada, Takeshi. 2004. "Event Analysis of *Claim* Making in Mexico: How Are Social Protests Transformed into Political Protests?" *Mobilization* 9, no. 3: 241–57.

———. 2014. "Who Are the Active and Central Actors in the 'Rising Civil Society' in Mexico?" *Social Movement Studies* 13, no. 1: 127–57.

———. 2019. *Mexican Popular Contention Database (MPCD): Manual de uso e ingreso de datos.* Versión el 1 de julio de 2019. The University of Tokyo.

———. 2023. "Repertoires of Contention across Latin America." In *The Oxford Handbook of Latin American Social Movements*, edited by Federico M. Rossi, 658–75. Oxford: Oxford University Press.

Walton, John, and David Seddon. 1994. "Food Riots Past and Present." In *Free Markets and Food Riots: The Politics of Global Adjustment*, edited by John Walton and David Seddon, 23–54. Oxford: Blackwell.

Wang, Dan J., and Sarah A. Soule. 2012. "Social Movement Organizational Collaboration: Networks of Learning and the Diffusion of Protest Tactics, 1960–1995." *American Journal of Sociology* 117, no. 6: 1674–722.

Weyland, Kurt. 2009. "The Rise of Latin America's Two Lefts: Insights from Rentier State Theory." *Comparative Politics* 41, no. 2: 145–64.

Wiarda, Howard J. 2004. "Introduction: Whatever Happened to Corporatism and Authoritarianism in Latin America?" In *Authoritarianism and Corporatism in Latin America: Revisited*, edited by Howard J. Wiarda, 1–26. Gainesville: University Press of Florida.

Williams, Mark E. 2012. "The Path of Economic Liberalism." In Camp, *Oxford Handbook of Mexican Politics*, 744–76.

Williams, Rhys. 2004. "The Cultural Contexts of Collective Action: Constraints, Opportunities, and the Symbolic Life of Social Movements." In Snow et al., *Blackwell Companion to Social Movements*, 91–115.

Williamson, John. 1990. "What Washington Means by Policy Reform." In *Latin American Adjustment: How Much Has Happened?*, edited by John Williamson, 7–20. Washington, DC: Institute for International Economics.

Winn, Peter. 2004. *Victims of the Chilean Miracle: Workers and Neoliberalism in the Pinochet Era, 1973–2002.* Durham, NC: Duke University Press.

World Bank. 2022. "World Development Indicators." Washington, DC: World Bank. https://databank.worldbank.org/source/world-development-indicators.

Yashar, Deborah J. 1999. "Democracy, Indigenous Movements, and the Postliberal Challenge in Latin America." *World Politics* 52, no. 1: 76–104.

———. 2005. *Contesting Citizenship in Latin America: The Rise of Indigenous*

Movements and the Postliberal Challenge. Cambridge: Cambridge University Press.

Zajak, Sabrina. 2013. "A Political Economic View of Social Movements: New Perspectives and Open Questions." *Moving the Social* 50: 121-42.

Zanini, Débora, and Luciana Tatagiba. 2019. "Between the Streets and Facebook: Engaged Action in the Pro-Impeachment Campaign in Brazil (2014–2016)." In Ferrero et al., *Socio-Political Dynamics within the Crisis of the Left*, 95-116.

Zermeño, Sergio. 1990. "Crisis, Neoliberalism, and Disorder." In *Popular Movements and Political Change in Mexico*, edited by Joe Foweraker and Ann L. Craig, 160-80. Boulder, CO: Lynne Rienner.

———. 1998. *La sociedad derrotada: el desorden mexicano del fin de siglo*. Mexico City: Siglo XXI.

Zibechi, Raúl. 2003. *Genealogía de la revuelta: Argentina, la sociedad en movimiento*. Montevideo: Nordan.

Contributors

Paul Almeida is a professor of sociology at the University of California, Merced. His articles have appeared in the *American Journal of Sociology, Annual Review of Sociology, Social Forces, Social Problems, Mobilization*, and other scholarly outlets. Almeida's books include *Global Struggles and Social Change* (Johns Hopkins University Press, 2020, with Chris Chase-Dunn); *Social Movements: The Structure of Collective Mobilization* (University of California Press, 2019); *Mobilizing Democracy: Globalization and Citizen Protest* (Johns Hopkins University Press, 2014); *Waves of Protest: Popular Struggle in El Salvador, 1925–2005* (University of Minnesota Press, 2008); *Handbook of Social Movements across Latin America* (coedited with Allen Cordero, 2015); and *Latin American Social Movements: Globalization, Democratization and Transnational Networks* (coedited with Hank Johnston, 2006). He is currently the chair-elect of the Political Sociology section of the American Sociological Association.

Moisés Arce is the Scott and Marjorie Cowen Chair in Latin American Social Sciences and a professor in the Department of Political Science at Tulane University. He received his PhD in political science from the University of New Mexico in 2000. Professor Arce specializes in conflict processes and the politics of social and economic development. He is the author of *Market Reform in Society* (Pennsylvania State University Press, 2005), *Resource Extraction and Protest in Peru* (University of Pittsburgh Press, 2014), *Protest and Democracy* (University of Calgary Press, 2019, with Roberta Rice), *The Roots of Engagement* (Oxford University Press, 2021, with Michael Hendricks and Marc Polizzi), and numerous book chapters and journal articles. His research has been funded by the National Science Foundation and the Social Science Research Council. Professor Arce has served as a visiting Fulbright lecturer at the Pontificia Universidad Católica del Perú (2003) and as a visiting professor at the University of Tokyo (2014).

Mauricio Archila Neira is a full professor at the Universidad Nacional de Colombia, Bogotá Campus, and a coordinator of the Social Movements Team of the Centro de Investigación y Educación Popular (CINEP). He received his PhD in history from the State University of New York, Stony Brook, in 1991. He is a specialist in the labor and social history of Latin America and Colombia, with books in the area such as *Cultura e Identidad Obrera* (CINEP, 1991) and *Idas y venidas, vueltas y revueltas: Protestas sociales en Colombia, 1958–1990* (CINEP, 2003), winner of the Colombian National Award on Social Sciences in 2004. He is a coauthor of collective publications such as *Cuando la copa se rebosa: Luchas sociales en Colombia, 1975–2015* (CINEP, 2019); *"Hasta cuando soñemos": Extractivismo e interculturalidad en el sur de La Guajira* (CINEP, 2015); *Violencia contra el sindicalismo en Colombia, 1984–2010* (CINEP-PNUD, 2012); and other book chapters and journal articles.

Renzo Aurazo is a PhD student at Tulane University. His research focuses on contentious politics, selection of protest routines, social movements, and mobilization campaigns, with a regional focus on Latin America.

Andréia Galvão, PhD, is a professor of political science at the University of Campinas. She is the author of *Neoliberalismo e reforma trabalhista no Brasil* (2007) and coauthor of *Política e classes sociais no Brasil dos anos 2000* (2012) and *As bases sociais das novas centrais sindicais brasileiras* (2015). She works on labor relations, trade unionism, social movements. and collective action in Brazil, and she has published several articles on these topics. She is a member of the editorial committee of the journal *Crítica Marxista* and of the national coordination of REMIR (Network for Interdisciplinary Studies and Monitoring of Labor Reform).

Martha Cecilia García Velandia is a sociologist with a master's degree in urbanism and a researcher for the Centro de Investigación y Educación Popular (CINEP). She studies social protest, urban social movements, memories, and identities of subaltern groups in Colombia. Among her books are *Protestas relacionadas con la minería en Colombia, 2000–2015* (Glocon and CINEP, 2017) and *Las organizaciones y movilizaciones sociales por la defensa de los recursos y bienes naturales: Un desafío para la democracia y el desarrollo en América Latina* (DESCO, 2015). She is also a coauthor of *La crisis de la salud es anterior al COVID-19* (CINEP, 2020); *Cuando la copa se rebosa: Luchas sociales en Colombia, 1975–2015* (CINEP, 2019); *Tendencias de la movilización social en municipios críticos para el posconflicto* (CINEP, 2016); *"Hasta cuando soñemos": Extractivismo e interculturalidad en el sur de La Guajira* (CINEP, 2015); *Violencia contra el sindicalismo en Colombia, 1984–2010* (CINEP-PNUD, 2012), and numerous book chapters and journal articles.

Luis Rubén González Márquez is a PhD student in sociology at the University of California, Merced. His previous studies were in history and sociology in El Salvador and Ecuador. He worked as a researcher in the National Teachers Training Institute of El Salvador and an adjunct professor in the Social Science School at the University of El Salvador. For his doctoral studies, he received a Fulbright-LASPAU scholarship. His research interests are popular mobilization, political violence, and labor and environmental conflicts in Latin America.

María Inclán is a professor in the Political Studies Division at CIDE (Centro de Investigación y Docencia Económicas) in Mexico City. She received her PhD in 2005 from Pennsylvania State University. Professor Inclán specializes in conflict studies, democratization processes, and mobilizing campaigns. She is the author of *The Zapatista Movements and Mexico's Democratic Transition* (Oxford University Press, 2018) and numerous book chapters and journal articles.

Roberto Laserna obtained a doctorate from the University of California, Berkeley, with a thesis on "The Coca Boom and the Regional Development of Cochabamba." He received his BA in economics from the Universidad Mayor de San Simón and an MA in urban planning from the University of California, Berkeley. He has been a professor at the Universidad Mayor de

San Simón (Cochabamba, Bolivia), Universidad del Pacífico (Lima), and Princeton University (New Jersey). He is a principal investigator at the Centro de Estudios de la Realidad Económica y Social (CERES) in Cochabamba. In 1984, he established the Observatorio de Conflictos at CERES, which maintains a database on social events from 1970 to date using the print media. He has done consultancy work for the United Nations Development Programme (UNDP) on human development issues in Africa, Central America, and Eastern Europe. He is the author of several articles and books, among them *La Trampa del Rentismo*, *El Fracaso del Prohibicionismo*, *20 (Mis)conceptions on Coca and Cocaine*, and *Crisis, Democracy and Social Conflict*.

Margarita López Maya is a historian and has a PhD in social sciences from the Universidad Central de Venezuela. She is professor-researcher at the Center for Development Studies (CENDES) at the Universidad Central and a member of the Center of Political Studies of Universidad Católica Andrés Bello in Caracas. She was the vice president / president of the Latin American Studies Association from 2021 until 2023. Some of her prominent publications include *Venezuela: Del Viernes Negro al Referendo Revocatorio* (*Venezuela: From Black Friday to the Presidential Recall*) (Grupo Alfa, 2005); *Democracia Participativa en Venezuela: Orígenes, leyes, percepciones y desafíos* (*Participative Democracy in Venezuela: Origins, Laws, Perceptions and Challenges*) (Centro Gumilla, 2011); *El ocaso del chavismo: Venezuela 2005–2015* (*The Sunset of Chavism: Venezuela 2005–2015*) (Grupo Alfa, 2016); and *Democracia en Venezuela ¿Representativa, participativa o populista?* (*Democracy in Venezuela: Representative, Participative or Populist?*) (Grupo Alfa, 2021).

Rodrigo M. Medel is an assistant professor at the Faculty of Education and Social Sciences of the Universidad Andres Bello in Chile. His research interests revolve around political participation, social movements, protest, and labor strikes. He has lately focused on the relationship between electoral and nonelectoral political participation. His work has been published in *Latin American Politics and Society, Journal of Latin American Studies, Acta Politica, Social Science Quarterly, Critical Sociology, Social Movement*

Studies, and elsewhere. Medel completed his undergraduate studies in sociology at the University of Chile. He later obtained the degrees of Master in Sociology, Master in Political Science, and PhD in Political Science at the Pontificia Universidad Católica de Chile.

María De Jesus Mora is an assistant professor in the Sociology, Gerontology, and Gender Studies Department at California State University, Stanislaus. Her research centers on race, immigration, and social movements. She studies how racialized and immigrant groups mobilize against threats and the long-term organizing outcomes for immigrant rights social movements.

Santiago Ortiz earned his master and doctoral degrees in social sciences at FLACSO Ecuador. He was the Coordinator of the doctorate in social sciences, specialization in Andean Studies, at FLACSO Ecuador and a professor in the Department of Sociology and Gender Studies in the subjects of populism, citizenship, citizen participation, and state and local governments. He studies social movements and the Citizens' Revolution. He is a member of the Political Sociology Research Group.

Nicolás M. Somma (PhD, University of Notre Dame, Indiana) is an associate professor of the Instituto de Sociología at the Pontificia Universidad Católica de Chile, and he is an associate researcher at the Centre for Social Conflict and Cohesion Studies (COES). His research has appeared in journals such as *Party Politics*, *Social Movement Studies*, *American Behavioral Scientist*, *Latin American Politics and Society*, and *Comparative Politics*. Among other projects, he is leading a comparative study of labor movements in seventeen Latin American countries since 1990, as well as a macro-historical comparative analysis of institutions from the early civilizations to our era.

Luciana Tatagiba is an associate professor in the Department of Political Science and the Post-Graduate Program in Political Science at State University of Campinas (UNICAMP), São Paulo, Brazil. She was the associate director of the Brazilian Political Science Association (ABCP) from 2018 to

2020 and the coordinator of the Political Participation's Area in the Brazilian Political Science Association (ABCP) from 2017 to 2020, and she is currently a member of the Executive Committee of Brazilian Network of Women Scientists. Her research interests include social movements, protests, democracy, and participation in Brazil, with many publications on these areas. The newest one is the book *Socio-Political Dynamics within the Crisis of the Left: Argentina and Brazil* (2019).

Takeshi Wada is a professor in the Department of Area Studies and the director of the Latin American and Iberian Network for Academic Collaboration (LAINAC) at the University of Tokyo. He received his PhD in sociology from Columbia University in 2003. His areas of specialization include contentious politics and the sociology of development. His research has appeared in journals such as *Mobilization, Social Problems,* and *Social Movement Studies.* His research has been funded by the Japan Society for the Promotion of Science, the Toyota Foundation, and the National Science Foundation of the United States. He has served as a postdoctoral fellow at the Weatherhead Center for International Affairs, Harvard University (2003–2005), and as a visiting scholar at the Jack W. Peltason Center for the Study of Democracy, University of California, Irvine (2019).

Index

Convention on Human Rights of San
José, 83
Convergencia National, 167
co-optation, in Mexico, 39, 43, 299
Coordinadora Nacional Plan de
Ayala (CNPA), Mexico, 58–59
COPEI (Comité de Organización
Política Electoral Independiente), 167
corporatism, 39–41, 49, 56, 87, 299
Correa, Rafael, 15, 238, 242, 244–45,
248, 250, 255, 259, 261n6; with
Alianza País, 260n1; 30-S of
2010 and, 246, 249, 253, 261n8,
262n11
corruption, 68, 81, 135n11, 161, 251,
253, 254; Brazil, 30, 265, 268,
269, 274–76, 283, *285*, 291, 291n5,
305; Venezuela, 167, 172, 173
Costa Rica, 9, 10, 33n6, 135n5, 303;
collective action, 190–91, 195–
96, 200, 204; CUT, 151, 191–92;
DINADECO, 190–92, 197, *199*;
electricity prices, 29, 186, 190,
192–93, 197, *198*, 199–200, 204;
empirical results, 197–200, *198*,
199, *200*; methods, 195–97; neoliberalism, 190–93, 197–200, 205;
popular politics, 190–93; protest
events, *199*, *200*; Pueblo Unido,
191–93, 199, 204; roadblocks, 186,
192, 193, 200; strikes, 191–92
"Cost Brazil," 292n12
country-specific event datasets, 21–23
COVID-19 pandemic, 85, 101n12,
135n9, 181, 262n17
Creando Oportunidades (CREO)
movement, 262n11
crime, 115, 288, 293n16; Organic
Crime Law, 256; organized, 24,
39, 55, 68, 299, 310n2
cross-national datasets, 3, 6, 298

CTM (Confederación de Trabajadores de México), 40
CTP (Confederación de Trabajadores
del Perú), 151
Cuando la copa se rebosa (Archila
Neira), 134n1
Cuba, 33n4, 117, 135n5, 135n12, 282,
296
cultural claims, in Mexico, 53, 55, 69
currency devaluation, 41, 100n3, 272
CUT (Confederación Unitaria de Trabajadores), Costa Rica, 151,
191–92
CUT (Unified Workers' Central), Brazil, 280
CUT (Unitary Workers' Central),
Chile, 209, 210

data, 21, 83–84, 112, 196, 214
databases: BDLS, 26, 104, 108–12, 117,
121, 129, 133, 135n6; MPCD, 24,
46–49, 52, 71n7, 71n12; Observatory of Conflicts, 25, 29, 214, 231
Datafolha survey, 272
datasets: Base de Protestas Sociales
del Perú, 27, 139, 142; BDEBP, 27,
164–66, 168–72, *173*, 174, 181n3,
182nn6-9; CAAP, 30, 239, 241,
247–48, *249*, *251–55*, 255–56, *257*,
261n3, 262n13, 262n18; country-
specific event, 21–23; cross-
national, 3, 6, 298; longitudinal,
4; Observatory of Conflicts, 25,
29, 214, 231; print media, 23, 247;
PROVEA, 27, 164–66, 168–69,
169, 174, *174*, *177*, 178, 181n3,
182n6; summary of, *23*
Davis, Diane E., 222
deaths, 64, 172, 173, 186, 206n12, 209;
Baguazo, 160; Caracazo, 8, 166;
killing of women, 122; massacres, 43, 78, 289; murders, 119, 212

debt crisis, 5, 7, 41, 54, 144, 190, 200, 240

debtors: Chile with consumers and, 215, 218, 225, 228, 230, 232, 235; rights, 304, 305

dedazo ("big finger"), 39, 44

de-democratization, 27, 30, 265

deglobalization, 24, 301–2

deindustrialization, 106, 240, 259

De la Madrid, Miguel, 41

Delgado Guzmán, Álvaro, 129

Della Porta, Donatella, 267

democracy, 2, 10, 15, 26, 79–82, 94, 300. *See also* Varieties of Democracy Project

democratization, 5, 9–12, 24, *25*, 199, 307; de-democratization and, 27, 30, 265; market reforms and, 211–14. *See also* globalization and democratization

Democrat Party, Chile, 209

devaluation, of currency, 41, 100n3, 272

Díaz Ordaz, Gustavo, 43

diffuse groups and individuals, Brazil, 280, 283–84

Dirección Nacional de Desarrollo de la Comunidad (DINADECO), Costa Rica, 190–92, 197, *199*

the "disappeared," 115, 310n2

Domínguez, Jorge I., 70n4

drugs, 63, 68, 70, 108, 134n3, 299

Duque Márquez, Iván, 117, 118, 135n9

Earl, Jennifer, 32n2

Echeverría, Luis, 40–41, 53

economic and sectoral policy, Brazil, 289

economic globalization, 4, 6–12, 16–17, 31, 99, 112, 306; Chile and, 215, 237n1; defined, 32n1; deglobalization and, 24; neoliberalism

and, 185, 186, 189; Peru and, 140–42, 301; social consequences of, 1–2, 32; threats associated with, 186; Venezuela and, 164

economic liberalization: Bolivia and, 80; Brazil and, 304; Chile and, 208; Colombia and, 115, 116, 118, 133; economic globalization and, 9; Ecuador and, 242; farmers and, 206n1; Latin America and, 295–96, 298; Mexico and, 24, 37, 39, 41–43, *42*, 46, 48, 50, 52, 58, 60, 62, 64, 68–69, 299; opposition to, 185–86, 187, 188; Peru and, 138, 139, 141, 142, 148, 150, 162; political and, 24, 37, 39, *42*, 45–46, 48, 50, 52, 60, 64, 295–96, 298–99, 301, 303–4; reactive mobilization and, 16, 306; Venezuela and, 166, 302

economy: commodity boom, post-neoliberal regimes and growth in, 13–15; GDP, *13*, 13–15, 142, 144, 272, 292nn10–11; hybrid political-economic environment, 2, 10, 24, 31, 139–42, 153, 277, 305; Latin America with social indicators and, *13*; production chain, 134n4; Washington Consensus and, 7, 9, 11–14, 32n1, 80, 106, 115, 141–42, 166, 240

Ecuador, 2, 7, 10, 14, 30, 33n6, 84, 185, 186, 262n17; actions, 247–48, *254*, 254–55; actors, 247, 250–51, *251*; Alianza País, 242, 244–48, 250, 256, 258, 261n1, 261n10, 262n11; Citizens' Revolution, 238–39, 242–48, 254–60, 260n1; claims, 247, 251–54, *252*, *253*, 259; with class identity lost, 263n20; collective action, 239, 246; commodity boom, 238,

www.ingramcontent.com/pod-product-compliance
Lightning Source LLC
Chambersburg PA
CBHW020452270326
41926CB00008B/579